# READING THE AMERICAN PAST

## *Selected Historical Documents*
### *Volume II: From 1865*

# READING THE AMERICAN PAST

THIRD EDITION

*Selected Historical Documents*
*Volume II: From 1865*

MICHAEL P. JOHNSON
*Johns Hopkins University*

Bedford/St. Martin's    Boston ◆ New York

*For Bedford/St. Martin's*

*Executive Editor for History*: Mary V. Dougherty
*Director of Development for History*: Jane Knetzger
*Developmental Editors*: Louise Townsend, Dale Anderson
*Editorial Assistant*: Elizabeth Harrison
*Senior Production Supervisor*: Joe Ford
*Senior Marketing Manager*: Jenna Bookin Barry
*Project Management*: DeMasi Design and Publishing, Inc.
*Cover Design*: Donna Lee Dennison
*Cover Art*: *Italian Family on the Ferryboat Leaving Ellis Island*, 1905.
         Gelatin Silver print. From the *Ellis Island* series. By Lewis
         W. Hine. Reproduced by permission of the George
         Eastman House.
*Composition*: Macmillan India Limited
*Printing and Binding*: RR Donnelley & Sons Company

*President*: Joan E. Feinberg
*Editorial Director*: Denise B. Wydra
*Director of Marketing*: Karen Melton Soeltz
*Director of Editing, Design, and Production*: Marcia Cohen
*Manager, Publishing Services*: Emily Berleth

Manufactured in the United States of America.

0   9   8   7
j

For information, write: Bedford/St. Martin's, 75 Arlington Street, Boston, MA 02116   (617-399-4000)

ISBN-10:  0-312-40901-X
ISBN-13:  978-0-312-40901-2

**Acknowledgments**
*Acknowledgments and copyrights appear at the back of the book on pages 331–32, which constitute an extension of the copyright page.*

# PREFACE FOR INSTRUCTORS

Reading the American Past is a collection of compelling documents by people who made American history. The documents provide depth and breadth to textbook discussions of important events, ideas, and experiences in our nation's past. Organized chapter by chapter to parallel *The American Promise: A History of the United States*, Third Edition — the textbook to which I contribute — these documents offer teachers many historical voices and pedagogical choices. Above all, *Reading the American Past* seeks to ignite the sparks of historical imagination that every teacher hopes to see in students' eyes.

Reading a textbook discussion of Columbus's arrival in the New World, for example, gives students basic, up-to-date information that has been collected, sorted out, and synthesized over the past 500 years. But reading the words Columbus wrote in his log shortly after he stepped ashore in the Western Hemisphere recaptures as no textbook can that moment of profound, mutual surprise when fifteenth-century Europeans and the people they called Indians first encountered one another. As every historian knows, primary sources bridge from the present, when they are read, to the past, when they were written. They encourage students to venture across that span connecting present and past and to risk discovering a captivating and unexpected world.

Three basic principles guided my selection of documents. First and foremost, the sources highlight major events and significant perspectives of a given historical era. Second, I chose and edited documents to be accessible, interesting, and often surprising to survey course students. Third, I sought sources that lend themselves to analysis in classroom discussion and writing assignments — documents that vividly portray controversies marking a particular historical moment and that offer multiple avenues of interpretation.

To help students read and interpret the sources, consistently user-friendly editorial features appear. These features have been kept brief, providing just enough information to allow students to explore the sources and make their own discoveries. By minimizing editorial interventions, I hope to encourage students to focus on the documents and to become astonished, perplexed, and invigorated by what they read.

This new edition incorporates the insights and suggestions of teachers and students throughout the nation who have used *Reading the American Past*. Guided by their classroom experiences, I have increased the number of documents by 25 percent, adding one or more new documents per chapter, in order to diversify the historical voices from each era and to give students and teachers more choices for investigating major developments. The new documents provide greater attention to the West, native Americans, Spanish borderlands, and the global context of American history, as well as offering more coverage of the viewpoints of ordinary Americans, women and men, immigrants and natives, minorities and majorities, workers and bosses.

To help students read and analyze each document, "Questions for Reading and Discussion" point toward key passages in every text and encourage students to consider both the language of the document and its historical context. Likewise, every chapter concludes with thought-provoking "Comparative Questions" that ask students to consider ways the documents comment on one another and disclose the larger historical processes that shaped their era.

## FEATURES

*A wide variety of perspectives and sources.* The documents assembled here provide students with a generous cross-section of the diverse experiences that comprise the American past. The reflections of politicians and thieves, generals and privates, reformers and reprobates can be found here, along with those of the nation's countless ethnic and religious minorities. Classic sources such as John Winthrop's *Arbella* sermon (Document 4-1), George Kennan's "Long Telegram" (Document 26-2), and George W. Bush's national security strategy of preemptive war (Document 31-5) disclose the perspectives of influential leaders. The no-less-significant views of common people are revealed by such documents as a seventeenth-century catechism for Timucuan Indians in Florida (Document 3-2), eighteenth-century interviews with African slaves in the West Indies (Document 5-5), twentieth-century letters from American soldiers at war (Documents 22-3 and 25-4), and a twenty-first century al Qaeda training manual calling for *jihad* against infidels (Document 31-4). Diaries and court cases convey the immediacy of history as lived experience. Reminiscences and oral histories illuminate the past with memories of participants. Speeches, manifestos, congressional testimony, and White House tape recordings spotlight the ends and means of political power. Essays, addresses, poems, and passages from books offer the considered opinions of cultural leaders, whether captains of industry, novelists, poets, or social critics.

Since I am always on the lookout for outstanding documents to consider for future editions of *Reading the American Past*, please send any suggestions you may have to **ReadingAmericanPast@bedfordstmartins.com**. I promise to give serious consideration to every suggestion; as all teachers know, history is a collective effort.

*Allows instructors flexibility in the classroom.* The selections in *Reading the American Past* allow instructors to choose documents that best serve their teaching needs. Teachers might, for example, ask students to read documents in preparation for lectures, then refer to the assigned selections as they explain, say, the encounter between Europeans and native Americans, the tensions that led to the Civil War, or the origins and consequences of the Cold War. An instructor might devote a class to explicating a single source, such as the investigation of the conduct of Coronado's men during his exploration of the American Southwest (Document 2-5), or Reinhold Niebuhr's probing reflections about the meaning of Christianity in Detroit of the 1920s (Document 23-2), or the Central Intelligence Agency's President's Daily Brief that warned of terrorist attacks on the United States before September 11, 2001 (Document 31-3). All the documents are ideally suited for provoking discussions during lecture sessions or in section meetings. Students can be asked to adopt and defend the viewpoint of a given source, to attack it from the perspective of a historical contemporary, to dissect its assumptions and evasions, or to compare and contrast it with other sources. Selections might also be used for brief writing assignments, longer papers, or examinations. The documents open these and many other possibilities for inspiring students to investigate the American past.

*An Introduction for Students.* A short introduction at the outset of each volume explains the significance of documents for understanding history and outlines basic questions that students should ask themselves in order to decipher any primary source.

*Useful chapter apparatus.* A brief paragraph begins each chapter, setting the documents in the larger historical context detailed in the corresponding chapter of the textbook. A headnote precedes every document, identifying the source, explaining when it was produced, by whom, and why it presents a revealing point of view. Rather than cluttering documents with numerous explanatory notes, I have assumed that students will — and should — refer to a textbook for basic information about the people and events that appear in the sources.

*Questions that help students get the most out of the sources.* To guide students toward key passages and central ideas, "Questions for Reading and Discussion" follow each document. They are intended to help students identify fundamental points, analyze what a document means, and think about its larger historical significance. "Comparative Questions" at the end of each chapter ask students to ponder some of the similarities and differences among the chapter's documents, and to consider how the ideas, observations, and viewpoints expressed reveal the major historical developments of the time.

To see more clearly along the many angles of historical vision offered by the documents, students rely on the guidance, insight, and wisdom of their teachers. *Reading the American Past* gives instructors numerous opportunities to entice students to become active collaborators in the study of American history. Ideally, these documents will help persuade students that the American past is neither frozen in time nor entombed in books, but instead shapes their present and prefigures their future. Ideally, they will come to see that they do not simply read American history; they live it.

## ACKNOWLEDGMENTS

For help with this edition of *Reading the American Past* I am indebted to many people, but to none more than the following historians who have shared their professional insights and classroom experiences to suggest ways to make the documents more useful and informative for students and teachers throughout the country: Jamie Bronstein, New Mexico State University; S. Max Edelson, University of Illinois at Urbana–Champaign; Nicole Etcheson, University of Texas at El Paso; Eliga Gould, University of New Hampshire; Catherine Kaplan, Arizona State University; Jeffrey McClurken, Mary Washington College; Amy Murrell, State University of New York at Albany; Matthew Neugroschel, State University of New York at Albany; Edmund Wehrle, Eastern Illinois University; Richard Weiner, Indiana University–Purdue; Bradford Wood, Eastern Kentucky University; and Alice Yang Murray, University of California, Santa Cruz. I have also relied, as usual, on my coauthors of *The American Promise* — James L. Roark, Patricia Cline Cohen, Sarah Stage, and Susan M. Hartmann — for advice and suggestions. Although I have benefited from the support of all of these colleagues, I am nonetheless solely responsible for the final selection of documents and edited passages in this volume.

Many others contributed their energy and creativity to this project from the outset. Joan Feinberg and Chuck Christensen enthusiastically supported the publication of a collection of American history documents that aspired to the high standards readers have come to expect from Bedford/ St. Martin's. Louise Townsend brought to every page the sympathies of a historian and the balanced judgments of a seasoned editor. Emily Berleth shepherded the book throughout the production process; Cathy Jewel expertly copyedited the manuscript, attentive to the documents' numerous idiosyncrasies of spelling and phrasing; and Linda DeMasi supervised the transforming of typescript into book pages. Closer to home, Andrew Miller helped gather documents from obscure locations, and Sarah Elizabeth Johnson compiled a small mountain of copies from unwieldy volumes to allow thorough checking and proofreading. Anne Johnson offered a sympathetic ear and sound advice, lovingly tolerating my repeated seclusion with books and bytes.

# INTRODUCTION
# FOR STUDENTS

**D**ocuments allow us to peer into the past and learn what happened and what did not happen — crucial beginning points for understanding how and why the present came to be. It would be convenient if we did not need documents, if we could depend instead on our memory to tell us what happened. Unfortunately, memory is far from perfect, as we are reminded every time we misplace our keys. We not only forget things that did happen, but we also remember things that never occurred, such as erroneously thinking we put those keys right there on that shelf. Mark Twain once quipped, "When I was younger I could remember anything, whether it happened or not; but my faculties are decaying now, and soon I shall be so [old] I cannot remember any but the things that never happened."

Twain's witticism points to another important property of memory: It changes over time. Every good trial lawyer knows that memory is fragile, volatile, and subject to manipulation by our desires, intentions, and fears. Spin artists routinely perform not just on witness stands and at press conferences but whenever memory is reshaped to serve the needs of the present. Compounding the unreliability of memory are two stubborn realities: Most of the people who might remember something about what happened are dead, their memories erased forever; and no person, no single memory, ever knew all there is to know about what happened.

These flaws of memory might cause us to shrug wearily and conclude that it is impossible to determine what happened. But that conclusion would be wrong. Documents make it possible to learn a great deal — although not every last thing — about what really happened. Because documents are created by humans, they are subject to all the frailties of memory, with one vital exception. Documents do not change. Unlike memory, documents freeze words at a moment in time. Ideas, perceptions, emotions, and assumptions expressed in a document allow us to learn now about what happened then.

In effect, documents are a bridge from the present to the past. They allow us to cross over and to discover how we got from there to here.

Today you can stand where the audience stood in 1863 to listen to Abraham Lincoln's famous speech at the dedication of the cemetery for the Union soldiers killed at the battle of Gettysburg. Of course you can't hear Lincoln's voice, but you can read his words because the Gettysburg Address exists as a historical document; you can literally read this portion of the American past. The address transports the reader back to that crisp November day more than a century ago, the outcome of the war very much in doubt, when the president and commander-in-chief of more than a million men in blue uniforms explained in a few words his view of the meaning of the war for the nation and the world. Lincoln spoke of the immense sacrifice made by the soldiers at Gettysburg and evoked the nation's highest ideals in words that continue to inspire Americans long after the Civil War: "Four score and seven years ago our fathers brought forth on this continent, a new nation, conceived in Liberty, and dedicated to the proposition that all men are created equal. . . . [W]e here highly resolve that these dead shall not have died in vain — that this nation, under God, shall have a new birth of freedom — and that government of the people, by the people, for the people, shall not perish from the earth."

Because the Gettysburg Address survives in Lincoln's handwriting, we know not only what Lincoln said, but also what he did not say: for instance, that the thousands of dead soldiers at Gettysburg proved that the price of war was too high and it was time to negotiate a peace settlement. The address captured Lincoln's thoughts at that moment and preserved them, much like a historical snapshot. All documents have this property of stopping time, of indelibly recording the views of somebody at a specific moment in the past.

Documents record far more than the ideas of presidents. They disclose, for instance, Pueblo Indians' views of conquering Spaniards in the sixteenth century, accusations New Englanders made against suspected witches in the seventeenth century, the confessions of slave insurrectionists in the nineteenth century, the experiences of American soldiers in the twentieth century, and much, much more. These views and many others are recorded by the documents in this collection. They permit you to read the American past from the diversity of perspectives that contributed to the making of America: women and men, workers and bosses, newcomers and natives, slaves and masters, voters and politicians, moderates and radicals, activists and reactionaries, westerners and easterners, northerners and southerners, farmers and urbanites, the famous and the forgotten. These people created historical documents when they stole a spare moment to write a letter or record thoughts in a diary, when they talked to a scribbling friend or stranger, when they appeared in court or made a will, and when they delivered a sermon, gave a speech, or penned a manifesto. Examples of all these kinds of documents are included in *Reading the American Past*. Together, they make it possible for you to learn a great deal about what really happened.

From the almost limitless historical record, I chose documents that clearly and vividly express an important perspective about a major event or a widespread point of view during a certain historical era. I selected documents that are not only revealing but also often surprising, controversial, or troubling. My goal is to bring you face to face with the past through the eyes of the people who lived it.

*Reading the American Past* is designed to accompany *The American Promise: A History of the United States*. Each chapter in this volume parallels a chapter in *The American Promise*. The documents provide eyewitness accounts that broaden and deepen the textbook narrative. Chapter 16, for example, supplements the textbook discussion of Reconstruction with selections from the 1865 Mississippi Black Code, advertisements of former slaves seeking lost family members, resolutions of a black convention in Alabama in 1867, testimony of an African American Republican before the congressional committee investigating the Ku Klux Klan in 1871, and the report of a prominent white Republican about conditions in the South in 1875. As a rule, each chapter contains five documents; occasionally there are more shorter ones or fewer longer ones.

To help you read and understand the documents, a brief paragraph at the beginning of each chapter sketches the larger historical context explained in more detail in your textbook. Each document is also preceded by a headnote that identifies its source, explains when it was produced and by whom, and suggests why it is revealing. The questions that follow each selection point you toward key passages and fundamental ideas and ask you to consider both what a document says and what it means.

Making the most of these documents requires reading with care and imagination. Historians are interested in what a document says and what it reveals about the historical reality that is only partly disclosed by the document itself. A document might be likened to a window through which we may glimpse features of the past. A document challenges us to read and understand the words on the page as a way to look through the window and learn about the larger historical context.

Lincoln's Gettysburg Address, for example, hints that he believed many loyal Americans wondered whether the war was worth the effort, whether all those soldiers, as he said, "have died in vain." Lincoln's words do not explicitly say that many people thought the human tragedy of the war was too great, but that seems to be one of their meanings. His address attempted to answer such doubts by proclaiming the larger meaning of the war and the soldiers' deaths. His public statement of the noble ideals of the Union war effort hint at his private perception that many Americans had come to doubt whether the war had any meaning beyond the maiming or death of their loved ones.

To see such unstated historical reality in and through a document, readers must remain alert to exactly what the document says. The first step is to learn something about the era in which the document was written by reading *The American Promise* or another textbook of American history.

The next step is to read the document, keeping in mind three important questions: Who wrote the document? When was it written? Who was the intended audience? To help answer these questions, you will find useful information in the brief headnote and the questions that accompany each document, as well as in the concluding comparative questions that draw attention to similarities and differences among the documents in the chapter. But these editorial features are merely beginning points for your investigation of the documents. You should always proceed by asking who wrote a document, when, and for what audience.

Obviously, a document expresses the viewpoint of its author. Different people had different views about the same event. At Gettysburg, for example, the Confederacy suffered a painful defeat that weakened their ability to maintain their independence and to defend slavery. If Jefferson Davis, the president of the Confederacy, had delivered a Gettysburg Address, it would have been very different from Lincoln's. Documents also often convey their authors' opinions of the viewpoints of other people, including those who agree with them and those who don't. You should always ask, then: What does a document say about the viewpoint of the author? What does it say about the author's opinion about the views of other people? Does the document suggest the author's point of view was confined to a few people, shared by a substantial minority, or embraced by a great many Americans?

A document conveys valuable information about the time when it was written as well as about the author's point of view. Frequently, a person's point of view changes, making it critical to know exactly when a document was written in order to understand its meaning. When Lincoln delivered the Gettysburg Address, the outcome of the Civil War remained in doubt; seventeen months later, in April 1865, he was certain of Northern victory. The address expresses the urgency and uncertainty of the wartime crisis of 1863 rather than the relief and confidence of 1865. As you read every document, you should ask: How does the document reflect the time when it was written? What does it say about the events under way at the time? What does it suggest about how that particular time was perceived by the author and by other people?

In addition to considering who wrote a document and when, one must think about the intended audience. A politician may say one thing in a campaign speech and something quite different in a private letter to a friend. An immigrant might send a rosy account of life in America to family members in the Old Country — one that is at odds with many features of life in the New World. The intended audience shapes the message an author seeks to send. The author's expectations of what the audience wants to hear contribute to what a document says, how it is said, and what is left unsaid. Lincoln knew that his audience at Gettysburg included thousands of family members mourning the death of loved ones who "gave the last full measure of devotion" on the battlefield. He hoped his remarks would soothe the heartache of the survivors by ennobling the Union and those who died in its defense. To decipher any document, you should always ask: Who is the intended audience? How did the audience shape what the author says? Did consideration of the audience lead the author to emphasize some things and downplay or ignore others? How would the intended audience be likely to read the document? How would people who were not among the intended audience be likely to read it?

The meanings of words, like the viewpoints of individuals, also reflect their historical moment. For the most part, the documents in this collection were written in English and the authors' original spelling has been preserved (unless stated otherwise), even if it fails to conform to common usage today. Numerous documents have been translated into English from Spanish, Portuguese, Latin, German, Swedish, or one of several native American languages. But even documents originally written in English require you to translate the meaning of English words at the time the document was written into the meaning of English words today. Readers must guard against imputing today's meanings to yesterday's words. When Lincoln said "this nation" in the Gettysburg Address, he referred to the United States in 1863, a vastly different nation from the one founded four score and seven years earlier and from the one that exists today, almost a century and a half later. The word is the same, but the meaning varies greatly.

Although the meaning of many words remains relatively constant, if you are on the lookout for key words whose meanings have changed, you will discover otherwise hidden insights in the documents. You can benefit simply from exercising your historical imagination about the changing meaning of words. To Lincoln, the phrase "all men are created equal" did not have the same meaning that it did for women's rights leaders at the time, or for slaves or slave owners. You should always pay attention to the words used in a document and ask a final set of questions: How do the words in the document reflect the author, the time, and the intended audience? Would the same words have different meanings to other people at that time? Does the author's choice of words reveal covert assumptions and blind spots along with an overt message?

Historical documents provide readers not only with indelible markers of historical changes that have occurred. They also illuminate the role human beings played in making those changes. Documents instruct us about the achievements and limitations of the past as they inspire and caution us for the future. Documents also instill in us a strong sense of historical humility. Americans in the past were no less good and no more evil, no less right and no more wrong, than we are today. Their ideas, their experiences, and their times were different from ours in many respects. But they made the nation we inhabit. Ideally, the documents in *Reading the American Past* will give you an appreciation of what it took, and will continue to take, to make American history happen.

# CONTENTS

# READING
# THE AMERICAN
# PAST

*Selected Historical Documents*
*Volume II: From 1865*

# CHAPTER 16

# RECONSTRUCTION
## 1863–1877

During the turbulent years of Reconstruction, the character of freedom for former slaves was the subject of intense debate within the South and across the nation. Most Southern whites sought the most limited form of freedom for African Americans, as the black codes passed by several states suggested. Most former slaves sought to exercise their liberty to the full, as advertisements by former slaves seeking to reunite families and black conventions repeatedly declared. White vigilantes resorted to murder, lynching, and other acts of brutality to force blacks to limit their horizons. In the end, most Northern white Republicans concluded that once former slaves had the vote, the South — not the North or the federal government — should determine how best to define freedom and preserve order.

## DOCUMENT 16-1
## *Black Codes Enacted in the South*

*After the Civil War, the legal status of former slaves was defined by state legislatures throughout the South. In the months following General Robert E. Lee's surrender at Appomattox, white legislators devised laws to regulate and control former slaves. Known as black codes, these laws defined freedom for African Americans in terms that resembled slavery in many respects, as revealed in the following provisions of the Mississippi Black Code, enacted in November 1865.*

### *Mississippi Black Code,* November 1865

AN ACT to confer Civil Rights on Freedmen, and for other purposes.

Be it enacted by the Legislature of the State of Mississippi. That all freedmen, free negroes and mulattoes may sue and be sued, . . . in all the courts of law and equity of this State, and may acquire personal property . . . by descent or purchase, and may dispose of the same, in the same manner . . . that white persons

---

W. L. Fleming, ed., *Laws of Mississippi Documentary History of Reconstruction*, 2 vols. (Cleveland: A. H. Clark, 1865), 281–90.

may: Provided that the provisions of this section shall not be so construed as to allow any freedman, free negro or mulatto, to rent or lease any lands or tenements, except in incorporated towns or cities in which places the corporate authorities shall control the same. . . .

That all freedmen, free negroes and mulattoes may intermarry with each other. . . . That all freedmen, free negroes and mulattoes, who do now and have heretofore lived and cohabited together as husband and wife shall be taken and held in law as legally married, and the issue shall be taken and held as legitimate for all purposes. That it shall not be lawful for any freedman, free negro or mulatto to inter-marry with any white person; nor for any white person to inter-marry with any freedman, free negro or mulatto; and any person who shall so intermarry shall be deemed guilty of felony, and on conviction thereof, shall be confined in the State penitentiary for life. . . .

That . . . freedmen, free negroes and mulattoes are now by law competent witnesses . . . in civil cases . . . and they shall also be competent witnesses in all criminal prosecutions where the crime charged is alleged to have been committed by a white person upon or against the person or property of a freedman, free negro or mulatto. . . .

That every freedman, free negro and mulatto, shall, on the second Monday of January, one thousand eight hundred and sixty-six, and annually thereafter, have a lawful home or employment, and shall have written evidence thereof; as follows, to wit: if living in any incorporated city, town or village, a license from the mayor thereof; and if living outside of any incorporated city, town or village, from the member of the board of police of his beat, authorizing him or her to do irregular and job work, or a written contract . . . which licenses may be revoked for cause, at any time, by the authority granting the same. . . .

That all contracts for labor made with freedmen, free negroes and mulattoes, for a longer period than one month shall be in writing and in duplicate, attested and read to said freedman, free negro or mulatto, by a beat, city or county officer, or two disinterested white persons of the county in which the labor is to be performed . . . and if the laborer shall quit the service of the employer, before expiration of his term of service, without good cause, he shall forfeit his wages for that year, up to the time of quitting. . . .

That every civil officer shall, and every person may arrest and carry back to his or her legal employer any freedman, free negro or mulatto, who shall have quit the service of his or her employer before the expiration of his or her term of service without good cause, and said officer and person, shall be entitled to receive for arresting and carrying back every deserting employee aforesaid, the sum of five dollars, and ten cents per mile from the place of arrest to the place of delivery, [to] be paid by the employer. . . .

AN [A]CT to regulate the relation of Master and Apprentice, as related to Freedmen, Free Negroes, and Mulattoes.

Be it enacted by the Legislature of the State of Mississippi:

That it shall be the duty of all sheriffs, justices of the peace, and other civil officers of the several counties in this State, to report to the probate courts of their respective counties, semi-annually, at the January and July terms of said courts, all freedmen, free negroes and mulattoes, under the age of eighteen, within their respective counties, beats or districts, who are orphans, or whose parent or parents have not the means, or who refuse to provide for and support said minors, and thereupon it shall be the duty of said probate court, to order the clerk of said court to apprentice said minors to some competent and suitable person, on such terms as the court may direct. . . . Provided, that the former owner of said minors shall have the preference. . . .

That . . . the said court shall require the said master or mistress to execute bond and security, payable to the State of Mississippi, conditioned that he or she shall furnish said minor with sufficient food and clothing, to treat said minor humanely, furnish medical attention in case of sickness; [and to] teach or cause to be taught him or her to read and write, if under fifteen years old. . . . Provided, that said apprentice shall be bound by indenture, in case of males until they are twenty-one years old, and in case of females until they are eighteen years old. . . .

That in the management and control of said apprentices, said master or mistress shall have power to inflict such moderate corporeal chastisement as a father or guardian is allowed to inflict on his or her child or ward at common law. . . .

That if any apprentice shall leave the employment of his or her master or mistress, without his or her consent, said master or mistress may pursue and recapture said apprentice, and bring him or her before any justice of the peace of the county, whose duty it shall be to remand said apprentice to the service of his or her master or mistress; and in the event of a refusal on the part of said apprentice so to return, then said justice shall commit said apprentice to the jail of said county. . . .

That if any person entice away any apprentice from his or her master or mistress, or shall knowingly employ an apprentice, or furnish him or her food or clothing, without the written consent of his or her master or mistress, or shall sell or give said apprentice ardent spirits, without such consent, said person so offending shall be deemed guilty of a high misdemeanor, and shall, on conviction thereof before the county court, be punished as provided for the punishment of persons enticing from their employer hired freedmen, free Negroes or mulattoes. . . .

AN ACT to amend the Vagrant Laws of the State.

Be it further enacted,

That all freedmen, free negroes and mulattoes in this State, over the age of eighteen years, found on the second Monday in January, 1866, or thereafter, with no lawful employment or business, or found unlawfully assembling themselves together either in the day or night time, and all white persons so assembling with [them] on terms of equality, or living in adultery or fornication with a freedwoman, free negro, or mulatto, shall be deemed vagrants, and on conviction thereof, shall be fined in the sum of not exceeding, in the case of a freedman, free negro or mulatto, fifty dollars, and a white man two hundred dollars, and imprisoned at the discretion of the court, the free negro not exceeding ten days, and the white man not exceeding six months. . . .

That . . . in case any freedman, free negro or mulatto, shall fail for five days after the imposition of any fine or forfeiture upon him or her for violation of any of the provisions of this act, to pay the same, that it shall be, and is hereby made the duty of the sheriff of the proper county to hire out said freedman, free negro or mulatto, to any person who will, for the shortest period of service, pay said fine or forfeiture and all costs: Provided, a preference shall be given to the employer, if there be one, in which case the employer shall be entitled to deduct and retain the amount so paid from the wages of such freedman, free negro or mulatto, then due or to become due. . . .

AN ACT to punish certain offences. . . .

Be it enacted by the Legislature of the State of Mississippi:

That no freedman, free negro or mulatto . . . shall keep or carry fire-arms of any kind, or any ammunition, dirk or bowie knife, and on conviction thereof, in the county court, shall be punished by fine, not exceeding ten dollars, and pay the costs of such proceedings, and all such arms or ammunition shall be forfeited to the informer, and it shall be the duty of every civil and military officer to arrest any freedman, free negro or mulatto found with any such arms or ammunition, and cause him or her to be committed for trial in default of bail. . . .

That any freedman, free negro or mulatto, committing riots, routs, affrays, trespasses, malicious mischief, cruel treatment of animals, seditious speeches, insulting gestures, language or acts, or assaults on any person, disturbances of the peace, exercising the function of a minister of the Gospel, without a license from some regularly organized church, vending spirituous or intoxicating liquors, or committing any other misdemeanor . . . shall, upon conviction thereof, in the county court, be fined, not less than ten dollars, and not more than one hundred dollars, and may be imprisoned, at the discretion of the court, not exceeding thirty days. . . .

That if any white person shall sell, lend or give to any freedman, free negro or mulatto, any firearms, dirk or bowie-knife, or ammunition, or any spirituous or intoxicating liquors, such person or persons so offending, upon conviction thereof, in the county court of his or her county, shall be fined, not exceeding fifty dollars, and may be imprisoned, at the discretion of the court, not exceeding thirty days. . . .

That all the penal and criminal laws now in force in this State, defining offences and prescribing the mode of punishment for crimes and misdemeanors committed by slaves, free negroes or mulattoes, be and the same are hereby re-enacted, and declared to be in full force and effect, against freedmen, free negroes and mulattoes, except so far as the mode and manner of trial and punishment have been changed or altered by law. . . .

That if any freedman, free negro or mulatto, convicted of any of the misdemeanors provided against in this act, shall fail or refuse, for the space of five days after conviction, to pay the fine and costs imposed, such person shall be hired out by the sheriff or other officer, at public outcry, to any white person who will pay said fine and all costs, and take such convict for the shortest time.

## QUESTIONS FOR READING AND DISCUSSION

1. What civil rights, if any, did these laws confer on freed black men and women?
2. Why did the laws repeatedly refer to "freedmen, free negroes and mulattoes"?
3. In what ways did these laws limit the freedom of African Americans in Mississippi? Were these laws different from the laws governing slaves? If so, how and why?
4. Did former masters exercise any control over their former slaves? To what extent did these laws limit the freedom of white Mississippians?
5. What do these laws suggest about white Southerners' anxieties and fears regarding the end of slavery? In what ways did the laws envision postemancipation society differing from antebellum slavery?

## DOCUMENT 16-2

# Former Slaves Seek to Reunite Their Families

*With freedom, former slaves tried to reunite families slavery had separated. Some freed people traveled far and wide searching for kinfolk. Others appealed for help from the Freedmen's Bureau or enlisted literate friends to write letters of inquiry. But hundreds of former slaves placed advertisements in newspapers, asking for help in locating lost family members. The advertisements below appeared in the* Christian Recorder, *the weekly newspaper of the African Methodist Episcopal Church in Philadelphia. The ads provide a glimpse of the scars of slavery and the meanings of freedom for millions of former slaves.*

## Advertisements from the Christian Recorder, 1865–1870

January 25, 1865

INFORMATION WANTED

Jacob Brown wishes to find his sister and friends, from whom he was sold about eight years ago. He belonged to George Fisher, of Hardy County, Va., near Morefield. His sister Louisa, who was sold with him into Louisiana, has been back home once. She left three children, named respectively Peter, Isaac, and Moses. She is in New Orleans, and is anxious to hear of them. Another sister remained, named Arena or "Arenir," whose husband was named Paul Peterson. His uncles were Richard and Jacob Cassam, owned by McCoy.

Any person knowing any thing of them will confer a great favor upon the undersigned, who is their young brother, and who escaped from imprisonment in the jail, at Winchester, Va., by writing such information as shall unite those separated by slavery.

Respectfully,
Jacob Brown,
Baton Rouge, Louisiana

July 29, 1865

INFORMATION WANTED

Information is wanted of Cayrel Robinson, who left Liberty, Clay County, Missouri, about four years ago, to join the Union army at Wyandotte, Kansas; and he has not been heard from since. Any information of his whereabouts will be thankfully received by his wife.

Mrs. Fannie Robinson
Care of P. C. Cooper
Box 1129
Davenport, Iowa

*Christian Recorder*, 1865–1870.

August 5, 1865

INFORMATION WANTED

Edith Chappel left Columbia, South Carolina, on February 20th, 1865, with the army of Gen. Sherman, from the residence of Mrs. Henry Lyons. Her aunt, Fannie Bostick, can be found with

Mr. A. L. Hart
827 Lombard St.
Philadelphia

November 18, 1865

NOTICE

Information wanted of my two brothers Nelson, and Wesley Smothers, and my six sisters, Mary Ann Russell, Harriet, Matilda, Elizabeth, Henrietta, and Cornelia Smothers.

They formerly belonged to Ruth Rigla, who resided two miles from the Old Harper's Ferry Road, Frederick County, Md.

In 1837, we were all sold to South Carolina. I have not seen them since. Any information will be thankfully received by

Rev. Cyrus Boey
Oswego, N.Y.

March 10, 1866

INFORMATION WANTED

By a mother concerning her children. Mrs. Elizabeth Williams, who now resides in Marysville, California, was formerly owned, together with her children viz.: Lydia, William, Allen, and Parker, by one John Petty, who lived about six miles from the town of Woodbury, Franklin County, Tennessee. At that time she was the wife of Sandy Rucker, and was familiarly known as Betsy, sometimes called Betsy Petty.

About twenty-five years ago, the mother was sold to Mr. Marshal Stroud, by whom some twelve or fourteen years later, she was, for the second time since purchased by him, taken to Arkansas. She has never seen the above named children since. Any information given concerning them, however, will be very gratefully received by one whose love for her children survives the bitterness and hardships of many long years spent in slavery.

Preachers in the neighborhood of Woodbury, Tennessee, are especially requested to make inquiry, and communicate any information they may deem valuable either by letter or through the columns of the "Recorder."

April 7, 1866

INFORMATION WANTED

Of the children of Hagar Outlaw, who went from Wake Forest. Three of them, (their names being Cherry, Viny, and Mills Outlaw,) were bought by Abram Hester. Noah Outlaw was taken to Alabama by Joseph Turner Hillsborough. John Outlaw was sold to George Vaughan. Eli Outlaw was sold by Joseph Outlaw. He acted as watchman for old David Outlaw. Thomas Rembry Outlaw was taken away by Wm. Outlaw. Julia Outlaw was sold in New Orleans by Dr. Outlaw. I live in Raleigh, and I hope they will think enough of their mother to come and look for her, as she is growing old, and needs help. She will be glad to see them again at [illegible word]. The place is healthy, and they can all do well here. As the hand of time steals over me now so rapidly, I wish to see my dear ones once more clasped to their mother's heart as in days of yore. Come to the capital of North Carolina, and you will find your mother there, eagerly awaiting her loved ones.

Hugh Outlaw, if you should find any or all of my children, you will do me an incalculable favor by immediately informing them that their mother still lives.

May 5, 1866

INFORMATION WANTED

Of the oldest daughter Jane's children. One son by the name of Andrew, another by the name of Ransom, and another by the name of George, who were taken from me and sold when they were very small.

Also two others, (twins) one called Martha Ann and the other had no name. The name of the father of these children is Washington. He belonged to a man in Franklinton, Ky., whose name was Joseph Kearney.

The mother of these children belonged to a man in Franklin Co., Ky., by the name of Seth Ward, her name is Charity Ward, wife of Washington Kearney, who was killed by a fall from a wagon. Any information concerning any of the above will be thankfully received by addressing

W. A. Bookram
Franklinton, North Carolina

June 9, 1866

INFORMATION WANTED

Charles Metts wishes to hear from his family. His wife's name is Jane, and his children are named Margaret, Drucilla, Elizabeth, and Chas. Henry. He has not seen them for ten years. The last he heard from them was when in the Rebel Army. They were at Columbia, S.C. He could not get a chance to go to see them. He came on to Philadelphia, and is now living here.

Baptist ministers at Columbia, S.C., will please make inquiry concerning the above family. All information will be thankfully received by addressing

Chas. Metts
Care of R. A. Black
"Christian Recorder" Office.
Philadelphia, Pa.

July 14, 1866

INFORMATION WANTED

Lewis Wade wishes to learn the whereabouts of his wife, Lucy, and three children, named respectively, Benjamin, Harriet and Charlotte. He left them in 1850, they then being in Rockbridge county, Virginia. He belonged to Wm. Thompson, while his wife and children belonged to James Watts. Any information respecting them will be thankfully received by the subscriber at Chatham, Canada West, — and Heaven will bless the hand that guides the wanderers home.

Chatham, Canada West

August 11, 1866

INFORMATION WANTED

Phoebe Ann Jackson, formerly Phoebe Nichols is desirous of informing her brother, Thomas G. Nichols, of Galveston, Texas, of her location in Richmond, Va.

Her proper name was Nichols. She was called Robertson, her eldest brother being known by that name.

In the family, beside father and mother, there were twelve brothers and three sisters. Nancy and Peter Robertson were sold to New Orleans; Brother Samuel went to Georgia. Mother could only learn that Francis and Thomas were on the same boat. Mother and father have since died, as also our stepfather, whose name was Africa Hanes.

Address
Phoebe Ann Jackson
1015 Marshall street, corner 11th
Richmond, Va.

September 22, 1866

INFORMATION WANTED

Information wanted of the whereabouts of my husband, Richard Jones, and my two sons, John and Thomas. We were separated in the woods, near a place called Alleywhite, in November, 1862. I was carried back to Suffolk by the Union troops. I have heard nothing of them since.

We were owned by Birven Jones, of Smithfield, Suffolk County, Virginia. I am the granddaughter of old Tom Peet Wilson. I am much in want at this time. Ministers will please read this notice in the churches.

Matilda Jones
Direct to Anthony Bowen
Agent, *Christian Recorder*
No. 85 E St., betw'n 9th and 10th (Island)
Washington, D.C.

November 17, 1866

INFORMATION WANTED

Information wanted of Silvey Lynch, wife of Sandy Lynch, who was carried away from Carolina county, Virginia, by her "master," Wm. Goodman, in 1862. Her maiden name is Silvey Wilkins. She took with her three children. The name of the eldest is Jane; the next eldest is Henrietta; and the youngest is a boy named Alexander.

When my wife was taken away, I was in the army, performing the duties of a servant. My wife was formerly claimed as the property of one Nicholas Wilkins. She is of the Baptist persuasion. Any information concerning her whereabouts will be thankfully received from any one who will please address a letter to

Sandy Lynch
Care of Rev. J. R. V. Thomas
Box 90
Portsmouth, Virginia

March 23, 1867

INFORMATION WANTED

Information wanted of John and Lavinia Teamer, or Teamoh, who were sold in 1853, from Richmond, Va., by one John Lindsay, formally of Fortress Monroe, Va. John was nine years old, and Lavinia eight, at the time of the sale. Their mother Sarah was sold by the same party to Rosinfield, of Richmond, Va. It was thought they were sold to Texas. Ministers of the Christian Church will please inquire, as any information of the parties, will be thankfully received by their father.

Geo. Teamoh
Portsmouth, Va.
P.O. Box 152

November 2, 1867

INFORMATION WANTED

Canton, Ind., Oct. 19, 1867

John Grantson and Albert Thurston Robinson, brothers, aged respectively about 16 and 13 years, were sent from Missouri to Kentucky in the year 1863. Andrew Robinson, of Clay County, Missouri, was the owner of the boys' father, Coyed Robinson, whose wife, Frances was owned by Whiton Drew, of the same County and State, and after his death fell to his son, Dalphin Drew, who, in 1860, sold her to a man by the name of Pitcher, the former owner of her mother. This man formerly lived in Platt city, Platt county, Missouri. Albert, the youngest boy, was brought to Kentucky in August, 1863, by Dalphin Drew's wife, as nurse for her babe. John the elder boy, and his sister, Mary Eliza, with several others, were sent there a few months later to the care of Washington Gordon, Logan County, Kentucky. From thence they came back here a few months since, intending to get back to Missouri as soon as possible; but the parents may be elsewhere now. A kind, elderly colored man, by the name of Peter Garland, has voluntarily taken charge of them, and placed them in comfortable, but transient homes, but they wish very much to be united to their relatives.

Susan Trueblood

P.S. If any one should wish further information, they can write to me, and I will give it, if possible. My address is Canton, Washington, Co., Indiana.

May 8, 1869

INFORMATION WANTED

Of my son Charles Blackwell. He was sold from me in Lancaster county, Virginia, ten years ago, when quite young. He was sold from the estate of Mr. Joseph Beacham to Mr. Lewis Dix, and then taken to Mississippi. I am an old man and need the companionship of my son. Any assistance in securing information of his whereabouts will be thankfully received. Ministers in Mississippi and throughout the entire country will please read in their churches. Address information to my address,

Lewis Blackwell
Lancaster Court House, Virginia

April 2, 1870

INFORMATION WANTED

Information wanted of Sarah Williams, who I left at Halifax Court House, Va., about 25 years ago. She belonged to a man whose name was William Early, who kept a dry-goods store. Any information of her will be thankfully received by her sister, Martha Ann Good, who was taken away from Nathan Dexter, who kept a hotel at Halifax, at 12 o'clock at night, when quite small, and sold in Alabama, but who now lives at 225 Currant Alley, Philadelphia, Pa.

N.B. Ministers in the South, please read in your churches.

July 2, 1870

INFORMATION WANTED

Of my sisters, Jennette, Eliza, Caroline, America, and Elizabeth, and of my brother Harry. Also of our mother, whose name was Dinah Hickson. They were sold from Liberty, Mo., over 30 years ago, and the last time I heard of them they were on Red River. They belonged to Andy Hickson, and were sold to a man named Francis Benware. Any information of these parties will be gladly received by Moses Hickson,

Now Moses Sisseney
St. Joseph, Mo., Box 507

N.B. Pastors of churches will please read this.

December 10, 1870

INFORMATION WANTED

Of my mother Isabella, my sister Sallie, and of my grandmother, named Minna. I left them in Georgia about thirty years ago. They belonged to a man named Joe Marshall; my mother belonged to a man named Wm. Bell. They lived near Green Brier Meeting House. Any information address, Jas. Bell, Helena, Ark.

QUESTIONS FOR READING AND DISCUSSION

1. How did the people who placed these ads expect readers to recognize their lost family members?
2. What audiences did the people who placed these ads intend to reach? What was the significance of statements such as, "Ministers in Mississippi and throughout the entire country will please read in their churches"?
3. What do these ads suggest about slavery? What do these ads suggest about family relationships among slaves?
4. Do you think such ads actually helped to reunite families? Why or why not? What do these ads suggest about the meanings of freedom for former slaves?

DOCUMENT 16-3

# A Black Convention in Alabama

*Beginning in 1867, state governments throughout the old Confederacy were reorganized under the auspices of Reconstruction legislation passed by Congress, which was controlled by Northern Republicans. Congressional Reconstruction empowered former slaves by granting them the right to vote and permitting their views to be expressed through such traditional political processes as parties, conventions, campaigns, and elections. Across the South, African Americans assembled in conventions and hammered out resolutions that defined their own views of freedom, as revealed in the following address drawn up at a convention in Mobile, Alabama, and published in 1867.*

## Address of the Colored Convention to the People of Alabama, 1867

As there seems to be considerable difference of opinion concerning the "legal rights of the colored man," it will not be amiss to say that we claim exactly *the same rights, privileges and immunities as are enjoyed by white men* — we ask nothing more and will be content with nothing less. *All legal* distinctions between the races are now abolished. The word white is stricken from our laws, and every privilege which white men were formerly permitted to enjoy, merely because they were white men, now that word is stricken out, we are entitled to on the ground that we are men. *Color can no longer be pleaded for the purpose of curtailing privileges, and every public right, privilege and immunity is enjoyable by every individual member of the public.* This is the touchstone that determines all these points. So long as a park or a street is a public park or street the entire public has the right to use it; so long as a car or a steamboat is a public conveyance, it must carry all who come to it, and serve all alike who pay alike. The law no longer knows white nor black, but simply men, and consequently we are entitled to ride in public conveyances, hold office, sit on juries and do everything else which we have in the past been prevented from doing solely on the ground of our color. . . .

We have said that we intend to claim all our rights, and we submit to our white friends that it is the height of folly on their part to withhold them any longer. One-half of the voters in Alabama are black men, and in a few months there is to be an entire reorganization of the State government. The new officers — legislative, executive and judicial — will owe their election largely, if not mainly to the colored people, and every one must see clearly that the voters will then be certain to require and the officers to compel a cessation of all illegal discriminations. The question which every man now illegally discriminating against us has to decide is whether it is politic to insist upon gratifying prejudices . . . with the certainty by so doing, of incurring the lasting displeasure of one-half of the voting population of the State. We can stand it if they can, but we assure them that they are being watched closely, and that their conduct will be remembered when we have power.

There are some good people who are always preaching patience and procrastination. They would have us wait a few months, years, or generations, until the whites voluntarily give us our rights, but we do not intend to wait one day longer than we are absolutely compelled to. Look at our demands, and then at theirs. We ask of them simply that they surrender unreasonable and unreasoning prejudice; . . . that they consent to allow others as well as themselves to prosper and be happy. But they would have us pay for what we do not get; tramp through the broiling sun or pelting rain, or stand upon a platform, while empty seats

---

"Address of the Colored Convention to the People of Alabama," Montgomery *Daily State Sentinel*, May 21, 1867.

mockingly invite us to rest our wearied limbs; our sick must suffer or submit to indignity; we must put up with inconvenience of every kind; and the virtuous aspirations of our children must be continually checked by the knowledge that no matter how upright their conduct, they will be looked on as less worthy of respect than the lowest wretch on earth who wears a white skin. We ask you — only while in public, however — to surrender your prejudices, — nothing but prejudices; and you ask us to sacrifice our personal comfort, health, pecuniary interests, self-respect, and the future prospects of our children. The men who make such requests must suppose us devoid of spirit and of brains, but find themselves mistaken. Solemnly and distinctly, we again say to you, men of Alabama, that we will not submit voluntarily to such infamous discrimination, and if you will insist upon tramping on the rights and outraging the feelings of those who are so soon to pass judgment upon you, then upon your own heads will rest the responsibility for the effect of your course.

All over the state of Alabama — all over the South indeed — the colored people have with singular unanimity, arrayed themselves under the Republican banner, upon the Republican platform, and it is confidently predicted that nine-tenths of them will vote the Republican ticket. Do you ask, why is this? We answer, because:

1. The Republican Party opposed and prohibited the extension of slavery.
2. It repealed the fugitive slave law.
3. It abolished slavery in the District of Columbia.
4. It abolished slavery in the rebellious states.
5. It abolished slavery throughout the rest of the Union.
6. It put down rebellion against the Union.
7. It passed the Freedmen's Bureau Bill and the Civil Rights Bill.
8. It enfranchised the colored people of the District of Columbia.
9. It enfranchised the colored people of the nine territories.
10. It enfranchised the colored people of the ten rebel states.
11. It provided for the formation of new constitutions and state governments in those ten states.
12. It passed new homestead laws, enabling the poor to obtain land.

In short, it has gone on, step by step, doing first one thing for us and then another, and it now proposes to enfranchise our people all over the Union. It is the only party which has ever attempted to extend our privileges, and as it has in the past always been trying to do this, it is but natural that we should trust it for the future.

While this has been the course of the Republican Party, the opposition has unitedly opposed every one of these measures, and it also now opposes the enfranchisement of our people in the North. Everywhere it has been against us in the past, and the great majority of its voters hate us as cordially now as ever before. It is sometimes alleged that the Republicans of the North have not been actuated by love for us in what they have done, and therefore that we should not join them; we answer that even if that were true they certainly never professed to hate us and the opposition party has always been denouncing the "d——n nigger and abolitionist" with equal fervor. When we had no votes to give, the opposition placed us and the Republicans in the same boat, and now we reckon we'll stay in it. It may be and probably is true that some men acting with the Republican Party have cared nothing for the principles of that party; but it is also certainly true that ninety-nine-hundredths of all those who were conscientiously in favor of our rights were and are in the Republican Party, and that the great mass of those who hated, slandered and abused us were and are in the opposition party.

The memories of the opposition must be short indeed, to have forgotten their language of the past twenty years but we have *not* forgotten it.

But, say some of the members of the opposition party, "We intend to turn over a new leaf, and will hereafter give you all your rights." Perhaps they would, but we prefer not to put the new wine of political equality into the old bottles of "sectional animosity" and "caste feeling." We are somewhat fearful that those who have always opposed the extensions of rights are not sincere in their professions. . . .

Another fact should be borne in mind. While a few conservatives are making guarded promises to us the masses of that party are cursing us, and doing all they can to "make the d —— d niggers stay in their place." If we were, therefore, to join that party, it would be simply as servants, and not as equals. Some leaders, who needed our votes might treat us decently, but the great majority would expect us to stay at home until election day, and then vote as our employers dictated. This we respectfully decline doing. It seems to us safest to have as little as possible to do with those members of the community who delight to abuse us, and they are nearly, if not quite, all to be found in the ranks of the opposition party. . . .

It cannot be disguised, however, that many men calling themselves conservatives are disposed to use unfair means to carry their points. The press . . . contain numerous threats that those colored people who do not vote as their employers command, will be discharged; that the property-holders will combine, import white laborers, and discharge their colored hands, etc. Numerous instances have come to our knowledge of persons who have already been discharged because they attended Republican meetings, and great numbers more have been threatened. "Vote as we command, or starve," is the argument these men propose to make [use] of, and with it they expect to succeed.

In this expectation they will be mistaken, and we warn them before it is prosecuted any further, that their game is a dangerous one for themselves. The property which they hold was nearly all earned by the sweat of our brows — not theirs. It has been forfeited to the Government by the treason of its owners, and is liable to be confiscated whenever the Republican Party demands it. The great majority of that party is now opposed to confiscation, but if the owners of property use the power which it gives them to make political slaves of the poor, a cry will go up to Congress which will make the party a unit for confiscation.

Conservatives of Alabama, do you propose to rush upon certain destruction? Are you mad, that you threaten to pursue a policy which could only result in causing thousands of men to cry out to their leaders, "Our wives and little ones are starving because we stood by you; because we would not be slaves!" When the nation abolished slavery, you used your local governments to neutralize and defeat its action, and the nation answered by abolishing your governments and enfranchising us. If you now use your property to neutralize or defeat this, its last act, it will answer by taking away the property you are only allowed to retain through its unparalleled mercy and which you have proved yourselves so unworthy of retaining. . . .

So complete, indeed, will be our victory, that our opponents will become disheartened unless they can divide us. This is the great danger which we have to guard against. . . . In nominations for office we expect that there will be no discriminations on account of color by either wing, but that the most capable and honest men will always be put in nomination. We understand full well that our people are too deficient in education to be generally qualified to fill the higher offices, but when qualified men are found, they must not be rejected for being black.

This lack of education, which is the consequence of our long servitude, and which so diminishes our powers for good, should not be allowed to characterize our children when they come upon the stage of action, and we therefore earnestly call upon every member of the Republican Party to demand the establishment of a thorough system of common schools throughout the State. It will benefit every citizen of the State, and, indeed, of the Union, for the well-being of each enures to the advantage of all. In a Republic, education is especially necessary, as the ignorant are always liable to be led astray by the arts of the demagogue.

With education secured to all; with the old and helpless properly cared for; with justice everywhere impartially administered, Alabama will commence a career of which she will have just cause to be proud. We shall all be prosperous and happy. The sad memories of the past will be forgotten amid the joys of the present and the prospect of the future.

QUESTIONS FOR READING AND DISCUSSION

1. How did the Alabama Colored Convention define the "legal rights of the colored man"? Were they different from the legal rights of white men?

2. The convention favored the Republican party. Why were Republicans preferable to Democrats? What did the convention mean by stating, "we prefer not to put the new wine of political equality into the old bottles of 'sectional animosity' and 'caste feeling'"?

3. How did the convention propose to use political power to realize the opportunities presented by emancipation? To what extent did their address recommend punitive measures against former slaveholders and ex-Confederates? To what extent did they recommend policies specifically to aid freed men and women?

# DOCUMENT 16-4

# Klan Violence against Blacks

*White vigilantes often terrorized African Americans after emancipation. The campaign of terror intensified with congressional Reconstruction and the mobilization of black voters in the Republican party. The violence attracted the attention of Congress, which held committee hearings throughout the South in 1871 to investigate the Ku Klux Klan. The following testimony of Elias Hill — a black preacher and teacher who lived in York County, South Carolina — illustrates the tactics and purposes of white vigilantes.*

# Elias Hill

## *Testimony before Congressional Committee Investigating the Ku Klux Klan,* 1871

[The committee included a brief description of Hill.] Elias Hill is a remarkable character. He is crippled in both legs and arms, which are shriveled by rheumatism; he cannot walk, cannot help himself, has to be fed and cared for personally by others; was in early life a slave, whose freedom was purchased, his father buying his mother and getting Elias along with her, as a burden of which his master was glad to be rid. Stricken at seven years old with disease, he never was afterward able to walk, and he presents the appearance of a dwarf with the limbs of a child, the body of a man, and a finely developed intellectual head. He learned his letters and to read by calling the school children into the cabin as they passed, and also learned to write. He became a Baptist preacher, and after the war engaged in teaching colored children, and conducted the business correspondence of many of his colored neighbors. He is a man of blameless character, of unusual intelligence, speaks good English, and we put the story of his wrongs in his own language:

On the night of the 5th of last May, after I had heard a great deal of what they had done in that neighborhood, they came. It was between 12 and 1 o'clock at night when I was awakened and heard the dogs barking, and something walking, very much like horses. As I had often laid awake listening for such persons, for they had been all through the neighborhood, and disturbed all men and many women, I supposed that it was them. They came in a very rapid manner, and I could hardly tell whether it was the sound of horses or men. At last they came to my brother's door, which is in the same yard, and broke open the door and attacked his wife, and I heard her screaming and mourning. I could not understand what they said, for they were talking in an outlandish and unnatural tone, which I had heard they generally used at a negro's house. I heard them knocking around in her house. I was lying in my little cabin in the yard. At last I heard them have her in the yard. She was crying and the Ku-Klux were whipping her to make her tell where I lived. I heard her say, "Yon is his house." She has told me since that they first asked who had taken me out of her house. They said, "Where's Elias?" She said, "He doesn't stay here; yon is his house." They were then in the yard, and I had heard them strike her five or six licks when I heard her say this. Some one then hit my door. It flew open. One ran in the house, and stopping about the middle of the house, which is a small cabin, he turned around, as it seemed to me as I lay there awake, and said, "Who's here?" Then I knew they would take me, and I answered, "I am here." He shouted for joy, as it seemed, "Here he is! Here he is! We have found him!" and he threw the bedclothes off of me and caught me by one arm, while another man took me by the other and they carried me into the yard between the houses, my brother's and mine, and put me on the ground beside a boy. The first thing they asked me was, "Who did that burning? Who burned our houses?" — gin-houses, dwelling houses and such. Some had been

U. S. Congress, *Report of the Joint Select Committee to Inquire into the Condition of Affairs in the Late Insurrectionary States* (Washington, D.C., 1872), 1: 44–46.

burned in the neighborhood. I told them it was not me; I could not burn houses; it was unreasonable to ask me. Then they hit me with their fists, and said I did it, I ordered it. They went on asking me didn't I tell the black men to ravish all the white women. No, I answered them, They struck me again with their fists on my breast, and then they went on, "When did you hold a night-meeting of the Union League,[1] and who were the officers? Who was the president?" I told them I had been the president, but that there had been no Union League meeting held at that place where they were formerly held since away in the fall. This was the 5th of May. They said that Jim Raney, that was hung, had been at my house since the time I had said the League was last held, and that he had made a speech. I told them that he had not, because I did not know the man. I said, "Upon honor." They said I had no honor, and hit me again. They went on asking me hadn't I been writing to Mr. A. S. Wallace, in Congress, to get letters from him. I told them I had. They asked what I had been writing about? I told them, "Only tidings." They said, with an oath, "I know the tidings were d —— d good, and you were writing something about the Ku-Klux, and haven't you been preaching and praying about the Ku-Klux?" One asked, "Haven't you been preaching political sermons?" Generally, one asked me all the questions, but the rest were squatting over me — some six men I counted as I lay there, Said one, "Didn't you preach against the Ku-Klux," and wasn't that what Mr. Wallace was writing to me about? "Not at all," I said. "Let me see the letter,"said he; "what was it about?" I said it was on the times. They wanted the letter. I told them if they would take me back into the house, and lay me in the bed, which was close adjoining my books and papers, I would try and get it. They said I would never go back to that bed, for they were going to kill me. "Never expect to go back; tell us where the letters are." I told them they were on the shelf somewhere, and I hoped they would not kill me. Two of them went into the house. . . . They staid in there a good while hunting about and then came out and asked me for a lamp. I told them there was a lamp somewhere. They said "Where?" I was so confused I said I could not tell exactly. They caught my leg — you see what it is — and pulled me over the yard, and then left me there, knowing I could not walk nor crawl, and all six went into the house. I was chilled with the cold lying in the yard at that time of night, for it was near 1 o'clock, and they had talked and beat me and so on until half an hour had passed since they first approached. After they had staid in the house for a considerable time, they came back to where I lay and asked if I wasn't afraid at all. They pointed pistols at me all around my head once or twice, as if they were going to shoot me, telling me they were going to kill me; wasn't I ready to die, and willing to die? Didn't I preach? That they came to kill me — all the time pointing pistols at me. This second time they came out of the house, after plundering the house, searching for letters, they came at me with these pistols, and asked if I was ready to die. I told them that I was not exactly ready; that I would rather live; that I hoped they would not kill me that time. They said they would; I had better prepare. One caught me by the leg and hurt me, for my leg for forty years has been drawn each year, more and more year by

---

[1]**Union League:** Republican organization that helped mobilize African American voters.

year, and I made moan when it hurt so. One said "G——d d——n it, hush!" He had a horsewhip, and he told me to pull up my shirt, and he hit me. He told me at every lick, "Hold up your shirt." I made a moan every time he cut with the horsewhip. I reckon he struck me eight cuts right on the hip bone; it was almost the only place he could hit my body, my legs are so short — all my limbs drawn up and withered away with pain. I saw one of them standing over me or by me motion to them to quit. They all had disguises on. I then thought they would not kill me. One of them then took a strap, and buckled it around my neck and said, "Let's take him to the river and drown him.". . . After pulling the strap around my neck, he took it off and gave me a lick on my hip where he had struck me with the horsewhip. One of them said, "Now, you see, I've burned up the d—— d letter of Wallace's and all," and he brought out a little book and says, "What's this for?" I told him I did not know; to let me see with a light and I could read it. They brought a lamp and I read it. It was a book in which I had keep an account of the school. I had been licensed to keep a school. I read them some of the names. He said that would do, and asked if I had been paid for those scholars I had put down. I said no. He said I would now have to die. I was somewhat afraid, but one said not to kill me. They said "Look here! Will you put a card in the paper next week like June Moore and Sol Hill?" They had been prevailed on to put a card in the paper to renounce all republicanism and never vote. I said, "If I had the money to pay the expense, I could." They said I could borrow, and gave me another lick. They asked me, "Will you quit preaching?" I told them I did not know. I said that to save my life. They said I must stop that republican paper that was coming to Clay Hill. It has been only a few weeks since it stopped. The republican weekly paper was then coming to me from Charleston. It came to my name. They said I must stop it, quit preaching, and put a card in the newspaper renouncing republicanism, and they would not kill me; but if I did not they would come back the next week and kill me. With that one of them went into the house where my brother and my sister-in-law lived, and brought her to pick me up. As she stooped down to pick me up one of them struck her, and as she was carrying me into the house another struck her with a strap. She carried me into the house and laid me on the bed. Then they gathered around and told me to pray for them. I tried to pray. They said, "Don't you pray against Ku-Klux, but pray that God may forgive Ku-Klux. Don't pray against us. Pray that God may bless and save us." I was so chilled with cold lying out of doors so long and in such pain I could not speak to pray, but I tried to, and they said that would do very well, and all went out of the house.

### Questions for Reading and Discussion

1. What did the Klan want from Hill? Why did they not kill him?
2. The Klan was concerned about Hill's preaching, teaching, and newspaper reading? Why?
3. Why did the Klan use such brutal violence against Hill and his relatives? According to Hill, how had others been treated by the Klan? Does it appear that the Klan randomly chose people to terrorize? Why or why not?
4. What significance, if any, should be attributed to the Klan's demand that Hill "pray that God may forgive [the] Ku-Klux"? For what did they seek forgiveness? Why?

DOCUMENT 16-5

# A Northern Republican's Report on Reconstruction

*By 1875, many Republican leaders in the North concluded that Reconstruction had done enough for former slaves. Concerned about the political consequences throughout the nation of federal support for Southern, mostly black, Republicans, they decided that the best way to achieve order and stability in the South, as well as in the North, was to permit home rule in the former slave states. The disillusionment of many Northern Republicans about Reconstruction and the conviction that Southern blacks had to defend themselves with their own meager resources were illustrated in the observations — excerpted here — of Charles Nordhoff, a Northern journalist, who spent five months traveling across the South in 1875.*

## Charles Nordhoff
### The Cotton States, 1875

To make clear my point of view, it is proper to say that I am a Republican, and have never voted any other Federal ticket than the Republican; I have been opposed to slavery as long as I have had an opinion on any subject . . . ; and I am a thorough believer in the capacity of the people to rule themselves, even if they are very ignorant, better than any body else can rule them.

The following, then, are the conclusions I draw from my observations in the Cotton States:

There is not, in any of the States of which I speak, any desire for a new war; any hostility to the Union; any even remote wish to re-enslave the blacks; any hope or expectation of repealing any constitutional amendment, or in any way curtailing the rights of the blacks as citizens. The former slave-holders understand perfectly that the blacks can not be re-enslaved. . . .

That the Southern whites should rejoice over their defeat, now, is impossible. That their grandchildren will, I hope and believe. What we have a right to require is, that they shall accept the situation; and that they do. What they have a right to ask of us is, that we shall give them a fair chance under the new order of things; and that we have so far too greatly failed to do. . . .

The Southern Republicans seem to me unfair and unreasonable in another way. They complain constantly that the Southern whites still admire and are faithful to their own leaders; and that they like to talk about the bravery of the South during the war, and about the great qualities of their leading men. There seems to me something childish, and even cowardly, in this complaint. . . .

In all the States I have seen, the Republican reconstructors did shamefully rob the people. In several of them they continue to do so. . . .

As to "intimidation," it is a serious mistake to imagine this exclusively a Democratic proceeding in the South. It has been practiced in the last three years quite as much, and even more rigorously, by the Republicans. The negroes are the most

Charles Nordhoff, *The Cotton States in the Spring and Summer of 1875* (New York: D. A. Appleton & Co., 1876).

savage intimidators of all. In many localities which I visited, it was as much as a negro's life was worth to vote the Democratic ticket. . . . That there has also been Democratic intimidation is undeniable; but it does not belong to the Southern Republicans to complain of it.

Wherever one of these States has fallen under the control of Democrats, this has been followed by important financial reforms; economy of administration; and . . . by the restoration of peace and good-will. . . .

The misconduct of the Republican rulers in all these States has driven out of their party the great mass of the white people, the property-owners, tax-payers, and persons of intelligence and honesty. At first a considerable proportion of these were ranged on the Republican side. Now . . . the Republican party consists almost exclusively of the negroes and the Federal office-holders. . . .

Thus has been perpetuated what is called the "color-line" in politics, the Democratic party being composed of the great mass of the whites, including almost the entire body of those who own property, pay taxes, or have intelligence; while the Republican party is composed almost altogether of the negroes, who are, as a body, illiterate, without property, and easily misled by appeals to their fears, and to their gratitude to "General Grant," who is to them the embodiment of the Federal power.

This division of political parties on the race or color-line has been a great calamity to the Southern States.

It had its origin in the refusal of the Southern whites, after the war, to recognize the equal political rights of the blacks; and their attempts, in State legislatures, to pass laws hostile to them. This folly has been bitterly regretted by the wiser men in the South. . . .

The color-line is maintained mostly by Republican politicians, but they are helped by a part of the Democratic politicians, who see their advantage in having the white vote massed upon their side. . . .

Inevitably in such cases there must be a feeling of hostility by the whites toward the blacks, and it is an evidence of the good nature of the mass of whites that, in the main, they conduct themselves toward the blacks kindly and justly. They concentrate their dislike upon the men who have misled and now misuse the black vote, and this I can not call unjust. It is commonly said, "The negroes are not to blame; they do not know any better."

On the other hand, as the feeling is intense, it is often undiscriminating, and includes the just with the unjust among the Republicans. . . . [It] will last just as long as the color-line is maintained, and as long as Republicans maintain themselves in power by the help of the black vote, and by Federal influence. . . .

There was, in those Southern States which I have visited, for some years after the war and up to the year 1868, or in some cases 1870, much disorder, and a condition of lawlessness toward the blacks — a disposition . . . to trample them underfoot, to deny their equal rights, and to injure or kill them on slight or no provocations. The tremendous change in the social arrangements of the Southern States required time as well as laws and force to be accepted. The Southern whites had suffered a defeat which was sore to bear, and on top of this they saw their slaves — their most valuable and cherished property — taken away and made free, and not only free, but their political equals. One needs to go into the far South to know what this really meant, and what deep resentment and irritation it inevitably bred. . . .

I believe that there was, during some years, a necessity for the interference of the Federal power to repress disorders and crimes which would otherwise have spread, and inflicted, perhaps, irretrievable blows on society itself. But, after all, I am persuaded time was the great and real healer of disorders, as well as differences. We of the North do not always remember that even in the farthest South there were large property interests, important industries, many elements of civilization which can not bear long-continued disorders; and, moreover, that the men of the South are Americans, like ourselves, having, by nature or long training a love of order and permanence, and certain, therefore, to reconstitute society upon the new basis prescribed to them, and to do it by their own efforts, so soon as they were made to feel that the new order of things was inevitable. . . .

No thoughtful man can examine the history of the last ten years in the South, as he may hear it on the spot and from both parties, without being convinced that it was absolutely necessary to the security of the blacks, and the permanent peace of the Southern communities, to give the negro, ignorant, poor, and helpless as he was, every political right and privilege which any other citizen enjoys. That he should vote and that he should be capable of holding office was necessary, I am persuaded, to make him personally secure, and, what is of more importance, to convert him from a *freedman* into a *free man*.

That he has not always conducted himself well in the exercise of his political rights is perfectly and lamentably true; but this is less his fault than that of the bad white men who introduced him to political life. But, on the other hand, the vote has given him what nothing else could give — a substantive existence; it has made him a part of the State. . . .

General manhood suffrage is undoubtedly a danger to a community where, as in these States, the entire body of ignorance and poverty has been massed by adroit politicians upon one side. . . .

But the moment the color-line is broken, the conditions of the problem are essentially changed. Brains and honesty have once more a chance to come to the top. The negro, whose vote will be important to both parties, will find security in that fact. No politician will be so silly as to encroach upon his rights, or allow his opponents to do so; and the black man appears to me to have a sense of respectability which will prevent him, unencouraged by demagogues, from trying to force himself into positions for which he is unfit. He will have his fair chance, and he has no right to more.

Whenever the Federal interference in all its shapes ceases, it will be found, I believe, that the negroes will not at first cast a full vote; take away petty Federal "organizers," and the negro, left face to face with the white man, hearing both sides for the first time; knowing by experience, as he will presently, that the Democrat is not a monster, and that a Democratic victory does not mean his reenslavement, will lose much of his interest in elections. . . .

Of course, as soon as parties are re-arranged on a sound and natural basis, the negro vote will re-appear; for the leaders of each party, the Whig or Republican and the Democrat, will do their utmost to get his vote, and therein will be the absolute security of the black man. I believe, however, that for many years to come, until a new generation arrives at manhood perhaps, and, at any rate, until the black man becomes generally an independent farmer, he will be largely influenced in his political affiliations by the white. He will vote as his employer, or the planter from whom he rents land, or the white man whom he most trusts, and with whom, perhaps, he deposits his savings, tells him is best for his own interest. . . . But, at any rate, he will vote or not, as he pleases. And it is far better for him that he should act under such influences than that his vote should be massed against the property and intelligence of the white people to achieve the purposes of unscrupulous demagogues. . . .

These are my conclusions concerning those Southern States which I have seen. If they are unfavorable to the Republican rule there, I am sorry for it.

## QUESTIONS FOR READING AND DISCUSSION

1. What did Nordhoff mean by observing that Southern whites "accept the situation"? What "fair chance" did they "have a right to ask of" Northerners, and why had Northerners "greatly failed" to grant it?
2. Nordhoff criticized southern Republicans as "unfair and unreasonable." Why? To what standards had they failed to conform?
3. To what extent, according to Nordhoff, were "negroes . . . the most savage intimidators of all"? What were the consequences of Republican rule in the South? Did Nordhoff believe Reconstruction was necessary and justifiable? Why?
4. How did Nordhoff believe order could be established in the South? In his opinion, what would happen to black voters when home rule was established in the South?

## COMPARATIVE QUESTIONS

1. How do the views of former slaves expressed by white Mississippians in their state's black code differ from those of the Black Convention in Alabama? To what extent do the two documents express contrasting conceptions of freedom? To what extent do they contrast with the meanings of freedom documented in the advertisements from the *Christian Recorder*?
2. To what extent do Nordhoff's observations justify the Klan's campaign of terror against black Republicans like Hill? To what extent do Nordhoff's conclusions endorse the activities of Hill and other Republicans?
3. In what ways do Nordhoff's conclusions about the South differ from those of black and white Southerners in the other documents in this chapter? What explains the differences?
4. Documents in this chapter provide evidence that Reconstruction profoundly challenged fundamental assumptions among Northerners and Southerners, whites and blacks. Judging from these documents, what assumptions were challenged, and how, if at all, did those assumptions change during Reconstruction?

# CHAPTER 17

# BUSINESS AND POLITICS IN THE GILDED AGE
## 1870–1895

The growth of huge corporations during the Gilded Age concentrated great power in the hands of wealthy industrialists and financiers. Their power to hire and fire employees, to make or break the fortunes of many, and to shape the economic fate of the nation raised the question of how the principles of democracy should apply to corporations. Should the government attempt to regulate the relations between labor and capital? Should lawmakers set rates for public services such as railroads or telegraphs? What should be done about the growing disparity between rich and poor? Did wealthy capitalists have special social obligations? Captains of industry and their supporters answered these questions by declaring that things were as they should be, as illustrated in the first four selections that follow. Critics pointed out that the actual relations between government and industry were very different from the laissez-faire claims of business leaders, as the fifth selection documents.

## DOCUMENT 17-1
### *John D. Rockefeller Defends His Oil Trust*

*With one million dollars, John D. Rockefeller incorporated the Standard Oil Company in 1870 and within a few years the company achieved a near monopoly in the oil business in the United States. By combining more than seventy corporations under his control, Rockefeller created a massive trust that generated profits that gave him a personal fortune of more than a billion dollars. Rockefeller's success and the monopoly practices of Standard Oil attracted both proponents and critics. Rockefeller explained the virtues of industrial combinations to a congressional commission in 1899. Rockefeller's testimony, excerpted below, illustrates the logic of competition, efficiency, and necessity common among Gilded Age industrialists.*

# Testimony to the U.S. Industrial Commission, 1899

Q. Did the Standard Oil Company or other affiliated interests at any time before 1887 receive from the railroads rebates on freight shipped, or other special advantages?

A. The Standard Oil Company of Ohio, of which I was president, did receive rebates from the railroads prior to 1880, but received no special advantages for which it did not give full compensation. The reason for rebates was that such was the railroads' method of business. A public rate was made and collected by the railway companies, but so far as my knowledge extends, was never really retained in full, a portion of it was repaid to the shippers as a rebate. By this method the real rate of freight which any shipper paid was not known by his competitors nor by other railway companies, the amount being in all cases a matter of bargain with the carrying company. Each shipper made the best bargain he could, but whether he was doing better than his competitor was only a matter of conjecture. Much depended upon whether the shipper had the advantage of competition of carriers. The Standard Oil Company of Ohio, being situated at Cleveland, had the advantage of different carrying lines, as well as of water transportation in the summer, and taking advantage of those facilities made the best bargains possible for its freights. All the other companies did the same, their success depending largely upon whether they had the choice of more than one route. The Standard sought also to offer advantages to the railways for the purpose of lessening rates of freight. It offered freights in large quantity, carloads and trainloads. It furnished loading facilities and discharging facilities. It exempted railways from liability for fire. For these services it obtained contracts for special allowances on freights. These never exceeded, to the best of my personal recollections, 10 per cent. But in almost every instance it was discovered subsequently that our competitors had been obtaining as good, and, in some instances, better rates of freight than ourselves. . . .

Q. About what percentage of the profits of the Standard Oil Company came from special advantages given by the railroads. . . .

A. No percentage of the profits of the Standard Oil Company came from advantages given by railroads at any time. Whatever advantage it received in its constant efforts to reduce rates of freight was deducted from the price of oil. The advantages to the Standard from low freight rates consisted solely in the increased volume of its business arising from the low price of its products. . . .

Q. Has the Standard Oil Company received any financial favors from any railroad since 1887?

A. To my knowledge, none whatever.

Q. Has the ownership of stock in railroad companies by officers of the Standard Oil Company given the Standard advantages with those railroads over its competitors?. . . .

A. It has not. Stockholders and officers of the Standard have invested in stock of railway companies. But in no instance have they done so for the purpose of influencing the policy of the railway companies, nor to the best of my knowledge

U.S. Industrial Commission, *Preliminary Report on Trusts and Industrial Combinations,* 56th Congress, 1st Session (December 30, 1899), Document No. 476, Part 1, 794–97.

and belief has any attempt ever been made through such ownership to influence any railway in favor of the Standard.

Q. To what advantages, or favors, or methods of management do you ascribe chiefly the success of the Standard Oil Company?

A. I ascribe the success of the Standard to its consistent policy to make the volume of its business large through the merits and cheapness of its products. It has spared no expense in finding, securing, and utilizing the best and cheapest methods of manufacture. It has sought for the best superintendents and workmen and paid the best wages. It has not hesitated to sacrifice old machinery and old plants for new and better ones. It has placed its manufactories at the points where they could supply markets at the least expense. It has not only sought markets for its principal products, but for all possible by-products, sparing no expense in introducing them to the public. It has not hesitated to invest millions of dollars in methods for cheapening the gathering and distribution of oils by pipe lines, special cars, tank steamers, and tank wagons. It has erected tank stations at every important railroad station to cheapen the storage and delivery of its products. It has spared no expense in forcing its products into the markets of the world among people civilized and uncivilized. It has had faith in American oil, and has brought together millions of money for the purpose of making it what it is, and holding its markets against the competition of Russia and all the many countries which are producers of oil and competitors against American oil.

Q. What are, in your judgment, the chief advantages from industrial combinations (a) financially to stockholders; (b) to the public?

A. All the advantages which can be derived from a cooperation of persons and aggregation of capital. Much that one man can not do alone two can do together, and once admit the fact that cooperation, or, what is the same thing, combination, is necessary on a small scale, the limit depends solely upon the necessities of business. Two persons in partnership may be a sufficiently large combination for a small business, but if the business grows or can be made to grow, more persons and more capital must be taken in. The business may grow so large that a partnership ceases to be a proper instrumentality for its purposes, and then a corporation becomes a necessity. In most countries, as in England, this form of industrial combination is sufficient for a business coextensive with the parent country, but it is not so in this country. Our Federal form of government making every corporation created by a State foreign to every other State, renders it necessary for persons doing business through corporate agency to organize corporations in some or many of the different States in which their business is located. Instead of doing business through the agency of one corporation they must do business through the agencies of several corporations. If the business is extended to foreign countries, and Americans are not today satisfied with home markets alone, it will be found helpful and possibly necessary to organize corporations in such countries, for Europeans are prejudiced against foreign corporations as are the people of many of our States. These different corporations thus become cooperating agencies in the same business and are held together by common ownership of their stocks.

It is too late to argue about the advantages of industrial combinations. They are a necessity. And if Americans are to have the privilege of extending their business in all the States of the Union, and into foreign countries as well, they are a necessity on a large scale, and require the agency of more than one corporation. Their chief advantages are:

(1)  Command of necessary capital.
(2)  Extension of limits of business.
(3)  Increase of number of persons interested in the business.
(4)  Economy in the business.
(5)  Improvements and economies which are derived from knowledge of many interested persons of wide experience.
(6)  Power to give the public improved products at less prices and still make profit for stockholders.
(7)  Permanent work and good wages for laborers.

I speak from my experience in the business with which I have been intimately connected for about 40 years. Our first combination was a partnership and afterwards a corporation in Ohio. That was sufficient for a local refining business. But dependent solely upon local business we should have failed years ago. We were forced to extend our markets and to seek for export trade. This latter made the seaboard cities a necessary place of business, and we soon discovered that manufacturing for export could be more economically carried on at the seaboard, hence refineries at Brooklyn, at Bayonne, at Philadelphia, and necessary corporations in New York, New Jersey, and Pennsylvania.

We soon discovered as the business grew that the primary method of transporting oil in barrels could not last. The package often cost more than the contents and the forests of the country were not sufficient to supply the necessary material for an extended length of time. Hence we devoted attention to other methods of transportation, adopted the pipe-line system, and found capital for pipe-line construction equal to the necessities of the business.

To operate pipe lines required franchises from the States in which they were located, and consequently corporations in those States, just as railroads running through different States, are forced to operate under separate State charters. To perfect the pipe-line system of transportation required in the neighborhood of fifty millions of capital. This could not be obtained or maintained without industrial combination. The entire oil business is dependent upon this pipe-line system. Without it every well would shut down and every foreign market could be closed to us.

The pipe-line system required other improvements, such as tank cars upon railways, and finally the tank steamer. Capital had to be furnished for them and corporations created to own and operate them.

Every step taken was necessary in the business if it was to be properly developed, and only through such successive steps and by such an industrial combination is America today enabled to utilize the bounty which its land pours forth, and to furnish the world with the best and cheapest light ever known, receiving in return . . . from foreign lands nearly $50,000,000 per year, most of which is distributed in payment of American labor.

I have given a picture rather than a detail of the growth of one industrial combination. It is a pioneer, and its work has been of incalculable value. There are other American products besides oil for which the markets of the world can be opened, and legislators will be blind to our best industrial interests if they unduly hinder by legislation the combination of persons and capital requisite for the attainment of so desirable an end.

Q. What are the chief disadvantages or dangers to the public arising from them?

A. The dangers are that the power conferred by combination may be abused; that combinations may be formed for speculation in stocks rather than for conducting business, and that for this purpose prices may be temporarily raised instead of being lowered. These abuses are possible to a greater or less extent in all combinations, large or small, but this fact is no more of an argument against combinations than the fact that steam may explode is an argument against steam. Steam is necessary and can be made comparatively safe. Combination is necessary and its abuses can be minimized; otherwise our legislators must acknowledge their incapacity to deal with the most important instrument of industry. Hitherto most legislative attempts have been an effort not to control but to destroy; hence their futility.

### QUESTIONS FOR READING AND DISCUSSION

1. According to John D. Rockefeller, why did trusts, or "combinations," form? What did he mean by, "It is too late to argue about the advantages of industrial combinations"?

2. Whose interests did trusts such as Standard Oil serve? How did the company pursue those interests? Did Rockefeller's arguments apply to the oil business alone? Why or why not?

3. Rockefeller stated that "power conferred by combination may be abused." What abuses of power did he point out? Did he overlook other abuses?

4. Rockefeller declared that Standard Oil "spared no expense in forcing its products into markets of the world." Did Rockefeller attribute the company's success in the United States to "forcing its products into markets"? What accounted for the company's domestic success, according to Rockefeller?

5. To what extent did competition explain industrial combinations, according to Rockefeller? Did he believe trusts like Standard Oil attempted to limit or even eliminate competition?

## DOCUMENT 17-2

# Jay Gould on Capital and Labor

*Concerned about numerous strikes in industry after industry, the U.S. Senate initiated in 1882 a broad investigation of the relations between labor and capital. Senators traveled throughout the nation and took testimony from workers and bosses, the unemployed and employers. In 1883, Senator Henry W. Blair of New Hampshire questioned Jay Gould, a multimillionaire railroad tycoon and stock speculator. At the time of the testimony excerpted here, Gould's holdings included the Union Pacific Railroad, the Western Union Telegraph Company, and many other enterprises.*

## Testimony before the U.S. Senate, 1883

Senator Blair: We have had a man six feet high, who has driven a truck team, and who has more intellectual capacity than half, or perhaps any, of the members of Congress, offering here before this committee to agree under contract to work

U.S. Congress, Senate, *Report of the Senate Committee upon the Relations between Labor and Capital* (Washington, D.C.: Government Printing Office, 1885), 47–133.

diligently and faithfully for the next twenty years for anybody who would give him employment and agree to maintain himself and his family. That man said he had been unable to get anything ahead, and could not find a chance to work; that he was hungry, and his family were hungry, and that he didn't know what to do; and it was represented to us here that he was one of a large class. He said that folks told him to go West; but such a man cannot go West, if he tells the truth about his situation, and even if he were to adopt the plan you suggest, his family certainly could not accompany him, driving a mule on the canal tow-path. . . .

Jay Gould: Well, I know there are a great many cases of actual suffering in a large city like this, and in all large cities. It is a very difficult thing to say exactly how you are to everybody's condition. I have noticed, though, that generally if men are temperate and industrious they are pretty sure of success. In cases such as the one you describe I could almost always go back behind the scenes and find a cause for such a person's "misfortunes."

Blair: There has been testimony before us that the feeling generally between employers and employees throughout the country is one of hostility, especially on the part of the employees toward those whom they designate as monopolists. From your observation, what do you think is really the feeling as a general rule between those two classes?

Gould: I think that if left alone they would mutually regulate their relations. I think there is no disagreement between the great mass of the employees and their employers. These societies that are gotten up magnify these things and create evils which do not exist — create trouble which ought not to exist.

Blair: Of the men who conduct business enterprises and wield the power of capital in this country today, what proportion do you think are what are called "self-made men"?

Gould: I think they are all "self-made men"; I do not say self-made exactly, for the country has grown and they have grown up with it. In this country we have no system of heirlooms or of handing down estates. Every man has to stand here on his own individual merit.

Blair: What is the proportion of those men who have made their own fortunes pecuniarily, such as they are?

Gould: I think they are nearly all of that class. I think, that according to my observation in the field that I have been in, nearly every one that occupies a prominent position has come up from the ranks, worked his own way along up. . . .

Blair: . . . Won't you please give us, . . . as fully as you see fit . . . your idea in regard to the establishment of a postal telegraph for the purpose of supplanting or rivaling the existing telegraphic systems of the country now controlled by private ownership?

Gould: Well, I think that control by the government in such things is contrary to our institutions. A telegraph system, of all businesses in the world, wants to be managed by skilled experts. Our government is founded on a political idea; that is, that the party in power shall control the patronage; and if the government controlled the telegraph, the heads of the general managers and the superintendents would come off every four years, if there was a change in politics — at least as often as that — and you would not have any such efficient service as you have now. The very dividend of the Western Union depends upon the company doing the business well, keeping her customers, and developing the business. But if the government controlled it — why if the Democrats were in power it would be a Democratic telegraph, and if the Republicans came into power it would be a Republican telegraph, and if the great Reformers came in I don't know what they would do with it. I think they would —

Blair: [Interposing.] It will not be very important to decide that until they come in.

Gould: No, sir. . . .

Blair: Would you regard a corporate property like that of the Western Union, which is based upon a franchise to which the public are a party, as standing upon the same ground with reference to its right to create an increase of earning power that a piece of private property stands upon where there is no franchise obtained from the public?

Gould: I look upon corporate property in this way. I make a great difference between corporate property and private property. Corporate property is clothed with public rights and has duties to the public, and I regard those duties as paramount, really, to the rights of the stockholders. A corporation has first to perform its public obligations and the business that it was created to do; but when you have gone to that extent, then beyond that, I put it upon the same ground as private property. I judge of its value by its net earning power, the same as I judge of any private property; because I have faith in the government — I have faith in the republican institutions under which we live.

Blair: Right upon that point, is one of those public rights of which you speak — the right to exercise the power of reducing, regulating, or controlling the charges which the corporation may make for the services which it renders to the public and for which the public pays.

Gould: They can regulate those charges within the limits of legislative direction. For instance, if the legislature should come in and fix a limit, that becomes the law of the corporation. The legislature can regulate the rates to be imposed. That is the great hold of the public upon corporations. If unreasonable rates are established or unreasonable regulations made by a corporation, the legislature can come in and control them, and its directions are paramount. For instance, if there was a great clamor that the Western Union Company was charging unreasonable rates, it would be perfectly fair for the legislature to come in and examine into that question, and if they found the rates or regulations unreasonable, to control them by legislative action. Their control is paramount to every other control. But that would be a very different thing from the government going into the business of telegraphing and destroying the property of her own citizens. . . .

Blair: Do you think there would be any opposition made to a general national law regulating the fares and freight charges upon interstate commerce?

Gould: Well, I don't know about that. I think the freer you allow things to be the better. They regulate themselves. The laws of supply and demand, production and consumption, enter into and settle those matters. . . . I know that some years ago, when I was connected with the Chicago and Northwestern road, the states of Wisconsin and some of the other states passed what were called the "Granger laws"; but they repealed them afterwards, because they found on practical investigation that that legislation was tending to frighten capital away from those states, and to retard their development. Finding that to be so, in order to bring back confidence they repealed the laws and left the roads free to work out their own success. . . .

A corporation is only another name for the means which we have discovered of allowing a poor man to invest his income in a great enterprise. In other words, instead of one man owning any of these great properties in bulk, they are divided into small shares, so that the man who has got only $200 or $500 or $5,000, or whatever it may be, can own an interest in proportion to his capital. That is what a corporation means.

Blair: Then, in your opinion, the natural operation of the laws of descent as they exist in this country is to guard the community against any danger from the perpetuation of associated corporate wealth, or of great individual fortunes in the future?

Gould: Yes, sir; I do not think there is any need to be afraid of capital; capital is [not] scary. What you have got to fear is large, ignorant masses of population; I don't think the liberties of the people have anything to fear from capital. Capital is conservative and scary; but what you have to fear in a republican government like ours, where there is no military control, is large masses of uneducated, ignorant people.

Blair: Do you think there is any danger to this country in that direction?

Gould: I think we are accumulating great masses of such people from abroad. Whether we have a system that will educate them up rapidly enough I do not know.

Blair: If there was to be any legislation in any direction on this general question, don't you think that it might as well be in the direction of educating the people as in any other?

Gould: I think that is what we should do — educate the masses, elevate their moral standards. I think that is the only protection we can have for a long period in the future. When the people are educated and intelligent you have nothing to fear from them.

Blair: Do you think that to do that would accomplish more for labor than anything else we could do?

Gould: Yes, sir; because education fits a man so that if he does not like one field of labor he can go to another. Business is constantly changing, and where there is an excess of one class of labor there is very likely to be a lack of another class, and if a man is properly educated he can turn his hand to a great many different things. . . .

Blair: Do you think that the large employers of labor, the manufacturing corporations, the transportation companies, the telegraph companies, and so on, and also individuals who employ help in large masses and who necessarily classify their help, paying them different rates of wages, according to classes rather than according to their individual merits do you think that they might profitably ingraft upon their business some system of assurance, or some method by which a portion of the earnings of the laborers should be contributed to a fund, and perhaps a proportion of the profit of capital also, to secure the working people against want in seasons of nonemployment, and against the disabilities resulting from accident, sickness, or old age? Could something of that kind be introduced which would be of benefit to the laboring people?

Gould: The trouble about that is that the drones would get control of the money and spend it, in nine cases out of ten. It is a good thing in theory, but I fear it would not work well in practice.

## QUESTIONS FOR READING AND DISCUSSION

1. According to Gould, "if men are temperate and industrious they are pretty sure of success." How, then, did Gould explain the masses of poor working-class people?

2. What did Gould mean by "self-made men"? To what extent did he consider himself such a man?

3. Why did he oppose government ownership of Western Union? What did he

believe were the "public obligations" of corporations? How did corporations "regulate themselves"? Why did Gould think government regulation caused, rather than solved, problems?

4. Gould declared that "there is no disagreement between the great mass of the employees and their employers." How did he explain the "hostility" mentioned by Blair? How might Gould's own employees have replied to his statement?

## Document 17-3

# *William Graham Sumner on Social Obligations*

*Many Americans wondered what to do about those who suffered more than they benefitted from the phenomenal economic development of the Gilded Age. Should one give spare change to a beggar? Should one donate money to a home for unwed mothers? Should the government somehow help those who needed it? William Graham Sumner, a Yale professor whose ideas attracted a large national audience, answered these questions in his 1883 book,* What Social Classes Owe to Each Other, *excerpted here.*

## *What Social Classes Owe to Each Other,* 1883

There is no possible definition of "a poor man." A pauper is a person who cannot earn his living; whose producing powers have fallen positively below his necessary consumption; who cannot, therefore, pay his way. A human society needs the active co-operation and productive energy of every person in it. A man who is present as a consumer, yet who does not contribute either by land, labor, or capital to the work of society, is a burden. On no sound political theory ought such a person to share in the political power of the State. He drops out of the ranks of workers and producers. Society must support him. It accepts the burden, but he must be cancelled from the ranks of the rulers likewise. So much for the pauper. About him no more need be said. But he is not the "poor man.". . .

Neither is there any possible definition of "the weak." Some are weak in one way, and some in another; and those who are weak in one sense are strong in another. In general, however, it may be said that those whom humanitarians and philanthropists call the weak are the ones through whom the productive and conservative forces of society are wasted. They constantly neutralize and destroy the finest efforts of the wise and industrious, and are a dead-weight on the society in all its struggles to realize any better things. . . .

Under the names of the poor and the weak, the negligent, shiftless, inefficient, silly, and imprudent are fastened upon the industrious and prudent as a responsibility and a duty. On the one side, the terms are extended to cover the idle, intemperate, and vicious, who, by the combination, gain credit which they do not deserve, and which they could not get if they stood alone. On the other hand, the terms are extended to include wage-receivers of the humblest rank, who are degraded by the combination. . . .

William Graham Sumner, *What Social Classes Owe to Each Other* (New York: Harper & Brothers, 1883), 84–90.

The humanitarians, philanthropists, and reformers, looking at the facts of life as they present themselves, find enough which is sad and unpromising in the condition of many members of society. They see wealth and poverty side by side. They note great inequality of social position and social chances. They eagerly set about the attempt to account for what they see, and to devise schemes for remedying what they do not like. In their eagerness to recommend the less fortunate classes to pity and consideration they forget all about the rights of other classes; they gloss over all the faults of the classes in question, and they exaggerate their misfortunes and their virtues. They invent new theories of property, distorting rights and perpetrating injustice, as any one is sure to do who sets about the readjustment of social relations with the interests of one group distinctly before his mind, and the interests of all other groups thrown into the background. When I have read certain of these discussions I have thought that it must be quite disreputable to be respectable, quite dishonest to own property, quite unjust to go one's own way and earn one's own living, and that the only really admirable person was the good-for-nothing. The man who by his own effort raises himself above poverty appears, in these discussions, to be of no account. The man who has done nothing to raise himself above poverty finds that the social doctors flock about him, bringing the capital which they have collected from the other class, and promising him the aid of the State to give him what the other had to work for. In all these schemes and projects the organized intervention of society through the State is either planned or hoped for, and the State is thus made to become the protector and guardian of certain classes. The agents who are to direct the State action are, of course, the reformers and philanthropists. . . . [O]n the theories of the social philosophers to whom I have referred, we should get a new maxim of judicious living: Poverty is the best policy. If you get wealth, you will have to support other people; if you do not get wealth, it will be the duty of other people to support you.

No doubt one chief reason for the unclear and contradictory theories of class relations lies in the fact that our society, largely controlled in all its organization by one set of doctrines, still contains survivals of old social theories which are totally inconsistent with the former. In the Middle Ages men were united by custom and prescription into associations, ranks, guilds, and communities of various kinds. These ties endured as long as life lasted. Consequently society was dependent, throughout all its details, on status, and the tie, or bond, was sentimental. In our modern state, and in the United States more than anywhere else, the social structure is based on contract, and status is of the least importance. Contract, however, is rational — even rationalistic. It is also realistic, cold, and matter-of-fact. A contract relation is based on a sufficient reason, not on custom or prescription. It is not permanent. It endures only so long as the reason for it endures. In a state based on contract sentiment is out of place in any public or common affairs. It is relegated to the sphere of private and personal relations. . . .

A society based on contract is a society of free and independent men, who form ties without favor or obligation, and cooperate without cringing or intrigue. A society based on contract, therefore, gives the utmost room and chance for individual development, and for all the self-reliance and dignity of a free man. That a society of free men, co-operating under contract, is by far the strongest society which has ever yet existed; that no such society has ever yet developed the full measure of strength of which it is capable; and that the only social improvements which are now conceivable lie in the direction of more complete realization of a society of free men united by contract, are points which cannot be controverted.

It follows, however, that one man, in a free state, cannot claim help from, and cannot be charged to give help to, another. . . .

Every honest citizen of a free state owes it to himself, to the community, and especially to those who are at once weak and wronged, to go to their assistance and to help redress their wrongs. Whenever a law or social arrangement acts so as to injure any one, and that one the humblest, then there is a duty on those who are stronger, or who know better, to demand and fight for redress and correction. . . .

We each owe it to the other to guarantee rights. Rights do not pertain to results, but only to chances. They pertain to the conditions of the struggle for existence, not to any of the results of it; to the pursuit of happiness, not to the possession of happiness. It cannot be said that each one has a right to have some property, because if one man had such a right some other man or men would be under a corresponding obligation to provide him with some property. Each has a right to acquire and possess property if he can. . . . If we take rights to pertain to results, and then say that rights must be equal, we come to say that men have a right to be equally happy, and so on in all the details. Rights should be equal, because they pertain to chances, and all ought to have equal chances so far as chances are provided or limited by the action of society. This, however, will not produce equal results, but it is right just because it will produce unequal results — that is, results which shall be proportioned to the merits of individuals. We each owe it to the other to guarantee mutually the chance to earn, to possess, to learn, to marry, etc., etc., against any interference which would prevent the exercise of those rights by a person who wishes to prosecute and enjoy them in peace for the pursuit of happiness. If we generalize this, it means that All-of-us ought to guarantee rights to each of us. . . .

The only help which is generally expedient, even within the limits of the private and personal relations of two persons to each other, is that which consists in helping a man to help himself. This always consists in opening the chances. . . .

Now, the aid which helps a man to help himself is not in the least akin to the aid which is given in charity. If alms are given, or if we "make work" for a man, or "give him employment," or "protect" him, we simply take a product from one and give it to another. If we help a man to help himself, by opening the chances around him, we put him in a position to add to the wealth of the community by putting new powers in operation to produce. . . .

The men who have not done their duty in this world never can be equal to those who have done their duty more or less well. If words like wise and foolish, thrifty and extravagant, prudent and negligent, have any meaning in language, then it must make some difference how people behave in this world, and the difference will appear in the position they acquire in the body of society, and in relation to the chances of life. They may, then, be classified in reference to these facts. Such classes always will exist; no other social distinctions can endure. If, then, we look to the origin and definition of these classes, we shall find it impossible to deduce any obligations which one of them bears to the other. The class distinctions simply result from the different degrees of success with which men have availed themselves of the chances which were presented to them. Instead of endeavoring to redistribute the acquisitions which have been made between the existing classes, our aim should be to increase, multiply, and extend the chances. Such is the work of civilization. Every old error or abuse which is removed opens new chances of development to all the new energy of society. Every improvement in education, science, art, or government expands the chances of man on earth. Such expansion is no guarantee of equality. On the contrary, if there be liberty, some will profit by the chances eagerly and some will neglect them altogether. Therefore, the greater the chances, the more unequal will be the fortune of these two sets of men. So it ought to be, in all justice and right reason.

QUESTIONS FOR READING AND DISCUSSION

1. According to Sumner, what did one class owe to another? What defined classes?
2. What, according to Sumner, were the advantages of a "social structure . . . based on contract"? What was the relationship between contracts and freedom?
3. "Rights do not pertain to *results*, but only to *chances*," Sumner declared. Why was that distinction important to him? Why did increasing chances create greater inequality? Was great inequality therefore a sign of the health and strength of American society? Why or why not?
4. In Sumner's view, what was the proper role for government and politics in a society based on "justice and right reason"? In what ways might "agents who are to direct State action" have disagreed with him?

## DOCUMENT 17-4

# Andrew Carnegie Explains the Gospel of Wealth

*Gilded Age critics argued that the concentration of wealth in the bank accounts of the rich robbed workers of just compensation and gave the few too much power. Andrew Carnegie, one of the nation's leading industrialists and among the richest Americans of the era, defended the concentration of wealth. In an article published in 1889 — the source of the following selection — Carnegie declared that the wealthy knew best how to use their riches for the public welfare.*

## Wealth, 1889

The problem of our age is the proper administration of wealth, that the ties of brotherhood may still bind together the rich and poor in harmonious relationship. The conditions of human life have not only been changed, but revolutionized, within the past few hundred years. In former days there was little difference between the dwelling, dress, food, and environment of the chief and those of his retainers. The Indians are today where civilized man then was. . . . The contrast between the palace of the millionaire and the cottage of the laborer with us today measures the change which has come with civilization. This change, however, is not to be deplored, but welcomed as highly beneficial. It is well, nay, essential, for the progress of the race that the houses of some should be homes for all that is highest and best in literature and the arts, — and for all the refinements of civilization, rather than that none should be so. Much better this great irregularity than universal squalor. . . . The "good old times" were not good old times.

Andrew Carnegie, "Wealth," *North American Review* (1889).

Neither master nor servant was as well situated then as to-day. A relapse to old conditions would be disastrous to both — not the least so to him who serves — and would sweep away civilization with it. But whether the change be for good or ill, it is upon us, beyond our power to alter, and, therefore, to be accepted and made the best of. It is a waste of time to criticize the inevitable.

It is easy to see how the change has come. . . . In the manufacture of products we have the whole story. . . . Formerly, articles were manufactured at the domestic hearth, or in small shops which formed part of the household. The master and his apprentices worked side by side, the latter living with the master, and therefore subject to the same conditions. When these apprentices rose to be masters, there was little or no change in their mode of life, and they, in turn, educated succeeding apprentices in the same routine. There was, substantially, social equality, and even political equality, for those engaged in industrial pursuits had then little or no voice in the State.

The inevitable result of such a mode of manufacture was crude articles at high prices. To-day the world obtains commodities of excellent quality at prices which even the preceding generation would have deemed incredible. . . . The poor enjoy what the rich could not before afford. What were the luxuries have become the necessaries of life. The laborer has now more comforts than the farmer had a few generations ago. The farmer has more luxuries than the landlord had, and is more richly clad and better housed. The landlord has books and pictures rarer and appointments more artistic than the king could then obtain.

The price we pay for this salutary change is, no doubt, great. We assemble thousands of operatives in the factory, and in the mine, of whom the employer can know little or nothing, and to whom he is little better than a myth. All intercourse between them is at an end. Rigid castes are formed, and, as usual, mutual ignorance breeds mutual distrust. Each caste is without sympathy with the other, and ready to credit anything disparaging in regard to it. Under the law of competition, the employer of thousands is forced into the strictest economies, among which the rates paid to labor figure prominently, and often there is friction between the employer and the employed, between capital and labor, between rich and poor. Human society loses homogeneity.

The price which society pays for the law of competition, like the price it pays for cheap comforts and luxuries, is also great; but the advantages of this law are also greater still than its cost — for it is to this law that we owe our wonderful material development, which brings improved conditions in its train. But, whether the law be benign or not, we must say of it, as we say of the change in the conditions of men to which we have referred: It is here; we cannot evade it; no substitutes for it have been found; and while the law may be sometimes hard for the individual, it is best for the race, because it insures the survival of the fittest in every department. We accept and welcome, therefore, as conditions to which we must accommodate ourselves, great inequality of environments; the concentration of business, industrial and commercial, in the hands of a few; and the law of competition between these, as being not only beneficial, but essential to the future progress of the race. . . .

What is the proper mode of administering wealth after the laws upon which civilization is founded have thrown it into the hands of the few? And it is of this great question that I believe I offer the true solution. It will be understood that fortunes are here spoken of, not moderate sums saved by many years of effort, the returns from which are required for the comfortable maintenance and education of families. This is not wealth, but only competence, which it should be the aim of all to acquire, and which it is for the best interests of society should be acquired. . . .

There remains . . . only one mode of using great fortunes; . . . in this we have the true antidote for the temporary unequal distribution of wealth, the reconciliation of the rich and the poor — a reign of harmony. . . . It is founded upon the present most intense Individualism, and the race is prepared to put it in practice by degrees whenever it pleases. Under its sway we shall have an ideal State, in which the surplus wealth of the few will become, in the best sense, the property of the many, because administered for the common good; and this wealth, passing through the hands of the few, can be made a much more potent force for the elevation of our race than if distributed in small sums to the people themselves. Even the poorest can be made to see this, and to agree that great sums gathered by some of their fellow-citizens and spent for public purposes, from which the masses reap the principal benefit, are more valuable to them than if scattered among themselves in trifling amounts through the course of many years. . . .

Poor and restricted are our opportunities in this life, narrow our horizon, our best work most imperfect; but rich men should be thankful for one inestimable boon. They have it in their power during their lives to busy themselves in organizing benefactions from which the masses of their fellows will derive lasting advantage, and thus dignify their own lives. The highest life is probably to be reached, not by such imitation of the life of Christ as Count Tolstoi gives us, but, while animated by Christ's spirit, by recognizing the changed conditions of this age, and adopting modes of expressing this spirit suitable to the changed conditions under which we live, still laboring for the good of our fellows, which was the essence of his life and teaching, but laboring in a different manner.

This, then, is held to be the duty of the man of wealth: To set an example of modest, unostentatious living, shunning display or extravagance; to provide moderately for the legitimate wants of those dependent upon him; and, after doing so, to consider all surplus revenues which come to him simply as trust funds, which he is called upon to administer, and strictly bound as a matter of duty to administer in the manner which, in his judgment, is best calculated to produce the most beneficial results for the community — the man of wealth thus becoming the mere trustee and agent for his poorer brethren, bringing to their service his superior wisdom, experience, and ability to administer, doing for them better than they would or could do for themselves. . . .

[O]ne of the serious obstacles to the improvement of our race is indiscriminate charity. It were better for mankind that the millions of the rich were thrown into the sea than so spent as to encourage the slothful, the drunken, the unworthy. Of every thousand dollars spent in so-called charity to-day, it is probable that nine hundred and fifty dollars is unwisely spent — so spent, indeed, as to produce the very evils which it hopes to mitigate or cure. . . .

[T]he best means of benefiting the community is to place within its reach the ladders upon which the aspiring can rise — free libraries, parks, and means of recreation, by which men are helped in body and mind; works of art, certain to give pleasure and improve the public taste; and public institutions of various kinds, which will improve the general condition of the people; in this manner returning their surplus wealth to the mass of their fellows in the forms best calculated to do them lasting good.

Thus is the problem of rich and poor to be solved. The laws of accumulation will be left free, the laws of distribution free. Individualism will continue, but the millionaire will be but a trustee for the poor, intrusted for a season with a great part of the increased wealth of the community, but administering it for the community far better than it could or would have done for itself. . . .

Such, in my opinion, is the true gospel concerning wealth, obedience to which is destined some day to solve the problem of the rich and the poor, and to bring "Peace on earth, among men good will."

### QUESTIONS FOR READING AND DISCUSSION

1. According to Carnegie, what were the revolutionary changes that made it possible for "the poor [to] enjoy what the rich could not before afford"?
2. What did Carnegie believe were the relative advantages and disadvantages of competition, the concentration of wealth, and the "law of competition"?
3. Why should the goal of the truly wealthy be to bring about "the reconciliation of the rich and the poor"? How should they accomplish that goal, according to Carnegie?
4. To what extent would "the millionaire" be a better "trustee for the poor" than government agencies, reform societies, or the poor themselves?

## DOCUMENT 17-5

# Henry Demarest Lloyd Attacks Monopolies

*Muckraking journalists attacked the pompous rhetoric of free markets and self-made men. They argued that the realities of the Gilded Age had more to do with monopolies and greed than with hard work and virtuous perseverance. Henry Demarest Lloyd, a Chicago muckraker, assailed monopolies in his book* Wealth against Commonwealth, *excerpted here. Lloyd contrasted the rhetoric of competition with the reality of monopolies and lambasted the wealthy for the evil social consequences of their gains. Lloyd articulated a widespread view among working people that, for them, the age was not gilded.*

## Wealth against Commonwealth, 1894

Nature is rich; but everywhere man, the heir of nature, is poor. Never in this happy country or elsewhere — except in the Land of Miracle, where "they did all eat and were filled" — has there been enough of anything for the people. Never since time began have all the sons and daughters of men been all warm, and all filled, and all shod and roofed. Never yet have all the virgins, wise or foolish, been able to fill their lamps with oil.

The world, enriched by thousands of generations of toilers and thinkers, has reached a fertility which can give every human being a plenty undreamed of even in the Utopias. But between this plenty ripening on the boughs of our civilization and the people hungering for it step the "cornerers," the syndicates, trusts, combinations, with the cry of "over-production" — too much of everything. Holding back the riches of earth, sea, and sky from their fellows who famish and freeze in the dark, they declare to them that there is too much light and warmth and food.

---

Henry Demarest Lloyd, *Wealth against Commonwealth* (New York: Harper, 1894).

They assert the right, for their private profit, to regulate the consumption by the people of the necessaries of life, and to control production, not by the needs of humanity, but by the desires of a few for dividends. The coal syndicate thinks there is too much coal. There is too much iron, too much lumber, too much flour — for this or that syndicate.

The majority have never been able to buy enough of anything; but this minority have too much of everything to sell.

Liberty produces wealth, and wealth destroys liberty. . . . Our bignesses — cities, factories, monopolies, fortunes, which are our empires, are the obesities of an age gluttonous beyond its powers of digestion. Mankind are crowding upon each other in the centres, and struggling to keep each other out of the feast set by the new sciences and the new fellowships. Our size has got beyond both our science and our conscience. The vision of the railroad stockholder is not far-sighted enough to see into the office of the General Manager; the people cannot reach across even a ward of a city to rule their rulers; Captains of Industry "do not know" whether the men in the ranks are dying from lack of food and shelter; we cannot clean our cities nor our politics; the locomotive has more man-power than all the ballot-boxes, and millwheels wear out the hearts of workers unable to keep up beating time to their whirl. If mankind had gone on pursuing the ideals of the fighter, the time would necessarily have come when there would have been only a few, then only one, and then none left. This is what we are witnessing in the world of livelihoods. . . . This era is but a passing phase in the evolution of industrial Caesars, and these Caesars will be of a new type — corporate Caesars. . . .

In an incredible number of the necessaries and luxuries of life, from meat to tombstones, some inner circle of the "fittest" has sought, and very often obtained, the sweet power which Judge Barrett [of the New York Supreme Court] found the sugar trust had: It "can close every refinery at will, close some and open others, limit the purchases of raw material (thus jeopardizing, and in a considerable degree controlling, its production), artificially limit the production of refined sugar, enhance the price to enrich themselves and their associates at the public expense, and depress the price when necessary to crush out and impoverish a foolhardy rival."

Laws against these combinations have been passed by Congress and by many of the States. There have been prosecutions under them by the State and Federal governments. The laws and the lawsuits have alike been futile. . . .

Nothing has been accomplished by all these appeals to the legislatures and the courts, except to prove that the evil lies deeper than any public sentiment or public intelligence yet existent, and is stronger than any public power yet at call.

What we call Monopoly is Business at the end of its journey. The concentration of wealth, the wiping out of the middle classes, are other names for it. To get it is, in the world of affairs, the chief end of man. . . .

If our civilization is destroyed . . . , it will not be by . . . barbarians from below. Our barbarians come from above. Our great money-makers have sprung in one generation into seats of power kings do not know. The forces and the wealth are new, and have been the opportunity of new men. Without restraints of culture, experience, the pride, or even the inherited caution of class or rank, these men, intoxicated, think they are the wave instead of the float, and that they have created the business which has created them. To them science is but a never-ending repertoire of investments stored up by nature for the syndicates, government but a fountain of franchises, the nations but customers in squads, and a million the unit of a new arithmetic of wealth written for them. They claim a power without control, exercised through forms which make it secret, anonymous, and perpetual. The possibilities of its gratification have been widening before them without interruption since they began, and even at a thousand millions they will feel no satiation and will see no place to stop. They are gluttons of luxury and power, rough, unsocialized, believing that mankind must be kept terrorized. Powers of pity die out of them, because they work through agents and die in their agents, because what they do is not for themselves. . . .

By their windfall of new power they have been forced into the position of public enemies. Its new forms make them seem not to be within the jurisdiction of the social restraints which many ages of suffering have taught us to bind about the old powers of man over man. A fury of rule or ruin has always in the history of human affairs been a characteristic of the "strong men" whose fate it is to be in at the death of an expiring principle. The leaders who, two hundred years ago, would have been crazy with conquest, to-day are crazy with competition. To a dying era some man is always born to enfranchise it by revealing it to itself. Men repay such benefactors by turning to rend them. Most unhappy is the fate of him whose destiny it is to lead mankind too far in its own path. Such is the function of these men, such will be their lot, as that of those for whom they are building up these wizard wealths. . . .

Business motived by the self-interest of the individual runs into monopoly at every point it touches the social life — land monopoly, transportation monopoly, trade monopoly, political monopoly in all its forms, from contraction of the currency to corruption in office. The society in which in half a lifetime a man without a penny can become a hundred times a millionaire is as over-ripe, industrially, as was, politically, the Rome in which the most popular bully could lift himself from the ranks of the legion on to the throne of the Caesars. Our rising issue is with business. Monopoly is business at the end of its journey. It has got there. The irrepressible conflict is now as distinctly with business as the issue so lately met was with slavery. Slavery went first only because it was the cruder form of business.

Against the principles, and the men embodying them and pushing them to extremes — by which the powers of government, given by all for all, are used as franchises for personal aggrandizement; by which, in the same line, the common toil of all and the common gifts of nature, lands, forces, mines, sites, are turned from service to selfishness, and are made by one and the same stroke to give gluts to a few and impoverishment to the many — we must plan our campaign. The yacht of the millionaire incorporates a million days' labor which might have been given to abolishing the slums, and every day it runs the labor of hundreds of men is withdrawn from the production of helpful things for humanity, and each of us is equally guilty who directs to his own pleasure the labor he should turn to the wants of others. Our fanatic of wealth reverses the rule that serving mankind is the end and wealth an incident, and has made wealth the end and the service an accident, until he can finally justify crime itself if it is a means to the end — wealth — which has come to be the supreme good; and we follow him.

It is an adjudicated fact of the business and social life of America that to receive the profits of crime and cherish the agents who commit it does not disqualify for fellowship in the most "solid" circles — financial, commercial, religious, or social. It illustrates . . . the "morbid" character of modern business that the history of its most brilliant episodes must be studied in the vestibules of the penitentiary. The riches of the combinations are the winnings of a policy which, we have seen, has certain constant features. Property to the extent of uncounted millions has been changed from the possession of the many who owned it to the few who hold it:

1. Without the knowledge of the real owners.
2. Without their consent.
3. With no compensation to them for the value taken.
4. By falsehood, often under oath.
5. In violation of the law.

Our civilization is builded on competition, and competition evolves itself crime — to so acute an infatuation has the lunacy of self-interest carried our dominant opinion. We are hurried far beyond the point of not listening to the new conscience which, pioneering in moral exploration, declares that conduct we think right because called "trade" is really lying, stealing, murder. . . . Two social energies have been in conflict, and the energy of reform has so far proved the weaker. We have chartered the self-interest of the individual as the rightful sovereign of conduct; we have taught that the scramble for profit is the best method of administering the riches of earth and the exchange of services. Only those can attack this system who attack its central principle, that strength gives the strong in the market the right to destroy his neighbor. Only as we have denied that right to the strong elsewhere have we made ourselves as civilized as we are. And we cannot make a change as long as our songs, customs, catchwords, and public opinions tell all to do the same thing if they can. Society, in each person of its multitudes, must recognize that the same principles of the interest of all being the rule of all, of the strong serving the weak, of the first being the last — "I am among you as one that serves" — which have given us the home where the weakest is the one surest of his rights and of the fullest service of the strongest, and have given us the republic in which all join their labor that the poorest may be fed, the weakest defended, and all educated and prospered, must be applied where men associate in common toil as wherever they associate. Not until then can the forces be reversed which generate those obnoxious persons — our fittest.

Our system, so fair in its theory and so fertile in its happiness and prosperity in its first century, is now, following the fate of systems, becoming artificial, technical, corrupt; and, as always happens in human institutions, after noon, power is stealing from the many to the few. Believing wealth to be good, the people believed the wealthy to be good. But, again in history, power has intoxicated and hardened its possessors, and Pharaohs are bred in counting-rooms as they were in palaces. Their furniture must be banished to the world-garret, where lie the out-worn trappings of the guilds and slavery and other old lumber of human institutions.

## QUESTIONS FOR READING AND DISCUSSION

1. Why, according to Lloyd, was "nature . . . rich" and "man . . . poor"? What were the social consequences of "bignesses"? How did competition contribute to monopolies?
2. According to Lloyd, who were the "barbarians . . . from above," and why were they barbarians? What did Lloyd object to about "corporate Caesars"?

3. Why did laws and courts fail to control monopolies? How did monopolies compare to slavery?

4. Why was wealth against commonwealth? How, according to Lloyd, might those interested in commonwealth strike back against wealth?

## COMPARATIVE QUESTIONS

1. How did Andrew Carnegie's views of the obligations of wealthy people compare with those of William Graham Sumner, John D. Rockefeller, and Jay Gould?

2. Carnegie and Henry Demarest Lloyd offered sharply contrasting characterizations of rich people and the social consequences of their wealth. What accounted for their differences? How would Lloyd have replied to Carnegie and vice versa?

3. What can you detect about Rockefeller's, Gould's, Sumner's, and Carnegie's views of democracy? How did Lloyd's views of democracy differ? To what extent did these men believe democracy and freedom were compatible? What did they think was the proper source of political power?

4. Each of the documents in this chapter focuses on the striking inequalities among Americans in the Gilded Age. To what extent did these authors perceive inequality as a problem, and what did they propose to do about it? To what extent did they believe in the ideal of equality? Why?

# CHAPTER 18

# THE WEST IN THE GILDED AGE

## 1870–1900

After the Civil War, hundreds of thousands of migrants settled the prairies, the mountain West, and the Pacific coast, most of them moving westward, although some Mexicans moved north and others — such as the Chinese — moved east. Native Americans displaced from their tribal lands into reservations sought to resist cultural extermination. The uprooting that accompanied this restless movement strengthened some ties while weakening or breaking others. The struggles of Chinese immigrants, farmers, Texas ranchers, Mexicans, and native Americans to come to terms with the consequences of western migration and settlement are disclosed in the following documents.

## DOCUMENT 18-1

## *Observations of Chinese Immigrants*

*Immigrants as well as native-born Americans flocked to the American West. Immigrants came from Europe, Central and South America, and Asia, especially China. In 1866 and 1867, James F. Rusling, an army officer, traveled throughout the West while the transcontinental railroad was still under construction, mostly by Chinese laborers. In the following excerpt from his travel report, Rusling described the Chinese community in San Francisco. Adopting terminology common among native-born Americans, Rusling often referred to Chinese immigrants as John Chinaman or John. He contrasted the immigrants with other residents of the West. His observations reveal distinctive features of community life among Chinese immigrants in the West as well as some of the ways they were perceived by native-born Americans.*

### James F. Rusling

### *Across America,* 1866–1867

We found the Chinese everywhere on the street and in the houses, in pretty much all occupations except the highest, and were constantly amazed at their general thrift and intelligence. . . .

James F. Rusling, *Across America* (New York: Sheldon, 1874), 225–26, 300–18.

All wore the collarless Chinese blouse, looped across the breast, not buttoned — that of the poorer classes of coarse blue stuff, but of the richer of broadcloth. Otherwise, they dressed outwardly chiefly as Americans. Here and there a Chinese hat, such as you see in the tea-prints, appeared, but not often — the American felt-hat being the rule, stove-pipes never. A good many still wore the Chinese shoe, wooden-soled, with cotton uppers; but the American boot and shoe were fast supplanting this, especially among the out-door classes, such as mechanics and laborers. Pig-tails were universal, generally hanging down, but often coiled about the head, under the hat, so as to be out of the way and attract less attention. In features, of course, they were all true Mongolians; but here and there were grand faces, worthy of humanity anywhere. Their food consists chiefly of fish and rice; but the wealthier classes indulge freely in poultry and beef, and the Chinese taste for these was constantly on the increase. The old stories of their dog and rat diet are evidently myths, at least here in America. Intelligent Californians laugh at such reports as antediluvian, and say their Chinese neighbors are only too glad to eat the very best, if they can only get it.

Everybody gave them credit for sobriety, intelligence, and thrift, the three great master qualities of mankind, practically speaking; and without them the industry of the Pacific Coast, it was conceded, would soon come to a stand-still. All are expert at figures, all read and write their own tongue, and nearly all seemed intent on mastering English, as quickly and thoroughly as possible. When not at work or otherwise occupied, they were usually seen with a book in their hands, and seemed much given to reading and study.

Their chief vices were gambling, and opium-smoking; but these did not seem to prevail to the extent we had heard, and appeared really less injurious, than the current vices of other races on the Coast, all things considered. The statistics of the city and Coast somehow were remarkably in their favor, showing a less percentage of vagrancy and crime among these heathens, than any other part of the population, notwithstanding the absurd prejudices and barbarous discriminations against them.

Their quickness to learn all American ways, even when not able to speak our tongue, was very surprising. They engaged in all household duties, ran errands, worked at trades, performed all kinds of manual labor, and yet as a rule, their only dialect was a sort of chow-chow or "Pigeon English." "Pigeon" is said to be the nearest approach a Chinaman can make to *"business,"* and hence "Pigeon English" really means *business* English. Most of the words are English, more or less distorted; a few, however, are Chinese Anglicized. They always use *l* for *r* — thus *lice* for "rice"; *mi* for "I," and abound in terminal "ee's." *Chop-chop* means "very fast"; *maskee,* "don't mind." . . .

The great Chinese Emigration and Banking Companies . . . are five . . . in all, the Yung-Wo, the Sze-Yap, the Sam-Yap, the Yan-Wo, and the Ning-Yung. They contract with their countrymen in China to transport them to America, insure them constant work while here at fixed wages, and at the expiration of their contract return them to China again, dead or alive, if so desired. They each have a large and comfortable building in San Francisco, where they board and lodge their members, when they first arrive, or when sick, or out of work, or on a visit from the interior. Chinese beggars are rare on the Coast, and our public hospitals contain no Chinese patients, although John before landing has always to pay a "hospital-tax" of ten dollars. This is what it is called out there; but, of course, it is a robbery and swindle, which the Golden State ought promptly to repeal. These great Companies also act, as express-agents and bankers, all over the Coast. In all the chief towns and mining districts, wherever you enter a Chinese quarter or camp, you will find a representative of one or more of them, who will procure anything a Chinaman needs, from home or elsewhere; and faithfully remit to the Flowery Kingdom [China] whatever he wants to send, even his own dead body. Both parties appear to keep their contracts well — a breach of faith being seldom recorded. Here, surely, is evidence of fine talent for organization and management — the best tests of human intellect and capacity — and a hint at the existence of sterling qualities, which the English-speaking nations are slow to credit other races with. Such gigantic schemes, such far-reaching plans, such harmonious workings, and exact results, imply a genius for affairs, that not even the Anglo-Saxon can afford to despise, and which all others may ponder with profit. A race that can plan and execute such things as these, must have some vigor and virility in it, whatever its other peculiarities. . . .

We were driven out to the Mission Woolen Mills, where Donald McLennan, a Massachusetts Scotch-Yankee, was converting California wool into gold. The climate being so favorable to sheep, the wool-product of the coast was already large, and everywhere rapidly increasing. I mention all these things in order to emphasize the fact, that out of the 450 persons then employed about these Mills, 350 were Chinamen. For the heavier work, Americans or Europeans were preferred; but the more delicate processes, we were assured, Chinamen learned more quickly and performed more deftly, besides never becoming drunk, or disorderly, or going on a "strike." We saw them at the looms, engaged in the most painstaking and superb pieces of workmanship, and they could not have been more attentive and exact, if they had been a part of the machinery itself. And yet, these one hundred Anglo-Saxons were paid $2,95 per day, coin, while the three hundred and fifty Chinamen received only $1,10 per day, coin, though the average work of each was about the same. Without this cheap labor of John Chinaman, these Mills would have had to close up; with it, they were run at a profit, and at the same time were a great blessing and credit to the Pacific Coast in every way. So, also, the Central Pacific Railroad was then being pushed through and over the Sierra Nevadas, by some ten thousand Chinamen, working for one dollar per day each, in coin, and finding themselves, when no other labor could be had for less than two dollars and a half per day. . . . It was simply a question with the Central [Pacific Railroad] directors, whether to build the road or not. Without John, it was useless to attempt it, as the expense would have bankrupted the company, even if other labor could have been had, which was problematical. With him, the road is already a fact accomplished; and in view of possible contingencies, nationally and politically, who shall say we have completed it an hour too soon? Here are practical results, not shadowy theories — of such a character, too, as should give one pause, however anti-Chinese, and ought to outweigh a world of prejudices. . . .

Next we explored the famous Barbary Coast [of San Francisco]. . . . Here in narrow, noisome alleys are congregated the wretched Chinese women, that are imported by the ship-load, mainly for infamous purposes. As a class, they are small in stature, scarcely larger than an American girl of fourteen, and usually quite plain. . . . They may be seen on the street any day in San Francisco, bonnetless, fan in hand, hobbling along in their queer little shoes, perfect fac-similes of the figures you see on lacquered ware imported from the Orient. They are not more immodest, than those of our own race, who ply the same vocation in

Philadelphia and New York; and their fellow-countrymen, it seemed, behaved decently well even here. But here is the great resort of sailors, miners, "long-shore-men, and the floating population generally of San Francisco, and the brutality and bestiality of the Saxon and the Celt here all comes suddenly to the surface, as if we were fiends incarnate." . . .

The Chinese temple, synagogue, or "Josh House," of which we had heard such conflicting reports, stands . . . in the heart of the city. It is a simple structure of brick, two or three stories high, and would attract little or no attention, were it not for a plain marble slab over the entrance, with "Sze-Yap Asylum" carved upon it, in gilt letters, and the same repeated in Chinese characters. It was spoken of as a "Heathen Synagogue," a "Pagan Temple," etc., and we had heard much ado about it . . . long before reaching San Francisco. But, in reality, it appeared to be only an asylum or hospital, for the unemployed and infirm of the Sze-Yap Emigration Company; with a small "upper chamber," set apart for such religious services, as to them seemed meet. The other companies all have similar hospitals or asylums, but we visited only this one. The first room on the ground-floor seemed to be the business-room or council-chamber of the company, and this was adorned very richly with crimson and gold. Silk-hangings were on the walls, arm-chairs elaborately carved along the sides, and at the end on a raised platform stood a table and chair, as if ready for business. The room adjoining seemed to be the general smoking and lounging room of the members of the company. Here several Chinamen lay stretched out, on rude but comfortable lounges, two smoking opium, all the rest only cigarritos — taking their afternoon siesta. Back of this were the dining-room, kitchen, etc., but we did not penetrate thither. A winding stairs brought us to the second floor, and here was the place reserved for religious purposes, — an "upper chamber" perhaps twenty by thirty feet, or even less. Its walls and ceiling were hung with silk, and here and there were placards, inscribed with moral maxims from Confucius and other writers, much as we suspend the same on the walls of our Sunday-school rooms, with verses on them from *our* Sacred writings. These mottoes, of course, were in Chinese; but they were said to exhort John to virtue, fidelity, integrity, the veneration of ancestors, and especially to admonish the young men not to forget, that they were away from home, and to do nothing to prejudice the character of their country in the eyes of foreigners. A few gilded spears and battle-axes adorned either side, while overhead hung clusters of Chinese lanterns, unique and beautiful. Flowers were scattered about quite profusely, both natural and artificial — the latter perfect in their way. At the farther end of the room, in "a dim religious light," amid a barbaric array of bannerets and battle-axes, stood their sacred Josh — simply a Representative Chinaman, perhaps half life-size, with patient pensive eyes, long drooping moustaches, and an expression doubtless meant for sublime repose or philosophic indifference. Here all orthodox Chinamen in San Francisco, connected with the Sze-Yap company, were expected to come at least once a year, and propitiate the deity by burning a slip of paper before his image. There was also some praying to be done, but this was accomplished by putting printed prayers in a machine run by clock-work. Tithes there were none — at least worth mentioning. Altogether, this seemed to be a very easy and cheap religion; and yet, easy as it was, John did not seem to trouble himself much about it. The place looked much neglected, as if worshippers were scarce, and devotees infrequent. A priest or acolyte, who came in and trimmed the ever-burning lamp, without even a bow or genuflection to Josh, was the only person about the "Temple," while we were there. The dormitories and apartments for the sick and infirm, we were told, were on this same floor and above; but we did not visit them. This Josh-worship, such as it is, seemed to be general among the Chinese, except the handful gathered into the various Christian churches; but it did not appear to be more than a ceremony. The truth is, John is a very practical creature, and was already beginning to understand, that he is in a new land and among new ideas. Surely, our vigorous, aggressive California Christians stand in no danger from such Pagan "Temples," and our all-embracing nationality can well afford to tolerate them, as China in turn tolerates ours.

QUESTIONS FOR READING AND DISCUSSION

1. How did the immigrants exhibit the "great master qualities of mankind"? What did Rusling's specification of "master qualities" suggest about his ideas and those of "everybody"?

2. According to Rusling, in what ways did immigrants confront prejudices in California? Did he exhibit his own prejudices? According to Rusling, were both Chinese and Americans "races" with their own "peculiarities"?

3. What contributions were the immigrants making to the West, according to Rusling? What did the immigrants achieve for themselves? Why was it significant that, according to Rusling, "John is a very practical creature"?

4. Rusling contrasted immigrant men and women. Why? What were the distinctive features of family and religious life among the immigrants?

5. Because Rusling could not read or speak Chinese, how reliable were his observations? How did he get his information? What or whose perspectives were missing from his report?

## DOCUMENT 18-2

# Swedish Immigrants on the Kansas Prairie

*Settlers raced to western farms after the Civil War. Some pulled up stakes in an eastern state and moved on. Others immigrated from Europe, lured by the prospects of a better life. Gustaf Lindgren; his wife, Ida; and their five children left Sweden for Lake Sibley, a small settlement in Kansas. Ida's brother, Magnus; his wife, Johanna; and other Swedes accompanied the Lindgrens. Ida's letters to her mother and sister in Sweden described experiences shared by many rural families on the move. Ida wrote in Swedish; English translations from excerpts of her letters follow.*

## Ida Lindgren
### Letters, 1870–1874

15 May 1870

What shall I say? Why has the Lord brought us here? Oh, I feel so oppressed, so unhappy! Two whole days it took us to get here and they were not the least trying part of our travels. We sat on boards in the work-wagon, packed in so

H. Arnold Barton, ed., *Letters from the Promised Land: Swedes in America, 1840–1914* (Minneapolis: University of Minnesota Press, 1975), 143–55.

tightly that we could not move a foot, and we drove across endless, endless prairies, on narrow roads; no, not roads, tracks like those in the fields at home when they harvested grain. No forest but only a few trees which grow along the rivers and creeks. And then here and there you see a homestead and pass a little settlement. The closer we came to Lake Sibley the more desolate the country seemed and the roads were altogether frightful, almost trackless. When we finally saw Lake Sibley, at twelve o'clock at night, it consisted of four houses, two larger ones and two small, very small, as well as two under construction. The rooms Albinson had written he wished to rent us were not available but we were quartered here in Albinson's attic. The attic is divided into three rooms but with no doors; I have hung up a sheet in front of our "door." When I immediately asked, after we arrived, to go up with the children and put them to bed, there was no table, no chair, no bed, nothing, and there we were to stay! I set the candle on the floor, sat down beside it, took the children in my lap and burst into tears. I feel about to do so now too, I cannot really pull myself together and the Albinsons appear quite uncomfortable every time they see me. The Indians are not so far away from here, I can understand, and all the men you see coming by, riding or driving wagons, are armed with revolvers and long carbines, and look like highway robbers. . . .

Gustaf is out with Magnus and Albinson to look at the land he bought and to see if there is any that Magnus would like to have. . . .

5 January 1871

. . . I must tell you about our Christmas! On "Little Christmas Eve," Sylvan (he had been in Chicago but came here to celebrate Christmas with us) and Tekla Littorin (she is employed four miles on the other side of Manhattan) arrived, then we all went over to Magnus and his family for Christmas Eve. They had everything so fine and cozy, three rooms downstairs and the attic all in order, and a Christmas tree of green cedar with candles and bonbons and apples on it, and the coffee table set, so it was really Christmas-like, and because of that I could not tear my thoughts away from you and from my old home and the tears kept welling up! . . . Then we had a few Christmas presents, the finest was a rocking chair which Magnus and his family gave us. From Gustaf I got two serving dishes, since we had none before, from Olga a rolling pin for cookies and three dozen clothespins to hang up wet clothes with when you do laundry, from Hugo a pair of woolen mittens, from Littorin a knitting bag, from Hedenskog material for a little sofa which we have made for the children to sleep on, from Carlson a pair of fire tongs.

I gave Magnus and the family a sofa cover, which I sewed last summer to exhibit, and a couple of pictures of Gustaf Vasa which we had with us. Hugo gave them a pair of drinking glasses and Olga gave Magnus a pipe pouch and Johanna clothespins like those I got. Helge had himself sewn a little lamp mat for them. I gave Gustaf a pair of real coarse, strong gloves for working, and Olga, Hugo, and Helge had gotten together to buy him a hat. Olga and Hugo had earned the money themselves that they used for Christmas presents.

After we had eaten our rice pudding and Christmas cookies, we sang a few hymns and "Hosianna," and then we broke up, though we all slept there, all the bachelors in the attic, Magnus and family in the kitchen, Gustaf, the younger children, and myself in the bedroom, and Olga, Tekla, and their hired girl in the parlor.

We stayed until the morning after the second day of Christmas and then we went home. Tekla, Ida, and Anna stayed on there, and so instead we took their hired girl and their hired man to help us slaughter our pig, which we were to have for New Year's, when Magnus and his family were to come to us. After we had finished with the slaughtering, I got started with laundry while we had Johanna's hired girl here, for it had been so cold that we had not been able to do any washing for some weeks, so now we had so much laundry. *Washing* is the worst work I have to do, for my hands can't take it and they have been so miserable, swollen and raw, that all the knuckles bled, but now it is better. . . .

All my menfolk are out in the woods today to cut fence rails, they took lunch with them so I don't know how long they will be away. . . . Now, dear Mamma, I will end for today, for I must tidy up a little here in the room before they come back from the woods, since it is Twelfth Night, and then I must skin two small hares for this evening. . . .

9 February 1871

. . . Magnus was here for a while this morning, so I can send greetings from them. They are well, but their hired girl has left so that Johanna now has to do everything herself, as I do. With the difference, however, that they are only two plus their hired man, while we are ten to bake and cook and wash up for every day, and worst of all, to wash clothes for. There is not much time for me to sit and do any handwork. America may be good in many respects, but certainly not for having servants. For no matter how good they may be in Sweden, as soon as they reach America's free soil they become far from good and want instead to be gentlemen and ladies themselves, and would rather be waited on than wait on others. It is hard to get used to this and therefore I think it is better to be one's own maid, though one gets awfully tired sometimes in both the back and legs. And my hands will not really accustom themselves to these tasks; they are sometimes roses, sometimes burrs, but never lilies smooth as satin. . . .

18 October 1871

. . . I was alone at home with the younger children, for Hugo had ridden over to Lindesfrid in the morning to help with the corn picking there, and around noon there was such a smell and smoke from burnt grass that I immediately suspected there was a prairie fire somewhere. Suddenly the smoke was so thick and ashes flew around (it was blowing up a real storm and the wind lay this way), that I couldn't see the nearest hills. I believed then that the fire was right upon us, so I ran in and gathered up the silver and Gustaf's watch and a little money all in a bundle, and put Anna on my arm and took Ida by the hand and ran through the woods down to the river. Oh, Mamma, how my heart pounded! I felt I could do nothing else, alone as I was with my little ones, for I believed that with the force with which the fire was moving today, it would go across the cornfield and set off all six haystacks and then there would be no saving the house. And then the woods were close by and there are now so many dry leaves that I felt there was no safety there. No, only in the river, there must I fly; if the fire should come so close to us I would take both children in my arms and go as far out into the water as I could: that was what I thought.

But first we sat down on the bank; Anna did not understand the danger, but Ida cried so bitterly that I had to try to calm her, fearful as I was myself. I told them, "We should pray to the Lord that He protect us." And so I prayed as well as I could, and the children repeated after me, and last of all we prayed for rain — for it had now been dry for several months and everything was so dried out that the fire could range freely, and no autumn grain could be sowed either until rain came. We sat there a couple of hours; once I took water in a spoon to drink but could not for it was black with ash that had flown here. When I thought the smoke had become less, I had the children sit where they were and I went up onto a rise to look.

Behold, there stood our house and home and the six haystacks unharmed, but a few that were out in the field and were intended for the owner were burned up, and the fire flamed on the other side on the hills and dales. We then went home and when we came in we fell on our knees and thanked the Lord who had protected us and our house and home. A little while later Hugo came: they had seen the fire coming toward us and Gustaf had sent him to help me, and a half hour or hour later Lindgren came himself, for all danger was far from past. I now felt so calm and glad, but they had to be out with water and rags with others to fight the fire until late at night, when all danger was over here. How far the fire later continued, we don't know, but many, many people had their hay burned up and we also had two small stacks at Lindesfrid that were lost. At Magnus's no hay burned but a section of fence. . . .

25 August 1874

. . . We have not had rain since the beginning of June, and then with this heat and often strong winds as well, you can imagine how everything has dried out. There has also been a general lamentation and fear for the coming year. We have gotten a fair amount of wheat, rye, and oats, for they are ready so early, but no one here will get corn or potatoes. We have a few summer potatoes but many don't even have that, and we thought and hoped we would get a good crop of other potatoes, but will evidently get none. Instead of selling the oats and part of the rye as we had expected, we must now use them for the livestock, since there was no corn. We are glad we have the oats (for many don't have any and must feed wheat to the stock) and had hoped to have the corn leaves to add to the fodder. But then one fine day there came millions, trillions of grasshoppers in great clouds, hiding the sun, and coming down onto the fields, eating up *everything* that was still there, the leaves on the trees, peaches, grapes, cucumbers, onions, cabbage, everything, everything. Only the peach stones still hung on the trees, showing what had once been there.

They are not the kind of grasshoppers we see in Sweden but are large, grayish ones. Now most of them have moved southward, to devastate other areas since there was nothing more to consume here. Certainly it is sad and distressing and depressing for body and soul to find that no matter how hard one drudges and works, one still has nothing, less than nothing.

Don't you think, Mamma, that I could bear a little bit of *success*? I think myself that I could well manage a little, but the Lord sees best what we need and therefore He daily strikes and humiliates us, now in one way, now in another. But still He has not crushed our stubborn hearts. As burdened as I feel, my heart is still not weighed down, it still rises up from time to time.

QUESTIONS FOR READING AND DISCUSSION

1. Why did Ida Lindgren "feel so oppressed, so unhappy" upon arriving in Lake Sibley? Can you detect what she expected to find there? What was the significance of her observation that her hands were "sometimes roses, sometimes burrs, but never lilies smooth as satin"?

2. In what ways did the Lindgrens cooperate with their friends and neighbors? The people Lindgren mentioned in her letters were almost all other Swedes. What does that suggest about settlement patterns and cultural norms on the Kansas prairie?

3. What did the gifts exchanged at the Christmas celebration reveal about the Lindgrens' daily lives and aspirations?

4. Lindgren wrote that "America may be good in many respects, but certainly not for having servants." What was the problem with servants? In what respects did she believe America may be good? How might she have defined "a little bit of *success*"?

## DOCUMENT 18-3

# *Texas Rangers on the Mexican Border*

*Texas Rangers patrolled South Texas against cattle rustlers and vigilantes. Organized as state law enforcement officials in 1874, the Rangers had existed unofficially since the 1830s and had fought in the campaigns for Texas independence and in the Civil War. The Rangers often repressed lawlessness among both whites and Mexicans along the Texas–Mexico border, as described in the following selection from a memoir by Ranger N. A. Jennings. The document recounts forms of rough and ready law enforcement common in Texas and other parts of the West, especially in encounters between white Americans and people of color, whether or not they were American citizens.*

## N. A. Jennings
### *A Texas Ranger,* 1875

We went by easy stages across the country to Corpus Christi, the pretty little old town on the Gulf of Mexico. We were ordered there because Mexican raiders had come across the Rio Grande and spread terror throughout that part of Texas.

We arrived at Corpus Christi on the morning of April 22, 1875, and found the country in the wildest state of excitement. We were told how large bands of raiders were coming from every direction to lay waste the countryside and burn the town. The most extravagant rumors found ready credence from the terrorized people. The civil authorities seemed helpless. Large parties of mounted and well-armed men, residents of Nueces County, were riding over the country, committing the most brutal outrages, murdering peaceable Mexican farmers and stockmen who had lived all their lives in Texas. These murderers called themselves vigilance committees and pretended that they were acting in the cause of law and order. . . .

---

N. A. Jennings, *A Texas Ranger* (New York: Scribners, 1899), 129–43.

It seemed that the excitement had been first caused by a raid made by Mexicans (from Mexico) in the neighborhood of Corpus Christi. These raiders had stolen cattle and horses, burned ranch houses, murdered men and ravished women, and then escaped back to Mexico. The excitement which followed was seized upon by a number of white men living in Nueces County as a fitting time to settle up old scores with the Mexican residents of that and some of the adjoining counties. Many of these Mexicans, it must be admitted, had been making a livelihood by stealing and skinning cattle, and the sheriffs and constables had failed to make any efforts to detect and punish them.

On the evening of April 24th a report was brought in that a party of raiders from Mexico had been seen at La Para about sixty miles from Corpus Christi. [Captain Leander H.] McNelly at once started with the troop to that place and arrived the following day. There we learned that the party reported to be Mexican raiders was really a posse of citizens from Cameron County, under a deputy sheriff, and that they "had come out to protect the people of La Para from further outrages from the citizens of Nueces County," meaning certain lawless bands organized in Nueces County.

McNelly ordered the deputy sheriff to take his posse back and disband it. After some demurring on the part of the posse, this was done. We went into camp and McNelly sent scouting parties out in every direction to disband the various vigilance committees and "regulators" which were roaming through the country.

On April 26th two companies of white men, commanded by T. Hynes Clark and M. S. Culver, cattlemen, came to our camp and said they wanted to cooperate with the Rangers.

"We need no one to cooperate with us," said the Captain. "I have heard that some of you men are the very ones accused of a number of outrages committed on Mexican citizens of this State, and you must disband at once and not reassemble, except at the call and under the command of an officer of the State. If you don't do as I say, you will have us to fight."

The Texans didn't like this high-handed way of talking and were disposed at first to dispute McNelly's authority, but the Captain showed them very quickly that he meant business and they disbanded. . . .

On May 20th we moved down the Rio Grande. We found the frontier in a state of great excitement. Reports of a dozen different raiding parties would be brought in daily and the scouting parties had no rest. I was in the saddle almost continually. At night we would either camp where we happened to be, or continue riding, in the attempt to head off some party of raiders of whom we had heard. Many of the reports of raiders brought to us were groundless, but the greater number were true. Through fear of the robbers, the law-abiding citizens withheld information which would have insured the capture of the marauders.

The people said that large droves of cattle and horses were stolen and driven across the Rio Grande into Mexico almost nightly. This, we found, had been going on for years. The United States military authorities had never made a determined effort to put a stop to the wholesale stealing, although the raiders at times would pass close to the frontier posts.

McNelly continued to keep out scouting parties of Rangers, and this course had the effect of lessening the number of raids, but not of wholly putting an end to them.

While we were encamped . . . a Mexican brought the information to Captain McNelly that a party of raiders was crossing into Texas, below Brownsville. . . .

McNelly at once ordered us to saddle up, and within fifteen minutes we were trotting after him and a Mexican guide over the prairie. . . .

It was three days . . . before we managed to head off the raiders. They had fourteen men and we had eighteen, including Captain McNelly. We found them with the cattle on a little bit of wooded rising ground surrounded by a swamp. . . . They were drawn up in line and were evidently expecting us. When they saw us, they drew off behind the rising ground and fired at a range of about one hundred and fifty yards with carbines.

"Boys," said Captain McNelly, "the only way we can get at those thieves is to cross through the mud of the swamp and ride them down. I don't think they can shoot well enough to hit any of us, but we'll have to risk that. Don't fire at them until you're sure of killing every time."

Following the Captain, we started across the swamp for the little hill, the Mexican marauders continually firing at us. When we got near the hill, the Captain put spurs to his horse and we followed him with a yell as we flew through the mud and up the hill. The Mexicans answered our yell with one of defiance and a volley. At first, we thought they had not done any execution, but we soon saw they had aimed only too well, for three of our horses went crashing to the ground, one after the other, throwing their riders over their heads. . . .

Then came a single shot from the Mexicans, and one of the Rangers . . . popularly known in the troop as "Sonny," threw his arms above his head, reeled in his saddle for a moment and fell headlong to the ground. We all saw him fall and the sight roused a fury in our hearts that boded ill for the men in front of us.

The Mexicans fired at us again, but this time did no harm. The next instant we were upon them, shooting and yelling like demons. They stood their ground for a moment only; then turned and fled. As they went they leaned forward on their horses' necks and fired back at us, but they were demoralized by the fury of our onslaught and could hit nothing.

Crack! bang! bang! went our revolvers, and at nearly every shot one of the raiders went tumbling from his saddle. We had ridden hard to get to that place and our horses were played out, but we never thought of giving up the chase on that account. The remembrance of poor young Smith's face, as he threw up his hands and reeled from his horse, was too fresh in our minds for us to think of anything but revenge.

Some of our enemies were well mounted, but even these we gradually overhauled. We flew over the prairie at a killing pace, intent only on avenging our comrade's death. When we finally did halt, our horses were ready to drop from exhaustion; but the work had been done — every man of the raiders but one was dead. . . .

The Mexican guerrilla chief, Cortina[1] . . . was a Mexican general, and at the head of all the cattle raiding. He had a contract to deliver in Cuba six hundred head of Texas cattle every week. About three thousand robbers were under him, and he was virtually the ruler of the Mexican border. . . .

We recovered 265 stolen cattle after the fight. We procured a wagon and took the body of young Smith to Brownsville. The next day the bodies of the thirteen dead Mexicans were brought to Brownsville and laid out in the plaza. Nearly the

---

[1]**Cortina:** Refers to Juan Nepomuceno Cortinas, a famous Mexican leader on the Texas-Mexican border.

entire population of Matamoras, the Mexican town immediately across the Rio Grande from Brownsville, came over to see their dead countrymen. The Mexicans were very angry, and we heard many threats that Cortina would come across with his men and kill us all. McNelly sent back word to Cortina that he would wait for him and his men. Cortina's bandits outnumbered the Rangers and the United States forces . . . about ten to one at that time. . . .

We gave Smith a fine military funeral. The Mexican raiders were all buried in one trench. The Mexican inhabitants of the town stood in their doorways and scowled at us whenever we passed, but they were afraid to express their hatred openly. They contented themselves with predicting that Cortina would come over and kill us. . . .

At the time of which I write, Matamoras [i.e., Matamoros] was full of Mexican soldiers, and Cortina had put the place under martial rule. No person was allowed on the streets after sunset, except by special permit; that is, no Mexican was allowed on the streets. For some reason best known to Cortina, Americans were not included in the rule, and the Mexican sentries had orders to pass Americans. The Rangers were not slow to take advantage of this state of affairs, and we paid frequent visits to Matamoras after nightfall. We went there for two reasons: to have fun, and to carry out a set policy of terrorizing the Mexicans at every opportunity. Captain McNelly assumed that the more we were feared, the easier would be our work of subduing the Mexican raiders; so it was tacitly understood that we were to gain a reputation as fire-eating, quarrelsome dare-devils as quickly as possible, and to let no opportunity go unimproved to assert ourselves and override the "Greasers." Perhaps everyone has more or less of the bully inherent in his make-up, for certain it is that we enjoyed this work hugely.

"Each Ranger was a little standing army in himself," was the way [one ranger] . . . put it to me, speaking, long afterward, of those experiences. The Mexicans were afraid of us, collectively and individually, and added to the fear was a bitter hatred. . . .

The news of our big fight with the raiders reached everyone's ears, and none was so bold as to attempt to resist our outrages upon the peace and dignity of the community, for such they undoubtedly were. But we accomplished our purpose. In a few weeks we were feared as men were never before feared on that border, and, had we given the opportunity, we should undoubtedly have been exterminated by the Mexicans, but there was "method in our madness," and we never gave them the chance to get the better of us.

## Questions for Reading and Discussion

1. Why were white men in Nueces County committing "brutal outrages" and what did the Rangers do about it, according to N. A. Jennings? Who were "regulators" and what did they seek?

2. There "was method in our madness," Jennings declared. What did he mean? What goals did the Rangers hope to achieve with their methods? Were the methods lawful? Just? Justified?

3. Who were "Greasers," according to Jennings? How did they differ from other people? What attitudes did Mexicans have toward the Rangers and why, according to Jennings?

4. What conclusions does Jennings's memoir suggest about violence, racism, law, and justice along the Texas–Mexico border? Do you think Jennings's account describes typical or atypical behavior and attitudes?

## Document 18-4

# *In-mut-too-yah-lat-lat Describes White Encroachment*

*The steady encroachment of white settlers on native American lands reached a crescendo after 1870. Soldiers who had fought in the Civil War now tried to confine tribes into reservations. In 1877, the chief of the Chute-pa-lu, or Nez Percés, resisted the U.S. government's demands that his tribe relinquish their land. In-mut-too-yah-lat-lat, or Chief Joseph as he was called by the whites, fought against overwhelming odds, was defeated, and with his tribe was moved to Fort Leavenworth, then to Baxter Springs, Kansas, and finally to Indian Territory. In 1879, In-mut-too-yah-lat-lat explained to a white audience why he fought. His explanation, excerpted here, described experiences shared by countless other native Americans.*

## Chief Joseph

### *Speech to a White Audience, 1879*

My friends, I have been asked to show you my heart. I am glad to have a chance to do so. I want the white people to understand my people. Some of you think an Indian is like a wild animal. This is a great mistake. I will tell you all about our people, and then you can judge whether an Indian is a man or not. I believe much trouble and blood would be saved if we opened our hearts more. I will tell you in my way how the Indian sees things. . . .

My name is In-mut-too-yah-lat-lat (Thunder Traveling over the Mountains). I am chief of the Wal-lam-wat-kin band of Chute-pa-lu, or Nez Percés (nose-pierced Indians). I was born in eastern Oregon, thirty-eight winters ago. My father was chief before me. When a young man, he was called Joseph by Mr. Spaulding, a missionary. He died a few years ago. There was no stain on his hands of the blood of a white man. He left a good name on the earth. He advised me well for my people.

Our fathers gave us many laws, which they had learned from their fathers. These laws were good. They told us to treat all men as they treated us; that we should never be the first to break a bargain; that it was a disgrace to tell a lie; that we should speak only the truth; that it was a shame for one man to take from another his wife, or his property without paying for it. We were taught to believe that the Great Spirit sees and hears everything, and that he never forgets; that hereafter he will give every man a spirit-home according to his deserts: if he has been a good man, he will have a good home; if he has been a bad man, he will have a bad home. This I believe, and all my people believe the same.

We did not know there were other people besides the Indian until about one hundred winters ago, when some men with white faces came to our country. They brought many things with them to trade for furs and skins. They brought tobacco, which was new to us. They brought guns with flint stones on them, which frightened our women and children. Our people could not talk with these white-faced men, but they used signs which all people understand. These men were Frenchmen, and they called our people "Nez Percés," because they wore rings in their noses for ornaments. Although very few of our people wear them now, we are still called by

"An Indian's Views of Indian Affairs" *North American Review,* 128 (April 1879), 412–33.

the same name. . . . The first white men of your people who came to our country were named Lewis and Clark. They also brought many things that our people had never seen. They talked straight, and our people gave them a great feast, as a proof that their hearts were friendly. These men were very kind. They made presents to our chiefs and our people made presents to them. We had a great many horses, of which we gave them what they needed, and they gave us guns and tobacco in return. All the Nez Percés made friends with Lewis and Clark, and agreed to let them pass through their country, and never to make war on white men. This promise the Nez Percés have never broken. No white man can accuse them of bad faith, and speak with a straight tongue. It has always been the pride of the Nez Percés that they were the friends of the white men. When my father was a young man there came to our country a white man [Mr. Spaulding] who talked spirit law. He won the affections of our people because he spoke good things to them. At first he did not say anything about white men wanting to settle on our lands. Nothing was said about that until about twenty winters ago, when a number of white people came into our country and built houses and made farms. At first our people made no complaint. They thought there was room enough for all to live in peace, and they were learning many things from the white men that seemed to be good. But we soon found that the white men were growing rich very fast, and were greedy to possess everything the Indian had. My father was the first to see through the schemes of the white men, and he warned his tribe to be careful about trading with them. He had suspicion of men who seemed so anxious to make money. I was a boy then, but I remember well my father's caution. He had sharper eyes than the rest of our people.

Next there came a white officer [Governor Stevens], who invited all the Nez Percés to a treaty council. After the council was opened he made known his heart. He said there were a great many white people in the country, and many more would come; that he wanted the land marked out so that the Indians and white men could be separated. If they were to live in peace it was necessary, he said, that the Indians should have a country set apart for them, and in that country they must stay. My father, who represented his band, refused to have anything to do with the council, because he wished to be a free man. He claimed that no man owned any part of the earth, and a man could not sell what he did not own.

Mr. Spaulding took hold of my father's arm and said, "Come and sign the treaty." My father pushed him away, and said: "Why do you ask me to sign away my country? It is your business to talk to us about spirit matters, and not to talk to us about parting with our land." Governor Stevens urged my father to sign his treaty, but he refused. "I will not sign your paper," he said; "you go where you please, so do I; you are not a child, I am no child; I can think for myself. No man can think for me. I have no other home than this. I will not give it up to any man. My people would have no home. Take away your paper. I will not touch it with my hand."

My father left the council. Some of the chiefs of the other bands of the Nez Percés signed the treaty, and then Governor Stevens gave them presents of blankets. My father cautioned his people to take no presents, for "after a while," he said, "they will claim that you have accepted pay for your country." Since that time four bands of the Nez Percés have received annuities from the United States. My father was invited to many councils, and they tried hard to make him sign the treaty, but he was firm as the rock, and would not sign away his home. His refusal caused a difference among the Nez Percés.

Eight years later [1863] was the next treaty council. A chief called Lawyer, because he was a great talker, took the lead in this council, and sold nearly all the Nez

Percés country. . . . In this treaty Lawyer acted without authority from our band. He had no right to sell the Wallowa . . . country. That had always belonged to my father's own people, and the other bands had never disputed our right to it. . . .

In order to have all people understand how much land we owned, my father planted poles around it and said: "Inside is the home of my people — the white man may take the land outside. Inside this boundary all our people were born. It circles around the graves of our fathers, and we will never give up these graves to any man."

The United States claimed they had bought all the Nez Percés country outside of Lapwai Reservation, from Lawyer and other chiefs, but we continued to live in this land in peace until eight years ago, when white men began to come inside the bounds my father had set. We warned them against this great wrong, but they would not leave our land, and some bad blood was raised. The white men represented that we were going upon the war-path. They reported many things that were false.

The United States Government again asked for a treaty council. . . . It was then that I took my father's place as chief. In this council I made my first speech to white men. I said to the agent who held the council:

"I did not want to come to this council, but I came hoping that we could save blood. The white man has no right to come here and take our country. We have never accepted any presents from the Government. Neither Lawyer nor any other chief had authority to sell this land. It has always belonged to my people. It came unclouded to them from our fathers, and we will defend this land as long as a drop of Indian blood warms the hearts of our men."

The agent said he had orders, from the Great White Chief at Washington, for us to go upon the Lapwai Reservation, and that if we obeyed he would help us in many ways. "You must move to the agency," he said. I answered him: "I will not. I do not need your help; we have plenty and we are contented and happy if the white man will let us alone. The reservation is too small for so many people with all their stock. You can keep your presents; we can go to your towns and pay for all we need; we have plenty of horses and cattle to sell, and we won't have any help from you; we are free now; we can go where we please. Our fathers were born here. Here they lived, here they died, here are their graves. We will never leave them." The agent went away, and we had peace for a little while. . . .

Year after year we have been threatened, but no war was made upon my people until General Howard came to our country two years ago [1877] and told us that he was the white war-chief of all that country. He said: "I have a great many soldiers at my back. . . . The country belongs to the Government, and I intend to make you go upon the reservation.". . .

I said to General Howard: ". . . I do not believe that the Great Spirit Chief gave one kind of men the right to tell another kind of men what they must do."

## QUESTIONS FOR READING AND DISCUSSION

1. In what ways did Chute-pa-lu laws differ from white laws? Did the two groups share some beliefs about laws? What was the significance of "spirit law," and how did it differ from other laws, if at all?

2. How did whites gain control of some Chute-pa-lu land? To what extent did conflicting concepts of land ownership divide the Chute-pa-lu from whites and from one another?

3. In-mut-too-yah-lat-lat told General Howard, "I do not believe that the Great Spirit Chief gave one kind of men the right to tell another kind of men what they must do." What gave General Howard "the right" to insist that the Chute-pa-lu "go upon a reservation," regardless of their wishes? To what extent was the conflict between the Chute-pa-lu and the federal government rooted in disagreements about what "kind of men" Americans were and could be?

## DOCUMENT 18-5

# *A Plea to "Citizenize" Indians*

*Indian reservations, some white reformers believed, isolated native Americans and prevented them from acquiring the benefits of American life. In 1887 the federal government launched boarding schools designed to remove young Indians from their homes and families on reservations and, as Richard Pratt — the leader of one such school — declared, "citizenize" them. In a speech to a group of reformers in 1892, Pratt described the vices of reservations and the virtues of schooling that would bring young native Americans into the mainstream of American society. Pratt's remarks illustrate the combination of ideas about racial and cultural superiority common among white Americans of the era.*

## Richard Pratt

## *"Kill the Indian . . . and save the man,"* 1892

A great general[1] has said that the only good Indian is a dead one. . . . In a sense, I agree with the sentiment, but only in this: that all the Indian there is in the race should be dead. Kill the Indian in him, and save the man.

We are just now making a great pretence of anxiety to civilize the Indians. I use the word "pretence" purposely, and mean it to have all the significance it can possibly carry. Washington believed that commerce freely entered into between us and the Indians would bring about their civilization, and Washington was right. He was followed by Jefferson, who inaugurated the reservation plan. Jefferson's reservation was to be the country west of the Mississippi; and he issued instructions to those controlling Indian matters to get the Indians there, and let the Great River be the line between them and the whites. Any method of securing removal — persuasion, purchase, or force — was authorized.

Jefferson's plan became the permanent policy. The removals have generally been accomplished by purchase, and the evils of this are greater than those of all the others combined. . . .

It is a sad day for the Indians when they fall under the assaults of our troops . . . but a far sadder day is it for them when they fall under the baneful influences

---

*Official Report of the Nineteenth Annual Conference of Charities and Correction* (1892), 46–59; reprinted in Richard H. Pratt, "The Advantages of Mingling Indians with Whites," in *Americanizing the American Indians: Writings by the "Friends of the Indian" 1880–1900* (Cambridge, MA: Harvard University Press, 1973), 260–71.

[1]Pratt refers to Philip Sheridan, a high-ranking Union general during the Civil War, overall commander of army forces in the West from 1867 to 1883, and general-in-chief of the army from 1883 to 1888.

of a treaty agreement with the United States whereby they are to receive large annuities, and to be protected on reservations, and held apart from all association with the best of our civilization. The destruction is not so speedy, but it is far more general. . . .

"Put yourself in his place" is as good a guide to a proper conception of the Indian and his cause as it is to help us to right conclusions in our relations with other men. For many years we greatly oppressed the black man, but the germ of human liberty remained among us and grew, until, in spite of our irregularities, there came from the lowest savagery into intelligent manhood and freedom among us more than seven millions of our population, who are to-day an element of industrial value with which we could not well dispense. However great this victory has been for us, we have not yet fully learned our lesson nor completed our work; nor will we have done so until there is throughout all of our communities the most unequivocal and complete acceptance of our own doctrines, both national and religious. Not until there shall be in every locality throughout the nation a supremacy of the Bible principle of the brotherhood of man and the fatherhood of God, and full obedience to the doctrine of our Declaration that "we hold these truths to be self-evident, that all men are created free and equal, with certain inalienable rights," and of the clause in our Constitution which forbids that there shall be "any abridgment of the rights of citizens on account of race, color, or previous condition." I leave off the last two words "of servitude," because I want to be entirely and consistently American.

Inscrutable are the ways of Providence. Horrible as were the experiences of its introduction, and of slavery itself, there was concealed in them the greatest blessing that ever came to the Negro race — seven millions of blacks from cannibalism in darkest Africa to citizenship in free and enlightened America; not full, not complete citizenship, but possible — probable — citizenship, and on the highway and near to it.

There is a great lesson in this. The schools did not make them citizens, the schools did not teach them the language, nor make them industrious and self-supporting. Denied the right of schools, they became English-speaking and industrious through the influences of association. Scattered here and there, under the care and authority of individuals of the higher race, they learned self-support and something of citizenship, and so reached their present place. No other influence or force would have so speedily accomplished such a result. Left in Africa, surrounded by their fellow savages, our seven millions of industrious black fellow-citizens would still be savages. Transferred into these new surroundings and experiences, behold the result. They became English-speaking and civilized, because forced into association with English-speaking and civilized people; became healthy and multiplied, because they were property; and industrious, because industry, which brings contentment and health, was a necessary quality to increase their value.

The Indians under our care remained savage, because forced back upon themselves and away from association with English-speaking and civilized people, and because of our savage example and treatment of them. . . .

We have never made any attempt to civilize them with the idea of taking them into the nation, and all of our policies have been against citizenizing and absorbing them. . . .

A public school system especially for the Indians is a tribal system; and this very fact says to them that we believe them to be incompetent, that they must not attempt to cope with us. Such schools build up tribal pride, tribal purposes, and tribal demands upon the government. They formulate the notion that the government owes them a living and vast sums of money; and by improving their education on these lines, but giving no other experience and leading to no aspirations beyond the tribe, leaves them in their chronic condition of helplessness, so far as reaching the ability to compete with the white race is concerned. . . .

Indian schools are just as well calculated to keep the Indians intact as Indians as Catholic schools are to keep the Catholics intact. Under our principles we have established the public school system, where people of all races may become unified in every way, and loyal to the government; but we do not gather the people of one nation into schools by themselves, and the people of another nation into schools by themselves, but we invite the youth of all peoples into all schools. We shall not succeed in Americanizing the Indian unless we take him in in exactly the same way. . . .

[A]nother influence . . . in Indian matters . . . is the missionary as a citizenizing influence upon the Indians. The missionary goes to the Indian; he learns the language; he associates with him; he makes the Indian feel he is friendly, and has great desire to help him; he even teaches the Indian English. But the fruits of his labor, by all the examples that I know, have been to strengthen and encourage him to remain separate and apart from the rest of us. Of course, the more advanced, those who have a desire to become civilized, and to live like white men, who would with little encouragement go out into our communities, are the first to join the missionary's forces. They become his lieutenants to gather in others. The missionary must necessarily hold on to every help he can get to push forward his schemes and plans, so that he may make a good report to his Church; and, in order to enlarge his work and make it a success, he must keep his community together. Consequently, any who care to get out into the nation, and learn from actual experience what it is to be civilized, what is the full length and breadth and height and depth of our civilization, must stay and help the missionary. The operation of this has been disastrous to any individual's escape from the tribe, has vastly and unnecessarily prolonged the solution of the question, and has needlessly cost the charitable people of this country large sums of money, to say nothing of the added cost to the government, the delay in accomplishing their civilization, and their destruction caused by such delay. . . .

We make our greatest mistake in feeding our civilization to the Indians instead of feeding the Indians to our civilization. America has different customs and civilizations from Germany. What would be the result of an attempt to plant American customs and civilization among the Germans in Germany, demanding that they shall become thoroughly American before we admit them to the country? Now, what we have all along attempted to do for and with the Indians is just exactly that, and nothing else. We invite the Germans to come into our country and communities, and share our customs, our civilization, to be of it; and the result is immediate success. Why not try it on the Indians? Why not invite them into experiences in our communities? Why always invite and compel them to remain a people unto themselves?

It is a great mistake to think that the Indian is born an inevitable savage. He is born a blank, like all the rest of us. Left in the surroundings of savagery, he grows to possess a savage language, superstition, and life. We, left in the surroundings of civilization, grow to possess a civilized language, life, and purpose. Transfer the infant white to the savage surroundings, he will grow to possess a savage language, superstition, and habit. Transfer the savage-born infant to the surroundings of civilization, and he will grow to possess a civilized language and habit. These results have been established over and over again beyond all question; and it is also well established that those advanced in life, even to maturity, of either class, lose already acquired qualities belonging to the side of their birth, and gradually take on those of the side to which they have been transferred.

As we have taken into our national family seven millions of Negroes, and as we receive foreigners at the rate of more than five hundred thousand a year, and assimilate them, it would seem that the time may have arrived when we can very properly make at least the attempt to assimilate our two hundred and fifty thousand Indians. . . .

Theorizing citizenship into people is a slow operation. What a farce it would be to attempt teaching American citizenship to the negroes in Africa. They could not understand it; and, if they did, in the midst of such contrary influences, they could never use it. Neither can the Indians understand or use American citizenship theoretically taught to them on Indian reservations. They must get into the swim of American citizenship. They must feel the touch of it day after day, until they become saturated with the spirit of it, and thus become equal to it.

When we cease to teach the Indian that he is less than a man; when we recognize fully that he is capable in all respects as we are, and that he only needs the opportunities and privileges which we possess to enable him to assert his humanity and manhood; when we act consistently towards him in accordance with that recognition; when we cease to fetter him to conditions which keep him in bondage, surrounded by retrogressive influences; when we allow him the freedom of association and the developing influences of social contact — then the Indian will quickly demonstrate that he can be truly civilized, and he himself will solve the question of what to do with the Indian.

## QUESTIONS FOR READING AND DISCUSSION

1. Why did Pratt oppose reservations? How would schools achieve Pratt's goal to "Kill the Indian . . . and save the man"?
2. What did Pratt mean by asserting that "our greatest mistake [is] in feeding our civilization to the Indians instead of feeding the Indians to our civilization"? Did he consider education or Christianity mistakes for Indians? Why or why not?
3. What lessons did Pratt draw from the experiences of African Americans? Did he believe they represented a success story for his goal of "citizenizing"?
4. What assumptions about civilization and race did Pratt make? What assumptions did he make about white Americans, native Americans, African Americans, and Catholics? For him, what was the goal of "citizenizing"?

## COMPARATIVE QUESTIONS

1. How did Ida Lindgren's experiences compare with those of In-mut-too-yah-lat-lat, the Texas Rangers, and the Mexicans they fought? To what extent did they have different concepts of property, ownership, law, and social order?
2. What similarities and differences characterized the immigrant experiences of the Chinese in San Francisco, the Lindgrens in Kansas, the Mexicans in Texas, and native Americans?

3. Do the documents in this chapter suggest that Americans in the West had conflicting ideas about civilization and race? Why or why not?

4. Based on the documents in this chapter, what part did migrants' assumptions about their familiar worlds play in their adjustments to their new lives in the West? To what extent did their experiences in America cause them to change their old assumptions and to become — in their own eyes — Americans?

# CHAPTER 19

# THE CITY AND ITS WORKERS
## 1870–1900

The economic achievements of the Gilded Age did not appear to be miraculous to working people. Factory workers knew that profits often meant low wages, long hours, and frequent unemployment. Domestic servants knew how much work it took to supply their employers with the comforts of home. Immigrants streamed into America where they hoped to find jobs, security, and a new life. Union members knew that strikes might win them a share of gains in productivity. As the following documents illustrate, the Gilded Age looked different when viewed from the shop floor rather than the corner office.

## DOCUMENT 19-1

## *A Textile Worker Explains the Labor Market*

*Wageworkers had jobs as long as they could be hired. Employers laid off workers during business slumps or replaced those whose jobs could be done more cheaply by a machine or a worker with a lower wage. In 1883, Thomas O'Donnell, who had worked as a mule spinner (operating a machine that spun cotton fibers into yarn) for eleven years in textile mills in Fall River, Massachusetts, testified before the U.S. Senate Committee on Relations between Capital and Labor. O'Donnell explained to Senator Henry W. Blair of New Hampshire what is was like to be a working man in the 1880s.*

## Thomas O'Donnell
## *Testimony before a U.S. Senate Committee,* 1885

Senator Blair: Are you a married man?

Thomas O'Donnell: Yes, sir; I am a married man; have a wife and two children. I am not very well educated. I went to work when I was young, and have been working ever since in the cotton business; went to work when I was about eight or nine years old. I was going to state how I live. My children get

---

U. S. Congress, Senate, *Report of the Senate Committee upon the Relations between Labor and Capital* (Washington, D.C.: Government Printing Office, 1885).

along very well in summer time, on account of not having to buy fuel or shoes or one thing and another. I earn $1.50 a day and can't afford to pay a very big house rent. I pay $1.50 a week for rent, which comes to about $6.00 a month.

Blair: That is, you pay this where you are at Fall River?

O'Donnell: Yes, Sir.

Blair: Do you have work right along?

O'Donnell: No, sir; since that strike we had down in Fall River about three years ago I have not worked much more than half the time, and that has brought my circumstances down very much.

Blair: Why have you not worked more than half the time since then?

O'Donnell: Well, at Fall River if a man has not got a boy to act as "back-boy" it is very hard for him to get along. In a great many cases they discharge men in that work and put in men who have boys.

Blair: Men who have boys of their own?

O'Donnell: Men who have boys of their own capable enough to work in a mill, to earn $.30 or $.40 a day.

Blair: Is the object of that to enable the boy to earn something for himself?

O'Donnell: Well, no; the object is this: They are doing away with a great deal of mule-spinning there and putting in ring-spinning, and for that reason it takes a good deal of small help to run this ring work, and it throws the men out of work. . . . For that reason they get all the small help they can to run these ring-frames. There are so many men in the city to work, and whoever has a boy can have work, and whoever has no boy stands no chance. Probably he may have a few months of work in the summer time, but will be discharged in the fall. That is what leaves me in poor circumstances. Our children, of course, are very often sickly from one cause or another, on account of not having sufficient clothes, or shoes, or food, or something. And also my woman; she never did work in a mill; she was a housekeeper, and for that reason she can't help me to anything at present, as many women do help their husbands down there, by working, like themselves. . . .

Blair: How much [work] have you had within a year?

O'Donnell: Since Thanksgiving I happened to get work in the Crescent Mill, and worked there exactly thirteen weeks. I got just $1.50 a day, with the exception of a few days that I lost because in following up mule-spinning you are obliged to lose a day once in a while; you can't follow it up regularly.

Blair: Thirteen weeks would be seventy-eight days, and, at $1.50 a day, that would make $117, less whatever time you lost?

O'Donnell: Yes. I worked thirteen weeks there and ten days in another place, and then there was a dollar I got this week, Wednesday.

Blair: Taking a full year back can you tell how much you have had?

O'Donnell: That would be about fifteen weeks' work. . . .

Blair: That would be somewhere about $133, if you had not lost any time?

O'Donnell: Yes, sir.

Blair: That is all you have had?

O'Donnell: Yes, sir.

Blair: To support yourself and wife and two children?

O'Donnell: Yes, sir.

Blair: Have you had any help from outside?

O'Donnell: No, sir.

Blair: Do you mean that yourself and wife and two children have had nothing but that for all this time?

O'Donnell: That is all. I got a couple dollars' worth of coal last winter, and the wood I picked up myself. I goes around with a shovel and picks up clams and wood.

Blair: What do you do with the clams?

O'Donnell: We eat them. I don't get them to sell, but just to eat, for the family. That is the way my brother lives, too, mostly. He lives close by us.

Blair: How many live in that way down there?

O'Donnell: I could not count them, they are so numerous. I suppose there are one thousand down there.

Blair: A thousand that live on $150 a year?

O'Donnell: They live on less.

Blair: Less than that?

O'Donnell: Yes; they live on less than I do.

Blair: How long has that been so?

O'Donnell: Mostly so since I have been married.

Blair: How long is that?

O'Donnell: Six years this month.

Blair: Why do you not go West on a farm?

O'Donnell: How could I go, walk it?

Blair: Well, I want to know why you do not go out West on a $2,000 farm, or take up a homestead and break it and work it up, and then have it for yourself and family?

O'Donnell: I can't see how I could get out West. I have got nothing to go with.

Blair: It would not cost you over $1,500.

O'Donnell: Well, I never saw over a $20 bill, and that is when I have been getting a month's pay at once. If someone would give me $1,500 I will go. . . .

Blair: Are you a good workman?

O'Donnell: Yes, sir.

Blair: Were you ever turned off because of misconduct or incapacity or unfitness for work?

O'Donnell: No, sir.

Blair: Or because you did bad work?

O'Donnell: No, sir.

Blair: Or because you made trouble among the help?

O'Donnell: No, sir. . . .

Blair: How old are you?

O'Donnell: About thirty.

Blair: Is your health good?

O'Donnell: Yes, sir.

Blair: What would you work for if you could get work right along; if you could be sure to have it for five years, staying right where you are?

O'Donnell: Well, if I was where my family could be with me, and I could have work every day I would take $1.50, and be glad to. . . .

Blair: You spoke of fuel — what do you have for fuel?

O'Donnell: Wood and coal.

Blair: Where does the wood come from?

O'Donnell: I pick it up around the shore — any old pieces I see around that are not good for anything. There are many more that do the same thing.

Blair: Do you get meat to live on much?

O'Donnell: Very seldom.

Blair: What kinds of meat do you get for your family?

O'Donnell: Well, once in a while we get a piece of pork and some clams and make a clam chowder. That makes a very good meal. We sometimes get a piece of corn beef or something like that. . . .

Blair: What have you eaten?

O'Donnell: Well, bread mostly, when we could get it; we sometimes couldn't make out to get that, and have had to go without a meal.

Blair: Has there been any day in the year that you have had to go without anything to eat?

O'Donnell: Yes, sir, several days.

Blair: More than one day at a time?

O'Donnell: No. . . .

Blair: What have the children got on in the way of clothing?

O'Donnell: They have got along very nicely all summer, but now they are beginning to feel quite sickly. One has one shoe on, a very poor one, and a slipper, that was picked up somewhere. The other has two odd shoes on, with the heel out. He has got cold and is sickly now.

Blair: Have they any stockings?

O'Donnell: He had got stockings, but his feet comes through them, for there is a hole in the bottom of the shoe.

Blair: What have they got on the rest of their person?

O'Donnell: Well, they have a little calico shirt — what should be a shirt; it is sewed up in some shape — and one little petticoat, and a kind of little dress.

Blair: How many dresses has your wife got?

O'Donnell: She has got one since she was married, and she hasn't worn that more than half a dozen times; she has worn it just going to church and coming back. She is very good in going to church, but when she comes back she takes it off, and it is pretty near as good now as when she bought it.

Blair: She keeps that dress to go to church in?

O'Donnell: Yes, sir.

Blair: How many dresses aside from that has she?

O'Donnell: Well, she got one here three months ago.

Blair: What did it cost?

O'Donnell: It cost $1.00 to make it and I guess about a dollar for the stuff, as near as I can tell . . . she has an undershirt that she got given to her, and she has an old wrapper, which is about a mile too big for her; somebody gave it to her. . . . That is all that I know that she has. . . .

Blair: Do you see any way out of your troubles — what are you going to do for a living — or do you expect to have to stay right there?

O'Donnell: Yes. I can't run around with my family.

Blair: You have nowhere to go to, and no way of getting there if there was any place to go to?

O'Donnell: No, sir; I have no means nor anything, so I am obliged to remain there and try to pick up something as I can.

Blair: Do the children go to school?

O'Donnell: No, sir; they are not old enough; the oldest child is only three and a half; the youngest one is one and a half years old.

Blair: Is there anything else you wanted to say?

O'Donnell: Nothing further, except that I would like some remedy to be got

to help us poor people down there in some way. Excepting the government decides to do something with us we have a poor show. We are all, or mostly all, in
good health; that is, as far as the men who are at work go.

Blair: You do not know anything but mule-spinning, I suppose?

O'Donnell: That is what I have been doing, but I sometimes do something
with pick and shovel. I have worked for a man at that, because I am so put on. I
am looking for work in a mill. The way they do there is this: There are about
twelve or thirteen men that go into a mill every morning, and they have to stand
their chance, looking for work. The man who has a boy with him he stands the
best chance, and then, if it is my turn or a neighbor's turn who has no boy, if
another man comes in who has a boy he is taken right in, and we are left out. I
said to the boss once it was my turn to go in, and now you have taken on that
man; what am I to do; I have got two little boys at home, one of them three years
and a half and the other one year and a half old, and how am I to find something
for them to eat; I can't get my turn when I come here. He said he could not do
anything for me. I says, "Have I got to starve; ain't I to have any work?" They are
forcing these young boys into the mills that should not be in mills at all; forcing
them in because they are throwing the mules out and putting on ring-frames.
They are doing everything of that kind that they possibly can to crush down the
poor people — the poor operatives there.

### QUESTIONS FOR READING AND DISCUSSION

1. What wages did O'Donnell earn? Why didn't he work more? How did he account for his poverty? To what extent did O'Donnell possess freedom to negotiate for better wages and working conditions?

2. O'Donnell requested "some remedy to . . . help us poor people." What remedies did he appear to favor? What remedies might have improved his
prospects of employment?

3. Why did he believe the employers were doing "everything . . . that they possibly can to crush down the poor people"? How might employers have
responded?

4. How representative do you think O'Donnell and his family were of working-
class Americans in the late nineteenth century?

## DOCUMENT 19-2

# Domestic Servants
# on Household Work

*Millions of women worked in factories and shops during the Gilded Age. Millions
more worked as domestic servants for people who could afford to pay somebody else to
do the household chores. Many women preferred to become factory laborers or shop
clerks rather than domestic servants. In the 1880s, journalist Helen Campbell inter-
viewed a number of former servants to try to find out why. A selection of Campbell's
interviews follows.*

## Interviews with Journalist Helen Campbell, 1880s

First on the list stands Margaret M———, an American, twenty-three years old, and for five years in a paper-box factory. Seven others nodded their assent, or added a word here and there as she gave her view, two of them Irish-Americans who had had some years in the public schools.

"It's freedom that we want when the day's work is done. I know, some nice girls, Bridget's cousins, that make more money and dress better and everything for being in service. They're waitresses, and have Thursday afternoon out and part of every other Sunday. But they're never sure of one minute that's their own when they're in the house. Our day is ten hours long, but when it's done it's done, and we can do what we like with the evenings. That's what I've heard from every nice girl that ever tried service. You're never sure that your soul's your own except when you are out of the house, and I couldn't stand that a day. Women care just as much for freedom as men do. Of course they don't get so much, but I know I'd fight for mine."

"Women are always harder on women than men are," said a fur sewer, an intelligent American about thirty. "I got tired of always sitting, and took a place as chambermaid. The work was all right and the wages good, but I'll tell you what I couldn't stand. The cook and the waitress were just common, uneducated Irish, and I had to room with one and stand the personal habits of both, and the way they did at table took all my appetite. I couldn't eat, and began to run down; and at last I gave notice, and told the truth when I was asked why. The lady just looked at me astonished: 'If you take a servant's place, you can't expect to be one of the family,' she said. 'I never asked it,' I said; 'all I ask is a chance at common decency.' 'It will be difficult to find an easier place than this,' she said, and I knew it; but ease one way was hardness another, and she couldn't see that I had any right to complain. That's one trouble in the way. It's the mixing up of things, and mistresses don't think how they would feel in the same place."

Third came an Irish-American whose mother had been cook for years in one family, but who had, after a few months of service, gone into a jute-mill, followed gradually by five sisters.

"I hate the very words 'service' and 'servant,'" she said. "We came to this country to better ourselves, and it's not bettering to have anybody ordering you round."

"But you are ordered in the mill."

"That's different. A man knows what he wants, and doesn't go beyond it; but a woman never knows what she wants, and sort of bosses you everlastingly. If there was such a thing as fixed hours it might be different, but I tell every girl I know, 'Whatever you do, don't go into service. You'll always be prisoners and always looked down on.' You can do things at home for them as belongs to you that somehow it seems different to do for strangers. Anyway, I hate it, and there's plenty like me."

"What I minded," said a gentle, quiet girl, who worked at a stationer's, and who had tried household service for a year, — "what I minded was the awful

Helen Campbell, *Prisoners of Poverty* (1900); reprinted in *Root of Bitterness: Documents in the Social History of American Women*, ed. Nancy F. Cott (Boston: Northeastern University Press, 1996), 322–26.

lonesomeness. I went for general housework, because I knew all about it, and there were only three in the family. I never minded being alone evenings in my own room, for I'm always reading or something, and I don't go out hardly at all, but then I always know I can, and that there is somebody to talk to if I like. But there, except to give orders, they had nothing to do with me. It got to feel sort of crushing at last. I cried myself sick, and at last I gave it up, though I don't mind the work at all. . . ."

"Oh, nobody need to tell me about poor servants," said an energetic woman of forty, Irish-American, and for years in a shirt factory. "Don't I know the way the hussies'll do, comin' out of a bog maybe, an' not knowing the names even, let alone the use, of half the things in the kitchen, and asking their twelve and fourteen dollars a month? Don't I know it well, an' the shame it is to 'em! but I know plenty o' decent, hard-workin' girls too, that give good satisfaction, an' this is what they say. They say the main trouble is, the mistresses don't know, no more than babies, what a day's work really is. A smart girl keeps on her feet all the time to prove she isn't lazy, for if the mistress finds her sitting down, she thinks there can't be much to do and that she doesn't earn her wages. Then if a girl tries to save herself or is deliberate, they call her slow. They want girls on tap from six in the morning till ten and eleven at night. 'Tisn't fair. And then, if there's a let-up in the work, maybe they give you the baby to see to. I like a nice baby, but I don't like having one turned over to me when I'm fit to drop scrabbling to get through and sit down a bit. . . . Women make hard mistresses, and I say again, I'd rather be under a man, that knows what he wants. That's the way with most."

"I don't see why people are surprised that we don't rush into places," said a shop-girl. "Our world may be a very narrow world, and I know it is; but for all that, it's the only one we've got, and right or wrong, we're out of it if we go into service. A teacher or cashier or anybody in a store, no matter if they have got common-sense, doesn't want to associate with servants. Somehow you get a sort of smooch. Young men think and say, for I have heard lots of them, 'Oh, she can't amount to much if she hasn't brains enough to make a living outside of a kitchen!' You're just down once [and] for all if you go into one."

"I don't agree with you at all," said a young teacher who had come with her. "The people that hire you go into kitchens and are not disgraced. What I felt was, for you see I tried it, that they oughtn't to make me go into livery. I was worn out with teaching, and so I concluded to try being a nurse for a while. I found two hard things: one, that I was never free for an hour from the children, for I took meals and all with them, and any mother knows what a rest it is to go quite away from them, even for an hour; and the other was that she wanted me to wear the nurse's cap and apron. She was real good and kind; but when I said, 'Would you like your sister, Miss Louise, to put on cap and apron when she goes out with them?' she got very red, and straightened up. 'It's a very different matter,' she said; 'you must not forget that in accepting a servant's place you accept a servant's limitations.' That finished me. I loved the children, but I said, 'If you have no other thought of what I am to the children than that, I had better go.' I went, and she put a common, uneducated Irish girl in my place. . . ."

"I've tried it," said one who had been a dressmaker and found her health going from long sitting. "My trouble was, no conscience as to hours; and I believe you'll find that is, at the bottom, one of the chief objections. My first employer was a smart, energetic woman, who had done her own work when she was first married and knew what it meant, or you'd think she might have known. But she had no more thought for me than if I had been a machine. She'd sit in her sitting room on the second floor and ring for me twenty times a day to do little things, and she wanted me up till eleven to answer the bell, for she had a great deal of company. I had a good room and everything nice, and she gave me a great many things, but I'd have spared them all if only I could have had a little time to myself. I was all worn out, and at last I had to go. There was another reason. I had no place but the kitchen to see my friends. I was thirty years old and as well born and well educated as she, and it didn't seem right. The mistresses think it's all the girls' fault, but I've seen enough to know that women haven't found out what justice means, and that a girl knows it, many a time, better than her employer. Anyway, you couldn't make me try it again."

"My trouble was," said another, who had been in a cotton-mill and gone into the home of one of the mill-owners as chambermaid, "I hadn't any place that I could be alone a minute. We were poor at home, and four of us worked in the mill, but I had a little room all my own, even if it didn't hold much. In that splendid big house the servants' room was over the kitchen, hot and close in summer, and cold in winter, and four beds in it. We five had to live there together, with only two bureaus and a bit of a closet, and one washstand for all. There was no chance to keep clean or your things in nice order, or anything by yourself, and I gave up. Then I went into a little family and tried general housework, and the mistress taught me a great deal, and was good and kind, only there the kitchen was a dark little place and my room like it, and I hadn't an hour in anything that was pleasant and warm. A mistress might see, you'd think, when a girl was quiet and fond of her home, and treat her different from the kind that destroy everything; but I suppose the truth is, they're worn out with that kind and don't make any difference. It's hard to give up your whole life to somebody else's orders, and always feel as if you was looked at over a wall like; but so it is, and you won't get girls to try it, till somehow or other things are different."

### QUESTIONS FOR READING AND DISCUSSION

1. What did these women object to about their experiences as domestic servants? Why did some consider factory work preferable to domestic service?
2. Why did these former servants think that "women are always harder on women [servants] than men are"? Why did a servant woman often "know what justice means . . . better than her employer"?
3. Several of these women testified about their desire for freedom. What kind of freedom did they seek, and how did they hope to attain it?
4. Given the many dissatisfactions of household service, why did these women become servants? In what ways did their experiences conflict with their expectations and those of their employers?

## DOCUMENT 19-3

# A Romanian Jew Emigrates to America

*European immigrants flooded into American cities in the late nineteenth century, each with a story and a hope. Michael Gold, the son of one of these immigrants, recalled the story of his father, Herman, about why he came to America. Gold's recounting of his father's journey to New York City described the mixed motives, misleading information, and unexpected experiences encountered by most immigrants.*

# Michael Gold
## *Jews without Money,* 1890s

My father, a house painter, was a tall lively man with Slavic cheek bones and a red mustache. . . . He was born near Yassy, Roumania. . . .

"I was always in trouble in Roumania" said my father. ". . . I was always fighting and drinking, and my father did not know what to do with me. . . .

"Why did I choose to come to America?" asked my father of himself gravely. . . . "I will tell you why: it was because of envy of my dirty thief of a cousin, that Sam Kravitz, may his nose be eaten by the pox.

"All this time, while I was disgracing my family, Sam had gone to America, and was making his fortune. Letters came from him, and were read throughout our village. Sam, in two short years, already owned his own factory for making suspenders. He sent us his picture. It was marveled at by every one. Our Sam no longer wore a fur cap, a long Jewish coat and peasant boots. No. He wore a fine gentleman's suit, a white collar like a doctor, store shoes and a beautiful round fun-hat called a derby.

"He suddenly looked so fat and rich, this beggarly cobbler's son! I tell you, my liver burned with envy when I heard my father and mother praise my cousin Sam. I knew I was better than him in every way, and it hurt me. I said to my father, 'Give me money. Let me go at once to America to redeem myself. I will make more money than Sam, I am smarter than he is. You will see!'

"My mother did not want me to go. But my father was weary of my many misfortunes, and he gave me the money for the trip. So I came to America. It was the greatest mistake in my life. . . .

"How full I was of all the . . . stories that were told in my village about America! In America, we believed, people dug under the streets and found gold anywhere. In America, the poorest ragpicker lived better than a Roumanian millionaire. In America, people did little work, but had fun all day.

"I had seen two pictures of America. They were shown in the window of a store that sold Singer Sewing Machines in our village. One picture had in it the tallest building I had ever seen. It was called a skyscraper. At the bottom of it walked the proud Americans. The men wore derby hats and had fine mustaches and gold watch chains. The women wore silks and satins, and had proud faces like queens. Not a single poor man or woman was there; every one was rich.

"The other picture was of Niagara Falls. You have seen the picture on postcards; with Indians and cowboys on horses, who look at a rainbow shining over the water. . . .

"In my family were about seventy-five relatives. All came to see me leave Roumania. There was much crying. But I was happy, because I thought I was going to a land of fun.

"The last thing my mother did, was to give me my cousin's address in New York, and say: 'Go to Sam. He will help you in the strange land.'

"But I made up my mind I would die first rather than ask Sam for help.

"Well, for eleven days our boat rocked on the ocean. I was sick, but I wrote out a play . . . and dreamed of America.

Michael Gold, *Jews without Money* (New York: H. Liverwright, 1930), 81–110.

"They gave us dry herring and potatoes to eat. The food was like dung and the boat stank like a big water closet. But I was happy.

"I joked all the way. One night all of us young immigrants held a singing party. One young Roumanian had an accordion. We became good friends, because both of us were the happiest people on the boat.

"He was coming to a rich uncle, a cigarmaker who owned a big business, he said. When he learned I had no relatives in America, he asked me to live at his uncle's with him. I agreed, because I liked this boy.

"*Nu*, how shall I tell how glad we were when after eleven days on the empty ocean we saw the buildings of New York?

"It looked so nice and happy, this city standing on end like a child's toys and blocks. It looked like a land of fun, a game waiting for me to play.

"And in Ellis Island, where they kept us overnight, I slept on a spring bed that had no mattress, pillow or blankets. I was such a greenhorn that I had never seen a spring before. I thought it was wonderful, and bounced up and down on it for fun.

"Some one there taught me my first American words. All night my friend Yossel and I bounced up and down on the springs and repeated the new funny words to each other.

"Potato! he would yell at me. Tomato! I would answer, and laugh. Match! he would say. All right! I would answer. Match! all right! go to hell! potato! until every one was angry at us, the way we kept them awake with our laughing and yelling.

"In the morning his uncle came for us and took us home in a horsecar.

"I tell you my eyes were busy on that ride through the streets. I was looking for the American fun.

"*Nu*, I will not mention how bad I felt when I saw the cigarmaker uncle's home. It was just a big dirty dark room in the back of the cigar store where he made and sold cigars. He, his wife and four children lived in that one room.

"He was not glad to have me there, but he spread newspapers on the floor, and Yossel and I slept on them.

"What does it matter, I thought, this is not America. To-morrow morning I will go out in the streets, and see the real American fun.

"The next morning Yossel and I took a long walk. That we might not be lost, we fixed in our minds the big gold tooth of a dentist that hung near the cigar shop.

"We walked and walked. I will not tell you what we saw, because you see it every day. We saw the East Side. To me it was a strange sight. I could not help wondering, where are all the people running? What is happening? And why are they so serious? When does the fun start? . . .

"I was such a greenhorn I believed the elevated train traveled all over America, to Niagara Falls and other places. We rode up and down on it all day. I paid the fare.

"I had some money left. I also bought two fine derby hats from a pushcart; one for Yossel, and one for me. They were a little big, but how proud we felt in these American fun-hats.

"No one wears such hats in Roumania. Both of us had pictures taken in the American fun-hats to send to our parents.

"This foolishness went on for two weeks. Then all my money was gone. So the cigarmaker told me I should find a job and move out from his home. So I found a job for seven dollars a month in a grocery store. I lived over the store, I rose at five o'clock, and went to bed at twelve in the night. My feet became large and red with standing all day. The grocerman, may the worms find him, gave me nothing to eat but dry bread, old cheese, pickles and other stale groceries. I soon became sick and left that job.

"For a week I sat in Hester Park without a bite of food. And I looked around me, but was not unhappy. Because I tell you, I was such a greenhorn, that I still thought fun would start and I was waiting for it.

"One night, after sleeping on the bench, I was very hungry in the morning and decided to look up my rich cousin, Sam Kravitz. I hated to do this, but was weak with fasting. So I came into my cousin's shop. To hide my shame I laughed out loud.

"'Look, Sam, I am here,' I laughed. 'I have just come off the boat, and am ready to make my fortune.'

"So my cousin Sam gave me a job in his factory. He paid me twenty-five cents a day.

"He had three other men working for him. He worked himself. He looked sick and sharp and poor and not at all like the picture of him in the fun-hat he had sent to Roumania.

"Nu, so your father worked. I got over my greenhorn idea that there was nothing but fun in America. I learned to work like every one else. I grew thin as my cousin.

"Soon I came to understand it was not a land of fun. It was a Land of Hurry-Up. There was no gold to be dug in the streets here. Derbies were not fun-hats for holidays. They were work-hats. Nu, so I worked! With my hands, my liver and sides! I worked!

"My cousin Sam had fallen into a good trade. With his machines he manu-factured the cotton ends of suspenders. . . . There was much money to be made, I saw that at once.

"But my cousin Sam was not a good business man. He had no head for fig-ures and his face was like vinegar. None of his customers liked him.

"Gradually, he let me go out and find business for him. I was very good for this. Most of the big suspender shops were owned by Roumanians who had known my father. They greeted me like a relative. I drank wine with them, and passed jokes. So they gave me their orders for suspender ends.

"So one day, seeing how I built up the business, Sam said: 'You shall be my partner. We are making a great deal of money. Leave the machine, Herman. I will take care of the inside shop work. You go out every day, and joke with our cus-tomers and bring in the orders.'

"So I was partners with my cousin Sam. So I was very happy. I earned as much as thirty dollars a week; I was at last a success.

"So a matchmaker came, and said I ought to marry. So he brought me to your momma and I saw at once that she was a kind and hard-working woman. So I decided to marry her and have children.

"So this was done.

"It was then I made the greatest mistake of my life.

"Always I had wanted to see that big water with the rainbow and Indians called Niagara Falls.

"So I took your momma there when we married. I spent a month's wages on the trip. I showed America to your momma. We enjoyed ourselves.

"In a week we came back. I went to the shop the next morning to work again. I could not find the shop. It had vanished. I could not find Sam. He had stolen the shop.

"I searched and searched for Sam and the shop. My heart was swollen like a sponge with hate. I was ready to kill my cousin Sam.

"So one day I found him and the shop. I shouted at him, 'Thief, what have you done?' He laughed. He showed me a paper from a lawyer proving that the shop was his. All my work had been for nothing. It had only made Sam rich.

"What could I do? So in my hate I hit him with my fist, and made his nose bleed. He ran into the street yelling for a policeman. I ran after him with a stick, and beat him some more. But what good could it do? The shop was really his, and I was left a pauper.

"So now I work as a house painter. I work for another man, I am not my own master now. I am a man in a trap.

"But I am not defeated. I am a man with a strong will. . . . I am certain to be rich!"

#### QUESTIONS FOR READING AND DISCUSSION

1. Herman Gold decided to go to America "because of envy" of his cousin. What did Gold envy? Why?
2. What was the image of America among Gold's family and friends in Romania? On what was it based? How did that image shape Gold's experiences once he arrived in the United States? To what extent did living in America change that image for Gold and his Romanian family members?
3. In what ways did kinship and ethnicity influence Gold's expectations and experiences?
4. Did Gold become a success? Why or why not? Why did he believe that "I am certain to be rich"?

## DOCUMENT 19-4

# Labor Contractors and Italian Immigrants

*In theory, wages gave working people the freedom to decide whether or not to work at a certain job. If wages were high enough, a worker took the job on the terms offered; if wages were too low, a worker refused the job and went elsewhere for employment. In reality, wages could restrict rather than expand workers' freedom, as illustrated by the following selection from a New York journalist's account of common labor practices by contractors who hired Italian immigrant laborers. The account spotlighted many differences between theories of free markets and free labor and the actual experiences of working-class Americans.*

### S. Merlino

### Italian Immigrants and Their Enslavement, 1893

The Italian laborer does more than his share of work and receives less than his share of earnings; for as a matter of fact, the laws enacted with regard to this matter oppress the laborer and assist rather than hamper the contractor. Even supposing

---

S. Merlino, "Italian Immigrants and Their Enslavement," *The Forum* (April 1893), 184–90.

that the contractor does not succeed in importing contract labor, he finds in the market a large number of men entirely at his mercy, with not even the weak support of a promise to defend themselves against his greed. The few dollars which the immigrant possesses on landing are skillfully taken out of his pocket by the hotel-keeper before the hotel-keeper gives him a chance to work. When he is reduced to absolute indigence, the lowest kind of work imaginable is offered him and he has to accept it. He walks through Mulberry Street and sees a crowd around a bar in a basement. He enters the basement and finds a man employing men for a company. He adds his name to the list without knowing anything about the work he will be called upon to do, or about the place where he is to be transported, or about the terms of his engagement. Perhaps, however, he passes a banker's establishment and stops to read on a paper displayed at the window a demand for two hundred laborers, supplemented with the significant assurance that the place of work is not far distant. He enters, enlists, takes his chances, and falls in the snare set for him.

I once witnessed the departure of a party of laborers and I shall never forget the sight. In foul Mulberry Street a half-dozen carts were being loaded with bundles of the poorest clothes and rags. One man after another brought his things; women and children lounged about, and the men gathered together in small groups, chattering about the work, their hopes, and their fears. For these men *fear*. They have heard of the deceit practised upon those who have preceded them and of their sufferings. Each man carried a tin box containing stale bread and pieces of loathsome cheese and sausage, his provision for the journey. Some had invested whatever money they had in buying more of such food, because, as they told me, everything was so much dearer at the contractor's store. The sausage, for instance, which, rotten as it was, cost them four cents a pound in New York, was sold for twenty cents a pound at the place of their work. Presently our conversation was interrupted by the appearance of the contractor; the groups dissolved, the men took leave of their wives and friends, kissed once more their children, and made a rush for the carts. Then the train started for the railroad station, where the laborers were to be taken to their unknown destination. Of course, this destination and the wages and the nature of the work have been agreed upon in some informal way. But the contract is a sham. I do not believe there is a single instance in which a contract was honestly fulfilled by the contractor. When we think of law-breakers we instinctively refer to the lowest classes. But the contractors are systematic law-breakers. As a rule, the laborer is faithful to the letter of his engagement, even when he feels wronged or deceived.

The contractor is sure to depart from the terms of the contract either as to wages, or hours of labor, or the very nature of the work. Contractors have been known to promise employment, to pocket their fees, and then to lead the men to lonely places and abandon them. Some employment agencies agree with the employers that the men shall be dismissed under pretext after a fortnight or two of work, in order that the agents may receive new fees from fresh recruits. As a rule, however, the men obtain more work than they want or can stand. The contractor, who has acted thus far as an employment agent, now assumes his real functions. Him alone the employer (a railroad or some other company) recognizes, and all wages are paid to him. He curtails these for his own benefit, first by ten or twenty per cent or more, and he retains another portion to reimburse himself for the money he has spent for railway fares and other items. Wages are generally paid at the end of the second fortnight; the first fortnight they remain unpaid till the end of the work, in guarantee of the fulfilment of the contract by the laborer. Meanwhile the men have to live, and to obtain food they increase their debt with the contractor, who keeps a "pluck-me-store," where the laborers are bound to purchase all their provisions, inclusive of the straw on which they sleep. The prices charged are from twenty-five to one hundred per cent and upward above the cost of the goods to the seller, and the quality is as bad as the price is high. At sunset the work ceases and the men retire to a shanty, very much like the steerage of a third-class emigrant ship, the men being packed together in unclean and narrow berths. The shanty is no shelter from wind or rain. Only recently the shanty where the Chicago National Gas-Pipe Company huddled its Italian workmen, near Logansport, Ind., was blown down by a wind-storm and several men were killed. Neither the number nor the names of the dead were known, as Italian laborers are designated only by figures.

The brutality of the contractors toward their subjects baffles description. The contractor is a strongly-built, powerful man; he has acquired the habit of command, is well armed, protected by the authorities, supported by such of his employees as he chooses to favor, and, sad to say, by the people, who are hostile to the laborers. He often keeps guards armed with Winchester rifles to prevent his men from running away. His power has the essential characteristics of a government. He fines his men and beats and punishes them for any attempted resistance to his self-constituted authority. On Sunday he may either force them to attend church service or keep them at work. I have been told of contractors who taxed their men to make birthday presents to their wives. A feudal lord would not have expected more from his vassals.

There are numerous cases where the contractor objects to paying wages. One day last July, as I was walking in King's Bridge, near New York City, I met two laborers loitering in the rear of their shanty. They were evidently afraid to talk, and it was with much difficulty that I learned from them that they were the only members of a gang of about two hundred who had dared to strike work, because their contractor had employed them for three months without paying them. I made my way to the shanty and entered into conversation with a woman who was engaged in cooking. She told me, with tears, that she had saved a little money and had invested it in feeding the men. "Now, if the contractor will not pay us," she said, "I shall be ruined." I denounced the outrage in the Italian press of New York, but ineffectually. A few days later some Italians who worked in a locality near Deal Lake, New Jersey, failing to receive their wages, captured the contractor and shut him up in the shanty, where he remained a prisoner until the county sheriff came with a *posse* to his rescue. I could mention a half-dozen more such cases, all recent. The latest came to my knowledge in Cleveland, Ohio. A contractor had run away with the money, and neither the press nor an attorney employed by the men succeeded in compelling the company which employed him to pay the workmen. Old laborers have the same tale to tell. Nearly all have the same experience. Every one will grant that robbing a poor man of his well-earned wages is a shameful crime; yet in no instance, to my knowledge, has a contractor been made to suffer for his fraud. He generally disappears for a few days and starts again in another place. In this way many, no doubt, have been enriched.

But this is not the worst form of outrage of which contractors are guilty. There have been cases where Italian laborers have suffered actual slavery, and in trying to escape have been fired upon by the guards and murdered, as happened not long ago in the Adirondacks. A similar case was told to me by one of the victims. He said:

"We started from New York on November 3, 1891, under the guidance of two bosses. We had been told we should go to Connecticut to work on a railroad and earn one dollar and seventy-five cents per day. We were taken, instead, to South Carolina, first to a place called Lambs(?) and then after a month or so to the 'Tom Tom' sulphate mines. The railroad fare was eight dollars and eighty-five cents; this sum, as well as the price of our tools, nearly three dollars, we owed the bosses. We were received by an armed guard, which kept constant watch over us, accompanying us every morning from the barracks to the mines and at night again from the work to our shanty. . . . Part of our pay went toward the extinction of our debt; the rest was spent for as much food as we could get at the 'pluck-me' store. We got only so much as would keep us from starvation. Things cost us more than twice or three times their regular price. Our daily fare was coffee and bread for breakfast, rice with lard or soup at dinner-time, and cheese or sausage for supper. Yet we were not able to pay off our debt; so after a while we were given only bread, and with this only to sustain us we had to go through our daily work. By and by we became exhausted, and some of us got sick. Then we decided to try, at the risk of our lives, to escape. Some of us ran away, eluding the guards. After a run of an hour I was exhausted and decided to stay for the night in the woods. We were, however, soon surprised by the appearance of the bosses and two guards. They thrust guns in our faces and ordered us to return to work or they would shoot us down. We answered that we would rather die than resume our former life in the mine. The bosses then sent for two black policemen, who insisted that we should follow them. We went before a judge, who was sitting in a bar-room. The judge asked if there was any written contract, and when he heard that there wasn't, said he would let us go free. But the bosses, the policemen, and the judge then held a short consultation, and the result was that the bosses paid some money (I believe it was forty-five dollars), the policemen put the manacles on our wrists, and we were marched off. At last, on April 1, we were all dismissed on account of the hot weather. My comrades took the train for New York. I had only one dollar, and with this, not knowing either the country or the language, I had to walk to New York. After forty-two days I arrived in the city utterly exhausted." . . .

At best, the workman, after years of hard labor, saves just enough money to purchase his return ticket, or possibly a hundred dollars more to pay off the debts contracted in his absence by his family, or to buy up the small farm which was foreclosed by the government because he failed to pay the land tax. The boss or contractor, the hotel-keeper, and the banker accumulate fortunes and buy villas or palaces in their native towns, whither they eventually return after the time has passed when their sentence to punishment is no longer valid, covered with all the honor and glory accruing from the possession of wealth.

### Questions for Reading and Discussion

1. How did laws "oppress the laborer" and "assist . . . the contractor"? Why were laborers "at the mercy" of contractors? How were contractors similar to "a government" for workers?

2. Merlino believed "the contract is a sham." Why? What could laborers do to change the terms of their jobs?

3. How did the freedoms of contractors differ from those of laborers? To what extent did wages give workers freedom? What was the significance of a "pluck-me-store"?

4. In what ways did Italian laborers suffer from "actual slavery"? To what extent did their ethnicity influence their experiences as workers?

DOCUMENT 19-5

# George Washington Plunkitt Explains Politics

*Political machines ruled big cities, and none was more successful — or notorious — than New York's Tammany Hall. George Washington Plunkitt, a loyal Tammany boss, liked to hold court at the county courthouse shoeshine stand, explaining how things really worked to anyone willing to listen. In 1897, a freelance journalist, William L. Riordon, began recording Plunkitt's remarks and followed him for a day to see what he did. Riordon's account appeared in the* New York Evening Post *and was later published in the volume* Plunkitt of Tammany Hall *in 1905. Plunkitt's statements are excerpted here, followed by Riordon's diary of one day in the life of a big-city boss.*

## William L. Riordon
### *Plunkitt of Tammany Hall,* 1905

Everybody is talkin' these days about Tammany men growin' rich on graft, but nobody thinks of drawin' the distinction between honest graft and dishonest graft. There's all the difference in the world between the two. Yes, many of our men have grown rich in politics. I have myself. I've made a big fortune out of the game, and I'm gettin' richer every day, but I've not gone in for dishonest graft — blackmailin' gamblers, saloon-keepers, disorderly people, etc. — and neither has any of the men who have made big fortunes in politics.

There's an honest graft, and I'm an example of how it works. I might sum up the whole thing by sayin': "I seen my opportunities and I took 'em."

Just let me explain by examples. My party's in power in the city, and it's goin' to undertake a lot of public improvements. Well, I'm tipped off, say, that they're going to lay out a new park at a certain place.

I see my opportunity and I take it. I go to that place and I buy up all the land I can in the neighborhood. Then the board of this or that makes its plan public, and there is a rush to get my land, which nobody cared particular for before.

Ain't it perfectly honest to charge a good price and make a profit on my investment and foresight? Of course, it is. Well, that's honest graft. . . .

It's just like lookin' ahead in Wall Street or in the coffee or cotton market. It's honest graft, and I'm lookin' for it every day in the year. I will tell you frankly that I've got a good lot of it, too. . . .

I seen my opportunity and I took it. I haven't confined myself to land; anything that pays is in my line. . . .

I've told you how I got rich by honest graft. Now, let me tell you that most politicians who are accused of robbin' the city get rich the same way.

They didn't steal a dollar from the city treasury. They just seen their opportunities and took them. That is why, when a reform administration comes in and spends a half million dollars in tryin' to find the public robberies they talked about in the campaign, they don't find them.

The books are always all right. The money in the city treasury is all right. Everything is all right. All they can show is that the Tammany heads of departments

---

William L. Riordon, *Plunkitt of Tammany Hall* (New York: McClure, Phillips & Co., 1905).

looked after their friends, within the law, and gave them what opportunities they could to make honest graft. Now, let me tell you that's never going to hurt Tammany with the people. Every good man looks after his friends, and any man who doesn't isn't likely to be popular. If I have a good thing to hand out in private life, I give it to a friend. Why shouldn't I do the same in public life? . . .

There's the biggest kind of a difference between political looters and politicians who make a fortune out of politics by keepin' their eyes wide open. The looter goes in for himself alone without considerin' his organization or his city. The politician looks after his own interests, the organization's interests, and the city's interests all at the same time. See the distinction? . . .

The Irish was born to rule, and they're the honestest people in the world. Show me the Irishman who would steal a roof off an almshouse! He don't exist. Of course, if an Irishman had the political pull and the roof was much worn, he might get the city authorities to put on a new one and get the contract for it himself, and buy the old roof at a bargain — but that's honest graft. . . .

One reason why the Irishman is more honest in politics than many Sons of the Revolution is that he is grateful to the country and the city that gave him protection and prosperity when he was driven by oppression from the Emerald Isle. . . . His one thought is to serve the city which gave him a home. He has this thought even before he lands in New York, for his friends here often have a good place in one of the city departments picked out for him while he is still in the old country. Is it any wonder that he has a tender spot in his heart for old New York when he is on its salary list the mornin' after he lands? . . .

[H]ave you ever thought what would become of the country if the bosses were put out of business, and their places were taken by a lot of cart-tail orators and college graduates? It would mean chaos. . . .

This is a record of a day's work by Plunkitt:

2 A.M.    Aroused from sleep by the ringing of his door bell; went to the door and found a bartender, who asked him to go to the police station and bail out a saloon-keeper who had been arrested for violating the excise law. Furnished bail and returned to bed at three o'clock.

6 A.M.    Awakened by fire engines passing his house. Hastened to the scene of the fire, according to the custom of the Tammany district leaders, to give assistance to the fire sufferers, if needed. Met several of his election district captains who are always under orders to look out for fires, which are considered great vote-getters. Found several tenants who had been burned out, took them to a hotel, supplied them with clothes, fed them, and arranged temporary quarters for them until they could rent and furnish new apartments.

8:30 A.M.    Went to the police court to look after his constituents. Found six "drunks." Secured the discharge of four by a timely word with the judge, and paid the fines of two.

9 A.M.    Appeared in the Municipal District Court. Directed one of his district captains to act as counsel for a widow against whom dispossess proceedings had been instituted and obtained an extension of time. Paid the rent of a poor family about to be dispossessed and gave them a dollar for food.

11 A.M.    At home again. Found four men waiting for him. One had been discharged by the Metropolitan Railway Company for neglect of duty, and wanted the district leader to fix things. Another wanted a job on the road. The third sought a place on the Subway and the fourth, a plumber, was looking for work with the Consolidated Gas Company. The district leader spent nearly three hours fixing things for the four men, and succeeded in each case.

3 P.M.    Attended the funeral of an Italian as far as the ferry. Hurried back to make his appearance at the funeral of a Hebrew constituent. Went conspicuously to the front both in the Catholic church and the synagogue, and later attended the Hebrew confirmation ceremonies in the synagogue.

7 P.M.    Went to district headquarters and presided over a meeting of election district captains. Each captain submitted a list of all the voters in his district, reported on their attitude toward Tammany, suggested who might be won over and how they could be won, told who were in need, and who were in trouble of any kind and the best way to reach them. District leader took notes and gave orders.

8 P.M.    Went to a church fair. Took chances on everything, bought ice-cream for the young girls and the children. Kissed the little ones, flattered their mothers and took their fathers out for something down at the corner.

9 P.M.    At the club-house again. Spent $10 on tickets for a church excursion and promised a subscription for a new church-bell. Bought tickets for a base-ball game to be played by two nines from his district. Listened to the complaints of a dozen pushcart peddlers who said they were persecuted by the police and assured them he would go to Police Headquarters in the morning and see about it.

10:30 P.M.    Attended a Hebrew wedding reception and dance. Had previously sent a handsome wedding present to the bride.

12 P.M.    In bed.

That is the actual record of one day in the life of Plunkitt.

## QUESTIONS FOR READING AND DISCUSSION

1. According to Plunkitt, what was "honest graft"? How did it differ from dishonest graft or from ordinary business deals?
2. What did reformers object to about Tammany and honest graft? What did Tammany's supporters object to about reformers? How did political bosses differ from bosses at places of employment?
3. How did Tammany win the loyalty of voters? In what ways did it matter to Tammany that many New Yorkers were immigrants?

4. Why did Plunkitt think chaos would result "if the bosses were put out of business, and their places taken by a lot of cart-tail orators and college graduates"?

5. To Plunkitt, what was politics? Did Riordon seem to have a different view of politics?

## COMPARATIVE QUESTIONS

1. What portrait of bosses emerges from the descriptions in these documents? How did bosses differ from working people? Why?

2. To what extent did Thomas O'Donnell's experiences with factory work compare with the experiences of women domestic servants, Herman Gold, and Italian contract laborers?

3. How were Plunkitt's notions of politics influenced by the experiences of immigrants like Herman Gold and the Italian contract laborers? How were immigrants' experiences influenced by politics as practiced by Plunkitt?

4. How did the people described in these documents define economic justice and injustice? In their views, what might lead to greater justice? Politics? Unions? Bosses? Religion?

5. These documents focus on the deep class divisions in American society in the late nineteenth century. Judging from these documents, what had created these divisions, and what might be done to bridge them? To what extent did working people share the ideals and aspirations of employers?

# CHAPTER 20

# DISSENT, DEPRESSION, AND WAR
## THE 1890s

Profound moral conflict generated intense strife during the 1890s. Many Americans believed that the basic principles of order in the economy, in society, and in politics were immoral and unjust. Numerous others believed the opposite. The Populists voiced some of the moral doubts, while their opponents reaffirmed their faith in the conventional virtues. This conflict was more than a debate, as African Americans, labor activists, and Filipino nationalists knew. The following documents disclose the contours of the moral conflict and some of its manifold consequences in the 1890s and beyond.

### DOCUMENT 20-1
## *Addressing the Crisis in Rural America*

*Hard times in agriculture pushed farmers in the Midwest and South to organize a wide variety of local reform movements. Selling their crops in distant markets for prices that often seemed to be rigged against them, shipping their produce on railroads that manipulated rates to their disadvantage, borrowing money for land and supplies at what seemed extravagant interest rates — these and other common experiences bred a sense of helplessness that many farmers came to believe could only be overcome by cooperation and organization. The Omaha Platform of the People's party, adopted at the first national convention in 1892, expressed many rural Americans' sense of crisis. The preamble preceding the platform, which follows, was written by Ignatius Donnelly, a Minnesota reform politician and one of the party's founders.*

# Populist Party Platform, July 4, 1892

## Preamble

Assembled upon the 116th anniversary of the Declaration of Independence, the People's Party of America, in their first national convention, invoking upon their action the blessing of Almighty God, puts forth, in the name and on behalf of the people of this country, the following preamble and declaration of principles:

The conditions which surround us best justify our cooperation: we meet in the midst of a nation brought to the verge of moral, political, and material ruin. Corruption dominates the ballot-box, the legislatures, the Congress, and touches even the ermine of the bench. The people are demoralized; most of the States have been compelled to isolate the voters at the polling-places to prevent universal intimidation or bribery. The newspapers are largely subsidized or muzzled; public opinion silenced; business prostrated; our homes covered with mortgages; labor impoverished; and the land concentrating in the hands of the capitalists. The urban workmen are denied the right of organization for self-protection; imported pauperized labor beats down their wages; a hireling standing army, unrecognized by our laws, is established to shoot them down, and they are rapidly degenerating into European conditions. The fruits of the toil of millions are boldly stolen to build up colossal fortunes for a few, unprecedented in the history of mankind; and the possessors of these, in turn, despise the republic and endanger liberty. From the same prolific womb of governmental injustice we breed the two great classes — tramps and millionaires.

The national power to create money is appropriated to enrich bondholders; a vast public debt, payable in legal tender currency, has been funded into gold-bearing bonds, thereby adding millions to the burdens of the people. Silver, which has been accepted as coin since the dawn of history, has been demonetized to add to the purchasing power of gold by decreasing the value of all forms of property as well as human labor; and the supply of currency is purposely abridged to fatten usurers, bankrupt enterprise, and enslave industry. A vast conspiracy against mankind has been organized on two continents, and it is rapidly taking possession of the world. If not met and overthrown at once, it forebodes terrible social convulsions, the destruction of civilization, or the establishment of an absolute despotism.

We have witnessed for more than a quarter of a century the struggles of the two great political parties for power and plunder, while grievous wrongs have been inflicted upon the suffering people. We charge that the controlling influences dominating both these parties have permitted the existing dreadful conditions to develop without serious effort to prevent or restrain them. Neither do they now promise us any substantial reform. They have agreed together to ignore in the coming campaign every issue but one. They propose to drown the outcries of a plundered people with the uproar of a sham battle over the tariff, so that capitalists, corporations, national banks, rings, trusts, watered stock, the demonetization of silver, and the oppressions of the usurers may all be lost sight of. They propose to sacrifice our homes, lives and children on the altar of mammon; to destroy the multitude in order to secure corruption funds from the millionaires.

*The People's Party Paper* (July 1892); reprinted in Norman Pollack, *The Populist Mind* (Old Tappan, NJ: Macmillan, 1967), 60–66.

Assembled on the anniversary of the birthday of the nation, and filled with the spirit of the grand general and chieftain who established our independence, we seek to restore the government of the Republic to the hands of "the plain people," with whose class it originated. We assert our purposes to be identical with the purposes of the National Constitution, "to form a more perfect union and establish justice, insure domestic tranquillity, provide for the common defence, promote the general welfare, and secure the blessings of liberty for ourselves and our posterity." We declare that this republic can only endure as a free government while built upon the love of the whole people for each other and for the nation; that it cannot be pinned together by bayonets; that the civil war is over, and that every passion and resentment which grew out of it must die with it; and that we must be in fact, as we are in name, one united brotherhood of freemen.

Our country finds itself confronted by conditions for which there is no precedent in the history of the world; our annual agricultural productions amount to billions of dollars in value, which must, within a few weeks or months, be exchanged for billions of dollars of commodities consumed in their production; the existing currency supply is wholly inadequate to make this exchange; the results are falling prices, the formation of combines and rings, the impoverishment of the producing class. We pledge ourselves, if given power, we will labor to correct these evils by wise and reasonable legislation, in accordance with the terms of our platform. We believe that the powers of government — in other words, of the people should be expanded (as in the case of the postal service) as rapidly and as far as the good sense of an intelligent people and the teachings of experience shall justify, to the end that oppression, injustice, and poverty shall eventually cease in the land.

While our sympathies as a party of reform are naturally upon the side of every proposition which will tend to make men intelligent, virtuous, and temperate, we nevertheless regard these questions — important as they are — as secondary to the great issues now pressing for solution, and upon which not only our individual prosperity but the very existence of free institutions depends; and we ask all men to first help us to determine whether we are to have a republic to administer before we differ as to the conditions upon which it is to be administered; believing that the forces of reform this day organized will never cease to move forward until every wrong is remedied, and equal rights and equal privileges securely established for all the men and women of this country.

## Platform

We declare, therefore,

First. That the union of the labor forces of the United States this day consummated shall be permanent and perpetual; may its spirit enter all hearts for the salvation of the republic and the uplifting of mankind!

Second. Wealth belongs to him who creates it, and every dollar taken from industry without an equivalent is robbery. "If any will not work, neither shall he eat." The interests of rural and civic labor are the same; their enemies are identical.

Third. We believe that the time has come when the railroad corporations will either own the people or the people must own the railroads; and, should the government enter upon the work of owning and managing all railroads, we should favor an amendment to the Constitution by which all persons engaged in the government service shall be placed under a civil service regulation of the most rigid character, so as to prevent the increase of the power of the national administration by the use of such additional government employees.

First, *Money*. We demand a national currency, safe, sound, and flexible, issued by the general government only, a full legal tender for all debts, public and private, and that, without the use of banking corporations, a just, equitable, and efficient means of distribution direct to the people, at a tax not to exceed two per cent per annum, to be provided as set forth in the sub-treasury plan of the Farmers' Alliance, or a better system; also, by payments in discharge of its obligations for public improvements.

(a) We demand free and unlimited coinage of silver and gold at the present legal ratio of sixteen to one.

(b) We demand that the amount of circulating medium be speedily increased to not less than fifty dollars per capita.

(c) We demand a graduated income tax.

(d) We believe that the money of the country should be kept as much as possible in the hands of the people, and hence we demand that all state and national revenues shall be limited to the necessary expenses of the government economically and honestly administered.

(e) We demand that postal savings banks be established by the government for the safe deposit of the earnings of the people and to facilitate exchange.

Second, *Transportation*. Transportation being a means of exchange and a public necessity, the government should own and operate the railroads in the interest of the people.

(a) The telegraph and telephone, like the post-office system, being a necessity for the transmission of news, should be owned and operated by the government in the interest of the people.

Third, *Land*. The land, including all the natural sources of wealth, is the heritage of the people, and should not be monopolized for speculative purposes, and alien ownership of land should be prohibited. All land now held by railroads and other corporations in excess of their actual needs, and all lands now owned by aliens, should be reclaimed by the government and held for actual settlers only.

## Resolutions

Whereas, Other questions have been presented for our consideration, we hereby submit the following, not as a part of the platform of the People's party, but as resolutions expressive of the sentiment of this convention.

1. *Resolved*, That we demand a free ballot and a fair count in all elections, and pledge ourselves to secure it to every legal voter without federal intervention, through the adoption by the States of the unperverted Australian or secret ballot system.
2. *Resolved*, That the revenue derived from a graduated income tax should be applied to the reduction of the burden of taxation now resting upon the domestic industries of this country.
3. *Resolved*, That we pledge our support to fair and liberal pensions to ex-Union soldiers and sailors.
4. *Resolved*, That we condemn the fallacy of protecting American labor under the present system, which opens our ports to the pauper and criminal classes of the world, and crowds out our wage-earners; and we denounce the present

ineffective laws against contract labor, and demand the further restriction of undesirable immigration.

5. *Resolved,* That we cordially sympathize with the efforts of organized workingmen to shorten the hours of labor, and demand a rigid enforcement of the existing eight-hour law on government work, and ask that a penalty clause be added to the said law.

6. *Resolved,* That we regard the maintenance of a large standing army of mercenaries, known as the Pinkerton system, as a menace to our liberties, and we demand its abolition; and we condemn the recent invasion of the Territory of Wyoming by the hired assassins of plutocracy, assisted by federal officials.

7. *Resolved,* That we commend to the favorable consideration of the people and the reform press the legislative system known as the initiative and referendum.

8. *Resolved,* That we favor a constitutional provision limiting the office of President and Vice-President to one term, and providing for the election of senators of the United States by a direct vote of the people.

9. *Resolved,* That we oppose any subsidy or national aid to any private corporation for any purpose.

10. *Resolved,* That this convention sympathizes with the Knights of Labor and their righteous contest with the tyrannical combine of clothing manufacturers of Rochester, [Minnesota,] and declares it to be the duty of all who hate tyranny and oppression to refuse to purchase the goods made by said manufacturers, or to patronize any merchants who sell such goods.

## QUESTIONS FOR READING AND DISCUSSION

1. According to the Populist platform, why was the nation on "the verge of moral, political, and material ruin"? What had the two major parties done about those problems?

2. What general principles did the Populists support, and what specific remedies did they propose? What was the proper role of government and of large corporations like railroads?

3. The Populists sought a "union of the labor forces of the United States." Who did they regard as their potential allies in such a union, and who would be excluded? Why?

4. The Populists declared that "the civil war is over, and that every passion and resentment which grew out of it must die with it" in order to emphasize their goal of "one united brotherhood of freemen." What were the implications of this statement for African Americans?

## DOCUMENT 20-2

# *White Supremacy in Wilmington, North Carolina*

*Black Southerners affiliated with the Republican party often cooperated with Populists to defeat Democrats. Such a fusion of Republicans and Populists carried North Carolina in 1894 and 1896, resulting in the election and appointment of a number of black officeholders, including the mayor and aldermen of Wilmington. In 1898, Democrats struck back with a campaign of terror and intimidation that culminated two days after their victory at the polls by what Gunner Jesse Blake called a "rebellion" that established white supremacy by killing at least twenty blacks. Blake, a Confederate veteran who participated in the "rebellion," recalled the event for a sympathetic white writer in the 1930s. Blake's narrative, excerpted here, illustrates the explosive racism that confronted Southern blacks every day and ultimately undermined the Populist revolt in the South.*

## Gunner Jesse Blake
## *Narrative of the Wilmington "Rebellion" of 1898*

"So, I am going to give you the inside story of this insurrection," he proceeded, "wherein the white people of Wilmington overthrew the constituted municipal authority overnight and substituted a reform rule, doing all this legally and with some needless bloodshed, to be sure, but at the same time they eliminated the Negroes from the political life of the city and the state. This Rebellion was the very beginning of Negro disfranchisement in the South and an important step in the establishment of 'White Supremacy' in the Southland. . . .

"The Rebellion was an organized resistance," Mr. Blake said, "on the part of the white citizens of this community to the established government, which had long irked them because it was dominated by 'Carpet Baggers' and Negroes, and also because the better element here wished to establish 'White Supremacy' in the city, the state and throughout the South, and thereby remove the then stupid and ignorant Negroes from their numerically dominating position in the government. . . .

"The older generation of Southern born men were at their wits' end. They had passed through the rigors of the North-South war and through the tyrannies of Reconstruction when Confiscation . . . of properties without due process of law, was the rule rather than the exception. They had seen 'Forty Acres and a Mule' buy many a Negro's vote.

"Black rapists were attacking Southern girls and women, those pure and lovely creatures who graced the homes in Dixie Land, and the brutes were committing this dastardly crime with more frequency while the majority of them were escaping punishment through the influence of the powers that be.

"These old Southern gentlemen had calculated that time and time only would remove the terrors of Reconstruction, a condition that was imposed upon the conquered Southerners by the victorious Northerners, but they were not willing to sit supinely by and see their girls and women assaulted by beastly brutes.

"The better element among the Northerners in the North could not want them and their little friends to grow up amid such conditions. . . .

"A group of nine citizens met at the home of Mr. Hugh MacRae and there decided that the attitude and actions of the Negroes made it necessary for them to take some steps towards protecting their families and homes in their immediate neighborhood, Seventh and Market Streets. . . .

"This group of citizens, . . . referred to as the 'Secret Nine,' divided the city into sections, placing a responsible citizen as captain in charge of each area. . . .

"The better element planned to gain relief from Negro impudence and domination, from grafting and from immoral conditions; the 'Secret Nine' and the white leaders marked time, hoping something would happen to arouse the citizenry to concerted action.

---

Harry Hayden, *The Wilmington Rebellion* (Wilmington, NC, 1936), 231–36.

"But the 'watch-and-wait policy' of the 'Secret Nine' did not obtain for long, as during the latter part of October [1898] there appeared in the columns of [t]he *Wilmington* (Negro) *Daily Record* an editorial, written by the Negro editor, Alex Manly, which aroused a state-wide revulsion to the city and state administrations then in the hands of the Republicans and Fusionists. The editorial attempted to justify the Negro rape fiends at the expense of the virtue of Southern womanhood."

Mr. Blake . . . read the following . . . editorial from [t]he *Wilmington Record*:

> Poor whites are careless in the matter of protecting their women, especially on the farm. They are careless of their conduct towards them, and our experience among the poor white people in the county teaches us that women of that race are not more particular in the matter of clandestine meetings with colored men, than are the white man and colored women.

Meetings of this kind go on for some time until the woman's infatuation, or the man's boldness, bring attention to them, and the man is lynched for rape.

> Every Negro lynched is called a "big, burly, black brute," when in fact, many of those who have been thus dealt with had white men for their fathers, and were not only not "black" and "burly," but were sufficiently attractive for white girls of culture and refinement to fall in love with them, as is very well known to all.

"That editorial," Mr. Blake declared . . . , "is the straw that broke Mister Nigger's political back in the Southland.". . .

"Excitement reigned supreme on election day and the day following," Mr. Blake said, adding that "the tension between the races was at the breaking point, as two Pinkerton detectives, Negroes, had reported to their white employers that the Negro women, servants in the homes of white citizens, had agreed to set fire to the dwellings of their employers, and the Negro men had openly threatened to 'burn the town down' if the 'White Supremacy' issue was carried in the political contest. The very atmosphere was surcharged with tinder, and only a spark, a misstep by individuals of either race, was needed to set the whites and the blacks at each other's throats.

"When Mr. Hugh MacRae was sitting on his porch on Market Street on the afternoon of the election, he saw a band of 'Red Shirts,' fifty in number, with blood in their eyes; mounted upon fiery and well caparisoned steeds and led by Mike Dowling, an Irishman, who had organized this band of vigilantes. The hot headed 'Red Shirts' paused in front of Mr. MacRae's home and the level headed Scotsman walked toward the group to learn what was amiss.

"Dowling told Mr. MacRae that they were headed for 'The Record' building to lynch Editor Manly and burn the structure. Mr. MacRae pleaded with Dowling and his 'Red Shirts' to desist in their plans. Messrs. MacRae, Dowling and other leaders of the 'Red Shirts' repaired across the street to Sasser's Drug store and there he, Mr. MacRae, showed them a 'Declaration of White Independence' that he had drawn up for presentation at a mass meeting of white citizens the next day.

"The 'Red Shirts' were finally persuaded by Mr. MacRae to abandon their plans for the lynching, but only after Mr. MacRae had called up the newspapers on the telephone and dictated a call for a mass meeting of the citizens for the next morning. . . .

"A thousand or more white citizens, representative of all walks of life . . . attended the mass meeting in the New Hanover county court house the next morning, November 10, at 11 o'clock.

"Colonel Alfred Moore Waddell, a mild mannered Southern gentleman, noted for his extremely conservative tendencies, was called upon to preside over the gathering. In addressing this meeting, Colonel Waddell said: . . . 'We will not live under these intolerable conditions. No society can stand it. We intend to change it, if we have to choke the current of Cape Fear River with (Negro) carcasses!'"

"*That* declaration," Mr. Blake said, "brought forth tremendous applause from the large gathering of white men at the mass meeting. . . .

"Colonel Waddell . . . announced that he heartily approved the set of resolutions which had been prepared by Mr. Hugh MacRae and which included the latter's 'Declaration of White Independence.'

"These resolutions were unanimously approved by the meeting, followed by a wonderful demonstration, the assemblage rising to its feet and cheering: 'Right! Right! Right!' and there were cries of 'Fumigate' the city with 'The Record' and 'Lynch Manly.'"

Blake then read the resolutions from the scrap book, as follows:

Believing that the Constitution of the United States contemplated a government to be carried on by an enlightened people; believing that its framers did not anticipate the enfranchisement of an ignorant population of African origin, and believing that those men of the state of North Carolina, who joined in framing the union, did not contemplate for their descendants subjection to an inferior race.

We, the undersigned citizens of the city of Wilmington and county of New Hanover, do hereby declare that we will no longer be ruled and will never again be ruled, by men of African origin.

This condition we have in part endured because we felt that the consequences of the war of secession were such as to deprive us of the fair consideration of many of our countrymen. . . .

"Armed with a Winchester rifle, Colonel Waddell ordered the citizens to form in front of the Armory for an orderly procession out to 'The Record' plant. . . .

"As this band of silent yet determined men marched up Market Street it passed the beautiful colonial columned mansion, the Bellamy home. From the balcony of this mansion, a Chief Justice of the United States Supreme Court, Salmon P. Chase, delivered an address shortly after Lincoln's tragic assassination, advocating Negro suffrage and thereby sowing the seeds that were now blossoming forth into a white rebellion.

"The printing press of 'The Record' was wrecked by the maddened white men, who also destroyed other equipment, and the type that had been used in producing the editorial that had reflected upon the virtue and character of Southern womanhood was scattered to the four winds by these men, who stood foursquare for the virtue of their women and for the supremacy of the white race over the African.

"Some lamps that had been hanging from the ceiling of the plant were torn down and thrown upon the floor, which then became saturated with kerosene oil; and then a member of the band struck a match, with the result that the two-story frame building was soon in flames.

"The leaders and most of the citizens had designed only to destroy the press," Mr. Blake averred, adding . . . "all of which proves that a mob, no matter how well disciplined, is no stronger than its weakest link.

"The crowd of armed men, which had destroyed the plant and building of the nefarious *Wilmington* (Negro) *Daily Record*, dispersed, repairing peacefully to their respective homes," Mr. Blake said. . . .

"But in about an hour the tension between the two races broke with the shooting of William H. (Bill) Mayo, a white citizen, who was wounded by the first shot that was fired in the Wilmington Rebellion as he was standing on the sidewalk near his home. . . . Mayo's assailant, Dan Wright, was captured by members of the Wilmington Light Infantry and the Naval Reserves after he had been riddled by 13 bullets. Wright died next day in a hospital.

"Then the 'Red Shirts' began to ride and the Negroes began to run. . . . The Africans, or at least those Negroes who had foolishly believed in the remote possibility of social equality with the former masters of their parents, began to slink before the Caucasians. They, the Negroes, appeared to turn primal, slinking away like tigers at bay, snarling as they retreated before the bristling bayonets, barking guns and flaming 'Red Shirts.'

"Six Negroes were shot down near the corner of Fourth and Brunswick Streets, the Negro casualties for the day — November 11, 1898 — totaling nine. One of these, who had fired at the whites from a Negro dance hall, 'Manhattan,' over in 'Brooklyn,' was shot 15 or 20 times. . . .

"One 'Red Shirt' said he had seen six Negroes shot down near the Cape Fear Lumber Company's plant and that their bodies were buried in a ditch. . . . Another 'Red Shirt' described the killing of nine Negroes by a lone white man, who killed them one at a time with his Winchester rifle as they filed out of a shanty door in 'Brooklyn' and after they had fired on him. . . . Another told of how a Negro had been killed and his body thrown in Cape Fear River after he had approached two white men on the wharf. . . .

"Other military units came to Wilmington to assist the white citizens in establishing 'White Supremacy' here. . . . Military organizations from as far South as New Orleans telegraphed offering to come here if their services were needed in the contest.

"When the Rebellion was in full blast 'The Committee of Twenty-five' appointed . . . a committee to call upon Mayor Silas P. Wright and the Board of Aldermen and demand that these officials resign. The mayor had expressed a willingness to quit, but not during the crisis. He changed his mind, however, when he saw white citizens walking the streets with revolvers in their hands. The Negroes, too, had suddenly turned submissive, they were carrying their hats in their hands. . . .

"African continued to cringe before Caucasian as the troops paraded the streets, as the guns barked and the bayonets flared, for a new municipal administration of the 'White Supremacy' persuasion had been established in a day! The old order of Negro domination over the white citizenry had ended."

## QUESTIONS FOR READING AND DISCUSSION

1. According to Blake, why did the "better element" want "to establish 'White Supremacy' in the city, the state, and throughout the South"? How did Blake's characterization of the behavior of African Americans serve his own political agenda?

2. Why did an editorial in the local newspaper precipitate violence, according to Blake? Who was offended by the editorial? Why?

3. Who was responsible for the violence? Why did it occur?

4. To what extent did the Declaration of White Independence express the views of all whites? How did the declaration undermine partisan loyalties of white voters?

## DOCUMENT 20-3

# *Pinkertons Defeated at Homestead*

*Corporations sometimes used private armies to defeat strikes. When strikers seized the Homestead steel mill in 1892, Henry Clay Frick hired an army of 300 men from the Pinkerton National Detective Agency, loaded them on barges, and ordered them to launch an amphibious attack on the mill. One of the Pinkerton men (called "guards," in reference to guarding the steel mill) later recalled for a congressional inquiry his experience as an industrial mercenary at Homestead. His testimony documents the bitter strife between working people and industrialists and their supporters during the 1890s.*

## *Pinkerton Guard Testimony, 1893*

We started out [in Chicago] . . . [and] we went into the three rear cars of the train very quickly. . . . [M]en who seemed to be detectives and not patrolmen, stationed themselves at the doors, and they prevented our exit, and they prevented the entrance of any outside parties who might wish to enter. . . .

We ran rather slowly — it was not a scheduled train — on to Cleveland. . . . There we waited for an hour and our three cars were joined to seven other cars of men from the east. We then, the whole train, went rapidly on. . . . During our trip we were not allowed to leave the cars at all, we were kind of prisoners. We did not have any rights. That might have been because they were afraid of union men, perhaps spies, who would telegraph ahead to Homestead. They wanted to get inside the works without bloodshed, but we had no rights whatever. Then we entered the boats, some 300 of us. There was two covered barges, like these Mississippi covered boats. . . .

We were told to fall in, and the roll of our names was called, and we were told to secure our uniforms, which consisted of coat, hat, vest, and pair of trousers. When we had secured our uniforms we were some distance down the river, and we were told to keep quiet, and the lights were turned out, and everything kept very quiet until we were given orders softly to arise. I was lying down about an hour when the order was sent around the boat for all the men to get ready to land. Then the captain called out for men who could handle rifles. I did not want to handle a rifle, and then he said we want two or three men here to guard the door with clubs, so I said I would do that, and I got over the table and got a club like a policeman's club to guard the side door — that was to prevent men from coming in boats and jumping on to our barge from the river. I stayed there while the men who could handle rifles were marched down to the open end of the boat, and I did not see anything more of them until the firing commenced. . . .

*United States Senate, Report No. 1280, 53d Congress, 2d Session.*

I had a curiosity to see what was going on on the bank. . . . I saw what appeared to be a lot of young men and boys on the bank, swearing and cursing and having large sticks. I did not see a gun or anything. They were swearing at our men. I did not see any more. . . . I heard a sharp pistol shot, and then there were 30, 40, or 100 of them, and our men came running and stampeding back as fast as they could and they got in the shelter of the door, and then they turned around and blazed away. It was so dark I could see the flames from the rifles easily. They fired about 50 shots — I was surprised to see them stand up, because the strikers were shooting also but they did not seem to be afraid of being hit. They had some shelter from the door. They fired in rather a professional manner I thought. The men inside the Chicago boat were rather afraid at hearing the rifles, and we all jumped for rifles that were laying on a table ready, and someone . . . opened a box of revolvers, and said, "all get revolvers," so I had now a Winchester rifle and a revolver. I called out to see if anybody had been hurt, and I saw a man there apparently strangling. He had been shot through the head and he died sometime afterwards, I think. . . . Of course it rather made us incensed to be shot at that way, but I kept out of danger as much as possible.

I was standing there when Nordrum came up, and he said to follow him, and I crossed over to the New York boat, where there were 40 men with rifles standing on the edge of the boat watching what was going on on shore. Nordrum spoke to the men on shore. He spoke in rather a loud manner — say a commanding manner. He said: "We are coming up that hill anyway, and we don't want any more trouble from you men." The men were in the mill windows. The mill is iron-clad. There were a few boys in sight, but the men were under shelter, all of them. I supposed I should have to go up the hill, and I didn't like the idea very well, because it was pretty nearly certain death, as I supposed. I thought it over in what little time I had, and I thought I would have to go anyway. While I was standing there, waiting for Nordrum to charge up the hill and we follow him, he went away, and he was gone quite a few minutes. I took advantage of that to look around the New York men's boat to see what was going on, and I saw about 150 of the New York men hiding in the aisle furthest from the shore. It was divided into bunks. They were hiding in the bunks — they were hiding under the mattresses; they didn't want to be told to shoulder a rifle and charge up the hill; they were naturally afraid of it. They were watchmen, and not detectives. Now the men who had the rifles were mostly [Pinkerton] detectives. There were 40 of the detectives, who I afterwards learned were regular employees of Pinkerton, but these other men were simply watchmen, and hired as watchmen, and told so, and nothing else. Seeing these men so afraid and cowering rather dispirited the rest of us, and those who had rifles — I noticed there seemed to be a fear among them all. I went to the end of the boat, and there I saw crowds on the bank, waving their hands, and all looking at the boat and appearing to be very frantic.

I judged we were going to have trouble and went back to the end where I had been placed and waited for Nordrum to come, but he did not turn up, and after I stood there about half an hour I concluded, as there was no one there to order us to do anything and as it was stated that the steam tug had pulled out, taking all those who had charge of us — I concluded I would look out for my life, and if anything was said about my leaving and not staying there I would say I did not intend to work for them any more; so I returned to the door I was told to guard, and in that place I stayed for the remainder of the day, during all the shooting and firing. I concluded if the boat was burned — we expected a thousand men would charge down the embankment and put us to massacre; that was what we expected all throughout the day — I concluded if the boat was burned I would defend my life with the other men. . . . During this firing there was a second battle. I was out of sight, but there were cracks of rifles, and our men replied with a regular fusilade. It kept up for ten minutes, bullets flying around as thick as hail, and men coming in shot and covered with blood. . . .

A good many of the men were thoroughly demoralized. They put on life-preservers and jumped under the tables and had no control over themselves whatever. Through the rest of the day there was this second battle when the strikers started the firing. There seemed to be sharpshooters picking us off. . . . [A]bout 12 o'clock barrels of burning oil were floating around the bank to burn us up, to compel us to go on the wharf and there shoot us down, but they didn't succeed because the oil was taken up by the water, and at about 1 o'clock a cannon was fired by the strikers. . . . At about 3 o'clock we heard something; we thought was a cannon, but it was dynamite. . . . It partially wrecked the other boat. A stick of it fell near me. It broke open the door of the aisles, and it smashed open the door, and the sharpshooters were firing directly at any man in sight. . . . Most of the men were for surrender at this time, but the old detectives held out and said, "If you surrender you will be shot down like dogs; the best thing to do is to stay here." We could not cut our barges loose because there was a fall below, where we would be sunk. We were deserted by our captains and by our tug, and left there to be shot. We felt as though we had been betrayed and we did not understand it, and we did not know why the tug had pulled off and didn't know it had come back. About 4 o'clock some one or other authorized a surrender. . . . [T]he strikers held that we should depart by way of the depot.

That surrender was effected, and I started up the embankment with the men who went out, and we were glad to get away and did not expect trouble; but I looked up the hill and there were our men being struck as they went up, and it looked rather disheartening. . . . I supposed there was not going to be any more crowds, but in front of the miners' cottages there were crowds of miners, women, etc., and as we all went by they commenced to strike at us again, and a man picked up a stone and hit me upon the ear . . . I got on further toward the depot and there were tremendous crowds on both sides and the men were just hauling and striking our men, and you would see them stumble as they passed by. I tried to get away from the crowd . . . , so I put my hat on and walked out of the line of Pinkerton men, but some one noticed me, and I started to run and about 100 got after me. I ran down a side street and ran through a yard. I ran about half a mile I suppose, but was rather weak and had had nothing to eat or drink and my legs gave out, could not run any further, and some man got hold of me by the back of my coat, and about 20 or 30 men came up and kicked me and pounded me with stones. I had no control of myself then. I thought I was about going and commenced to scream, and there were 2 or 3 strikers with rifles rushed up then and kept off the crowd and rushed me forward to a theater, and I was put in the theater and found about 150 of the Pinkerton men there, and that was the last violence offered me.

## QUESTIONS FOR READING AND DISCUSSION

1. Why did the Pinkerton men travel in secrecy? What did this Pinkerton guard mean by saying he had no rights? Once he was on the barge, what did he see on shore?

2. What was the Pinkerton man's opinion of the strikers? What was his view of the other Pinkerton detectives?

3. Why did he feel betrayed? What was his principal goal? What were the strengths and weaknesses of solidarity among the Pinkertons and among the strikers?

4. What happened to him after the Pinkerton men surrendered? Who saved him?

5. What did the use of the Pinkerton men by the Carnegie Steel Company suggest about the rule of law at Homestead?

## DOCUMENT 20-4

# Conflicting Views about Labor Unions

*Many employers vehemently opposed labor unions while many working people just as vehemently defended them and — more important — joined them. Bitter, often violent conflict between capital and labor over wages, working conditions, jobs, strikes, and boycotts fueled the debate. A forceful argument against labor unions was made in 1900 by N. F. Thompson, a representative of the Southern Industrial Convention and the Chamber of Commerce of Huntsville, Alabama, in testimony before the Industrial Commission on the Relations and Conditions of Capital and Labor. Samuel Gompers, who served as president of the American Federation of Labor almost continuously from 1886 to 1924, defended labor unions in a letter published in 1894 — six years before Thompson's testimony — in the union journal American Federationist. Gompers's letter responded to a judge who had issued an injunction against the leaders of the strike and boycott against the Pullman Company in 1894 and who subsequently called for federal troops to suppress the strike. The arguments made by Thompson and Gompers reveal clashing views of the period's industrial order, its strengths and weaknesses, achievements and failures, virtues and vices. The debate about labor unions also highlighted fundamental disagreements about the roles of capitalists, working people, and governments on the path toward progress.*

## N. F. Thompson

## Testimony before the Industrial Commission on the Relations and Conditions of Capital and Labor, 1900

Labor organizations are to-day the greatest menace to this Government that exists inside or outside the pale of our national domain. Their influence for disruption and disorganization of society is far more dangerous to the perpetuation of our Government in its purity and power than would be the hostile array on our borders of the army of the entire world combined. I make this statement from years of close study and a field of the widest opportunities for observation, embracing the principal industrial centers both of the North and the South. I make this statement entirely from a sense of patriotic duty and without prejudice against any class of citizens of our common country.

If I could make this statement any stronger or clearer, I would gladly do so, for it is not until an evil or a danger is made strongly apparent that adequate

*Report of the Industrial Commission on the Relations and Conditions of Capital and Labor*, vol. 7 (Washington, D.C.: U.S. Government Printing Office, 1901), 755–57; *American Federationist*, vol. 1 (September 1894), 150–52.

measures of relief are likely to be applied. That such a menace is real and not imaginary the most casual investigation of existing tendencies among the laboring classes will make the facts discernible. On every hand, and for the slightest provocation, all classes of organized labor stand ready to inaugurate a strike with all its attendant evils, or to place a boycott for the purpose of destroying the business of some one against whom their enmity has been evoked.

In addition to this, stronger ties of consolidation are being urged all over the country among labor unions with the view of being able to inaugurate a sympathetic strike that will embrace all classes of labor, simply to redress the grievances or right the wrong of one class, however remotely located or however unjust may be the demands of that class. To recognize such a power as this in any organization, or to permit such a theory to be advanced without a protest or counteracting influence, is so dangerous and subversive of government that it may justly be likened to the planting of deadly virus in the heart of organized society, death being its certain and speedy concomitant.

Organizations teaching such theories should be held as treasonable in their character and their leaders worse than traitors to their country. It is time for the plainest utterances on this subject, for the danger is imminent, and in view of the incidents that have occurred recently in strikes it can be considered little less than criminal in those who control public sentiment that such scenes are possible anywhere in this country.

This language may seem needlessly harsh and severe, but in some classes of diseases it is the sharpest knife that effects the speediest remedy, and so, in this case, if the public are to be awakened to their real danger the plainest speech becomes necessary.

No one questions the right of labor to organize for any legitimate purpose, but when labor organizations degenerate into agencies of evil, inculcating theories dangerous to society and claiming rights and powers destructive to government, there should be no hesitancy in any quarter to check these evil tendencies even if the organizations themselves have to be placed under the ban of law.

That these organizations are thus degenerating is seen in the following facts:

(1) Many labor leaders are open and avowed socialists and are using labor organizations as the propaganda of socialistic doctrines.

(2) These organizations are weakening the ties of citizenship among thousands of our people in that they have no other standard of community obligations than what these organizations inculcate.

(3) They are creating widespread disregard for the rights of others equally as entitled to the protection of organized society as their own, as evidenced in every strike that occurs and the increasing arbitrariness of labor demands on their employers.

(4) They are destroying respect for law and authority among the working classes, as many have no higher conception of these than such as are embodied in the commands and demands of labor organizations and labor leaders.

(5) They are educating the laboring classes against the employing classes, thus creating antagonisms between those whose mutuality of interests should be fostered and encouraged by every friend of good government; for the success of government hangs on no less a basis than the harmony and happiness of the people, embracing alike employers and the employed.

(6) They are demanding of Federal, State, and municipal authorities class legislation and class discrimination utterly at variance with the fundamental principles of our Government, in that they are demanding of these various authorities the employment of only union labor, thus seeking to bring the power of organized society to crush out all nonunion workers.

(7) They are destroying the right of individual contract between employees and employers and forcing upon employers men at arbitrary wages, which is unjust alike to other labor more skilled, and to capital, which is thus obliged to pay for more than it receives in equivalent.

(8) They demand the discharge of men who risk life to protect employers' interests during strikes to reinstate those who were formerly employed, but who have been instrumental, directly or indirectly, in the destruction of life and property, thereby placing a premium upon disloyalty and crime.

(9) They are bringing public reproach upon the judicial tribunals of our Country by public abuse of these tribunals and often open defiance of their judgments and decrees, thus seeking to break down the only safeguards of a free people. . . .

A further law should be enacted that would make it justifiable homicide for any killing that occurred in defense of any lawful occupation, the theory of our government being that anyone has a right to earn an honest living in this country, and any endeavor to deprive one of that right should be placed in the same legal status with deprivation of life and property.

## Samuel Gompers

## *Letter to the* American Federationist, 1894

You say that . . . you believe in labor organizations within such lawful and reasonable limits as will make them a service to the laboring man, and not a menace to the lawful institutions of the country. . . .

You would certainly have no objection . . . to workingmen organizing, and in their meetings discuss perhaps "the origin of man," benignly smiling upon each other, and declaring that all existing things are right, going to their wretched homes to find some freedom in sleep from gnawing hunger. You would have them extol the virtues of monopolists and wreckers of the people's welfare. You would not have them consider seriously the fact that more than two million of their fellows are unemployed, and though willing and able, cannot find the opportunity to work, in order that they may sustain themselves, their wives and their children. You would not have them consider seriously the fact that Pullman who has grown so rich from the toil of his workingmen, that he can riot in luxury, while he heartlessly turns these very workmen out of their tenements into the streets and leave to the tender mercies of corporate greed. Nor would you have them ponder upon the hundreds of other Pullmans of different names.

You know, or ought to know, that the introduction of machinery is turning into idleness thousands, faster than new industries are founded, and yet, machinery certainly should not be either destroyed or hampered in its full development. The laborer is a man, he is made warm by the same sun and made cold — yes, colder — by the same winter as you are. He has a heart and brain, and feels and knows the human and paternal instinct for those depending upon him as keenly as do you.

What shall the workers do? Sit idly by and see the vast resources of nature and the human mind be utilized and monopolized for the benefit of the comparative few? No. The laborers must learn to think and act, and soon, too, that only by the power of organization, and common concert of action, can either their manhood be maintained, their rights to life (work to sustain it) be recognized, and liberty and rights secured.

Since you say that you favor labor organizations within certain limits, will you kindly give to thousands of your anxious fellow citizens what you believe the workers could and should do in their organizations to solve this great problem? Not what they should not do. . . .

I am not one of those who regards the entire past as a failure. I recognize the progress made and the improved conditions of which nearly the entire civilized world are the beneficiaries. I ask you to explain . . . how is it that thousands of able-bodied, willing, earnest men and women are suffering the pangs of hunger? We may boast of our wealth and civilization, but to the hungry man and woman and child our progress is a hollow mockery, our civilization a sham, and our "national wealth" a chimera.

You recognize that the industrial forces set in motion by steam and electricity have materially changed the structure of our civilization. You also admit that a system has grown up where the accumulations of the individual have passed from his control into that of representative combinations and trusts, and that the tendency in this direction is on the increase. How, then, can you consistently criticize the workingmen for recognizing that as individuals they can have no influence in deciding what the wages, hours of toil and conditions of employment shall be?

You evidently have observed the growth of corporate wealth and influence. You recognize that wealth, in order to become more highly productive, is concentrated into fewer hands, and controlled by representatives and directors, and yet you sing the old siren song that the working man should depend entirely upon his own "individual effort."

The school of *laissez faire*, of which you seem to be a pronounced advocate, has produced great men in advocating the theory of each for himself, and his Satanic Majesty taking the hindermost, but the most pronounced advocates of your school of thought in economics have, when practically put to the test, been compelled to admit that combination and organization of the toiling masses are essential both to prevent the deterioration and to secure an improvement in the condition of the wage earners.

If, as you say, the success of commercial society depends upon the full play of competition, why do not you and your confreres turn your attention and direct the shafts of your attacks against the trusts and corporations, business wreckers and manipulators in the food products—the necessities of the people. Why garland your thoughts in beautiful phrase when speaking of these modern vampires, and steep your pen in gall when writing of the laborers' efforts to secure some of the advantages accruing from the concentrated thought and genius of the ages? . . .

One becomes enraptured in reading the beauty of your description of modern progress. Could you have had in mind the miners of Spring Valley or Pennsylvania, or the clothing workers of the sweat shops of New York or Chicago when you grandiloquently dilate, "Who is not rich to-day when compared with his ancestors of a century ago? The steamboat and the railroad bring to his breakfast table the coffees of Java and Brazil, the fruit from Florida and California, and the steaks from the plains. The loom arrays him in garments and the factories furnish him with a dwelling that the richest contemporaries of his grandfather would have envied. With health and industry he is a prince."

Probably you have not read within the past year of babies dying of starvation at their mothers' breasts. More than likely the thousands of men lying upon the bare stones night after night in the City Hall of Chicago last winter escaped your notice. You may not have heard of the cry for bread that was sounded through this land of plenty by thousands of honest men and women. But should these and many other painful incidents have passed you by unnoticed, I am fearful that you may learn of them with keener thoughts with the coming sleets and blasts of winter.

You say that "labor cannot afford to attack capital." Let me remind you that labor has no quarrel with capital, as such. It is merely the possessors of capital who refuse to accord to labor the recognition, the right, the justice which is the laborers' due, with whom we contend. . . .

Inquire from the thousands of women and children whose husbands or fathers were suffocated or crushed in the mines through the rapacious greed of stockholders clamoring for more dividends. Investigate the sweating dens of the large cities. Go to the mills, factories, through the country. Visit the modern tenement houses or hovels in which thousands of workers are compelled to eke out an existence. . . . Ascertain from employers whether the laborer is not regarded the same as a machine, thrown out as soon as all the work possible has been squeezed out of him.

Are you aware that all the legislation ever secured for the ventilation or safety of mines, factory or work-shop is the result of the efforts of organized labor? Do you know that the trade unions were the shield for the seven-year-old children . . . until they become somewhat older? And that the reformatory laws now on the statute books, protecting or defending . . . both sexes, young and old, from the fond care of the conquerors, were wrested from Congresses, legislatures and parliaments despite the Pullmans. . . .

By what right, sir, do you assume that the labor organizations do not conduct their affairs within lawful limits, or that they are a menace to the lawful institutions of the country? Is it because some thoughtless or overzealous member at a time of great excitement and smarting under a wrong may violate . . . a law or commit an improper act? Would you apply the same rule to the churches, the other moral agencies and organizations that you do to the organizations of labor? If you did, the greatest moral force of life to-day, the trade unions, would certainly stand out the clearest, brightest and purest. Because a certain class (for which you and a number of your colleagues on the bench seem to be the special pleaders) have a monopoly in their lines of trade, I submit that this is no good reason for their claim to have a monopoly on true patriotism or respect for the lawful institutions of the country.

Year by year man's liberties are trampled under foot at the bidding of corporations and trusts, rights are invaded and law perverted. In all ages wherever a tyrant has shown himself he has always found some willing judge to clothe that tyranny in the robes of legality, and modern capitalism has proven no exception to the rule.

You may not know that the labor movement as represented by the trades unions, stands for right, for justice, for liberty. You may not imagine that the issuance of an injunction depriving men of a legal as well as a natural right to protect themselves, their wives and little ones, must fail of its purpose. Repression or oppression never yet succeeded in crushing the truth or redressing a wrong.

In conclusion let me assure you that labor will organize and more compactly than ever and upon practical lines, and despite relentless antagonism, achieve for humanity a nobler manhood, a more beautiful womanhood and a happier childhood.

### QUESTIONS FOR READING AND DISCUSSION

1. Why were labor unions "the greatest menace to this Government," according to Thompson? How did Gompers's arguments respond to such claims? How did Thompson and Gompers differ in their views of strikes?

2. In what ways did labor unions violate the rights of others, according to Thompson? What workers' rights and liberties did Thompson recognize?

3. How did Gompers and Thompson differ in their beliefs about the benefits and liabilities of competition? Why was government important to each of them?

4. How did Gompers respond to accusations that labor unions were treasonous? Did Gompers oppose capitalism and industrialization?

5. How did Thompson and Gompers view the future? How did they differ in their assumptions about a just society?

### DOCUMENT 20-5

# Mark Twain on the Blessings-of-Civilization Trust

*Many Americans welcomed the war against Spain in 1898. The notion of American soldiers liberating colonists from a decaying monarchy had wide appeal. But the temptation to start an American overseas empire in the Philippines proved irresistible. Mark Twain wrote a bitter satire that ridiculed official claims that it was necessary to take over the Philippines in order to spread the virtues of American civilization to backward Filipinos, whom Twain termed the "Person Sitting in Darkness." Twain's satire made clear that the burgeoning American empire was a betrayal of fundamental national values. Selections from Twain's essay "To the Person Sitting in Darkness" follow.*

### To the Person Sitting in Darkness, February 1901

[S]hall we go on conferring our Civilization upon the peoples that sit in darkness, or shall we give those poor things a rest? Shall we bang right ahead in our old-time, loud, pious way, and commit the new century to the game; or shall we sober up and sit down and think it over first? Would it not be prudent to get our Civilization-tools together, and see how much stock is left on hand in the way of Glass Beads and Theology, and Maxim Guns and Hymn Books, and Trade-Gin

---

Mark Twain, "To the Person Sitting in Darkness," *North American Review* (February 1901), 461–73.

and Torches of Progress and Enlightenment (patent adjustable ones, good to fire villages with, upon occasion), and balance the books, and arrive at the profit and loss, so that we may intelligently decide whether to continue the business or sell out the property and start a new Civilization Scheme on the proceeds?

Extending the Blessings of Civilization to our Brother who Sits in Darkness has been a good trade and has paid well, on the whole; and there is money in it yet, if carefully worked but not enough, in my judgment, to make any considerable risk advisable. The People that Sit in Darkness are getting to be too scarce — too scarce and too shy. And such darkness as is now left is really of but an indifferent quality, and not dark enough for the game. The most of those People that Sit in Darkness have been furnished with more light than was good for them or profitable for us. We have been injudicious.

The Blessings-of-Civilization Trust, wisely and cautiously administered, is a Daisy. There is more money in it, more territory, more sovereignty, and other kinds of emolument, than there is in any other game that is played. But Christendom has been playing it badly of late years, and must certainly suffer by it, in my opinion. She has been so eager to get every stake that appeared on the green cloth, that the People who Sit in Darkness have noticed it — they have noticed it, and have begun to show alarm. They have become suspicious of the Blessings of Civilization. More — they have begun to examine them. This is not well. The Blessings of Civilization are all right, and a good commercial property; there could not be a better, in a dim light. In the right kind of a light, and at a proper distance, with the goods a little out of focus, they furnish this desirable exhibit to the Gentlemen who Sit in Darkness:

LOVE, LAW AND ORDER, JUSTICE, LIBERTY, GENTLENESS, EQUALITY, CHRISTIANITY, HONORABLE DEALING, PROTECTION TO THE WEAK, MERCY, TEMPERANCE, EDUCATION, and so on.

There. Is it good? Sir, it is pie. It will bring into camp any idiot that sits in darkness anywhere. But not if we adulterate it. It is proper to be emphatic upon that point. This brand is strictly for Export — apparently. *Apparently.* Privately and confidentially, it is nothing of the kind. Privately and confidentially, it is merely an outside cover, gay and pretty and attractive, displaying the special patterns of our Civilization which we reserve for Home Consumption, while *inside* the bale is the Actual Thing that the Customer Sitting in Darkness buys with his blood and tears and land and liberty. That Actual Thing is, indeed, Civilization, but it is only for Export. . . .

We all know that the Business is being ruined. The reason is not far to seek. It is because our Mr. McKinley [the President] . . . [has] been exporting the Actual Thing *with the outside cover left off.* This is bad for the Game. . . .

Now, my plan is . . . let us audaciously present the whole of the facts, shirking none. . . . This daring truthfulness will astonish and dazzle the Person Sitting in Darkness. . . . Let us say to him:

"Our case is simple. On the 1st of May, Dewey destroyed the Spanish fleet. This left the [Philippine] Archipelago in the hands of its proper and rightful owners, the Filipino nation. Their army numbered 30,000 men, and they were competent to whip out or starve out the little Spanish garrison; then the people could set up a government of their own devising. Our traditions required that Dewey should now set up his warning sign, and go away. But the Master of the Game happened to think of another plan — the European plan. He acted upon it. This was, to send out an army — ostensibly to help the native patriots put the finishing touch upon their long and plucky struggle for independence, but really to take their land away from them and keep it. That is, in the interest of Progress and Civilization. The plan developed, stage by stage, and quite satisfactorily. We entered into a military alliance with the trusting Filipinos, and they hemmed in Manila on the land side, and by their valuable help the place, with its garrison of 8,000 or 10,000 Spaniards, was captured — a thing which we could not have accomplished unaided at that time. We got their help by ingenuity. We knew they were fighting for their independence, and that they had been at it for two years. We knew they supposed that we also were fighting in their worthy cause — just as we had helped the Cubans fight for Cuban independence — and we allowed them to go on thinking so. *Until Manila was ours and we could get along without them.* Then we showed our hand. Of course, they were surprised — that was natural; surprised and disappointed; disappointed and grieved. To them it looked un-American; uncharacteristic; foreign to our established traditions. And this was natural, too; for we were only playing the American Game in public — in private it was the European. It was neatly done, very neatly, and it bewildered them. They could not understand it; for we had been so friendly — so affectionate. . . .

"We and the patriots having captured Manila, Spain's ownership of the Archipelago and her sovereignty over it were at an end — obliterated — annihilated — not a rag or shred of either remaining behind. It was then that we conceived the *divinely* humorous idea of buying both of these spectres from Spain! (It is quite safe to confess this to the Person Sitting in Darkness, since neither he nor any other sane person will believe it.) In buying those ghosts for twenty millions, we also contracted to take care of the friars and their accumulations. I think we also agreed to propagate leprosy and smallpox, but as to this there is doubt. But it is not important; persons afflicted with the friars do not mind other diseases.

"With our Treaty ratified, Manila subdued, and our Ghosts secured, we had no further use for Aguinaldo[1] and the owners of the Archipelago. We forced a war, and we have been hunting America's guest and ally through the woods and swamps ever since.". . .

Having now laid all the historical facts before the Person Sitting in Darkness, we should bring him to again, and explain them to him. We should say to him:

"They look doubtful, but in reality they are not. There have been lies; yes, but they were told in a good cause. We have been treacherous; but that was only in order that real good might come out of apparent evil. True, we have crushed a deceived and confiding people; we have turned against the weak and the friendless who trusted us; we have stamped out a just and intelligent and well-ordered republic; we have stabbed an ally in the back and slapped the face of a guest; we have bought a Shadow from an enemy that hadn't it to sell; we have robbed a trusting friend of his land and his liberty; we have invited our clean young men to shoulder a discredited musket and do bandit's work under a flag which bandits have been accustomed to fear, not to follow; we have debauched America's honor and blackened her face before the world; but each detail was for the best.

---

[1]Emilio Aguinaldo (1869–1964), who led Filipino insurrectionists against Spanish rule, initially welcomed American intervention in the Philippines but soon organized an armed rebellion against American domination.

We know this. The Head of every State and Sovereignty in Christendom and ninety per cent of every legislative body in Christendom, including our Congress and our fifty State Legislatures, are members not only of the church, but also of the Blessings-of-Civilization Trust. This world-girdling accumulation of trained morals, high principles, and justice, cannot do an unright thing, an unfair thing, an ungenerous thing, an unclean thing. It knows what it is about. Give yourself no uneasiness; it is all right."

Now then, that will convince the Person. You will see. It will restore the Business. . . .

And as for a flag for the Philippine Province, it is easily managed. We can have a special one . . . : we can have just our usual flag, with the white stripes painted black and the stars replaced by the skull and cross-bones.

## QUESTIONS FOR READING AND DISCUSSION

1. What was the "Blessings-of-Civilization Trust"? How would it benefit "the People who Sit in Darkness"?

2. What did Twain mean by the "Civilization . . . only for Export"? How and why did the export version differ from the domestic variety?

3. Why did American involvement in the Philippines threaten to ruin the Blessings-of-Civilization-Trust? How was the policy toward the Philippines different from policy toward Cuba?

4. What did Aguinaldo and other Filipinos think about American policy? Did they experience the blessings of American civilization promoted by the trust?

5. Twain's satire contrasts the rhetoric of American imperialists with the realities of imperialism. Can you identify what Twain believed about imperialism and American ideals? In what ways did Twain's proposal for a Philippine flag reflect his views?

## COMPARATIVE QUESTIONS

1. To what extent did the Populists' concepts of justice, freedom, and equality agree with those of Samuel Gompers? How did they compare with those of the Pinkertons at Homestead and the Blessings-of-Civilization Trust?

2. How did N. F. Thompson's concepts of justice, freedom, and democracy compare with those of the Pinkertons and the leading white citizens in Wilmington, North Carolina? Did they differ from the ideals of the Blessings-of-Civilization Trust?

3. In what ways did the experiences of Filipinos compare with those of black Republicans in Wilmington? Does the comparison suggest a significant relationship between American racial oppression and imperialism?

4. Judging from the documents in this chapter, what ideals and values united Americans in the 1890s under the deep fissures of class, race, and region?

# CHAPTER 21

# PROGRESSIVE REFORM FROM THE GRASS ROOTS TO THE WHITE HOUSE
## 1890–1916

Progressives sought to reunite Americans, to overcome the many bitter divisions that separated rich and poor, employers and employees, native citizens and immigrants, adherents of one faith and those of all others. The settlement house movement reflected the desire to bridge divisions by bringing the ideas and energies of middle-class Americans to poor immigrant neighborhoods. Many Americans did not share the Progressives' aspiration to find some middle ground between conflicting groups. Members of labor unions and black Americans feared that the middle ground would be nothing more than the continuation of a status quo they found unacceptable. The following documents illustrate the attitudes and experiences that drew some people toward progressive reforms and that caused others to seek change by insisting on the recognition of fundamental differences among Americans.

## DOCUMENT 21-1
### *Jane Addams on Settlement Houses*

*Progressives engaged in many reform activities besides electoral politics. Settlement houses were among the most important centers of progressive reform. Jane Addams, founder of Chicago's Hull House, explained her motives in a paper she presented in 1892 to a group of women considering settlement work. In "The Subjective Necessity for Social Settlements," Addams revealed attitudes and perceptions that motivated many other progressive reformers.*

## *The Subjective Necessity for Social Settlements,* 1892

This paper is an attempt to analyze the motives which underlie a movement based, not only upon conviction, but upon genuine emotion, wherever educated young people are seeking an outlet for that sentiment of universal brotherhood, which the best spirit of our times is forcing from an emotion into a motive. These young people accomplish little toward the solution of this social problem, and bear the brunt of being cultivated into unnourished, oversensitive lives. They have been shut off from the common labor by which they live which is a great source of moral and physical health. They feel a fatal want of harmony between their theory and their lives, a lack of coordination between thought and action. I think it is hard for us to realize how seriously many of them are taking to the notion of human brotherhood, how eagerly they long to give tangible expression to the democratic ideal. These young men and women, longing to socialize their democracy, are animated by certain hopes which may be thus loosely formulated; that if in a democratic country nothing can be permanently achieved save through the masses of the people, it will be impossible to establish a higher political life than the people themselves crave; that it is difficult to see how the notion of a higher civic life can be fostered save through common intercourse; that the blessings which we associate with a life of refinement and cultivation can be made universal and must be made universal if they are to be permanent; that the good we secure for ourselves is precarious and uncertain, is floating in mid-air, until it is secured for all of us and incorporated into our common life. It is easier to state these hopes than to formulate the line of motives, which I believe to constitute the trend of the subjective pressure toward the Settlement. . . .

You may remember the forlorn feeling which occasionally seizes you when you arrive early in the morning a stranger in a great city: the stream of laboring people goes past you as you gaze through the plate-glass window of your hotel; you see hard workingmen lifting great burdens; you hear the driving and jostling of huge carts and your heart sinks with a sudden sense of futility. The door opens behind you and you turn to the man who brings you in your breakfast with a quick sense of human fellowship. You find yourself praying that you may never lose your hold on it all. . . . You turn helplessly to the waiter and feel that it would be almost grotesque to claim from him the sympathy you crave because civilization has placed you apart, but you resent your position with a sudden sense of snobbery. . . .

I have seen young girls suffer and grow sensibly lowered in vitality in the first years after they leave school. In our attempt . . . to give a girl pleasure and freedom from care we succeed, for the most part, in making her pitifully miserable. She finds "life" so different from what she expected it to be. She is besotted with innocent little ambitions, and does not understand this apparent waste of herself, this elaborate preparation, if no work is provided for her. There is a heritage of noble obligation which young people accept and long to perpetuate. The desire for action, the wish to right wrong and alleviate suffering haunts them daily. Society smiles at it indulgently instead of making it of value to itself. . . .

[F]rom babyhood the altruistic tendencies of these daughters are persistently cultivated. They are taught to be self-forgetting and self-sacrificing, to consider

Jane Addams, *Twenty Years at Hull House* (New York: Macmillan, 1910).

the good of the whole before the good of the ego. But when all this information and culture show results, when the daughter comes back from college and begins to recognize her social claim to the "submerged tenth," and to evince a disposition to fulfill it, the family claim is strenuously asserted; she is told that she is unjustified, ill-advised in her efforts. . . .

We have in America a fast-growing number of cultivated young people who have no recognized outlet for their active faculties. They hear constantly of the great social maladjustment, but no way is provided for them to change it, and their uselessness hangs about them heavily. . . . These young people have had advantages of college, of European travel, and of economic study, but they are sustaining this shock of inaction. They have pet phrases, and they tell you that the things that make us all alike are stronger than the things that make us different. They say that all men are united by needs and sympathies far more permanent and radical than anything that temporarily divides them and sets them in opposition to each other. . . .

This young life, so sincere in its emotion and good phrase and yet so undirected, seems to me as pitiful as the other great mass of destitute lives. One is supplementary to the other, and some method of communication can surely be devised. . . . Our young people feel nervously the need of putting theory into action, and respond quickly to the Settlement form of activity.

Other motives which I believe make toward the Settlement are the result of a certain renaissance going forward in Christianity. The impulse to share the lives of the poor, the desire to make social service, irrespective of propaganda, express the spirit of Christ, is as old as Christianity itself. . . .

I believe that there is a distinct turning among many young men and women toward this simple acceptance of Christ's message. They resent the assumption that Christianity is a set of ideas which belong to the religious consciousness, whatever that may be. They insist that it cannot be proclaimed and instituted apart from the social life of the community and that it must seek a simple and natural expression in the social organism itself. The Settlement movement is only one manifestation of that wider humanitarian movement which throughout Christendom . . . is endeavoring to embody itself, not in a sect, but in society itself.

I believe that this turning, this renaissance of the early Christian humanitarianism, is going on in America, in Chicago, if you please, without leaders who write or philosophize, without much speaking, but with a bent to express in social service and in terms of action the spirit of Christ. Certain it is that spiritual force is found in the Settlement movement, and it is also true that this force must be evoked and must be called into play before the success of any Settlement is assured. There must be the overmastering belief that all that is noblest in life is common to men as men, in order to accentuate the likenesses and ignore the differences which are found among the people whom the Settlement constantly brings into juxtaposition. . . .

In a thousand voices singing the Hallelujah Chorus in Handel's Messiah, it is possible to distinguish the leading voices, but the differences of training and cultivation between them and the voices of the chorus, are lost in the unity of purpose and in the fact that they are all human voices lifted by a high motive. This is a weak illustration of what a Settlement attempts to do. It aims, in a measure, to develop whatever of social life its neighborhood may afford, to focus and give form to that life, to bring to bear upon it the results of cultivation and training; but it receives in exchange for the music of isolated voices the volume and strength of the chorus. It is quite impossible for me to say in what proportion or degree the subjective necessity which led to the opening of Hull-House combined the three trends: first, the desire to interpret democracy in social terms; secondly, the impulse beating at the very source of our lives, urging us to aid in the race progress; and, thirdly, the Christian movement toward humanitarianism. . . .

The Settlement, then, is an experimental effort to aid in the solution of the social and industrial problems which are engendered by the modern conditions of life in a great city. It insists that these problems are not confined to any one portion of a city. It is an attempt to relieve, at the same time, the overaccumulation at one end of society and the destitution at the other; but it assumes that this overaccumulation and destitution is most sorely felt in the things that pertain to social and educational privileges. From its very nature it can stand for no political or social propaganda. . . . The one thing to be dreaded in the Settlement is that it lose its flexibility, its power of quick adaptation, its readiness to change its methods as its environment may demand. It must be open to conviction and must have a deep and abiding sense of tolerance. It must be hospitable and ready for experiment. It should demand from its residents a scientific patience in the accumulation of facts and the steady holding of their sympathies as one of the best instruments for that accumulation. It must be grounded in a philosophy whose foundation is on the solidarity of the human race, a philosophy which will not waver when the race happens to be represented by a drunken woman or an idiot boy. Its residents must be emptied of all conceit of opinion and all self-assertion, and ready to arouse and interpret the public opinion of their neighborhood. They must be content to live quietly side by side with their neighbors, until they grow into a sense of relationship and mutual interests. Their neighbors are held apart by differences of race and language which the residents can more easily overcome. They are bound to see the needs of their neighborhood as a whole, to furnish data for legislation, and to use their influence to secure it. In short, residents are pledged to devote themselves to the duties of good citizenship and to the arousing of the social energies which too largely lie dormant in every neighborhood given over to industrialism. . . .

I may be forgiven the reminder that the best speculative philosophy sets forth the solidarity of the human race; that the highest moralists have taught that without the advance and improvement of the whole, no man can hope for any lasting improvement in his own moral or material individual condition; and that the subjective necessity for Social Settlements is therefore identical with that necessity, which urges us on toward social and individual salvation.

## QUESTIONS FOR READING AND DISCUSSION

1. According to Addams, what was subjective about the necessity for social settlements? What did she see as major problems in her society?

2. In what ways did Addams believe settlements would make "universal" those "blessings which we associate with a life of refinement and cultivation"? What differences did she notice among people, and what did she identify as the unity underlying those differences?

3. To what extent did Addams think social settlements would serve the interests of educated middle-class women, as well as immigrants? How might immigrants have described their own and Addams's interests in settlement houses?

4. To what degree did settlement houses exemplify Progressive approaches to the solution of social and industrial problems?

## DOCUMENT 21-2

# *John D. Rockefeller Jr. Explains "The Best Thing for Us All"*

*In 1914, striking miners who belonged to the United Mine Workers of America were attacked at Ludlow, Colorado, by soldiers and strikebreakers controlled by the Colorado Fuel and Iron Company, owned by the Rockefellers' Standard Oil Company. The soldiers and strikebreakers burned the strikers' dwellings, killing dozens. The Ludlow Massacre exemplified the bitter conflict between western miners and large mining companies — Colorado Fuel and Iron was the largest industry in the state and the Rockefellers' Anaconda Mine employed three-fourths of all wage earners in the entire state of Montana. About a year after the Ludlow Massacre, John D. Rockefeller Jr. spoke to company officials and miners' representatives in Pueblo, Colorado, and outlined his vision of "the best thing for us all." Rockefeller's remarks conveyed the common view of corporate barons that what was best for their corporations was best for "us all."*

## *Speech to Colorado Fuel and Iron Officials and Employee Representatives,* October 2, 1915

Mr. President, and Fellow Members of the Colorado Fuel & Iron Company:

This is a red-letter day in my life. It is the first time I have ever had the good fortune to meet the representatives of the employees of this great company, its officers and mine superintendents, together, and I can assure you that I am proud to be here, and that I shall remember this gathering as long as I live. Had this meeting been held two weeks ago, I should have stood here as a stranger to many of you, recognizing few faces. Having had the opportunity last week of visiting all of the camps in the southern [Colorado] coal fields and of talking individually with practically all of the representatives, except those who were away; having visited in your homes, met many of your wives and children, we meet here not as strangers but as friends, and it is in that spirit of mutual friendship that I am glad to have this opportunity to discuss with you men our common interests. Since this is a meeting of the officers of the Company and the representatives of the employees, it is only by your courtesy that I am here, for I am not so fortunate as to be either one or the other; and yet I feel that I am intimately associated with you men, for in a sense I represent the stockholders and the directors. Before speaking of the plan of industrial cooperation to which our President referred, I

*Address by John D. Rockefeller Jr. Delivered at Pueblo, Colorado* (Denver: W. H. Kistler, 1915).

want to say just a few words outlining my view as to what different interests constitute a company or corporation.

Every corporation is composed of four parties. First, there are the stockholders; they put up the money which pays the wages, builds the plants, operates the business, and they appoint the directors to represent their interests in the corporation. We have, secondly, the directors, whose business it is to see that the chief executive officers of the Company are carefully and wisely selected, to plan out its larger and more important policies, particularly its financial policies, and generally to see to it that the company is wisely administered. And, thirdly, we have the officers of the company, whose duty it is to conduct the current operation of the business. While last, but by no means least — for I might just as well have started at the other end — we come to the employees, who contribute their skill and their work.

Now the interest of these four parties is a common one. An effort to advance one interest at the expense of any other, means loss to all, and when any one of the four parties in this corporation selfishly considers his own interest alone, and is disregardful of the interests of the other three parties, sooner or later disaster must follow. This little table [*exhibiting a square table with four legs*] illustrates my conception of a corporation; and there are several points in regard to the table to which I want to call your attention. First, you see that it would not be complete unless it had all four sides. Each side is necessary; each side has its own part to play. Now, if you imagine this table cut into quarters, and each quarter separated from the others, what would happen? All of them would fall down, for no one could stand alone, and you would have no table. But when you put the four sides together, you have a useful piece of furniture; you have a table.

Then, secondly, I call your attention to the fact that these four sides are all perfectly joined together; that is why we have a perfect table. Likewise, if the parties interested in a corporation are not perfectly joined together, harmoniously working together, you have a discordant and unsuccessful corporation. . . .

When you have a level table, or a corporation that is on the level, you can pile up earnings on it [*piling coins on the table*]. Now, who gets first crack at the earnings? You know that we in New York don't. Here come along the employees, and first of all they get their wages [*removing some of the coins*], every two weeks like clock-work, just what has been agreed on; they get the first chance at the pile. You men come ahead of the President, the officers, the stockholders and directors. You are the first to put a hand into the pile and take out what is agreed shall belong to you. You don't have to wait for your share; you don't have to take any chances about getting it. You know that there has never been a two-week period that you have worked when you have not been able to get your pay from this company; whatever happens, so long as the company is running, you get your pay.

And then the officers and superintendents come along, and they get theirs, they don't get it until after you have gotten yours [*removing more coins*].

Then come the directors, and they get their directors' fees [*removing the balance of the coins*] for doing their work in the company.

And, Hello! There is nothing left! This must be the Colorado Fuel & Iron Company! For never, men, since my father and I became interested in this company as stockholders, some twelve or fourteen years ago — never has there been one cent for the common stock. For fourteen years the common stockholder has seen your wages paid to you workers; has seen your salaries paid to you officers; has seen the directors draw their fees, and has not had one cent of return for the money that he has put into this company in order that you men might work and get your wages and salaries. How many men in this room ever heard that fact stated before? Is there a man among you? Well, there are mighty few among the workers who have heard it. What you have been told, what has been heralded from the Atlantic to the Pacific, is that those Rockefeller men in New York, the biggest scoundrels that ever lived, have taken millions of dollars out of this company on account of their stock owner- ship, have oppressed you men, have cheated you out of your wages, and "done" you in every way they could. That is the kind of "dope" you have been getting, and that is what has been spread all over this country. And when that kind of talk was going on, and there were disturbances in this part of the coun- try because the four sides of this table were not square and the table was not level, there were those who in the streets of New York and in public gather- ings, were inciting the crowd to "shoot John D. Rockefeller, Jr., down like a dog." That is the way they talked. . . .

This meeting has been called today for the purpose of seeing whether we can work out and agree upon, among ourselves here, some plan which will accomplish what I feel sure we all want to accomplish. I have been asked to explain the plan which is up for our consideration. I may say, men, that for years this great problem of labor and capital and of corporate relationships has engaged my earnest attention and study, while for the last eighteen months I have spent more of my time on the particular problems which confront this com- pany than I have put on any other one interest with which I am related. I have talked with all of the men whom I could get in touch with who have had experi- ence with or have studied these vital questions, I have conferred with experts, and I have tried in every way to get the best information I could looking toward the working out of some plan which would accomplish the result we are all striv- ing to attain. Nearly a year ago the officers of the company after having studied this question, with us in New York introduced, as you know, the beginning of such a plan, namely, the selection by the men at each camp of duly chosen repre- sentatives, to confer with the officers of the company in regard to matters of common interest. . . . I have visited every camp, with the exception of those on the western slope, and lack of time alone has prevented my getting over these to see you men. I have gone, as you know, to every camp in the southern fields, have talked privately with every superintendent, except one who was away, and with all of the representatives at each camp with the exception of two or three who were not available at the time; I have gone into scores of your homes and met your wives and children, and have seen how you live; I have looked at your gardens, and in camps where fences were only recently built have seen how ea- gerly you have planted gardens the moment opportunity was afforded, and how quickly you have gotten the grass to grow, also flowers and vegetables, and how the interest in your homes has thereby been increased. I inquired specifically about the water supply at each camp; I went down into several of the mines and talked with hundreds of the miners; I looked into the schools, talked with the teachers, inquired what educational advantages your children were getting. I asked what opportunities you men, my partners, had for getting together socially, and I visited some of your club-houses and saw plans for others. I went into your wash-houses and talked with the men before and after bathing. As you know, we have pretty nearly slept together — it has been reported that I slept in one of your nightshirts — I would have been proud had the report been true. If any man could have gone more carefully, more thoroughly, into the working and living conditions that affect you, my partners, I should be glad to have had him make me suggestions as to what further I might have done. . . .

I want to stay in Colorado until we have worked out some plan that we all agree is the best thing for us all, because there is just one thing that no man in this company can ever afford to have happen again, be he stockholder, officer, or employee, or whatever his position, and that is, another strike. I know we are all agreed about that, every last man of us, and I propose to stay here if it takes a year, until we have worked out among ourselves, right in our own family, some plan that we all believe is going to prevent any more disturbances, any more interruption of the successful operations of this great company in which we are all interested. . . .

**QUESTIONS FOR READING AND DISCUSSION**

1. Why did Rockefeller liken a corporation to a table? Did the table metaphor accurately capture the realities of the four parts of the corporation he described?
2. Rockefeller called the miners "my partners." What meaning did he try to express by such a term? To what extent was the term accurate? What might a Colorado Fuel and Iron miner have thought about the term? What "dope" was being said about Rockefeller?
3. Rockefeller argued that he and other stockholders had not had "one cent of return" on their investments in the company in twelve or fourteen years. Assuming for the sake of argument that this statement was true, did it mean that Rockefeller and other stockholders had not benefited from their ownership of the company? Why or why not?
4. Why did Rockefeller believe that he understood what was "the best thing for us all"? Did he believe that he had a special self-interest or point of view? Did his boasting about visiting miners and their families suggest that he realized they had different lives and interests from his?
5. Imagine that you were a miner who witnessed the Ludlow Massacre. How might you have responded to Rockefeller's remarks?

## DOCUMENT 21-3

# *Mother Jones on the Futility of Class Harmony*

*Progressive impulses to reconcile differences, to find common ground, and to reduce conflict rang false to labor union activists. Struggling to defend working people from industrial abuses, union organizers often viewed Progressive reforms as dangerous compromises that defeated the goals of working people. Mother Jones, a tireless organizer for the United Mine Workers, expressed in a public letter her opinion of the efforts of a Chicago socialite, Mrs. Potter Palmer, to reduce the strife between labor and capital. Born in 1830, Mother Jones began to attend meetings of the Knights of Labor in 1871 and participated in many of the most important labor conflicts of the next half-century.*

# Letter to Mrs. Potter Palmer, January 12, 1907

43 Welton Place, Chicago, Ill.
January 12, 1907.

Mrs. Potter Palmer
100 Lake Shore Drive
Chicago, Ill.

Dear Madam:

By the announcement of the daily press I learn that you are to entertain a number of persons who are to be present as representatives of two recognized classes of American citizens — the working class and the capitalist class, and that the purpose of this gathering is to choose a common ground on which the conflicting interests of these two classes may be harmonized and the present strife between the organized forces of these two classes may be brought to a peaceful and satisfactory end.

I credit you with perfect sincerity in this matter, but being fully aware that your environment and whole life has prevented you from seeing and understanding the true relationship of these two classes in this republic and the nature of the conflict which you think can be ended by such means as you are so prominently associated with, and with a desire that you may see and understand it in all its grim reality, I respectfully submit these few personal experiences for your kind consideration.

I am a workman's daughter, by occupation a dress-maker and school teacher, and during this last twenty-five years an active worker in the organized labor movement. During the past seventy years of my life I have been subject to the authority of the capitalist class and for the last thirty-five years I have been conscious of this fact. With the years' personal experience — the roughest kind best of all teachers — I have learned that there is an irrepressible conflict that will never end between the working-class and the capitalist-class, until these two classes disappear and the worker alone remains the producer and owner of the capital produced.

In this fight I wept at the grave of nineteen workers shot on the highways of Latterman, Pennsylvania in 1897. In the same place I marched with 5,000 women eighteen miles in the night seeking bread for their children, and halted with the bayonets of the Coal and Iron police who had orders to shoot to kill.

I was at Stanford Mountain, W.Va., in 1903 where seven of my brother workers were shot dead while asleep in their little shanties by the same forces.

I was in Colorado at the bull pens in which men, women and children were enclosed by the same forces, directed by that instrument of the capitalist class recently promoted by President [Theodore] Roosevelt, General Bell, who achieved some fame for his declaration that "in place of Habeas Corpus" he would give them "Post Mortems."

The same forces put me, an inoffensive old woman, in jail in West Virginia in 1902. They dragged me out of bed in Colorado in March, 1904, and marched me at the point of fixed bayonets to the border line of Kansas in the night-time. The same force took me from the streets of Price, Utah, in 1904, and put me in jail. They did this to me in my old age, though I have never violated the law of the land, never been tried by a court on any charge but once, and that was for speaking to my fellow workers, and then I was discharged by the federal court whose injunction I was charged with violating.

The capitalist class, whose representatives you will entertain, did this to me, and these other lawless acts have and are being committed every hour by this same class all over this land, and this they will continue to do till the working-class send their representatives into the legislative halls of this nation and by law take away the power of this capitalist class to rob and oppress the workers.

The workers are coming to understand this and the intelligent part of that class while respecting you, understand the uselessness of such conferences as will assemble in your mansion.

Permit me to quote from [Oliver] Goldsmith's "Deserted Village," where he says:

> Ill fares the land, to hast'ning ills a prey,
> Where wealth accumulates and men decay.

Quite appropriate to this fair land to-day.

Sincerely yours, for justice,
Mother Jones

## QUESTIONS FOR READING AND DISCUSSION

1. According to Jones, why was Palmer's meeting misguided?
2. Why did Jones believe that Palmer's life and environment prevented her from understanding class relationships? How might Palmer have responded to Jones's recounting of the "lawless acts" of capitalists?
3. How did Jones describe the "true relationship" between workers and capitalists? Why did she believe "an irrepressible conflict" existed between the classes? What was the source of her belief?
4. What common ground existed, if any, for reconciling the different views of Palmer and Jones?

## DOCUMENT 21-4

# *An Anonymous Man Explains Why He Is a Wobbly*

*Progressive reformers concentrated their attention on large cities, and most labor unions focused on big factories. Many working people moved from job to job in small towns, in western mining and logging camps, or from farm to farm as migratory laborers in fields of wheat, sugarbeets, grapes, or vegetables. The Industrial Workers of the World (IWW), formed in Chicago in 1905, tried to organize these scattered workers under the tent of "One Big Union" dedicated to overthrowing capitalism. The IWW — or Wobblies, as they were called — attracted many working people throughout the West. One of them wrote an anonymous account of why he became a Wobbly — an account that illustrates the appeal of revolutionary doctrines anathema to Progressives.*

## *Why I Am a Member of the I.W.W.,* 1922

I come from a part of Europe which furnishes a very large percentage of the loggers in the northwest.

As to my past I might say that life has offered me a very varied bill of fare. From my seventh to my fourteenth year I generally put in from seven to eight months a year at the "point of production." We kids in the sugar beet fields of southern Sweden began our day at 6 A.M. and were kept busy until 8 P.M., with three rests a day, totaling altogether two hours, making a twelve-hour day. You can easily imagine how much time we had for play or study and how physically fit we were for either.

So my childhood was lost and I was an old man at 14, when I struck a job in a grocery store, and at the age of 23 I found myself manager for quite a large business enterprise in my native country — a co-operative association composed of several thousand members. . . .

At the age of 25 I emigrated to the United States. To me it was not a question of journeying to some place where I hoped to gain fortune and fame. It was merely the satisfying of a desire for adventure and for knowledge of the world, a desire long suppressed for reasons of entirely personal nature. My first job in this country was in a packing plant at South St. Paul, Minn. There I received a splendid illustration of Upton Sinclair's book, "The Jungle," perhaps the most read book in Sweden at the time of my departure. It was a ten-hour day, with lots of overtime at regular pay, 16 1/2 cents per hour. Never do I see a sign advertising a certain brand of ham and bacon without thinking of the terrible high premium in sweat and blood, in misery and starvation, in ignorance and degeneration, the workers in those establishments have to pay before these products reach your table.

I turned down offers to again enter the commercial field back in Minnesota in order to be able to study another class of men, the man of the "wild west," as well as the wild west itself, and early in March, 1910, I headed for this coast.

I'll never forget my first experience in camp. It was a railroad camp up in the Rockies. I was tired after the hike with my bundle on my back, and attempted to sit down on a bed, the only furniture I could see that would furnish me a rest. Before I could accomplish the deed I was told in a very sharp voice in my mother tongue not to do so. I moved a little and tried another bed, when another Swede gave a similar command. After a third experiment which ended in a similar way, I got kind of peeved and began to lecture my countrymen a little as to civilized manners, when one of the boys explained: "We only warn you so as not to get lousy."

Suffice it to say that I made no more attempts to rest in that camp, but took a freight train that very evening and stayed two nights and one day in a box car before I, nearly froze to death, was dumped off at Hillyard, Wash., penniless, with no one I knew, and unable to speak a word in English.

Shortly after this incident I found myself in a logging camp in Idaho, across from the city of Coeur d'Alene. It was double beds two stories high, sleep on straw, work eleven to twelve hours per day, but the board was fairly good.

---

"Why I Am a Member of the I.W.W.," *Four L Bulletin* (1922); reprinted in *Rebel Voices: An I.W.W. Anthology,* ed. Joyce L. Kornbluh, (Ann Arbor: University of Michigan Press, 1964), 286–89.

I stayed there for several months, mostly because I wanted to stay away from my countrymen in order to learn the language. From there I went to British Columbia. Put in one year in a logging camp in the Frazer Valley and then one year and a half in a railroad camp on the Kettle Valley railroad. It was here I aligned myself with the I.W.W., and may I state that there was no delegate in that camp, and, to the best of my knowledge, not one member, I went over a hundred miles into Vancouver, B.C., to get that "little red card."

Why did I do it?

The reasons were many. While young I had associated myself with the prohibitionists, joining the Independent Order of Good Templars. I soon came to the conclusion that the liquor traffic itself is but a natural outgrowth of our existing social system, and that I could not abolish it without a fundamental change in society itself.

When working on the Kettle Valley road I observed quite a few interesting facts in this connection. Of over three thousand workers employed for a couple of years I doubt if there were two dozen men who left that job with sufficient funds to carry them for two months. The general routine was to work for a month, draw your check, go down to a little town named Hope (the most hopeless city I've seen) composed of two very large saloons, a couple of dirty rooming houses, a couple of stores and half a dozen houses of prostitution, and to spend, in a day or two, your every nickel in either the saloons or the brothels, usually in both. . . .

The I.W.W. seemed to me then and seems to me now the only group offering me any sensible program under which I could operate with a view to gaining these good things in life, and such changes in society as I desired. The I.W.W. declared that our real ruler is our boss. He decides our wages and thereby our standard of living, our pleasure or our misery, our education as well as the education of our children, our health and our comfort in life; in fact, he almost decides if we shall be allowed to live. The I.W.W. also told me that by uniting with my fellow-workers in the industry and all industries combined into One Big Union of all the workers, we could successfully combat our masters' One Big Union and gain the good things in life. We did not need to live in misery, we did not need to be ignorant for lack of time and access to study. And furthermore, we would become trained and organized for our final task, the control and management of industries. And as this program met my demands I naturally joined the I.W.W.

Some particular influences caused me to devote my whole life to the organization, and I am sure that perhaps thousands of others have been similarly influenced and simply forced to align themselves with the movement.

I knew a young fellow-worker in Seattle, by name Gust Johnson. He was only a little more than 20 years of age, a very quiet and very studious fellow. He surely had the courage of his convictions and he practiced what he preached to the limit of his ability. He was refined in manners, exceedingly clean, neat and orderly. He had been in the United States for about two years, when the Everett free-speech fight took place. He went on board the Verona to go with the bunch to Everett on the fifth of November, 1916, to assist in enforcing the constitutional right of free speech and free assemblage. In the shooting that followed Gust Johnson was the first one who fell with a bullet through his heart. Gust Johnson, who would hesitate even to kill a fly, Gust Johnson, to whom violence and disorder were an abhorrence.

I did what every one of you would have done for a true friend on whom such a cruel outrage had been committed. I threw myself into the harness and faithfully worked for the defense of the seventy-two victims, unjustly arrested, until the day of their release, and until the memory of Gust Johnson and the other four victims of the Everett tragedy stood shining bright before their relatives and their class.

During this defense work I got acquainted with another countryman of mine who toured the country in behalf of the I.W.W. His name is Ragnar Johanson. Ragnar has all the advantages in life which I lack. He is well educated, well built, handsome, a gifted orator and accomplished writer. Now, there is no intelligent human being who thinks that any question can be solved by violence. So Ragnar's theme has always been: "Violence signifies weakness; reason, strength." In hundreds of lectures I have heard this man urge his fellow-workers to educate themselves, to study and organize, but never have I heard him utter one word about using brutal force or violence to accomplish their ends. On the contrary he has always argued against all such teachings as being harmful and detrimental to the workers as a class or as individuals. Where is Ragnar Johanson now? He is serving ten years in the Leavenworth, Kan., federal prison, together with about seventy other fellow-workers who are my personal acquaintances or friends.

And lastly, although I am a foreigner, it is only because I am in America that I am an I.W.W. For, contrary to the belief of many, the I.W.W. is an outgrowth of advanced economic developments in America, and the Italian, the Russian or the Swede that you may find in the organization here would not have been "wobblies" had they remained in their native countries.

The economic law which says "that commodities shall be produced by that method which allows for the least expenditure of human labor" is the real ruler of society. This law cannot be abrogated by any combinations, trusts, monopolies, parties or organizations of any kind. . . . At present time production on large scale affords the greatest conformity to this law, hence the success of the trusts and the great industrial combinations. United States, with its immensely large natural resources and its shortage of labor power in years gone by has offered the best opportunity for the development of machine production on a large scale, while at the same time the aforesaid shortage of labor power has served as a spur to progress in this direction. The result is that no country in the world is so far advanced, industrially, as the U.S., particularly in leading industries, such as agriculture, mining, lumbering and manufacturing of machinery and means of locomotion.

The saving of labor power appears through a thorough going specialization of the work, through elimination of competition by means of amalgamations into large trusts whereby unnecessary labor in management in advertising, in salesmanship, and in distribution are avoided, and at the same time over-production with its loss of values in perishable goods, etc., is limited to a minimum. The trust is the bosses' One Big Union whereby they not only control the price on labor power, but also safeguard themselves against waste of labor power.

The I.W.W. is the result of the trust, the bosses' One Big Union. As the trust becomes universal, succeeds in organizing the industries internationally, so will the I.W.W. expand. As the trust is the logical outcome of technical progress in our mode of production, is a means by which commodities can be produced with a smaller expenditure of human labor than under a competitive system, so is the I.W.W. [an] outcome of the same forces whose object is to counteract the power of the trust and ultimately take full control of the trusts and the means of production for the benefit of mankind as a whole. Neither of them can be talked, written or legislated away. Let's make an effort to understand them and the underlying causes for their existence, and much suffering and much hatred will be avoided.

QUESTIONS FOR READING AND DISCUSSION

1. Why did this man decide to become a Wobbly? In what ways, if at all, did his work and his immigrant experiences influence his decision?
2. What were the differences between the two "One Big Unions" he described?
3. What goals did the I.W.W. have, and what tactics did its members use to reach those goals? How did their goals and tactics differ from those of bosses?
4. This man reported that many workers did not join the I.W.W. Why not? From the workers' perspective, what were the relative costs and benefits of I.W.W. membership?

## DOCUMENT 21-5

# Booker T. Washington on Racial Accommodation

*Most progressives showed little interest in changing race relations; many in fact actively supported white supremacy. Beset by the dilemmas of sharecropping, Jim Crow laws, disfranchisement, poverty, illiteracy, and the constant threat of violence, black Southerners had few champions among progressives. Booker T. Washington, perhaps the era's most celebrated black leader, spelled out a plan of racial accommodation as a path toward progress. In an address to white business leaders gathered at the Cotton States and International Exposition in Atlanta in 1895, Washington outlined ideas that remained at the center of debate among black Americans for decades.*

## The Atlanta Exposition Address, 1895

Mr. President and Gentlemen of the Board of Directors and Citizens,

One-third of the population of the South is of the Negro race. No enterprise seeking the material, civil, or moral welfare of this section can disregard this element of our population and reach the highest success. I but convey to you . . . the sentiment of the masses of my race when I say that in no way have the value and manhood of the American Negro been more fittingly and generously recognized than by the managers of this magnificent Exposition at every stage of its progress. It is a recognition that will do more to cement the friendship of the two races than any occurrence since the dawn of our freedom.

Not only this, but the opportunity here afforded will awaken among us a new era of industrial progress. Ignorant and inexperienced, it is not strange that in the first years of our new life we began at the top instead of at the bottom; that a seat in Congress or the state legislature was more sought than real estate or industrial skill; that the political convention or stump speaking had more attractions than starting a dairy farm or truck garden.

A ship lost at sea for many days suddenly sighted a friendly vessel. From the mast of the unfortunate vessel was seen a signal, "Water, water; we die of thirst!"

---

Booker T. Washington, *Up From Slavery* (New York: A. L. Burt Company, 1901).

The answer from the friendly vessel at once came back, "Cast down your bucket where you are.". . . The captain of the distressed vessel, at last heeding the injunction, cast down his bucket, and it came up full of fresh, sparkling water from the mouth of the Amazon River. To those of my race who depend on bettering their condition in a foreign land or who underestimate the importance of cultivating friendly relations with the Southern white man, who is their next-door neighbor, I would say: "Cast down your bucket where you are" — cast it down in making friends in every manly way of the people of all races by whom we are surrounded.

Cast it down in agriculture, mechanics, in commerce, in domestic service, and in the professions. And in this connection it is well to bear in mind that whatever other sins the South may be called to bear, when it comes to business, pure and simple, it is in the South that the Negro is given a man's chance in the commercial world, and in nothing is this Exposition more eloquent than in emphasizing this chance. Our greatest danger is that in the great leap from slavery to freedom we may overlook the fact that the masses of us are to live by the productions of our hands, and fail to keep in mind that we shall prosper in proportion as we learn to dignify and glorify common labour and put brains and skill into the common occupations of life; shall prosper in proportion as we learn to draw the line between the superficial and the substantial, the ornamental gewgaws of life and the useful. No race can prosper till it learns that there is as much dignity in tilling a field as in writing a poem. It is at the bottom of life we must begin, and not at the top. Nor should we permit our grievances to overshadow our opportunities.

To those of the white race who look to the incoming of those of foreign birth and strange tongue and habits for the prosperity of the South, were I permitted I would repeat what I say to my own race, "Cast down your bucket where you are." Cast it down among the eight millions of Negroes whose habits you know, whose fidelity and love you have tested in days when to have proved treacherous meant the ruins of your firesides. Cast down your bucket among these people who have, without strikes and labour wars, tilled your fields, cleared your forests, builded your railroads and cities, and brought forth treasures from the bowels of the earth, and helped make possible this magnificent representation of the progress of the South. Casting down your bucket among my people, helping and encouraging them as you are doing on these grounds, and to education of head, hand, and heart, you will find that they will buy your surplus land, make blossom the waste places in your fields, and run your factories. While doing this, you can be sure in the future, as in the past, that you and your families will be surrounded by the most patient, faithful, law-abiding, and unresentful people that the world has seen. As we have proved our loyalty to you in the past, in nursing your children, watching by the sick-bed of your mothers and fathers, and often following them with tear-dimmed eyes to their graves, so in the future, in our humble way, we shall stand by you with a devotion that no foreigner can approach, ready to lay down our lives, if need be, in defence of yours, interlacing our industrial, commercial, civil, and religious life with yours in a way that shall make the interests of both races one. In all things that are purely social we can be as separate as the fingers, yet one as the hand in all things essential to mutual progress. . . .

Nearly sixteen millions of hands will aid you in pulling the load upward, or they will pull against you the load downward. We shall constitute one-third and more of the ignorance and crime of the South, or one-third its intelligence and progress; we shall contribute one-third to the business and industrial prosperity of the South, or we shall prove a veritable body of death, stagnating, depressing, retarding every effort to advance the body politic. . . .

The wisest among my race understand that the agitation of questions of social equality is the extremest folly, and that progress in the enjoyment of all the privileges that will come to us must be the result of severe and constant struggle rather than of artificial forcing. No race that has anything to contribute to the markets of the world is long in any degree ostracized. It is important and right that all privileges of the law be ours, but it is vastly more important that we be prepared for the exercises of these privileges. The opportunity to earn a dollar in a factory just now is worth infinitely more than the opportunity to spend a dollar in an operahouse.

### QUESTIONS FOR READING AND DISCUSSION

1. What did Washington mean by "Cast down your bucket where you are"?
2. Washington expressed a distinctive vision of racial equality and progress in his famous statement, "In all things that are purely social we can be as separate as the fingers, yet one as the hand in all things essential to mutual progress." What were the implications of his vision for blacks who sought equality and progress? What significance did Washington attach to the words *separate* and *mutual*?
3. In what ways did Washington's argument appeal to his white audience? Would his speech have been different if he had been addressing a black audience? If so, how and why?
4. To what extent did Washington's speech exemplify the dilemmas of African Americans in the Progressive Era?

## DOCUMENT 21-6

# W. E. B. Du Bois on Racial Equality

*Many educated African Americans, especially in the North, objected to Booker T. Washington's policy of racial accommodation. In 1903, W. E. B. Du Bois attacked Washington's ideas and proposed alternatives that made sense to many black Americans, then and since. One of the organizers of the Niagara Movement and of the National Association for the Advancement of Colored People, Du Bois had earned a doctorate in history from Harvard and was a professor at Atlanta University when he published his criticisms of Washington, excerpted from his work* The Souls of Black Folk.

## Booker T. Washington and Others, 1903

Easily the most striking thing in the history of the American Negro since 1876 is the ascendancy of Mr. Booker T. Washington. It began at the time when war memories and ideals were rapidly passing; a day of astonishing commercial development was dawning; a sense of doubt and hesitation overtook the freedmen's sons, — then it was that his leading began. Mr. Washington came, with a simple definite programme, at the psychological moment when the nation was a little ashamed of having bestowed so much sentiment on Negroes, and was

---

W. E. B. Du Bois, *The Souls of Black Folk* (Chicago: A. C. McClurg & Company, 1903).

concentrating its energies on Dollars. His programme of industrial education, conciliation of the South, and submission and silence as to civil and political rights, was not wholly original. . . . But Mr. Washington first indissolubly linked these things; he put enthusiasm, unlimited energy, and perfect faith into this programme, and changed it from a by-path into a veritable Way of Life. . . .

It startled the nation to hear a Negro advocating such a programme after many decades of bitter complaint; it startled and won the applause of the South, it interested and won the admiration of the North; and after a confused murmur of protest, it silenced if it did not convert the Negroes themselves.

To gain the sympathy and cooperation of the various elements comprising the white South was Mr. Washington's first task; and [it] . . . seemed, for a black man, well-nigh impossible. And yet ten years later it was done in the word spoken at Atlanta: "In all things purely social we can be as separate as five fingers, and yet one as the hand in all things essential to mutual progress." This "Atlanta Compromise" is by all odds the most notable thing in Mr. Washington's career. The South interpreted it in different ways: the radicals received it as a complete surrender of the demand for civil and political equality; the conservatives, as a generously conceived working basis for mutual understanding. . . .

So Mr. Washington's cult has gained unquestioning followers, his work has wonderfully prospered, his friends are legion, and his enemies are confounded. To-day he stands as the one recognized spokesman of his ten million fellows, and one of the most notable figures in a nation of seventy million. . . .

But Booker T. Washington arose as essentially the leader not of one race but of two, — a compromiser between the South, the North, and the Negro. Naturally the Negroes resented, at first bitterly, signs of compromise which surrendered their civil and political rights, even though this was to be exchanged for larger chances of economic development. The rich and dominating North, however, was not only weary of the race problem, but was investing largely in Southern enterprises, and welcomed any method of peaceful cooperation. Thus, by national opinion, the Negroes began to recognize Mr. Washington's leadership; and the voice of criticism was hushed.

Mr. Washington represents in Negro thought the old attitude of adjustment and submission; but adjustment at such a peculiar time as to make his programme unique. This is an age of unusual economic development, and Mr. Washington's programme naturally takes an economic cast, becoming a gospel of Work and Money to such an extent as apparently almost completely to overshadow the higher aims of life. Moreover, this is an age when the more advanced races are coming in closer contact with the less developed races, and the race-feeling is therefore intensified; and Mr. Washington's programme practically accepts the alleged inferiority of the Negro races. Again, in our own land, the reaction from the sentiment of war time has given impetus to race-prejudice against Negroes, and Mr. Washington withdraws many of the high demands of Negroes as men and American citizens. . . .

In answer to this, it has been claimed that the Negro can survive only through submission. Mr. Washington distinctly asks that black people give up, at least for the present, three things,

First, political power,
Second, insistence on civil rights,
Third, higher education of Negro youth, —

and concentrate all their energies on industrial education, the accumulation of wealth, and the conciliation of the South. This policy has been courageously and insistently advocated for over fifteen years, and has been triumphant for perhaps ten years. As a result of this tender of the palm-branch, what has been the return? In these years there have occurred:

1. The disfranchisement of the Negro.
2. The legal creation of a distinct status of civil inferiority for the Negro.
3. The steady withdrawal of aid from institutions for the higher training of the Negro.

These movements are not, to be sure, direct results of Mr. Washington's teachings; but his propaganda has, without a shadow of doubt, helped their speedier accomplishment. The question then comes: Is it possible, and probable, that nine millions of men can make effective progress in economic lines if they are deprived of political rights, made a servile caste, and allowed only the most meagre chance for developing their exceptional men? If history and reason give any distinct answer to these questions, it is an, emphatic *No*. And Mr. Washington thus faces the triple paradox of his career:

1. He is striving nobly to make Negro artisans business men and property-owners; but it is utterly impossible, under modern competitive methods, for workingmen and property-owners to defend their rights and exist without the right of suffrage.
2. He insists on thrift and self-respect, but at the same time counsels a silent submission to civic inferiority such as is bound to sap the manhood of any race in the long run.
3. He advocates common-school and industrial training, and depreciates institutions of higher learning. . . .

This triple paradox in Mr. Washington's position is the object of criticism by two classes of colored Americans. One class is spiritually descended from Toussaint the Savior, through Gabriel, Vesey, and Turner,[1] and they represent the attitude of revolt and revenge; they hate the white South blindly and distrust the white race generally, and so far as they agree on definite action, think that the Negro's only hope lies in emigration beyond the borders of the United States. And yet, by the irony of fate, nothing has more effectively made this programme seem hopeless than the recent course of the United States toward weaker and darker peoples in the West Indies, Hawaii, and the Philippines, — for where in the world may we go and be safe from lying and brute force?

The other class of Negroes who cannot agree with Mr. Washington has hitherto said little aloud. . . . Such men feel in conscience bound to ask of this nation three things:

1. The right to vote.
2. Civic equality.
3. The education of youth according to ability.

---

[1]**Toussaint the Savior . . . Gabriel, Vesey, and Turner:** Toussaint L'Ouverture was a former slave rebel who led the Haitian Revolution in 1798. African Americans Gabriel Prosser, Denmark Vesey, and Nat Turner were executed for attempts to lead slave rebellions in the United States in 1800, 1822, and 1831, respectively.

They acknowledge Mr. Washington's invaluable service in counselling patience and courtesy in such demands; they do not ask that ignorant black men vote when ignorant whites are debarred, or that any reasonable restrictions in the suffrage should not be applied; they know that the low social level of the mass of the race is responsible for much discrimination against it, but they also know, and the nation knows, that relentless color prejudice is more often a cause than a result of the Negro's degradation; they seek the abatement of this relic of barbarism, and not its systematic encouragement and pampering by all agencies of social power. . . . They advocate, with Mr. Washington, a broad system of Negro common schools supplemented by thorough industrial training; but they are surprised that a man of Mr. Washington's insight cannot see that no educational system ever has rested or can rest on any other basis than that of the well equipped college and university, and they insist that there is a demand for a few such institutions throughout the South to train the best of the Negro youth as teachers, professional men, and leaders. . . .

They do not expect that the free right to vote, to enjoy civic rights, and to be educated, will come in a moment; they do not expect to see the bias and prejudices of years disappear at the blast of a trumpet; but they are absolutely certain that the way for a people to gain their reasonable rights is not by voluntarily throwing them away and insisting that they do not want them; that the way for a people to gain respect is not by continually belittling and ridiculing themselves; that, on the contrary, Negroes must insist continually, in season and out of season, that voting is necessary to modern manhood, that color discrimination is barbarism, and that black boys need education as well as white boys. . . .

[T]he distinct impression left by Mr. Washington's propaganda is, first, that the South is justified in its present attitude toward the Negro because of the Negro's degradation; secondly, that the prime cause of the Negro's failure to rise more quickly is his wrong education in the past; and, thirdly, that his future rise depends primarily on his own efforts. Each of these propositions is a dangerous half-truth. The supplementary truths must never be lost sight of: first, slavery and race-prejudice are potent if not sufficient causes of the Negro's position; second, industrial and common-school training were necessarily slow in planting because they had to await the black teachers trained by higher institutions , , , ; and, third, while it is a great truth to say that the Negro must strive and strive mightily to help himself, it is equally true that unless his striving be not simply seconded, but rather aroused and encouraged, by the initiative of the richer and wiser environing group, he cannot hope for great success.

In his failure to realize and impress this last point, Mr. Washington is especially to be criticised. His doctrine has tended to make the whites, North and South, shift the burden of the Negro problem to the Negro's shoulders and stand aside as critical and rather pessimistic spectators; when in fact the burden belongs to the nation, and the hands of none of us are clean if we bend not our energies to righting these great wrongs.

## QUESTIONS FOR READING AND DISCUSSION

1. According to Du Bois, what were the shortcomings of "the Atlanta Compromise"? What was compromised, and why? What consequences did the compromise have for black Americans?

2. In what ways did Washington's "gospel of Work and Money" involve a "triple paradox"?

3. What alternatives did Du Bois propose to Washington's plan? How did the political implications of Du Bois's proposals differ from those of Washington?

4. Who did Du Bois consider his audience? To what extent did Du Bois and Washington differ in their assessments of their white and black audiences?

## COMPARATIVE QUESTIONS

1. How did the views of Mother Jones, John D. Rockefeller Jr., and Mrs. Potter Palmer about the possibility of harmony between classes compare with those of Jane Addams?

2. To what extent did Booker T. Washington's ideas about progress for black Americans differ from the Wobbly's concept of One Big Union or from Mother Jones's belief in strikes?

3. In what ways did W. E. B. Du Bois's beliefs about the necessity of equality and political conflict compare with Addams's notions about the role of settlement houses?

4. The documents in this chapter provide evidence of both the aspirations and limitations of progressivism. Judging from these documents, to what extent did the limitations of progressive reforms arise from the character of progressive aspirations? In what ways, if at all, did the aspirations of progressives differ from those of capitalists, union organizers, and African Americans?

# CHAPTER 22

# WORLD WAR I: THE PROGRESSIVE CRUSADE AT HOME AND ABROAD

## 1914–1920

W ith the declaration of war against Germany in 1917, the United States unmistakably asserted its status as a major power in world affairs. European nations had admired American economic might for decades and watched the politics of the nation's constitutional democracy with interest for more than a century. Now, by entering the war and claiming a decisive voice in the peace, the United States took its place as one of the powerful industrial nations that would shape global history in the twentieth century. The following documents illustrate the idealism of President Woodrow Wilson and the bitter criticism of the war by American Socialists as well as the experience of combat, the postwar suppression of political radicals, and outbreaks of violence against African Americans.

## DOCUMENT 22-1

### President Woodrow Wilson Asks Congress for a Declaration of War

*For more than two years after the beginning of war in Europe in 1914, the United States maintained a policy of neutrality. In the spring of 1917, President Woodrow Wilson called an emergency session of Congress to ask for a declaration of war against Germany. Wilson's speech to Congress, excerpted here, outlined the reasons for America's entry into the war, explained what actions would be necessary to mobilize for warfare, and declared the noble motives for which the nation would fight.*

### Speech to Congress, April 2, 1917

I have called the Congress into extraordinary session because there are serious, very serious, choices of policy to be made, and made immediately, which it

*Congressional Record*, 65th Congr., special sess. (Washington, D.C.: U.S. Government Printing Office, 1917), vol. 55, pt. 1, 102–04.

was neither right nor constitutionally permissible that I should assume the responsibility of making.

On the third of February . . . I officially laid before you the extraordinary announcement of the Imperial German Government that on and after the first day of February it was its purpose to put aside all restraints of law or of humanity and use its submarines to sink every vessel that sought to approach either the ports of Great Britain and Ireland or the western coasts of Europe or any of the ports controlled by the enemies of Germany within the Mediterranean. That had seemed to be the object of the German submarine warfare earlier in the war, but since April of last year the Imperial Government had somewhat restrained the commanders of its undersea craft in conformity with its promise then given to us that passenger boats should not be sunk and that due warning would be given to all other vessels which its submarines might seek to destroy, when no resistance was offered or escape attempted. . . . The new policy has swept every restriction aside. Vessels of every kind, whatever their flag, their character, their cargo, their destination, their errand, have been ruthlessly sent to the bottom without warning and without thought of help or mercy for those on board, the vessels of friendly neutrals along with those of belligerents. . . .

I was for a little while unable to believe that such things would in fact be done by any government that had hitherto subscribed to the humane practices of civilized nations. . . . [T]he German Government has swept aside . . . all scruples of humanity or of respect for the understandings that were supposed to underlie the intercourse of the world. I am not now thinking of the loss of property involved, immense and serious as that is, but only of the wanton and wholesale destruction of the lives of non-combatants, men, women, and children, engaged in pursuits which have always, even in the darkest periods of modern history, been deemed innocent and legitimate. Property can be paid for; the lives of peaceful and innocent people cannot be. The present German submarine warfare against commerce is a warfare against mankind.

It is a war against all nations. American ships have been sunk, American lives taken, in ways which it has stirred us very deeply to learn of, but the ships and people of other neutral and friendly nations have been sunk and overwhelmed in the waters in the same way. There has been no discrimination. The challenge is to all mankind. Each nation must decide for itself how it will meet it. . . . Our motive will not be revenge or the victorious assertion of the physical might of the nation, but only the vindication of right, of human right, of which we are only a single champion. . . .

With a profound sense of the solemn and even tragical character of the step I am taking and of the grave responsibilities which it involves, but in unhesitating obedience to what I deem my constitutional duty, I advise that the Congress declare the recent course of the Imperial German Government to be in fact nothing less than war against the government and people of the United States; that it formally accept the status of belligerent which has thus been thrust upon it; and that it take immediate steps not only to put the country in a more thorough state of defense but also to exert all its power and employ all its resources to bring the Government of the German Empire to terms and end the war.

What this will involve is clear. It will involve the utmost practicable cooperation in counsel and action with the governments now at war with Germany, and, as incident to that, the extension to those governments of the most liberal financial credits, in order that our resources may so far as possible be added to theirs.

It will involve the organization and mobilization of all the material resources of the country to supply the materials of war and serve the incidental needs of the nation in the most abundant and yet the most economical and efficient way possible. It will involve the immediate full equipment of the navy in all respects but particularly in supplying it with the best means of dealing with the enemy's submarines. It will involve the immediate addition to the armed forces of the United States already provided for by law in case of war at least five hundred thousand men. . . .

While we do these things, these deeply momentous things, let us be very clear, and make very clear to all the world what our motives and our objects are. . . . Our object now, as then, is to vindicate the principles of peace and justice in the life of the world as against selfish and autocratic power and to set up amongst the really free and self-governed peoples of the world such a concert of purpose and of action as will henceforth ensure the observance of those principles. Neutrality is no longer feasible or desirable where the peace of the world is involved and the freedom of its peoples, and the menace to that peace and freedom lies in the existence of autocratic governments backed by organized force which is controlled wholly by their will, not by the will of their people. We have seen the last of neutrality in such circumstances. We are at the beginning of an age in which it will be insisted that the same standards of conduct and of responsibility for wrong done shall be observed among nations and their governments that are observed among the individual citizens of civilized states.

We have no quarrel with the German people. We have no feeling towards them but one of sympathy and friendship. It was not upon their impulse that their government acted in entering this war. It was not with their previous knowledge or approval. It was a war determined upon as wars used to be determined upon in the old, unhappy days when peoples were nowhere consulted by their rulers and wars were provoked and waged in the interest of dynasties or of little groups of ambitious men who were accustomed to use their fellow men as pawns and tools. . . .

A steadfast concert for peace can never be maintained except by a partnership of democratic nations. . . . It must be a league of honour, a partnership of opinion. . . . Only free peoples can hold their purpose and their honour steady to a common end and prefer the interests of mankind to any narrow interest of their own.

Does not every American feel that assurance has been added to our hope for the future peace of the world by the wonderful and heartening things that have been happening within the last few weeks in Russia? Russia was known by those who knew it best to have been always in fact democratic at heart, in all the vital habits of her thought, in all the intimate relationships of her people that spoke their natural instinct, their habitual attitude towards life. The autocracy that crowned the summit of her political structure, long as it had stood and terrible as was the reality of its power, was not in fact Russian in origin, character, or purpose; and now it has been shaken off and the great, generous Russian people have been added in all their naive majesty and might to the forces that are fighting for freedom in the world, for justice, and for peace. Here is a fit partner for a League of Honour.

One of the things that has served to convince us that the Prussian autocracy was not and could never be our friend is that from the very outset of the present war it has filled our unsuspecting communities and even our offices of government with spies and set criminal intrigues everywhere afoot against our national unity of counsel, our peace within and without, our industries and our commerce. Indeed it is now evident that its spies were here even before the war began; and it is unhappily not a matter of conjecture but a fact proved in our courts of justice that the intrigues which have more than once come perilously near to disturbing the peace and dislocating the industries of the country have been carried on at the instigation, with the support, and even under the personal direction of official agents of the Imperial Government accredited to the Government of the United States. . . .

We are now about to accept gauge of battle with this natural foe to liberty and shall, if necessary, spend the whole force of the nation to check and nullify its pretensions and its power. We are glad, now that we see the facts with no veil of false pretense about them, to fight thus for the ultimate peace of the world and for the liberation of its peoples, the German peoples included: for the rights of nations great and small and the privilege of men everywhere to choose their way of life and of obedience. The world must be made safe for democracy. Its peace must be planted upon the tested foundations of political liberty. We have no selfish ends to serve. We desire no conquest, no dominion. We seek no indemnities for ourselves, no material compensation for the sacrifices we shall freely make. We are but one of the champions of the rights of mankind. We shall be satisfied when those rights have been made as secure as the faith and the freedom of nations can make them. . . .

It is a distressing and oppressive duty, Gentlemen of the Congress, which I have performed in thus addressing you. There are, it may be, many months of fiery trial and sacrifice ahead of us. It is a fearful thing to lead this great peaceful people into war, into the most terrible and disastrous of all wars, civilization itself seeming to be in the balance. But the right is more precious than peace, and we shall fight for the things which we have always carried nearest our hearts, — for democracy, for the right of those who submit to authority to have a voice in their own governments, for the rights and liberties of small nations, for a universal dominion of right by such a concert of free peoples as shall bring peace and safety to all nations and make the world itself at last free. To such a task we can dedicate our lives and our fortunes, everything that we are and everything that we have, with the pride of those who know that the day has come when America is privileged to spend her blood and her might for the principles that gave her birth and happiness and the peace which she has treasured, God helping her, she can do no other.

## Questions for Reading and Discussion

1. What motivated Wilson to ask Congress for a declaration of war? Why was neutrality no longer acceptable?
2. In what ways would the "league of honor" Wilson proposed differ from more conventional alliances? Why were those differences important in this war?
3. Why did Wilson believe recent events in Russia were "wonderful and heartening"? How did they show that Russia was "democratic at heart"?
4. Wilson declared that "the world must be made safe for democracy." To what extent, according to Wilson, did this statement guide America's wartime goals and policies? To what degree was democracy at stake in the war?

## DOCUMENT 22-2

# Eugene V. Debs Attacks Capitalist Warmongers

*The Socialist party opposed American entry into World War I, calling it "a crime against the people of the United States." In June 1918, Eugene V. Debs, the party's perennial presidential candidate, spoke in Canton, Ohio, to a group of working people. In his speech, excerpted here, Debs explained that Socialists opposed the war not because they were pro-German but because they were anticapitalist. This speech precipitated Debs's arrest for violating the Espionage Act; he was convicted and sentenced to ten years in prison. In 1920, he campaigned for president from his prison cell.*

## Speech Delivered in Canton, Ohio, June 16, 1918

Why should a Socialist be discouraged on the eve of the greatest triumph in all the history of the Socialist movement? It is true that these are anxious, trying days for us all — testing days for the women and men who are upholding the banner of labor in the struggle of the working class of all the world against the exploiters of all the world. . . .

Are we opposed to Prussian militarism? Why, we have been fighting it since the day the Socialist movement was born; and we are going to continue to fight it, day and night, until it is wiped from the face of the earth. Between us there is no truce — no compromise. . . . Multiplied thousands of Socialists have languished in the jails of Germany because of their heroic warfare upon the despotic ruling class of that country. . . .

I hate, I loathe, I despise Junkers[1] and junkerdom. I have no earthly use for the Junkers of Germany, and not one particle more use for the Junkers in the United States.

They tell us that we live in a great free republic; that our institutions are democratic; that we are a free and self-governing people. This is too much, even for a joke. But it is not a subject for levity; it is an exceedingly serious matter.

To whom do the Wall Street Junkers in our country marry their daughters? After they have wrung their countless millions from your sweat, your agony and your life's blood, in a time of war as in a time of peace, they invest these untold millions in the purchase of titles of broken-down aristocrats, such as princes, dukes, counts, and other parasites and no-accounts. Would they be satisfied to wed their daughters to honest workingmen? To real democrats? Oh, no! . . .

These are the gentry who are today wrapped up in the American flag, who shout their claim from the housetops that they are the only patriots, and who have their magnifying glasses in hand, scanning the country for evidence of disloyalty, eager to apply the brand of treason to the men who dare to even whisper their opposition to junker rule in the United States. No wonder Sam Johnson declared that "patriotism is the last refuge of the scoundrel." He must have had

---

Jean Y. Tussey, ed., Eugene V. Debs, "Speech at Canton, Ohio," June 16, 1918, in *Eugene V. Debs Speaks* (New York: Pathfinder Press, 1970).

[1]**Junkers:** Members of the Prussian aristocracy, an especially militaristic and politically reactionary class in German society at that time.

this Wall Street gentry in mind, or at least their prototypes, for in every age it has been the tyrant, the oppressor, and the exploiter who has wrapped himself in the cloak of patriotism, or religion, or both to deceive and overawe the people. . . .

Socialism is a growing idea, an expanding philosophy. It is spreading over the entire face of the earth. It is as vain to resist it as it would be to arrest the sunrise on the morrow. It is coming, coming, coming all along the line. . . . It is the mightiest movement in the history of mankind. . . . It has enabled me . . . to feel life truly worth while; . . . to be class-conscious, and to realize that, regardless of nationality, race, creed, color, or sex, every man, every woman who toils, who renders useful service, every member of the working class without an exception, is my comrade, my brother and sister — and that to serve them and their cause is the highest duty of my life. . . .

[O]ur hearts are with the Bolsheviki of Russia. Those heroic men and women, those unconquerable comrades have by their incomparable valor and sacrifice added fresh lustre to the fame of the international movement. . . . The very first act of the triumphant Russian revolution was to proclaim a state of peace with all mankind, coupled with a fervent moral appeal, not to kings, not to emperors, rulers or diplomats, but to the people of all nations. . . .

Wars throughout history have been waged for conquest and plunder. . . . The feudal barons of the Middle Ages, the economic predecessors of the capitalists of our day, declared all wars. And their miserable serfs fought all the battles. The poor, ignorant serfs had been taught to revere their masters; to believe that when their masters declared war upon one another, it was their patriotic duty to fall upon one another and to cut one another's throats for the profit and glory of the lords and barons who held them in contempt. And that is war in a nutshell. The master class has always declared the wars; the subject class has always fought the battles. The master class has had all to gain and nothing to lose, while the subject class has had nothing to gain and all to lose — especially their lives. . . .

And here let me emphasize the fact — and it cannot be repeated, too often — that the working class who fight all the battles, the working class who make the supreme sacrifices, the working class, who freely shed their blood and furnish the corpses, have never yet had a voice in either declaring war or making peace. It is the ruling class that invariably does both. They alone declare war and they alone make peace. . . .

What a compliment it is to the Socialist movement to be persecuted for the sake of the truth! The truth alone will make the people free. And for this reason the truth must not be permitted to reach the people. The truth has always been dangerous to the rule of the rogue, the exploiter, the robber. So the truth must be ruthlessly suppressed. That is why they are trying to destroy the Socialist movement. . . .

We do not attack individuals. We do not seek to avenge ourselves upon those opposed to our faith. . . . There is no room in our hearts for hate, except for the system, the social system in which it is possible for one man to amass a stupendous fortune doing nothing, while millions of others suffer and struggle and agonize and die for the bare necessities of existence. . . .

To turn your back on the corrupt Republican party and the corrupt Democratic party — the gold-dust lackeys of the ruling class counts for something. It counts for still more after you have stepped out of those popular and corrupt capitalist parties to join a minority party that has an ideal, that stands for a principle, and fights for a cause. This will be the most important change you have ever made. . . .

Give me a hundred capitalists and let me ask them a dozen simple questions about the history of their own country and I will prove to you that they are as ignorant and unlettered as any you may find in the so-called lower class. They know little of history; they are strangers to science; they are ignorant of sociology and blind to art but they know how to exploit, how to gouge, how to rob, and do it with legal sanction. They always proceed legally for the reason that the class which has the power to rob upon a large scale has also the power to control the government and legalize their robbery. . . .

They are continually talking about your patriotic duty. It is not their but your patriotic duty that they are concerned about. There is a decided difference. Their patriotic duty never takes them to the firing line or chucks them into the trenches.

And now among other things they are urging you to "cultivate" war gardens, while at the same time a government war report just issued shows that practically 52 percent of the arable, tillable soil is held out of use by the land-lords, speculators, and profiteers. They themselves do not cultivate the soil. They could not if they would. Nor do they allow others to cultivate it. They keep it idle to enrich themselves, to pocket the millions of dollars of unearned incre-ment. Who is it that makes this land valuable while it is fenced in and kept out of use? It is the people. Who pockets this tremendous accumulation of value? The landlords. And these landlords who toil not and spin not are supreme among American "patriots." . . .

This lord who practically owns the earth tells you that we are fighting this war to make the world safe for democracy — he, who shuts out all humanity from his private domain; he, who profiteers at the expense of the people who have been slain and mutilated by multiplied thousands, under pretense of being the great Americans patriot. It is he, this identical patriot who is in fact the arch-enemy of the people; it is he that you need to wipe from power. It is he who is a far greater menace to your liberty and your well-being than the Prussian junkers on the other side of the Atlantic Ocean. . . .

[W]ar comes in spite of the people. When Wall Street says war the press says war and the pulpit promptly follows with its Amen. In every age the pulpit has been on the side of the rulers and not on the side of the people. . . .

Political action and industrial action must supplement and sustain each other. You will never vote the Socialist republic into existence. You will have to lay its foundations in industrial organization. The industrial union is the forerunner of industrial democracy. In the shop where the workers are associated is where in-dustrial democracy has its beginning. Organize according to your industries! . . .

Then unite in the Socialist party. Vote as you strike and strike as you vote. . . .

When we unite and act together on the industrial field and when we vote to-gether on election day we shall develop the supreme power of the one class that can and will bring permanent peace to the world. . . . We shall conquer the public power. We shall then transfer the title deeds of the railroads, the telegraph lines, the mines, mills, and great industries to the people in their collective capacity; we shall take possession of all these social utilities in the name of the people. We shall then have industrial democracy. We shall be a free nation whose govern-ment is of and by and for the people.

And now for all of us to do our duty! The clarion call is ringing in our ears and we cannot falter without being convicted of treason to ourselves and to our great cause.

Do not worry over the charge of treason to your masters, but be concerned about the treason that involves yourselves. Be true to yourself and you cannot be a traitor to any good cause on earth.

QUESTIONS FOR READING AND DISCUSSION

1. According to Debs, why were "these . . . anxious, trying days"? What was the significance of his slogan "Vote as you strike and strike as you vote"?

2. Why did Debs object to Wilson's pledge that the war would make the world safe for democracy? Did Debs and Wilson agree about the democratic possibilities of developments in Russia?

3. According to Debs, how should working-class people respond to the patriotic appeals of leaders? How should they avoid treason? In what way could peace be achieved?

4. Do you think Debs should have opposed the war, even though U.S. troops were fighting in it? Why or why not?

## DOCUMENT 22-3

# A Doughboy's Letter from the Front

*More than a million American soliders, "doughboys" in contemporary slang, fought fierce German resistance in decisive battles in the Argonne forest of northern France during the fall of 1918. One anonymous solider described his experiences to a friend back home in the following letter. The letter expresses the risks, fears, horrors, and exhilaration that many soldiers experienced in combat.*

## Anonymous Soldier
### *Letter to Elmer J. Sutters, 1918*

Cote D'Or France

Dear Old Bunkie,

Now don't go into epileptic fits or something like that when you read this letter, that is because I sent one to you as I know I haven't written you a letter for some time. Too busy with Uncle Sam's affairs just now and am working to beat hell.

I guess you would like to know of a few of my experiences over here while the scrimmage was on so I'll give you a few little yarns.

We were in the line up at Thiacourt (St. Michel Sector) at first and although we did no actual fighting as we were in reserve at first and then in support, we got a lot of strafing from Jerry[1] in the nature of Artillery fire and Air raids.

But in the Argonne Forest was where we got in it in earnest and even if I do say it myself, the good old Lightning (78th) Division will go down in history as second to none for the work they did there.

It was here, old man, that I got my first Hun[2] with the bayonet. That was on the day prior to taking Grandpre and we had just broke through the enemy first line defenses when this happened.

---

Anonymous Soldier to Elmer J. Sutters, 1918, in Andrew Carroll, ed., *War Letters: Extraordinary Correspondence from American Wars* (New York: Washington Square Press, 2001), 162–67.

[1,2]**Jerry; Hun:** Slang term for German soldiers.

We were pressing through a thicket when this big plug-ugly Hun suddenly loomed up in front of me and made a one-armed stab at me with his bayonet. You can make a hell of a long reach this way, but it's a rather awkward thrust as the bayonet makes the rifle heavy at the muzzle when you've got hold of your rifle at the small of the stock like this guy had. A homelier guy I never saw before in all my life and he'd make two in size compared to Dad and you know what a big man my old Dad is.

Well you can imagine that this bud did not catch me unawares.

I was ready for him. I thought I was going to have a pretty stiff one-sided fight on my hands, with the odds in his favor, but he was a cinch. Before I even realized it myself I parried off his blow and had him through the throat. It was my first hand to hand fight.

It was all over in a second, that is it for Jerry. He never even made a shriek. He went down like a log.

It was hand to hand all the way through that section of the woods as it was considered a vulnerable point, but we finally cleared them out and opened up the way for an attack on Grandpre itself. . . .

We took it, but at heavy cost. I lost a buddie in that last charge. If short five or ten yard dashes can be called a charge and I certainly didn't have much love for the Boches[3] after he went west. We can't mention any names of boys who were killed in our letters so I'll have to postpone it until I get home but he came from New Hampshire and a whiter fellow never lived. He was an only child too, old chap and his parents certainly have my sympathy.

Although I don't know his people I wrote a letter to them trying to make it as soft as I could. Well, he gave his all to the cause and you can't expect a fellow to do more. If a fellow goes down, its up to the next one to carry on and make them pay dearly for every life taken. You know what I mean.

I know that the first thing you would ask me when you see me again for the first if I was afraid. Now I am not going to stick my chest out and exclaim "Like hell I was" or anything of the sort. I sure was afraid, and you and any other chap would be too, but what I was afraid of most was that I would be yellow.

If a fellow gets a yellow streak and backs down the other boys won't have anything to do with him and that was what I was afraid of the most, of getting a yellow streak.

But I didn't. I was as plucky as any other doughboy and carried on all the way through and although I didn't get as much as a scratch I had many a close call. Enough of them to make a fellow's hair turn white. I crouched for three hours one night up to my waist in water in a shell hole waiting for our barrage to lift.

The water was like ice and there [were] four or five dead Huns floating around in it too. Not very pleasant, eh?

While sneaking about the ruins of Grandpre "Mopping Up" we came across a Prussian Chap in a ruined building with a rifle. He was a sniper, alive and the reason he was still there was because he could not get out although the opening was big enough for him to crawl through. During the bombardment the roof of the building had fell through in such a way as to pin him there by the feet and although he was practically uninjured he could not get himself free. I'll explain better when I see you, as I can tell it better than I can write it. He begged us to help him and although

---

[3]**Boches:** Slang term for German soldiers.

we had been cautioned against treatury [i.e., treachery] one of the fellows who was with me put down his rifle and started to crawl through to free him. The moment he got his head and shoulders through the hole which had been smashed by a shell, by the way, this Hun hauls off and lets him have a charge right square in the face.

Poor Dan never knew what happened. His face was unrecognizable. We did-n't do a thing but riddle that hole, we were that furious, and we didn't stop shoot-ing until our magazines were empty.

That Hun was the dirtiest skunk that every lived. . . . Dan was some husky boy and boasted of being a foot-ball player somewhere out in Tennessee where he came from. . . .

Up near Brickemay we ran into another pretty stiff proposition. We had to fight through the woods that seemed to be full of machine gun nests. We had just cleared out one of them with hand grenades and while we were sneaking up a rather steep hill, thickly wooded, we saw these Huns suddenly appear and run about a dozen paces and disappear down into a clearly camouflaged dug-out.

The Yanks were pressing the Huns hard, they were some of the Famous Prussian Guard too, and after these three birds had gone down into their hole we sneaked right up. There were three of us together, all Buck Privates. I took a hand grenade out of my bag, pulled out the retaining pin and heaved it down into the dug-out. . . . There was a helluva an explosion in about six seconds. I threw two more down to join the first and keep it company. Well after the big noise had stopped down there we crept down to investigate.

There was only one room down there, a big concrete affair and only one en-trance, the one we came down, and that room was a mess. There were fifteen dead Huns down there and the walls, floor and ceiling were splashed with red, so you can see what damage a hand grenade can do. I don't know whether my grenades killed them all, we didn't have time to ascertain, as we had to hurry right out again, but I know I got the three we saw beating it down there.

I was also with a detachment of men who took a dozen prisoners out of a dug-out and the worst of the whole thing was that they were only mere kids.

Just think of it old man. Mere kids, that is the most of them and they all expected to be killed immediately.

They were all scared stiff. We bagged the lot and sent them to the man under guard.

Well I was there to the finish old man and we had just mashed Fritz's[4] last resistance up near Sedan when we were relieved by a French Division who cap-tured Sedan next day. . . .

Fritz pulled off a peach of an air raid. . . . It was about 7:30 pm and quiet, yes very dark outside when the thing started and he came back again and again at regular intervals of ten minutes and bombed hell out of everything in sight, but what he really wanted to get . . . was our Supply and Ammunition Depots. . . . Now there is only one sane thing to do and I did it. Nothing heroic about it old man, just common sense and it wasn't the first time I did it either, even though my heart was trying to pound a hole through my ribs at the time. I went outside and walked out on the railroad and lay down flat in a shallow trench I had stum-bled upon . . . along the tracks and I stayed there all night too. It was an orga-nized raid, or rather a general raid and I saw the flashes from the exploding bomb all around me all night. . . . [O]ne bomb struck right near a small wooden shack where the Engineers use to store tools and blew that thing to hallaballoo.

---

[4]**Fritz:** Slang term for German Soldier.

That shed stood only about 100 or 150 yards from where I was laying . . . and a big piece of that shed came down ker-smak only six feet from where I was.

The next instant another landed right on the railroad and exploded with terrific force. . . .

This one burst about 500 yards away from me, but those things can kill at 1,000 yards and the concussion lifted me up out of this trench between the rails, about a foot or so in the air and I came down again ker-flump. It wasn't a pleasant sensation, but nothing hit me and that was better than anything. . . .

Well I guess this will be all for just now so with best regard and good wishes to you, Elmer, Mother Sutters, Pop, Mutt, and all the kyoodles. I close.

Your Old Friend and Comrade in Mischief

Dickwitch

P.S. Say you old slab of a lop-sided tin-eared Jackass, what's wrong with you anyhow. Got writer's cramp or what? Pick up a pen for the Love of Pete and write to your old buddie in France. Dick

### QUESTIONS FOR READING AND DISCUSSION

1. What was this soldier most afraid of? Why? What did his fear suggest about motivation for combat? What did he seem to mean by the term, "the cause"?

2. Did this doughboy take pride in killing "Huns"? Did he express regrets or doubts about killing? Why or why not?

3. To what extent did his combat experiences seem different from his prewar life? Did his prewar experiences and expectations seem to influence his life as a soldier?

DOCUMENT 22-4

# National Popular Justice League
# Criticizes the Red Scare

*The Bolshevik Revolution in Russia terrified many Americans. They feared communism would spread in the United States with the help of political radicals and immigrants. To suppress this Red menace, U. S. Attorney General A. Mitchell Palmer organized a series of raids to round up and deport immigrants suspected to be agents of communism. Palmer's raids violated civil liberties enshrined in the Constitution, as the National Popular Government League, a prominent group of lawyers, reported in 1920. The League's* Report on Illegal Practices of the Department of Justice, *excerpted here, revealed the methods used in the Red scare raids and charged that the raids, not those arrested, were un-American.*

## Report on Illegal Practices of the Department of Justice, 1920

TO THE AMERICAN PEOPLE:

For more than six months we, the undersigned lawyers, whose sworn duty it is to uphold the Constitution and Laws of the United States, have seen with

---

National Popular Government League, *Report on Illegal Practices of the Department of Justice* (New York: Arno Press, 1969).

growing apprehension the continued violation of that Constitution and breaking of those Laws by the Department of Justice of the United States government.

Under the guise of a campaign for the suppression of radical activities, the office of the Attorney General, acting by its local agents throughout the country, and giving express instructions from Washington, has committed continual illegal acts. Wholesale arrests both of aliens and citizens have been made without warrant or any process of law; men and women have been jailed and held *incommunicado* without access of friends or counsel; homes have been entered without search-warrant and property seized and removed, other property has been wantonly destroyed; workingmen and workingwomen suspected of radical views have been shamefully abused and maltreated. Agents of the Department of Justice have been introduced into radical organizations for the purpose of informing upon their members or inciting them to activities; these agents have even been instructed from Washington to arrange meetings upon certain dates for the express object of facilitating wholesale raids and arrests. In support of these illegal acts, and to create sentiment in its favor, the Department of Justice has also constituted itself a propaganda bureau, and has sent to newspapers and magazines of this country quantities of material designed to excite public opinion against radicals, all at the expense of the government and outside the scope of the Attorney General's duties.

We make no argument in favor of any radical doctrine as such, whether Socialist, Communist or Anarchist. No one of us belongs to any of these schools of thought. Nor do we now raise any question as to the Constitutional protection of free speech and a free press. We are concerned solely with bringing to the attention of the American people the utterly illegal acts which have been committed by those charged with the highest duty of enforcing the laws — acts which have caused widespread suffering and unrest, have struck at the foundation of American free institutions, and have brought the name of our country into disrepute.

These acts may be grouped under the following heads:

### (1) *Cruel and Unusual Punishments:*

The Eighth Amendment to the United States Constitution provides:

> Excessive bail shall not be required nor excessive fines imposed, nor cruel and unusual punishments inflicted.

Punishments of the utmost cruelty, and heretofore unthinkable in America, have become usual. Great numbers of persons arrested, both aliens and citizens, have been threatened, beaten with blackjacks, struck with fists, jailed under abominable conditions, or actually tortured.

### (2) *Arrests without Warrant:*

The Fourth Amendment to the Constitution provides:

> The right of the people to be secure in their persons, houses, papers, and effects, against unreasonable searches and seizures, shall not be violated, and no Warrants shall issue, but upon probable cause, supported by Oath or affirmation, and particularly describing the places to be searched, and the persons or things to be seized.

Many hundreds of citizens and aliens alike have been arrested in wholesale raids, without warrants or pretense of warrants. They have then either been released, or have been detained in police stations or jails for indefinite lengths of time while warrants were being applied for. This practice of making mass raids and mass arrests without warrant has resulted directly from the instructions, both written and oral, issued by the Department of Justice at Washington. . . .

### (3) Unreasonable Searches and Seizures:

In countless cases agents of the Department of Justice have entered the homes, offices, or gathering places of persons suspected of radical affiliations, and, without pretense of any search warrant, have seized and removed property belonging to them for use by the Department of Justice. In many of these raids property which could not be removed or was not useful to the Department was intentionally smashed and destroyed.

### (4) Provocative Agents:

We do not question the right of the Department of Justice to use its agents in the Bureau of Investigation to ascertain when the law is being violated. But the American people has never tolerated the use of under-cover provocative agents or "agents provocateurs," such as have been familiar in old Russia or Spain. Such agents have been introduced by the Department of Justice into the radical movements, have reached positions of influence therein, have occupied themselves with informing upon or instigating acts which might be declared criminal, and at the express direction of Washington have brought about meetings of radicals in order to make possible wholesale arrests at such meetings.

### (5) Compelling Persons to be Witnesses against Themselves:

The Fifth Amendment provides as follows:

> No person . . . shall be compelled in any criminal case to be a witness against himself, nor be deprived of life, liberty, or property, without due process of law.

It has been the practice of the Department of Justice and its agents, after making illegal arrests without warrant, to question the accused person and to force admissions from him by terrorism, which admissions were subsequently to be used against him in deportation proceedings. . . .

Since these illegal acts have been committed by the highest legal powers in the United States, there is no final appeal from them except to the conscience and condemnation of the American people. American institutions have not in fact been protected by the Attorney General's ruthless suppression. On the contrary, those institutions have been seriously undermined, and revolutionary unrest has been vastly intensified. No organizations of radicals acting through propaganda over the last six months could have created as much revolutionary sentiment in America as has been created by the acts of the Department of Justice itself.

Even were one to admit that there existed any serious "Red menace" before the Attorney General started his "unflinching war" against it, his campaign has been singularly fruitless. Out of the many thousands suspected by the Attorney General (he had already listed 60,000 by name and history on November 14, 1919, aliens and citizens) what do the figures show of net results? Prior to January 1, 1920, there were actually deported 263 persons. Since January 1 there have been actually deported 18 persons. Since January 1 there have been ordered deported an additional 529 persons, and warrants for 1,547 have been cancelled (after full hearings and consideration of the evidence) by Assistant Secretary of Labor Louis F. Post, to whose courageous reestablishment of American Constitutional Law in deportation proceedings are due the attacks that have been made upon him. The Attorney General has consequently got rid of 810 alien suspects, which, on his own showing, leaves him at least 59,160 persons (aliens and citizens) still to cope with.

It has always been the proud boast of America that this is a government of laws and not of men. Our Constitution and laws have been based on the simple elements of human nature. Free men cannot be driven and repressed; they must be led. Free men respect justice and follow truth, but arbitrary power they will oppose until the end of time. There is no danger of revolution so great as that created by suppression, by ruthlessness, and by deliberate violation of the simple rules of American law and American decency.

It is a fallacy to suppose that, any more than in the past, any servant of the people can safely arrogate to himself unlimited authority. To proceed upon such a supposition is to deny the fundamental American theory of the consent of the governed. Here is no question of a vague and threatened menace, but a present assault upon the most sacred principles of our Constitutional liberty. . . .

## Exhibit 1a

. . . SEMEON NAKHWAT, being duly sworn, deposes and says:

I was born in Grodno, Russia, and am thirty-three years old and unmarried.

In the autumn of 1919 I was a member of the Union of Russian Workers. I am not an anarchist, Socialist or Bolshevik and do not take much interest in political theories. I joined the Russian Workers because I was a workman speaking Russian and wanted to associate with other Russians and have the benefit of the social intercourse and instruction in mechanics which the society gave. By trade I am a machinist.

On November 8, 1919, I was at a meeting of Russians in Bridgeport, [Connecticut,] who had come together to discuss ways and means for buying an automobile to be used for instruction purposes. At that time I was employed by the American Brass Co. in Ansonia as a machinist, working a ten-hour day at 46 $1/2$ cents an hour. At the meeting I speak of, I was arrested with all the other men at the meeting, 63 in number. The arrest was made by Edward J. Hickey, a special agent of the Department of Justice, who had helping him about fourteen Bridgeport policemen in uniform and about nine Department of Justice agents in plain clothes. No warrant of arrest was shown me then or at any other time, nor did I see any warrant shown to anyone else who was arrested.

I was taken with the other men to the police station on Fairfield Avenue and held there three days, being in a cell with two other men. During these three days no one gave me any hearing or asked me any questions. I was then taken to Hartford, Conn., with about forty-eight of the men, being informed that the rest of those arrested had been released.

I was held in the Hartford Jail for six weeks without any hearing. In the seventh week I had one hearing before the Labor Department, which hearing was held in the Post Office Building, and was then returned to jail.

In the thirteenth week of my confinement Edward J. Hickey came into my cell and asked me to give him the address of a man called Boyko in Greenpoint,

Brooklyn. I did not know this man and told Hickey that I did not. Hickey thereupon struck me twice with his fist, once in the forehead and once in the jaw, whereupon I fell. He then kicked me and I became unconscious. Hickey is a big man, weighing two hundred pounds. For three weeks after this I suffered severe pain where I was kicked in the back. . . .

### Exhibit 2b

. . . MITCHEL LAVROWSKY, being duly sworn, deposes and says:

On the 7th day of November, 1919, I conducted a class in Russian at 133 East 15th Street, in the Borough of Manhattan, City of New York. At about 8:00 o'clock in the evening, while I was teaching algebra and Russian, an agent of the Department of Justice opened the door of the school, walked in with a revolver in his hands and ordered everybody in the school to step aside; then ordered me to step towards him. I wear eyeglasses and the agent of the Department of Justice ordered me to take them off. Then without any provocation, struck me on the head and simultaneously two others struck and beat me brutally. After I was beaten and without strength to stand on my feet, I was thrown downstairs and while I rolled down, other men, I presume also agents of the Department of Justice, beat me with pieces of wood, which I later found out were obtained by breaking the banisters. I sustained a fracture of my head, left shoulder, left foot, and right side.

QUESTIONS FOR READING AND DISCUSSION

1. According to the *Report*, how did the Red scare raids violate the Constitution? How might the attorney general have defended the raids?
2. Why was Semeon Nakhwat arrested and jailed? Why was Mitchel Lavrowsky rounded up?
3. What do the *Report* and the depositions suggest about the attitudes of the many Americans who supported the raids? In what ways did American experiences during World War I influence such attitudes?
4. In what ways might the Red scare raids have influenced political radicals and immigrants? Did the raids succeed or fail?

DOCUMENT 22-5

# An African American Responds to the Chicago Race Riot

*Race riots exploded in almost two dozen American cities during the summer of 1919. White mobs attacked African Americans indiscriminately, beating, shooting, and lynching them. Shortly after the bloody riot in Chicago, the governor of Illinois appointed a biracial commission to study the causes of the melee. Stanley B. Norvell, an African American Chicagoan, wrote the following letter to Victor F. Lawson, editor of the Chicago Daily News, who had just been appointed as one of the white members of the commission to study the riot. Norvell described whites' ignorance of blacks and pointed out that a "new Negro" had been created by the experiences of World War I and the continuing injustices of white racism.*

# Stanley B. Norvell
## *Letter to Victor F. Lawson, 1919*

My dear Mr. Lawson:

. . . I take it that the object of this commission is to obtain by investigation . . . the cause or causes of the friction between the two races that started the molecules of race hatred into such violent motion as to cause the heterogeneous mixture to boil over in the recent race riots.

Few white men know the cause, for the simple reason that few white men know the Negro as an entity. On the other hand, I daresay that almost any Negro that you meet on the street could tell you the cause, if he would, for it is doubtful — aye, very doubtful — if he would tell you, because Negroes have become highly suspicious of white men, even such white men as they deem their friends ordinarily. The Negro has always been and is now largely a menial dependent upon the white man's generosity and charity for his livelihood, and for this reason he has become an expert cajoler of the white man and a veritable artist at appearing to be that which he is not. To resort to the vernacular, "conning" the white man has become his profession, his stock in trade. Take for example the Negro in Chicago — and Chicago is fairly representative — sixty per cent of the male Negro population is engaged in menial and servile occupations such as hotel waiters, dining car waiters, sleeping car porters, barbershop porters, billiard room attendants, etc., where "tips" form the greater part of their remuneration. Thirty per cent are laborers and artisans, skilled and unskilled, governmental and municipal employees; while the remaining ten per cent are business and professional men.

Unfortunately it is always by the larger class — the menial, servitor and flunky class — that the race is judged. Even at that, we would not object to being judged by this class of our race, if those who did the judging had a thorough knowledge of the individuals who make up this class. Unfortunately they have not this knowledge nor can they get it except through the instrumentality of just such a commission as that to which you gentlemen have been assigned. The white man of America knows just about as much about the mental and moral calibre, the home life and social activities of this class of colored citizens as he does about the same things concerning the inhabitants of the thus far unexplored planet of Mars. . . . [W]ere you to ask any white man concerning these dusky servitors he . . . will discuss him in a general superficial sort of way and if you press him further you will be surprised to know that in spite of his years of acquaintance with the subject he knows absolutely nothing about intellect, ability, ambitions, the home life and environment of one with whom he has come into daily contact for years. He is just a "nigger" and he takes him for granted, as a matter of course. . . .

I can walk down the "Boul Mich" [Michigan Avenue in Chicago] and be surveyed by the most critical of Sherlock Holmeses and I will wager that none of them can accurately deduce what I am or what I represent. They cannot tell whether I am well off or hard up; whether I am educated or illiterate; whether I am a northerner or a southerner; whether I am a native born Negro or a foreigner;

Stanley B. Norvell to Victor F. Lawson, in William Tuttle, ed., "Views of a Negro during the Red Summer of 1919," *Journal of Negro History,* 51 (July 1966), 211–18.

whether I live among beautiful surroundings or in the squalor of the "black belt." I defy the shrewdest of your pseudo detectives to know whether I am a reputable citizen or whether I am a newly arrived crook. They cannot tell by looking at me what my income is. . . . The point is that I am only an ordinary, average Negro and that the white man is constantly making the mistake of discounting us and rating us too cheaply. He should wake up to the fact that brain is not peculiar to any race or nationality but is merely a matter of development. . . .

The further causes of the apparent increased friction between the two races, in my opinion is due to the gradual, and inevitable evolution — metamorphosis, if you please — of the Negro. The Negro has also progressed in knowledge by his study of the white man, while the white man blinded by either his prejudice or by his indifference has failed to study the Negro judiciously, and as a consequence, he knows no more about him than he did fifty years ago and still continues to judge him and to formulate opinions about him by his erstwhile standards. Today we have with us a new Negro. A brand new Negro, if you please. What opportunities have you better class white people for getting into and observing the homes of the better class of colored people[?] Yet the duties of the colored man in his menial capacities gives him an insight of your home life. As a suggestion, if I may be permitted to make one, I suggest that the white members of this commission make it their business to try to obtain an opportunity through some of the colored members of the commission to visit the homes of some of our better class people. You will find that "Uncle Tom" that charming old figure of literature contemporary with the war of the rebellion is quite dead now and that his prototypes are almost as extinct as is the great auk, the dodo bird, old Dobbin and the chaise. . . . This was all brought about by education. . . . When a young colored boy of Chicago goes through the eight grades of grammar school and wins the cherished . . . diploma; then through a four year high school course and wins a university scholarship; and then goes to college and wins a degree . . . and is highly popular and well received among his fellow classmates, it is a very difficult thing for him to get it into his head that he is inferior to anybody that has no more knowledge, ability nor money than himself. Regardless of what the eminent sociologists may say, and the fiery and usually groundless claims of the southern negrophile [negrophobe] to the contrary notwithstanding, there is no amount of logic, nor philosophy, nor ethnology, nor anthropology, nor sociology that can convince him to his own satisfaction that he is not the possessor of all the lesser and major attributes that go to make up a good citizen by all of the standards which our republican conventions hold near and dear.

Take the late war for example, and consider the effect that it has had upon the Negro, by and large. I believe that the mental attitude of the Negro that went to war is comparable in a certain degree to the mental attitude of most of the Negroes throughout the country; so far as the awakenings are concerned. The Negro of this country has gone through the same evolution that the white man has, in his own way; and in a large percentage of the total, that way is not far removed from the way the white man's mind thought out the matter or is thinking it out, especially the soldier mind. The Negro of our country . . . the Negro of the mass I mean, is comparable in his awakening and in his manner of thought after that awakening, to these white boys who went to war. The white soldiers — being young — had but little thought of anything but their immediate concerns, and the Negro, until lately, had but little thought of anything but his immediate concerns — being segregated. How I loathe that word.

Since the war the Negro has been jolted into thinking by circumstances. . . . [Negroes] have learned that there were treaties and boundaries and Leagues of Nations and mandatories, and Balkan states, and a dismembered Poland, a ravished Belgium, a stricken France, a soviet Russia and a republic in Ireland and so on, and they have . . . for the first time in their lives taken a peep of their own volition and purely because they wanted to know, into the workings of governmental things of those other countries, and have tried to reason out the possible real cause of all of this bloodshed and woe and misery along such international, allied and foreign government and other vague lines.

Now then, this has logically . . . brought us round to a sort of realization of how our government was made and is conducted. I venture to claim that any average Negro of some education, if closely questioned, and the questions were put to him in simple understandable form, will tell you that he finally has come to know that he counts as a part of his government, that he is a unit in it. It took a world war to get that idea into general Negro acceptance, but it is there now. Centuries of the dictum, which heretofore not many of us disputed, that, "This was a white man's country and that we were destined to always be hewers of wood and carriers of water," was set aside by circumstances and conditions and reactions and reflexes and direct contacts of this war. Negroes were pulled out of their ordinary pursuits all over the country and called upon to do things that they had to do because there was nobody at hand to do them, and those circumstances induced an awakening that must inevitably continue for all time.

The five hundred thousand Negroes who were sent overseas to serve their country were brought into contacts that widened both their perceptions and their perspectives, broadened them, gave them new angles on life, on government, and on what both mean. They are now new men and world men, if you please. . . .

What the Negro wants and what the Negro will not be satisfied with until he gets is that treatment and that recognition that accords him not one jot or tittle less than that which any other citizen of the United States is satisfied with. He has become tired of equal rights. He wants the same rights. He is tired of equal accommodations. He wants [the] same accommodations. He is tired of equal opportunity. He wants the same opportunity. He must and will have industrial, commercial, civil and political equality. America has already given him these inalienable rights, but she has not always seen to it that he has received them. America must see that the Negro is not deprived of any right that she has given him otherwise the gift is bare, and in view of her recent international exploits she will stand in grave danger of losing her national integrity in the eyes of Europe and she will be forced to admit to her European adversaries that her constitution is but a scrap of paper.

Social equality — that ancient skeleton in the closet of the southern negrophile [negrophobe], whose bones are always brought out and rattled ominously whenever the Negro question is discussed — is in no way a factor in the solution of the problem, but is a condition that will quite naturally exist when the problem is eventually solved — just a little prior to the millennium. Leastwise considering the unsettled condition of the world at large, the white man of this country has a great deal more to be sensibly alarmed about than the coming of social equality. Looking into the future I can see more ominous clouds on the horizon of this country's destiny than the coming of social equality.

When the Negro ponders the situation — and now he is beginning to seriously do that — it is with a feeling of poignant resentment that he sees his alleged inferiority constantly and blatantly advertised at every hand, by the press, the pulpit, the stage and by the glaring and hideous sign-boards of segregation. Try to imagine, if you can, the feelings of a Negro army officer, who clothed in the full panoply of his profession and wearing the decorations for valor of three governments, is forced to the indignity of a jim-crow car and who is refused a seat in a theatre and a bed in a hotel. Think of the feelings of a colored officer, who after having been graduated from West Point and having worked up step by step to the rank of colonel to be retired on account of blood pressure — and other pressure — in order that he might not automatically succeed to the rank of general officer. Try to imagine the smouldering hatred within the breast of an overseas veteran who is set upon and mercilessly beaten by a gang of young hoodlums simply because he is colored. Think of the feelings in the hearts of boys and girls of my race who are clean, intelligent and industrious who apply for positions only to meet with the polite reply that, "We don't hire niggers." Think how it must feel to pass at the top of the list and get notice of appointment to some nice civil service position that is paid for out of the taxes of the commonwealth, and upon reporting to assume the duties thereof, to be told that there has been a mistake made in the appointment.

When you think of these things, and consider them seriously it is easy to see the underlying, contributory causes of the friction that led up to the recent racial troubles. It is a well known fact that civilization is but a veneer which lightly covers the surface of mankind; that if slightly scratched, with the right kind of tool, a man will turn into a bloodthirsty savage in the twinkling of an eye. The overt act that is alleged to have started the recent conflagration, would not have in itself been sufficient to have ignited and exploded such vials of wrath had not the structure of society been long soaked in the inflammable gasolene of smouldering resentment.

As soon as the white man is willing to inform himself about the true status of the Negro as he finds him today, and is willing to take off the goggles of race prejudice and to study the Negro with the naked eye of fairness, and to treat him with justice and equity, he will come to the conclusion that the Negro has "arrived" and then voila, you have the solution to the problem.

We ask not charity but justice. We no longer want perquisites but wages, salary and commissions. Much has been said . . . [about] the white man's burden. We admit to having been a burden, just as an infant that cannot walk is at one time a burden. But in the natural order of things the infant soon ceases to be a burden and eventually grows up to be a crutch for the arm that once carried him. We feel that now we are able to take our first, feeble diffident steps, and we implore the white man to set his burden down and let us try to walk. Put us in your counting rooms, your factories and in your banks. The young people who went to school with us and who learned the three R's from the same blackboard as ourselves will surely not object to working with us after we have graduated. If they do, it will only be because they are not yet accustomed to the new conditions. That is nothing. People soon become accustomed to new things and things that seem at first preposterous soon become commonplace. We have surely proven by years of unrequited toil and by constant and unfaltering loyalty and fealty that we are worthy of the justice that we ask. For God's sake give it to us!

Stanley B. Norvell

QUESTIONS FOR READING AND DISCUSSION

1. According to Norvell, what were the causes of the Chicago race riot?

2. Why did few white men "know the Negro"? How did whites judge "the race"? Why could whites not "accurately deduce what I am or what I represent," according to Norvell?

3. What did Norvell mean by saying, "Today we have with us a new Negro"? How did education influence attitudes among blacks and whites? How did World War I contribute to new attitudes among African Americans?

4. How did "the goggles of race prejudice" shape the experiences of blacks and whites? What assumptions did Norvell make about the motivations of whites and blacks and how they might be changed?

COMPARATIVE QUESTIONS

1. In what ways did Woodrow Wilson's arguments about American war aims differ from Eugene V. Debs's views? What accounted for the differences? To what extent did Wilson and Debs differ from the views in the doughboy's letter?

2. To what extent were the raids against the Red menace an outgrowth of Wilson's wartime policies? Based on the documents in this chapter, how might Debs have explained the raids?

3. To what extent did Debs's advocacy of socialism address the issues raised by Stanley B. Norvell? Did Norvell endorse Debs's stance toward the war and other matters?

4. Wilson's wartime appeal to patriotism intensified domestic concerns about who was authentically American. Considering the documents in this chapter, what ideas do you think existed about who genuine Americans were, how they could be recognized, and what their duties and responsibilities were?

# CHAPTER 23

# FROM NEW ERA TO GREAT DEPRESSION
## 1920–1932

During the 1920s, complacency became an article of faith among many comfortable Americans. Things were as they should be, business was good, America was strong, and God was in his heaven. Republican presidents explained the logic of contentment that appealed to many voters. Beneath the gaze of the satisfied, however, other Americans felt disoriented and dissatisfied by the economic, political, social, racial, and ethnic status quo. For them, complacency was a problem, rather than a result of all problems having been solved.

## DOCUMENT 23-1

### President Calvin Coolidge on Government and Business

*The success of the Bolshevik Revolution frightened most American leaders and strengthened the appeal of the argument that government should not interfere with business. As governor of Massachusetts, Calvin Coolidge won national recognition in 1919 for using the state militia to break the Boston police strike, which he declared was an intolerable threat to public order. As president, Coolidge explained his concept of the proper relationship between government and business in an address, excerpted here, to the New York Chamber of Commerce in 1925.*

### Address before the New York Chamber of Commerce, November 19, 1925

This time and place naturally suggest some consideration of commerce in its relation to Government and society. We are finishing a year which can justly be said to surpass all others in the overwhelming success of general business. We

---

Calvin Coolidge, "Government and Business," in *Foundations of the Republic: Speeches and Addresses* (New York: C. Scribner's Sons, 1926).

are met not only in the greatest American metropolis, but in the greatest center of population and business that the world has ever known. . . .

The foundation of this enormous development rests upon commerce. New York is an imperial city, but it is not a seat of government. The empire over which it rules is not political, but commercial. The great cities of the ancient world were the seats of both government and industrial power. . . . In the modern world government is inclined to be merely a tenant of the city. Political life and industrial life flow on side by side, but practically separated from each other. When we contemplate the enormous power, autocratic and uncontrolled, which would have been created by joining the authority of government with the influence of business, we can better appreciate the wisdom of the fathers in their wise dispensation which made Washington the political center of the country and left New York to develop into its business center. They wrought mightily for freedom. . . .

I should put an even stronger emphasis on the desirability of the largest possible independence between government and business. Each ought to be sovereign in its own sphere. When government comes unduly under the influence of business, the tendency is to develop an administration which closes the door of opportunity; becomes narrow and selfish in its outlook, and results in an oligarchy. When government enters the field of business with its great resources, it has a tendency to extravagance and inefficiency, but, having the power to crush all competitors, likewise closes the door of opportunity and results in monopoly. It is always a problem in a republic to maintain on the one side that efficiency which comes only from trained and skillful management without running into fossilization and autocracy, and to maintain on the other that equality of opportunity which is the result of political and economic liberty without running into dissolution and anarchy. The general results in our country, our freedom and prosperity, warrant the assertion that our system of institutions has been advancing in the right direction in the attempt to solve these problems. We have order, opportunity, wealth, and progress.

While there has been in the past and will be in the future a considerable effort in this country of different business interests to attempt to run the Government in such a way as to set up a system of privilege, and while there have been and will be those who are constantly seeking to commit the Government to a policy of infringing upon the domain of private business, both of these efforts have been very largely discredited, and with reasonable vigilance on the part of the people to preserve their freedom do not now appear to be dangerous.

When I have been referring to business, I have used the word in its all-inclusive sense to denote alike the employer and employee, the production of agriculture and industry, the distribution of transportation and commerce, and the service of finance and banking. It is the work of the world. In modern life, with all its intricacies, business has come to hold a very dominant position in the thoughts of all enlightened peoples. Rightly understood, this is not a criticism, but a compliment. In its great economic organization it does not represent, as some have hastily concluded, a mere desire to minister to selfishness. The New York Chamber of Commerce is not made up of men merely animated with a purpose to get the better of each other. It is something far more important than a sordid desire for gain. It could not successively succeed on that basis. It is dominated by a more worthy impulse; its rests on a higher law. True business represents the mutual organized effort of society to minister to the economic requirements of civilization. It is an effort by which men provide for the material needs of each other. While it is not an end in itself, it is the important means for the attainment of a supreme end. It rests squarely on the law of service. It has for its main reliance truth and faith and justice. In its larger sense it is one of the greatest contributing forces to the moral and spiritual advancement of the race.

It is the important and righteous position that business holds in relation to life which gives warrant to the great interest which the National Government constantly exercises for the promotion of its success. This is not exercised as has been the autocratic practice abroad of directly supporting and financing different business projects, except in case of great emergency; but we have rather held to a democratic policy of cherishing the general structure of business while holding its avenues open to the widest competition, in order that its opportunities and its benefits might be given the broadest possible participation. . . . Those who are so engaged, instead of regarding the Government as their opponent and enemy, ought to regard it as their vigilant supporter and friend. . . .

Except for the requirements of safety, health and taxation, the law enters very little into the work of production. It is mostly when we come to the problems of distribution that we meet the more rigid exactions of legislation. The main reason why certain practices in this direction have been denounced is because they are a species of unfair competition on the one hand or tend to monopoly and restraint of trade on the other. The whole policy of the Government in its system of opposition to monopoly, and its public regulation of transportation and trade, has been animated by a desire to have business remain business. We are politically free people and must be an economically free people.

It is my belief that the whole material development of our country has been enormously stimulated by reason of the general insistence on the part of the public authorities that economic effort ought not to partake of privilege, and that business should be unhampered and free. This could never have been done under a system of freight-rate discriminations or monopolistic trade associations. These might have enriched a few for a limited period, but they never would have enriched the country, while on the firmer foundation of justice we have achieved even more ample individual fortunes and a perfectly unprecedented era of general prosperity. This has resulted in no small part from the general acceptance on the part of those who own and control the wealth of the Nation, that it is to be used not to oppress but to serve. It is that policy, sometimes perhaps imperfectly expressed and clumsily administered, that has animated the National Government. In its observance there is unlimited opportunity for progress and prosperity.

It would be difficult, if not impossible, to estimate the contribution which government makes to business. It is notorious that where the government is bad, business is bad. The mere fundamental precepts of the administration of justice, the providing of order and security, are priceless. The prime element in the value of all property is the knowledge that its peaceful enjoyment will be publicly defended. . . . It is really the extension of these fundamental rights that the Government is constantly attempting to apply to modern business. It wants its rightful possessors to rest in security, it wants any wrongs that they may suffer to have a legal remedy, and it is all the time striving through administrative machinery to prevent in advance the infliction of injustice.

These undoubtedly represent policies which are wise and sound and necessary. That they have often been misapplied and many times run into excesses, nobody can deny. Regulation has often become restriction, and inspection has too frequently been little less than obstruction. This was the natural result of those times in the past when there were practices in business which warranted severe disapprobation. It was only natural that when these abuses were reformed by an aroused public opinion a great deal of prejudice which ought to have been discriminating and directed only at certain evil practices came to include almost the whole domain of business, especially where it had been gathered into large units. After the abuses had been discontinued the prejudice remained to produce a large amount of legislation, which, however well meant in its application to trade, undoubtedly hampered but did not improve. It is this misconception and misapplication, disturbing and wasteful in their results, which the National Government is attempting to avoid. Proper regulation and control are disagreeable and expensive. They represent the suffering that the just must endure because of the unjust. They are a part of the price which must be paid to promote the cause of economic justice.

Undoubtedly if public vigilance were relaxed, the generation to come might suffer a relapse. But the present generation of business almost universally throughout its responsible organization and management has shown every disposition to correct its own abuses with as little intervention of the Government as possible. This position is recognized by the public, and due to the appreciation of the needs which the country has for great units of production in time of war, and to the better understanding of the service which they perform in time of peace, . . . a new attitude of the public mind is distinctly discernible toward great aggregations of capital. Their prosperity goes very far to insure the prosperity of all the country. The contending elements have each learned a most profitable lesson.

This development has left the Government free to advance from the problems of reform and repression to those of economy and construction. A very large progress is being made in these directions. Our country is in a state of unexampled and apparently sound and well distributed prosperity. . . .

As nations see their way to a safer economic existence, they will see their way to a more peaceful existence. Possessed of the means to meet personal and public obligations, people are reestablishing their self respect. The financial strength of America has contributed to the spiritual restoration of the world. It has risen into the domain of true business.

## Questions for Reading and Discussion

1. According to Coolidge, why should government and business have "the largest possible independence"? What were the dangers of failing to observe that principle?
2. Were there also dangers of absolutely no connection between government and business? What contributions did government make to "order and security"?
3. In what ways was business "one of the greatest contributing forces to the moral and spiritual advancement of the race"?
4. How had businesses changed since the imposition of government regulations and inspections? What did Coolidge mean by stating that "regulation and control" were "the suffering that the just must endure because of the unjust"?

## DOCUMENT 23-2

# Reinhold Niebuhr on Christianity in Detroit

*What meaning did Christianity have in an industrial society? Many Americans answered that question by affirming that Christianity and industrial capitalism were perfectly compatible. Businessmen went to church, and ministers preached the gospel of business. Reinhold Niebuhr, a young minister in Detroit, criticized the comfortable equation of Christianity with industrialization in a diary he kept between 1915 and 1928. In his diary, excerpted here, Niebuhr noted the frequent conflict between Christian ideals and the industrial realities he encountered in Detroit.*

## Diary Entries, 1925–1928

1925 We went through one of the big automobile factories today. So artificial is life that these factories are like a strange world to me though I have lived close to them for many years. The foundry interested me particularly. The heat was terrific. The men seemed weary. Here manual labor is a drudgery and toil is slavery. The men cannot possibly find any satisfaction in their work. They simply work to make a living. Their sweat and their dull pain are part of the price paid for the fine cars we all run. And most of us run the cars without knowing what price is being paid for them. . . .

We are all responsible. We all want the things which the factory produces and none of us is sensitive enough to care how much in human values the efficiency of the modern factory costs. Beside the brutal facts of modern industrial life, how futile are all our homiletical spoutings! The church is undoubtedly cultivating graces and preserving spiritual amenities in the more protected areas of society. But it isn't changing the essential facts of modern industrial civilization by a hair's breadth. It isn't even thinking about them.

The morality of the church is anachronistic. Will it ever develop a moral insight and courage sufficient to cope with the real problems of modern society? . . . We ministers maintain our pride and self-respect and our sense of importance only through a vast and inclusive ignorance. If we knew the world in which we live a little better we would perish in shame or be overcome by a sense of futility. . . .

1926 Several ministers have been commended for "courage" because they permitted labor leaders to speak in their churches who represented pretty much their own convictions and said pretty much what they had been saying for years.

It does seem pretty bad to have the churches lined up so solidly against labor and for the open shop policy[1] of the town. The ministers are hardly to blame, except if they are to be condemned for not bringing out the meaning of Christianity for industrial relations more clearly in their ministry previous to the

---

Reinhold Niebuhr, *Leaves from the Notebook of a Tamed Cynic* (Chicago: Willet, Clark & Colby, 1929).

[1]**open shop policy:** Anti-union law that permitted employers to hire workers who did not belong to a union, thereby preventing the union from representing all the workers of a given employer.

moment of crisis. As it was, few of the churches were sufficiently liberal to be able to risk an heretical voice in their pulpits. The idea that these A. F. of L. leaders are dangerous heretics is itself a rather illuminating clue to the mind of Detroit. I attended several sessions of the [labor] convention and the men impressed me as having about the same amount of daring and imagination as a group of village bankers. . . .

There are few cities in which wealth, suddenly acquired and proud of the mechanical efficiency which produced it, is so little mellowed by social intelligence. Detroit produces automobiles and is not yet willing to admit that the poor automata who are geared in on the production lines have any human problems.

Yet we differ only in degree from the rest of the country. The churches of America are on the whole thoroughly committed to the interests and prejudices of the middle classes. I think it is a bit of unwarranted optimism to expect them to make any serious contribution to the reorganization of society. . . .

If religion is to contribute anything to the solution of the industrial problem, a more heroic type of religion than flourishes in the average church must be set to the task. . . .

That resolution we passed in our pastors' meeting, calling upon the police to be more rigorous in the enforcement of law, is a nice admission of defeat upon the part of the church. Every one of our cities has a crime problem, not so much because the police are not vigilant as because great masses of men in an urban community are undisciplined and chaotic souls, emancipated from the traditions which guided their fathers and incapable of forming new and equally potent cultural and moral restraints. . . .

Perhaps the real reason that we live such chaotic lives in urban communities is because a city is not a society at all, and moral standards are formed only in societies and through the sense of mutual obligation which neighbors feel for one another. A big city is not a society held together by human bonds. It is a mass of individuals, held together by a productive process. Its people are spiritually isolated even though they are mechanically dependent upon one another. In such a situation it is difficult to create and preserve the moral and cultural traditions which each individual needs to save his life from anarchy.

All of us do not live in moral chaos. But in so far as we escape it, it is due to our loyalty to religious, moral and cultural traditions which have come out of other ages and other circumstances. That is why churches, Protestant, Catholic and Jewish, however irrelevant their ethical idealism may be to the main facts of an industrial civilization, are nevertheless indispensable. . . .

There is something very pathetic about the efforts of almost every one of our large cities to restore by police coercion what has been lost by the decay of moral and cultural traditions. But of course we do have to save ourselves from anarchy, even if it must be done by force. Only I think the church would do well to leave the police problem alone. If violence must be used temporarily, let the state do so without undue encouragement from the church. . . .

1927 Our city race commission has finally made its report after months of investigation and further months of deliberation on our findings. It has been a rare experience to meet with these white and colored leaders and talk over our race problems. The situation which the colored people of the city face is really a desperate one, and no one who does not spend real time in gathering the facts can have any idea of the misery and pain which exists among these people, recently migrated from the south and unadjusted to our industrial civilization. Hampered both by their own inadequacies and the hostility of a white world they have a desperate fight to keep body and soul together, to say nothing of developing those amenities which raise life above the brute level.

I wish that some of our romanticists and sentimentalists could sit through a series of meetings where the real social problems of a city are discussed. They would be cured of their optimism. A city which is built around a productive process and which gives only casual thought and incidental attention to its human problems is really a kind of hell. Thousands in this town are really living in torment while the rest of us eat, drink and make merry. What a civilization! . . .

Mother and I visited at the home of —— today where the husband is sick and was out of employment before he became sick. The folks have few connections in the city. They belong to no church. What a miserable existence it is to be friendless in a large city. And to be dependent upon a heartless industry. The man is about 55 or 57 I should judge, and he is going to have a desperate time securing employment after he gets well. These modern factories are not meant for old men. They want young men and they use them up pretty quickly. Your modern worker, with no skill but what is in the machine, is a sorry individual. After he loses the stamina of youth, he has nothing to sell. . . .

According to the ethics of our modern industrialism men over fifty, without special training, are so much junk. It is a pleasure to see how such an ethic is qualified as soon as the industrial unit is smaller and the owner has a personal interest in his men. . . . But unfortunately the units are getting larger and larger and more inhuman. . . .

The new Ford car is out. The town is full of talk about it. Newspaper reports reveal that it is the topic of the day in all world centers. Crowds storm every exhibit to get the first glimpse of this new creation. Mr. [Henry] Ford has given out an interview saying that the car has cost him about a hundred million dollars and that after finishing it he still has about a quarter of a billion dollars in the bank.

I have been doing a little arithmetic and have come to the conclusion that the car cost Ford workers at least fifty million in lost wages during the past year. No one knows how many hundreds lost their homes in the period of unemployment, and how many children were taken out of school to help fill the depleted family exchequer, and how many more children lived on short rations during this period. Mr. Ford refuses to concede that he made a mistake in bringing the car out so late. He has a way of impressing the public even with his mistakes. We are now asked to believe that the whole idea of waiting a year after the old car stopped selling before bringing out a new one was a great advertising scheme which reveals the perspicacity of this industrial genius. But no one asks about the toll in human lives.

What a civilization this is! Naïve gentlemen with a genius for mechanics suddenly become the arbiters over the lives and fortunes of hundreds of thousands. Their moral pretentions are credulously accepted at full value. No one bothers to ask whether an industry which can maintain a cash reserve of a quarter of a billion ought not make some provision for its unemployed. It is enough that the new car is a good one. . . . The cry of the hungry is drowned in the song, "Henry has made a lady out of Lizzy.". . .

1928 It is almost impossible to be sane and Christian at the same time, and on the whole I have been more sane than Christian. . . . The church can really be a community of love and can give one new confidence in the efficacy of the principles of brotherhood outside of the family relation. The questions and qualms of conscience arise when one measures the church in its relationships to society, particularly to the facts of modern industry. It is at this point where it seems to me that we had better admit failure than to claim any victory. . . .

Modern industry, particularly American industry, is not Christian. The economic forces which move it are hardly qualified at a single point by really ethical considerations. If, while it is in the flush of its early triumphs, it may seem impossible to bring it under the restraint of moral law, it may strengthen faith to know that life without law destroys itself. If the church can do nothing else, it can bear witness to the truth until such a day as bitter experience will force a recalcitrant civilization to a humility which it does not now possess.

### QUESTIONS FOR READING AND DISCUSSION

1. Why did Niebuhr believe that the "morality of the church is anachronistic"? What did he consider to be the proper role of Christianity in industrial society? In what ways was "modern industry, particularly American industry . . . not Christian"?

2. What were the consequences of "the churches of America" being "thoroughly committed to the interests and prejudices of the middle classes"?

3. Niebuhr argued that "a city is not a society at all"? Why not? Why were the police important?

4. How did Henry Ford's new car exemplify the moral basis of business?

## DOCUMENT 23-3

# *The Ku Klux Klan Defends Americanism*

*During the 1920s, the Ku Klux Klan attracted hundreds of thousands throughout the nation with its defense of "true" Americans from threats allegedly posed by immigrants, blacks, Catholics, Jews, and dissenters. In the following excerpt from an essay published in the* North American Review, *the imperial wizard of the Klan, Hiram W. Evans, outlined who the KKK represented and why. Evans explained the Klan's racial definition of Americanism, a definition that seemed sensible to many native-born white Americans who never joined the KKK. Evans's essay disclosed the widespread sense that the familiar contours of American life were under assault and must, somehow, be defended.*

## Hiram W. Evans

## *The Klan's Fight for Americanism, 1926*

The Klan, therefore, has now come to speak for the great mass of Americans of the old pioneer stock. We believe that it does fairly and faithfully represent them, and our proof lies in their support. To understand the Klan, then, it is necessary to understand the character and present mind of the mass of old-stock

Hiram W. Evans, "The Klan's Fight for Americanism," *North American Review* 223 (March—April–May 1926).

Americans. The mass, it must be remembered, as distinguished from the intellectually mongrelized "Liberals."

These are, in the first place, a blend of various peoples of the so-called Nordic race, the race which, with all its faults, has given the world almost the whole of modern civilization. The Klan does not try to represent any people but these.

There is no need to recount the virtues of the American pioneers; but it is too often forgotten that in the pioneer period a selective process of intense rigor went on. From the first only hardy, adventurous and strong men and women dared the pioneer dangers; from among these all but the best died swiftly, so that the new Nordic blend which became the American race was bred up to a point probably the highest in history. This remarkable race character, along with the new-won continent and the new-created nation, made the inheritance of the old-stock Americans the richest ever given to a generation of men.

In spite of it, however, these Nordic Americans for the last generation have found themselves increasingly uncomfortable, and finally deeply distressed. There appeared first confusion in thought and opinion, a groping and hesitancy about national affairs and private life alike, in sharp contrast to the clear, straightforward purposes of our earlier years. There was futility in religion, too, which was in many ways even more distressing. Presently we began to find that we were dealing with strange ideas; policies that always sounded well, but somehow always made us still more uncomfortable.

Finally came the moral breakdown that has been going on for two decades. One by one all our traditional moral standards went by the boards, or were so disregarded that they ceased to be binding. The sacredness of our Sabbath, of our homes, of chastity, and finally even of our right to teach our own children in our own schools fundamental facts and truths were torn away from us. Those who maintained the old standards did so only in the face of constant ridicule.

Along with this went economic distress. The assurance for the future of our children dwindled. We found our great cities and the control of much of our industry and commerce taken over by strangers, who stacked the cards of success and prosperity against us. Shortly they came to dominate our government. The *bloc* system by which this was done is now familiar to all. Every kind of inhabitant except the Americans gathered in groups which operated as units in politics, under orders of corrupt, self-seeking and un-American leaders, who both by purchase and threat enforced their demands on politicians. Thus it came about that the interests of Americans were always the last to be considered by either national or city governments, and that the native Americans were constantly discriminated against, in business, in legislation and in administrative government.

So the Nordic American today is a stranger in large parts of the land his fathers gave him. Moreover, he is a most unwelcome stranger, one much spit upon, and one to whom even the right to have his own opinions and to work for his own interests is now denied with jeers and revilings. "We must Americanize the Americans," a distinguished immigrant said recently. Can anything more clearly show the state to which the real American has fallen in this country which was once his own?

Our falling birth rate, the result of all this, is proof of our distress. We no longer feel that we can be fair to children we bring into the world, unless we can make sure from the start that they shall have capital or education or both, so that they need never compete with those who now fill the lower rungs of the ladder of success. We dare no longer risk letting our youth "make its own way" in the conditions under which we live. So even our unborn children are being crowded out of their birthright.

All this has been true for years, but it was the World War that gave us our first hint of the real cause of our troubles, and began to crystallize our ideas. The war revealed that millions whom we had allowed to share our heritage and prosperity, and whom we had assumed had become part of us, were in fact not wholly so. They had other loyalties: each was willing — anxious! — to sacrifice the interests of the country that had given him shelter to the interests of the one he was supposed to have cast off; each in fact did use the freedom and political power we had given him against ourselves whenever he could see any profit for his older loyalty.

This, of course, was chiefly in international affairs, and the excitement caused by the discovery of disloyalty subsided rapidly after the war ended. But it was not forgotten by the Nordic Americans. They had been awakened and alarmed; they began to suspect that the hyphenism which had been shown was only a part of what existed; their quiet was not that of renewed sleep, but of strong men waiting very watchfully. And presently they began to form decisions about all those aliens who were Americans for profit only.

They decided that even the crossing of salt-water did not dim a single spot on a leopard; that an alien usually remains an alien no matter what is done to him, what veneer of education he gets, what oaths he takes, nor what public attitudes he adopts. They decided that the melting pot was a ghastly failure, and remembered that the very name was coined by a member of one of the races — the Jews — which most determinedly refuses to melt. They decided that in every way, as well as in politics, the alien in the vast majority of cases is unalterably fixed in his instincts, character, thought and interests by centuries of racial selection and development, that he thinks first for his own people, works only with and for them, cares entirely for their interests, considers himself always one of them, and never an American. They decided that in character, instincts, thought, and purposes — in his whole soul — an alien remains fixedly alien to America and all it means.

They saw, too, that the alien was tearing down the American standard of living, especially in the lower walks. It became clear that while the American can out-work the alien, the alien can so far under-live the American as to force him out of all competitive labor. So they came to realize that the Nordic can easily survive and rule and increase if he holds for himself the advantages won by strength and daring of his ancestors in times of stress and peril, but that if he surrenders those advantages to the peoples who could not share the stress, he will soon be driven below the level at which he can exist by their low standards, low living and fast breeding. And they saw that the low standard aliens of Eastern and Southern Europe were doing just that thing to us.

They learned, though more slowly, that alien ideas are just as dangerous to us as the aliens themselves, no matter how plausible such ideas may sound. With most of the plain people this conclusion is based simply on the fact that the alien ideas do not work well for them. Others went deeper and came to understand that the differences in racial background, in breeding, instinct, character and emotional point of view are more important than logic. So ideas which may be perfectly healthy for an alien may also be poisonous for Americans.

Finally they learned the great secret of the propagandists; that success in corrupting public opinion depends on putting out the subversive ideas without revealing their source. They came to suspect that "prejudice" against foreign ideas is really a protective device of nature against mental food that may be indigestible,

They saw, finally, that the alien leaders in America act on this theory, and that there is a steady flood of alien ideas being spread over the country, always carefully disguised as American.

As they learned all this the Nordic Americans have been gradually arousing themselves to defend their homes and their own kind of civilization. They have not known just how to go about it; the idealist philanthropy and good-natured generosity which led to the philosophy of the melting pot have died hard. Resistance to the peaceful invasion of the immigrant is no such simple matter as snatching up weapons and defending frontiers, nor has it much spectacular emotionalism to draw men to the colors.

The old-stock Americans are learning, however. They have begun to arm themselves for this new type of warfare. Most important, they have broken away from the fetters of the false ideals and philanthropy which put aliens ahead of their own children and their own race.

To do this they have had to reject completely — and perhaps for the moment the rejection is a bit too complete — the whole body of "Liberal" ideas which they had followed with such simple, unquestioning faith. The first and immediate cause of the break with Liberalism was that it had provided no defense against the alien invasion, but instead had excused it — even defended it against Americanism. Liberalism is today charged in the mind of most Americans with nothing less than national, racial and spiritual treason. . . .

We are a movement of the plain people, very weak in the matter of culture, intellectual support, and trained leadership. We are demanding, and we expect to win, a return of power into the hands of the everyday, not highly cultured, not overly intellectualized, but entirely unspoiled and not de-Americanized, average citizen of the old stock. Our members and leaders are all of this class — the opposition of the intellectuals and liberals who held the leadership, betrayed Americanism, and from whom we expect to wrest control, is almost automatic. . . .

Our critics have accused us of being merely a "protest movement," of being frightened; they say we fear alien competition, are in a panic because we cannot hold our own against the foreigners. That is partly true. We are a protest movement — protesting against being robbed. We are afraid of competition with peoples who would destroy our standard of living. We are suffering in many ways, we have been betrayed by our trusted leaders, we are half beaten already. But we are not frightened nor in a panic. We have merely awakened to the fact that we must fight for our own. We are going to fight — and win! . . .

QUESTIONS FOR READING AND DISCUSSION

1. What did Evans mean by "the American race"? How was such a "race" formed? Who composed it?
2. Why was "the Nordic American today . . . a stranger"? In what ways had a "moral breakdown" occurred, according to Evans? What part did World War I play?
3. Why was "hyphenism" important? In what sense was "the melting pot . . . a ghastly failure"? Why? How might an immigrant have responded to Evans's arguments?
4. Why did Evans believe "Liberalism" amounted to "national, racial, and spiritual treason"? What was the significance of "false ideals and philanthropy"? How might a "Liberal" have replied to Evans's criticisms?

## DOCUMENT 23-4

# Anzia Yesierska Describes a Vacation for "Worn-Out Mothers"

*Benevolent organizations offered to give working-class immigrants exposure to the comforts of middle-class life. Anzia Yesierska's story, excerpted below, recounts the experience of an immigrant mother who received a two-week vacation from housework from a charity. Yesierska emigrated from Poland in the 1890s, worked in factories as a young woman, refused to conform to her Jewish parents' conventional expectations, and became a writer. Her story illustrates the condescension and shame that often accompanied charity, as well as immigrants' understanding that the purveyors of charity often helped themselves.*

## The Free Vacation House, 1920

One day the visiting teacher from the school comes to find out for why don't I get the children ready for school in time; for why are they so often late.

I let out on her my whole bitter heart. I told her my head was on wheels from worrying. When I get up in the morning, I don't know on what to turn first: should I nurse the baby, or make Sam's breakfast, or attend on the older children. I only got two hands.

"My dear woman," she says, "you are about to have a nervous breakdown. You need to get away to the country for a rest and vacation."

"Gott im Himmel! [God in Heaven]" says I. "Don't I know I need a rest? But how? On what money can I go to the country?"

"I know of a nice country place for mothers and children that will not cost you anything. It is free."

"Free! I never heard from it."

"Some kind people have made arrangements so no one need pay," she explains.

Later, in a few days, I just finished up with Masha and Mendel and Frieda and Sonya to send them to school, and I was getting Aby ready for kindergarten, when I hear a knock on the door, and a lady comes in. She had a white starched dress like a nurse and carried a black satchel in her hand.

"I am from the Social Betterment Society," she tells me. "You want to go to the country?"

Before I could say something, she goes over to the baby and pulls out the rubber nipple from her mouth, and to me, she says, "You must not get the child used to sucking this; it is very unsanitary."

"Gott im Himmel!" I beg the lady. "Please don't begin with that child, or she'll holler my head off. She must have the nipple. I'm too nervous to hear her scream like that."

When I put the nipple back again in the baby's mouth, the lady takes herself a seat, and then takes out a big black book from her satchel. Then she begins to question me. What is my first name? How old I am? From where come I? How long I'm already in this country? Do I keep any boarders? What is my husband's

---

Anzia Yezierska, "The Free Vacation House," in *Hungry Hearts* (Boston and New York: Houghton Mifflin Company, 1920), 97–113.

first name? How old is he? How long he is in this country? By what trade he works? How much wages he gets for a week? How much money do I spend out for rent? How old are the children, and everything about them.

"My goodness!" I cry out. "For why is it necessary all this to know? For why must I tell you all my business? What difference does it make already if I keep boarders, or I don't keep boarders? If Masha had the whooping-cough or Sonya had the measles? Or whether I spend out for my rent ten dollars or twenty? . . ."

"We must make a record of all the applicants, and investigate each case," she tells me. "There are so many who apply to the charities, we can help only those who are most worthy."

"Charities!" I scream out. "Ain't the charities those who help the beggars out? I ain't no beggar. I'm not asking for no charity. My husband, he works." . . .

When she is gone I think to myself, I'd better knock out from my head this idea about the country. For so long I lived, I didn't know nothing about the charities. For why should I come down among the beggars now?

Then I looked around me in the kitchen. On one side was the big wash-tub with clothes, waiting for me to wash. On the table was a pile of breakfast dishes yet. In the sink was the potatoes, waiting to be peeled. The baby was beginning to cry for the bottle. Aby was hollering and pulling me to take him to kindergarten. I felt if I didn't get away from here for a little while, I would land in a crazy house, or from the window jump down. Which was worser, to land in a crazy house, jump from the window down, or go to the country from the charities?

In about two weeks later around comes the same lady with the satchel again in my house.

"You can go to the country to-morrow," she tells me. . . .

When we got into the train, I opened my eyes, and lifted up my head, and straightened out my chest, and again began to breathe. It was a beautiful, sunshiny day. I knocked open the window from the train, and the fresh-smelling country air rushed upon my face and made me feel so fine! I looked out from the window and instead of seeing the iron fire-escapes with garbage-cans and bedclothes, that I always seen when from my flat I looked — instead of seeing only walls and washlines between walls, I saw the blue sky, and green grass and trees and flowers. . . .

"Get away from me, my troubles!" I said. "Leave me rest a minute. Leave me breathe and straighten out my bones. Forget the unpaid butcher's bill. Forget the rent. Forget the wash-tub and the cook-stove and the pots and pans. Forget the charities! . . ."

By the time we came to the vacation house I already forgot all about my knock-down. I was again filled with the beauty of the country. I never in all my life yet seen such a swell house like that vacation house. Like the grandest palace it looked. . . . I never yet seen such an order and such a cleanliness. From all the corners from the room, the cleanliness was shining like a looking-glass. The floor was so white scrubbed you could eat on it. . . .

I was beginning to feel happy and glad that I come, when, Gott im Himmel! again a lady begins to ask us out the same questions what the nurse already asked me in my home and what was asked over again in the charity office. How much wages my husband makes out for a week? How much money I spend out for rent? Do I keep boarders? . . .

When she already got through asking us out everything, she gave to each of us a tag with our name written on it. She told us to tie the tag on our hand. Then like tagged horses at a horse sale in the street, they marched us into the dining-room. . . .

I soon forgot again all my troubles. For the first time in ten years I sat down to a meal what I did not have to cook or worry about. For the first time in ten years I sat down to the table like a somebody. Ah, how grand it feels, to have handed you over the eatings and everything you need. Just as I was beginning to like it and let myself feel good, in comes a fat lady all in white, with a teacher's look on her face. I could tell already, right away by the way she looked on us, that she was the boss from this place.

"I want to read you the rules from this house, before you leave this room," says she to us.

Then she began like this: We dassen't [i.e., shouldn't] stand on the front grass where the flowers are. We dassen't stay on the front porch. We dassen't sit on the chairs under the shady trees. We must stay always in the back and sit on those long wooden benches there. We dassen't come in the front sitting-room or walk on the front steps what have carpet on it — we must walk on the back iron steps. Everything on the front from the house must be kept perfect for the show for visitors. We dassen't lay down on the beds in the daytime, the beds must always be made up perfect for the show for visitors.

"Gott im Himmel!" thinks I to myself, "ain't there going to be no end to the things we dassen't do in this place?"

But still she went on. The children over two years dassen't stay around by the mothers. They must stay by the nurse in the play-room. By the meal-times, they can see their mothers. The children dassen't run around the house or tear up flowers or do anything. They dassen't holler or play rough in the play-room. They must always behave and obey the nurse.

. . . If I tried to remember the endless rules, it would only make me dizzy in the head. I was thinking for why, with so many rules, didn't they also have already another rule, about how much air in our lungs to breathe.

On every few days there came to the house swell ladies in automobiles. It was for them that the front from the house had to be always perfect. For them was all the beautiful smelling flowers. For them the front porch, the front sitting-room, and the easy stairs with the carpet on it.

Always when the rich ladies came the fat lady, what was the boss from the vacation house, showed off to them the front. Then she took them over to the back to look on us, where we was sitting together, on long wooden benches, like prisoners. I was always feeling cheap like dirt, and mad that I had to be there, when they smiled down on us.

"How nice for these poor creatures to have a restful place like this," I heard one lady say. . . .

The reason why I stayed out the whole two weeks is this: I think to myself, so much shame in the face I suffered to come here, let me at least make the best from it already. Let me at least save up for two weeks what I got to spend out for grocery and butcher for my back bills to pay out. And then also think I to myself, if I go back on Monday, I got to do the big washing; on Tuesday waits for me the ironing; on Wednesday, the scrubbing and cleaning, and so goes it on. How bad it is already in this place, it's a change from the very same sameness of what I'm having day in and day out at home. . . .

But at last the day for going out from this prison came. On the way riding back, I kept thinking to myself: "This is such a beautiful vacation house. For why do they make it so hard for us? When a mother needs a vacation, why must they tear the insides out from her first, . . . [and] when we live through the shame of the charities and when we come already to the vacation house, for why do they boss the life out of us with so many rules and bells? For why don't they let us lay down our heads on the bed when we are tired? For why must we always stick in the back, like dogs what have got to be chained in one spot? If they would let us walk around free, would we bite off something from the front part of the house?"

"If the best part of the house what is comfortable is made up for a show for visitors, why ain't they keeping the whole business for a show for visitors? For why do they have to fool in worn-out mothers, to make them think they'll give them a rest? Do they need the worn-out mothers as part of the show? I guess that is it, already."

### QUESTIONS FOR READING AND DISCUSSION

1. The mother in this story exclaims, "I ain't no beggar." Did the Social Betterment Society consider her a beggar? Why did they ask her so many questions?
2. What were the motives of the mother in going to the vacation house and staying there for two weeks? Did the mother admire the people who gave her this opportunity? Why or why not?
3. What were the motives of the benevolent people who ran the vacation house? Why did they have so many rules? Was the vacation house part of a desire to Americanize working-class mothers? Why or why not?
4. Why did the mother believe "they need the worn-out mothers as part of the show"? What was the purpose of the show? How did worn-out mothers serve that purpose?

## DOCUMENT 23-5

# Marcus Garvey Explains the Goals of the Universal Negro Improvement Association

*Ideals of racial pride and purity appealed to many African Americans. Tens of thousands joined Marcus Garvey's Universal Negro Improvement Association (UNIA) and many thousands more sympathized with Garvey's ideas. In this excerpt from an essay in a current periodical, Garvey explained the origins of the UNIA and why he believed its program of racial purity, separatism, and nationalism represented the best hope for the future. His essay reveals both aspirations and frustrations common among many African Americans during the 1920s.*

## The Negro's Greatest Enemy, 1923

I was born in the Island of Jamaica, British West Indies, on Aug. 17, 1887. My parents were black negroes. . . . I grew up with other black and white boys. I was never whipped by any, but made them all respect the strength of my arms. I got my education from many sources — through private tutors, two public schools, two grammar or high schools and two colleges. . . .

---

Marcus Garvey, "The Negro's Greatest Enemy," *Current History* 18 (September 1923), 951–57.

To me, at home in my early days, there was no difference between white and black. . . . We romped and were happy children playmates together. The little white girl whom I liked most knew no better than I did myself. We were two innocent fools who never dreamed of a race feeling and problem. As a child, I went to school with white boys and girls, like all other negroes. We were not called negroes then. I never heard the term negro used once until I was about fourteen.

At fourteen my little white playmate and I parted. Her parents thought the time had come to separate us and draw the color line. They sent her and another sister to Edinburgh, Scotland, and told her that she was never to write or try to get in touch with me, for I was a "nigger." It was then that I found for the first time that there was some difference in humanity, and that there were different races, each having its own separate and distinct social life. . . .

At maturity the black and white boys separated, and took different courses in life. I grew up then to see the difference between the races more and more. My schoolmates as young men did not know or remember me any more. Then I realized that I had to make a fight for a place in the world, that it was not so easy to pass on to office and position. Personally, however, I had not much difficulty in finding and holding a place for myself, for I was aggressive. At eighteen I had an excellent position as manager of a large printing establishment, having under my control several men old enough to be my grandfathers. But I got mixed up with public life. I started to take an interest in the politics of my country, and then I saw the injustice done to my race because it was black, and I became dissatisfied on that account. I went traveling to South and Central America and parts of the West Indies to find out if it was so elsewhere, and I found the same situation. I set sail for Europe to find out if it was different there, and again I found the same stumbling-block — "You are black." I read of the conditions in America. I read "Up From Slavery," by Booker T. Washington, and then my doom — if I may so call it — of being a race leader dawned upon me in London after I had traveled through almost half of Europe.

I asked, "Where is the black man's Government?" "Where is his King and his kingdom?" "Where is his President, his country, and his ambassador, his army, his navy, his men of big affairs?" I could not find them, and then I declared, "I will help to make them."

Becoming naturally restless for the opportunity of doing something for the advancement of my race, I was determined that the black man would not continue to be kicked about by all the other races and nations of the world, as I saw it in the West Indies, South and Central America and Europe, and as I read of it in America. My young and ambitious mind led me into flights of great imagination. I saw before me then, even as I do now, a new world of black men, not peons, serfs, dogs and slaves, but a nation of sturdy men making their impress upon civilization and causing a new light to dawn upon the human race. I could not remain in London any more. My brain was afire. There was a world of thought to conquer. I had to start ere it became too late and the work be not done. Immediately I boarded a ship at Southampton for Jamaica, where I arrived on July 15, 1914. The Universal Negro Improvement Association and African Communities (Imperial) League was founded and organized five days after my arrival, with the program of uniting all the negro peoples of the world into one great body to establish a country and Government absolutely their own. . . .

I got in touch with Booker Washington and told him what I wanted to do. He invited me to America and promised to speak with me in the Southern and other States to help my work. Although he died in the Fall of 1915, I made my arrangements and arrived in the United States on March 23, 1916.

Here I found a new and different problem. I immediately visited some of the then so-called negro leaders, only to discover, after a close study of them, that they had no program, but were mere opportunists who were living off their so-called leadership while the poor people were groping in the dark. I traveled through thirty-eight States and everywhere found the same condition. I visited Tuskegee [Alabama] and paid my respects to the dead hero, Booker Washington, and then returned to New York, where I organized the New York division of the Universal Negro Improvement Association. . . .

The organization under my Presidency grew by leaps and bounds. I started The Negro World. Being a journalist, I edited this paper free of cost for the association, and worked for them without pay until November, 1920. I traveled all over the country for the association at my own expense, and established branches until in 1919 we had about thirty branches in different cities. By my writings and speeches we were able to build up a large organization of over 2,000,000 by June, 1919, at which time we launched the program of the Black Star Line. . . .

The first year of our activities for the Black Star Line added prestige to the Universal Negro Improvement Association. Several hundred thousand dollars worth of shares were sold. Our first ship, the steamship Yarmouth, had made two voyages to the West Indies and Central America. The white press had flashed the news all over the world. I, a young negro, as President of the corporation, had become famous. My name was discussed on five continents. The Universal Negro Improvement Association gained millions of followers all over the world. By August, 1920, over 4,000,000 persons had joined the movement. A convention of all the negro peoples of the world was called to meet in New York that month. Delegates came from all parts of the known world. Over 25,000 persons packed the Madison Square Garden on Aug. 1 to hear me speak to the first International Convention of Negroes. It was a record-breaking meeting, the first and the biggest of its kind. The name of Garvey had become known as a leader of his race.

Such fame among negroes was too much for other race leaders and politicians to tolerate. My downfall was planned by my enemies. They laid all kinds of traps for me. They scattered their spies among the employees of the Black Star Line and the Universal Negro Improvement Association. Our office records were stolen. Employees started to be openly dishonest; we could get no convictions against them. . . . The ships' officers started to pile up thousands of dollars of debts against the company without the knowledge of the officers of the corporation. Our ships were damaged at sea, and there was a general riot of wreck and ruin. Officials of the Universal Negro Improvement Association also began to steal and be openly dishonest. I had to dismiss them. They joined my enemies, and thus I had an endless fight on my hands to save the ideals of the association and carry out our program for the race. My negro enemies, finding that they alone could not destroy me, resorted to misrepresenting me to the leaders of the white race, several of whom, without proper investigation, also opposed me. . . .

The temporary ruin of the Black Star Line has in no way affected the larger work of the Universal Negro Improvement Association, which now has 900 branches with an approximate membership of 6,000,000. This organization has succeeded in organizing the negroes all over the world and we now look forward to a renaissance that will create a new people and bring about the restoration of Ethiopia's ancient glory.

Being black, I have committed an unpardonable offense against the very light colored negroes in America and the West Indies by making myself famous as a negro leader of millions. In their view, no black man must rise above them, but I still forge ahead determined to give to the world the truth about the new negro who is determined to make and hold for himself a place in the affairs of men. The Universal Negro Improvement Association has been misrepresented by my enemies. They have tried to make it appear that we are hostile to other races. This is absolutely false. We love all humanity. We are working for the peace of the world which we believe can only come about when all races are given their due.

We feel that there is absolutely no reason why there should be any differences between the black and white races, if each stop to adjust and steady itself. We believe in the purity of both races. We do not believe the black man should be encouraged in the idea that his highest purpose in life is to marry a white woman, but we do believe that the white man should be taught to respect the black woman in the same way as he wants the black man to respect the white woman. It is a vicious and dangerous doctrine of social equality to urge, as certain colored leaders do, that black and white should get together, for that would destroy the racial purity of both.

We believe that the black people should have a country of their own where they should be given the fullest opportunity to develop politically, socially and industrially. The black people should not be encouraged to remain in white people's countries and expect to be Presidents, Governors, Mayors, Senators, Congressmen, Judges and social and industrial leaders. We believe that with the rising ambition of the negro, if a country is not provided for him in another 50 or 100 years, there will be a terrible clash that will end disastrously to him and disgrace our civilization. We desire to prevent such a clash by pointing the negro to a home of his own. We feel that all well disposed and broad minded white men will aid in this direction. It is because of this belief no doubt that my negro enemies, so as to prejudice me further in the opinion of the public, wickedly state that I am a member of the Ku Klux Klan, even though I am a black man.

I have been deprived of the opportunity of properly explaining my work to the white people of America through the prejudice worked up against me by jealous and wicked members of my own race. My success as an organizer was much more than rival negro leaders could tolerate. They, regardless of consequences, either to me or to the race, had to destroy me by fair means or foul. The thousands of anonymous and other hostile letters written to the editors and publishers of the white press by negro rivals to prejudice me in the eyes of public opinion are sufficient evidence of the wicked and vicious opposition I have had to meet from among my own people, especially among the very lightly colored. . . . No wonder, therefore, that the great white population of this country and of the world has a wrong impression of the aims and objects of the Universal Negro Improvement Association and of the work of Marcus Garvey.

Having had the wrong education as a start in his racial career, the negro has become his own greatest enemy. Most of the trouble I have had in advancing the cause of the race has come from negroes. Booker Washington aptly described the race in one of his lectures by stating that we were like crabs in a barrel, that none would allow the other to climb over, but on any such attempt all would continue to pull back into the barrel the one crab that would make the effort to climb out. Yet, those of us with vision cannot desert the race, leaving it to suffer and die.

Looking forward a century or two, we can see an economic and political death struggle for the survival of the different race groups. Many of our present-day national centres will have become over-crowded with vast surplus populations. The fight for bread and position will be keen and severe. The weaker and unprepared group is bound to go under. That is why, visionaries as we are in the Universal Negro Improvement Association, we are fighting for the founding of a negro nation in Africa, so that there will be no clash between black and white and that each race will have a separate existence and civilization all its own without courting suspicion and hatred or eyeing each other with jealousy and rivalry within the borders of the same country.

White men who have struggled for and built up their countries and their own civilizations are not disposed to hand them over to the negro or any other race without let or hindrance. It would be unreasonable to expect this. Hence any vain assumption on the part of the negro to imagine that he will one day become President of the Nation, Governor of the State or Mayor of the city in the countries of white men, is like waiting on the devil and his angels to take up their residence in the Realm on High and direct there the affairs of Paradise.

### QUESTIONS FOR READING AND DISCUSSION

1. What meanings did "race" have for Garvey? How did he envision the ideal relationship among races? Why was it "a vicious and dangerous doctrine" to urge that "black and white should get together"?
2. What goals did he have for the UNIA? How would "a new world of black men" be different from the world that existed?
3. How might a supporter of Booker T. Washington have responded to Garvey's arguments?
4. To what extent did Garvey's ideas reflect larger currents of thought during the 1920s? Were Garvey's ideas an expression of — or a challenge to — American ideals?

### COMPARATIVE QUESTIONS

1. How did Reinhold Niebuhr's view of industrial society and spiritual progress differ from those of Calvin Coolidge, Anzia Yesierska's immigrant mother, and Hiram W. Evans?
2. How did Evans's advocacy of the Ku Klux Klan compare with Marcus Garvey's promotion of the UNIA and Yesierska's account of charity for worn-out mothers?
3. What arguments might Coolidge have made to respond to the arguments of Niebuhr, Yesierska, Evans, and Garvey?
4. According to Coolidge, Niebuhr, Yesierska, Evans, and Garvey, what were the major divisions in American society, and what should be done, if anything, to repair them?

# CHAPTER 24

# THE NEW DEAL EXPERIMENT

## 1932–1939

The New Deal initiated an unprecedented array of government reforms in response to the unprecedented crisis of the Great Depression. Franklin D. Roosevelt had few specific plans other than to improvise constantly and experiment until something worked. The New Deal's willingness to identify problems and to try to solve them represented a departure from the laissez-faire policies of Roosevelt's Republican predecessors. Working people appreciated the New Dealers' efforts to help, but by the end of the 1930s many remained mired in hard times. The following documents illustrate Roosevelt's concept of what government could and should do, the hopes many working people had about what government would do, and criticisms of the New Deal's program from those who believed it went too far and those who faulted it for not going far enough.

## DOCUMENT 24-1

### *Franklin D. Roosevelt Proposes an Activist Government*

*The severity of the Great Depression made it almost certain that the Democratic presidential candidate, Franklin D. Roosevelt, would be elected in 1932. The severity of the Depression also made it profoundly uncertain what Roosevelt should or would do as president. On the campaign trail, Roosevelt delivered an ambitious speech to the Commonwealth Club in San Francisco that outlined his ideas about fundamental historical changes that required new relations between government, citizens, and the economy. Roosevelt's speech, excerpted here, proposed principles that underlie many New Deal initiatives.*

### *Speech to the Commonwealth Club, San Francisco,* 1932

Sometimes, my friends, particularly in years such as these, the hand of discouragement falls upon us. It seems that things are in a rut, fixed, settled, that

Samuel Rosenman, ed., *The Public Papers and Addresses of Franklin D. Roosevelt,* vol. 1, *The Genesis of the New Deal, 1928–1932* (New York: Random House, 1938).

the world has grown old and tired and very much out of joint. This is the mood of depression, of dire and weary depression.

But then we look around us in America, and everything tells us that we are wrong. America is new. It is in the process of change and development. It has the great potentialities of youth, and particularly is this true of the great West, and of this coast, and of California. . . .

The issue of Government has always been whether individual men and women will have to serve some system of Government or economics, or whether a system of Government and economics exists to serve individual men and women. . . .

Mr. [Thomas] Jefferson, in the summer of 1776, after drafting the Declaration of Independence . . . realized that the exercise of the property rights might so interfere with the rights of the individual that the Government, without whose assistance the property rights could not exist, must intervene, not to destroy individualism, but to protect it.

You are familiar with the great political duel which followed; and how [Alexander] Hamilton, and his friends, building toward a dominant centralized power were at length defeated in the great election of 1800, by Mr. Jefferson's party. Out of that duel came the two parties, Republican and Democratic, as we know them today.

So began, in American political life, the new day, the day of the individual against the system, the day in which individualism was made the great watchword of American life. . . .

It was in the middle of the nineteenth century that a new force was released and a new dream created. The force was what is called the industrial revolution, the advance of steam and machinery and the rise of the forerunners of the modern industrial plant. The dream was the dream of an economic machine, able to raise the standard of living for everyone; to bring luxury within the reach of the humblest; to annihilate distance by steam power and later by electricity, and to release everyone from the drudgery of the heaviest manual toil. It was to be expected that this would necessarily affect Government. Heretofore, Government had merely been called upon to produce conditions within which people could live happily, labor peacefully, and rest secure. Now it was called upon to aid in the consummation of this new dream. There was, however, a shadow over the dream. To be made real, it required use of the talents of men of tremendous will and tremendous ambition, since by no other force could the problems of financing and engineering and new developments be brought to a consummation.

So manifest were the advantages of the machine age, however, that the United States fearlessly, cheerfully, and, I think, rightly, accepted the bitter with the sweet. It was thought that no price was too high to pay for the advantages which we could draw from a finished industrial system. The history of the last half century is accordingly in large measure a history of a group of financial Titans, whose methods were not scrutinized with too much care, and who were honored in proportion as they produced the results, irrespective of the means they used. The financiers who pushed the railroads to the Pacific were always ruthless, often wasteful, and frequently corrupt; but they did build railroads, and we have them today. . . . As long as we had free land; as long as population was growing by leaps and bounds; as long as our industrial plants were insufficient to supply our own needs, society chose to give the ambitious man free play and unlimited reward provided only that he produced the economic plant so much desired.

During this period of expansion, there was equal opportunity for all and the business of Government was not to interfere but to assist in the development of industry. This was done at the request of business men themselves. The tariff was originally imposed for the purpose of "fostering our infant industry.". . . The railroads were subsidized, sometimes by grants of money, oftener by grants of land. . . . Some of my friends tell me that they do not want the Government in business. With this I agree; but I wonder whether they realize the implications of the past. For while it has been American doctrine that the Government must not go into business in competition with private enterprises, still it has been traditional, particularly in Republican administrations, for business urgently to ask the Government to put at private disposal all kinds of Government assistance. The same man who tells you that he does not want to see the Government interfere in business — and he means it, and has plenty of good reasons for saying so — is the first to go to Washington and ask the Government for a prohibitory tariff on his product. . . . Each group has sought protection from the Government for its own special interests, without realizing that the function of Government must be to favor no small group at the expense of its duty to protect the rights of personal freedom and of private property of all its citizens.

In retrospect we can now see that the turn of the tide came with the turn of the century. We were reaching our last frontier; there was no more free land and our industrial combinations had become great uncontrolled and irresponsible units of power within the State. Clear-sighted men saw with fear the danger that opportunity would no longer be equal; that the growing corporation, like the feudal baron of old, might threaten the economic freedom of individuals to earn a living. . . .

A glance at the situation today only too clearly indicates that equality of opportunity as we have known it no longer exists. Our industrial plant is built; the problem just now is whether under existing conditions it is not overbuilt. Our last frontier has long since been reached, and there is practically no more free land. More than half of our people do not live on the farms or on lands and cannot derive a living by cultivating their own property. There is no safety valve in the form of a Western prairie to which those thrown out of work by the Eastern economic machines can go for a new start. We are not able to invite the immigration from Europe to share our endless plenty. We are now providing a drab living for our own people. . . .

Just as freedom to farm has ceased, so also the opportunity in business has narrowed. . . . [A]rea after area has been preempted altogether by the great corporations, and even in the fields which still have no great concerns, the small man starts under a handicap. The unfeeling statistics of the past three decades show that the independent business man is running a losing race. Perhaps he is forced to the wall; perhaps he cannot command credit; perhaps he is "squeezed out". . . by highly organized corporate competitors, as your corner grocery man can tell you. Recently a careful study was made of the concentration of business in the United States. It showed that our economic life was dominated by some six hundred odd corporations who controlled two-thirds of American industry. Ten million small business men divided the other third. . . . Put plainly, we are steering a steady course toward economic oligarchy, if we are not there already.

Clearly, all this calls for a re-appraisal of values. A mere builder of more industrial plants, a creator of more railroad systems, an organizer of more corporations, is as likely to be a danger as a help. The day of the great promoter or the financial Titan, to whom we granted anything if only he would build, or develop, is over. Our task now is not discovery or exploitation of natural resources, or necessarily producing more goods. It is the soberer, less dramatic business of administering resources and plants already in hand, of seeking to reestablish foreign markets for our surplus production, of meeting the problem of underconsumption, of adjusting production to consumption, of distributing wealth and products more equitably, of adapting existing economic organizations to the service of the people. The day of enlightened administration has come. . . .

As I see it, the task of Government in its relation to business is to assist the development of an economic declaration of rights, an economic constitutional order. This is the common task of statesman and business man. It is the minimum requirement of a more permanently safe order of things.

Happily, the times indicate that to create such an order not only is the proper policy of Government, but it is the only line of safety for our economic structures as well. We know, now, that these economic units cannot exist unless prosperity is uniform, that is, unless purchasing power is well distributed throughout every group in the Nation. That is why even the most selfish of corporations for its own interest would be glad to see wages restored and unemployment ended and to bring the Western farmer back to his accustomed level of prosperity and to assure a permanent safety to both groups. That is why some enlightened industries themselves endeavor to limit the freedom of action of each man and business group within the industry in the common interest of all; why business men everywhere are asking a form of organization which will bring the scheme of things into balance, even though it may in some measure qualify the freedom of action of individual units within the business. . . .

I feel that we are coming to a view through the drift of our legislation and our public thinking in the past quarter century that private economic power is, to enlarge an old phrase, a public trust as well. I hold that continued enjoyment of that power by an individual or group must depend upon the fulfillment of that trust. The men who have reached the summit of American business life know this best; happily, many of these urge the binding quality of this greater social contract.

The terms of that contract are as old as the Republic, and as new as the new economic order.

Every man has a right to life; and this means that he has also a right to make a comfortable living. He may by sloth or crime decline to exercise that right; but it may not be denied him. We have no actual famine or dearth; our industrial and agricultural mechanism can produce enough and to spare. Our Government formal and informal, political and economic, owes to everyone an avenue to possess himself of a portion of that plenty sufficient for his needs, through his own work.

Every man has a right to his own property; which means a right to be assured, to the fullest extent attainable, in the safety of his savings. By no other means can men carry the burdens of those parts of life which, in the nature of things, afford no chance of labor; childhood, sickness, old age. In all thought of property, this right is paramount; all other property rights must yield to it. If, in accord with this principle, we must restrict the operations of the speculator, the manipulator, even the financier, I believe we must accept the restriction as needful, not to hamper individualism but to protect it.

These two requirements must be satisfied, in the main, by the individuals who claim and hold control of the great industrial and financial combinations which dominate so large a part of our industrial life. They have undertaken to be, not business men, but princes of property. I am not prepared to say that the system which produces them is wrong. I am very clear that they must fearlessly and competently assume the responsibility which goes with the power. . . .

[T]he responsible heads of finance and industry instead of acting each for himself, must work together to achieve the common end. They must, where necessary, sacrifice this or that private advantage; and in reciprocal self-denial must seek a general advantage. It is here that formal Government — political Government, if you choose — comes in. Whenever in the pursuit of this objective the lone wolf, the unethical competitor, the reckless promoter . . . whose hand is against every man's, declines to join in achieving an end recognized as being for the public welfare, and threatens to drag the industry back to a state of anarchy, the Government may properly be asked to apply restraint. Likewise, should the group ever use its collective power contrary to the public welfare, the Government must be swift to enter and protect the public interest.

The Government should assume the function of economic regulation only as a last resort, to be tried only when private initiative, inspired by high responsibility, with such assistance and balance as Government can give, has finally failed. As yet there has been no final failure, because there has been no attempt; and I decline to assume that this Nation is unable to meet the situation.

The final term of the high contract was for liberty and the pursuit of happiness. We have learned a great deal of both in the past century. We know that individual liberty and individual happiness mean nothing unless both are ordered in the sense that one man's meat is not another man's poison. We know that the old "rights of personal competency," the right to read, to think, to speak, to choose and live a mode of life, must be respected at all hazards. We know that liberty to do anything which deprives others of those elemental rights is outside the protection of any compact; and that Government in this regard is the maintenance of a balance, within which every individual may have a place if he will take it; in which every individual may find safety if he wishes it; in which every individual may attain such power as his ability permits, consistent with his assuming the accompanying responsibility. . . .

Faith in America, faith in our tradition of personal responsibility, faith in our institutions, faith in ourselves demand that we recognize the new terms of the old social contract. We shall fulfill them. . . . We must do so, lest a rising tide of misery, engendered by our common failure, engulf us all. But failure is not an American habit; and in the strength of great hope we must all shoulder our common load.

## Questions for Reading and Discussion

1. According to Roosevelt, what were the differences between the Republican and Democratic parties? In what ways were those differences pertinent in the current era?

2. Roosevelt observed that "equality of opportunity as we have known it no longer exists." Why was that so? What had provided equality of opportunity during the previous century?

3. Why had the "day of enlightened administration" arrived? What did Roosevelt believe was the government's proper function in the economy?

DOCUMENT 24-2

# *Working People's Letters to New Dealers*

President Roosevelt expressed sympathy for the plight of working people during the Depression. That sympathy, heard by millions in Roosevelt's fireside chats and frequent press conferences, helped to shape efforts to provide relief, to restore employment, and to regulate wages, hours, and working conditions. Feeling they had a friend in the White House, thousands of American working people wrote the president and other New Dealers, especially Secretary of Labor Frances Perkins. Those letters, excerpted here, illustrated the hard times many Americans continued to face long after the New Deal was under way.

## *Letter to Frances Perkins,* January 27, 1935

Winston-Salem, North Carolina

Dear Miss Perkins:

Please allow me to state some of the facts concerning our wages paid in the Tobacco factories first I want to call your attention to the firm I am working for. The Brown & Williamson Co; We make 40 hours a week and we don't average $10.00 per week for semi skilled labor in my department where the plug tobacco is manufactured we that are doing semi skilled labor make less than those doing common labor. [T]hey make around $12.00 per week while we make from $7.00 to $10.00 and maybe some few of us might make $13.00 once and a while. Now how can we be considered in the Presidents spending program when we don't make enough to live on and pay our just and honest debts. Please take notice Meat advanced from 6 cents to 16 cents sugar from 5 to 6 cents flour has almost doubled and house rent and every thing but our wages the idea of men young and middle age making less than $2.00 while we are piling up millions for the firms we work and the sad part of it is the majority are afraid to make an out cry about conditions. Now I think our great trouble lies in the fact that no[ body] ever investigates our working conditions and the greatest portion of us are colored people and I think every body hates a colored man. How can we support a family of 7 or 8 send our children to school and teach them citizen ship when capitalist choke us and make criminals out of some of us that might be a bit weak. Now Miss Perkins just think about our condition how hard it is to come up to the American Standard of living on less than $10.00 for 40 hours work and 7 or 8 in family or it seems that my race of people are not considered in the American Standard of living. Now most of my people are afraid to complain because some few years ago the R. J. Reynolds Tobacco Co. discharged every one that joined a union they were trying to organize here and for reason you can't find any union workers in the R. J. Reynolds firm among the colored people. . . . It seems that some investigations should be made. Now how can we pay our debts educate our children and if we have to call a doctor we don't have the money to

Gerald Markowitz and David Rosner, *"Slaves of the Depression": Workers' Letters about Life on the Job* (Ithaca, NY: Cornell University Press, 1987), 21–167.

pay him for his visit. . . . How can we get a square deal as our case is continued to be pushed a side. Please consider these facts Miss Perkins We are up against a hard proposition.

O. G.

## Letter to Frances Perkins, March 29, 1935

Brooklyn, New York

Dear Miss Perkins:

Reading about you as I do I have come to the understanding, that you are a fair and impartial observer of labor conditions in the United States. Well, I'll have to get a load off my chest, and tell you of the labor conditions in a place which is laughingly called a factory. We work in a Woolstock Concern. We handle discarded rags. We work, ten hours a day for six days. In the grime and dirt of a nation. We go home tired and sick — dirty — disgusted — with the world in general, work — work all day, low pay — average wage sixteen dollars. Tired in the train going home, sitting at the dinner table, too tired to even wash ourselves, what for — to keep body and souls together not to depend on charity. What of N.R.A.? What of everything —? We handle diseased rags all day. Tuberculosis roaming loose, unsanitary conditions —, slaves — slaves of the depression! I'm even tired as I write this letter —, a letter of hope —. What am I? I am young — I am twenty, a high school education — no recreation — no fun —. Pardon ma'am — but I want to live —! Do you deny me that right —? As an American citizen I ask you —, what — what must we do? Please investigate this matter. I sleep now, yes ma'am with a prayer on my lips, hoping against hope —, that you will better our conditions. I'll sign my name, but if my boss finds out —, well — Give us a new deal, Miss Perkins. . . .

Yours hoping,
J. G.

## Letter to Franklin D. Roosevelt, November 23, 1936

Paris, Texas

Dear President now that we have had a land Slide and done just what was best for our country & I will Say more done the only thing that could of bin done to Save this Country I do believe you Will Strain a point to help the ones who helped you mostly & that is the Working Class of People I am not smart or I would be in a different line of work & better up in ever way yet I will Know you are the one & only President that ever helped a Working Class of People I have Writen you several letters & have always received a answer from Some of you officials clerks or Some one & I will know you have to much to think about to answer a little man letter like my Self yet I will Say I and thousands of men just like me were in the fight for you & I for one will go down for you any day I am a White Man American age, 47 married wife 2 children in high School am a Finishing room foreman I mean a Working foreman & am in a furniture Factory here in Paris Texas where thaire is 175 to 200 Working & when the NRA came in I was Proud to See my fellow workmen Rec 30 Per hour in Place of 8 cents to 20 cents Per hour yet the NRA did not make any allowance for Skilled labor or foreman unless they rec as much as 35.00 [dollars] Per Week & very few Furniture Makers rec Such a Price I have bin with this firm for 25 years & they have Surly reaped the harvest. . . . I can't see for my life President why a man must toil & work his life out in Such factories 10 long hours ever day except Sunday for a small sum of 15 cents to 35 cents per hour & pay the high cost of honest & deason living expences is thaire any way in the world to help this one class of Laboring People just a little I admit this class of Working People should form a union but ever time it talked the big boy owners say we will close down then it is more releaf workers to take care of more expence to our Government and more trouble to you what we need is a law passed to shorten our hours at a living & let live scal & take more men off the Government expense & put them in the factories & get things to running normal but if a co cuts hours & then tells Foreman shove & push them & keeps putting out as much with short hours & driving the men like convicts it will never help a bit you have had your load & I well know it but please see if something can be done to help this one Class of Working People the factories are a man killer not venelated or kept up just a bunch of Republickins Grafters 90/100 of them Please help us some way I Pray to God for relief. I am a christian . . . and a truthful man & have not told you wrong & am for you to the end.

## *Letter to Frances Perkins,* July 27, 1937

Plaquemine, Louisiana

Dear Miss Perkins:

I am writing to you because I think you are pretty square to the average laboring man. but I am wondering if anyone has told you of the cruel and terrible condition that exist in this part of the country or the so called sugar cane belt in Louisiana. I am sure that it hasn t made any progress or improvement since slavery days and to many people here that toil the soil or saw mills as laboring men I am sure slavery days were much better for the black slaves had their meals for sure three times a day and medical attention at that. but if an American nowadays had that much he is a communist I am speaking of the labor not the ones that the government give a sugar bounty too but the real forgotten people for the ones the government give the sugar bounty too are the ones that really don't need it for those same people that has drawn the sugar bonus for two years has never gave an extra penny to their white and black slaves labor. I will now make an effort to give you an idea of the terrible inhuman condition.

I will first give you the idea of the sugar cane tenants and plantations poor laboring people. The bell rings at 2 A.M. in the morning when all should really be sleeping at rest. they work in the summer until 9 or 10 A.M. the reason they knock them off from the heat is not because of killing the labor from heat but they are afraid it kills the mule not the slave. Their wages runs from go 90¢ to $1.10 per day. Their average days per week runs from three to four days a week in other words people that are living in so called United States have to live on the about $4.00 per week standing of living in a so called American Community which is way below the Chinese standard of living for the Chinese at least have a cheaper food and clothing living but here one has to pay dear for food and clothing because these sugar cane slave owners not only give inhuman wages but the ones that work for them have to buy to their stores, which sells from 50 per cent to 60 per cent higher than the stores in town still these same people that are worst than the old time slave owners or yelling and hollering for more sugar protection, why should they get more when they don't pay their white and black slaves more. It is true they give the white and black slaves a place to live on. But Miss Perkins if you were to see these places they live on you'd swear that this is not our so call rich America with it high standing of living for I am sure that the lowest places in China or Mexico or Africa has better places to live in. These Southern Senators which are backed by the big shots will tell you it is cheaper to live in the South but have you investigated their living condition. Sometimes I don't wonder why some of these people don't be really communism but they are true Americans only they are living in such a low standing of living that one wouldn't believe they are living in the good old U.S.A.

Now regarding the saw mills of this town and other towns in this section but most particular this town they pay slightly more than the plantation but they get it back by charging more for food & clothing which they have to buy in their stores.

I am writing you this hoping that you will try to read it and understand the situation which if you think is not true you can send an investigator in this section of Louisiana that has American freedom of speech for some hasn't that speech in our so called free America. . . .

Thanking you for humanity sake.
R. J.

## *Letter to Franklin D. Roosevelt,* November 27, 1939

Detroit, Michigan

President Roosevelt
Dear Honorable Sir:

I am living in a city that should be one of the prized possessions of these United States of America but it isn't only to a small group of chiseling money mongers.

I and my husband are and have been Americans for three generations and we are proud of what our parents did also our grandparents to help America progress. They were builders of our country not destructers as is now going on to make the rich man richer and the poor man poorer in fact try and starve them in a land of plenty. We have six growing children that are all separated each one pining for each other and our hearts nearly broken because we cannot keep them all together.

We have tried so hard these past seven years we lost our furniture twice lost our car our insurance even my engagement ring and finally the wedding ring to buy groceries pay rent and for illness. Neither one of us are lazy he worked in steel mills auto factories painting dishwashing and anything he could get. I worked at waitress janitress selling to make a few dollars now my health is slowly ebbing. I was a widow when I married my present husband my first husband died shortly after the world war having served as a submarine chaser. I received a check for $1.00 for each day he served he died leaving me two lovely children. Why should descent American people be made suffer in this manner living in an attic room paying $5.00 per week and if its not paid out you go on the streets. Welfare has never solved these problems as there are far too many inefficient social workers also too much political graft for it to survive or even help survive. We are one family out of 100,000 that are in the same position right here in Detroit where the ones we labor for and help build up vast fortunes and estates do nothing but push us down farther. They cheat the government out of taxes hire foreign labor at lower rates and if we get discouraged and take some groceries to feed our family we must serve time.

They have 40 to 100 room houses with no children to make it even like a home while we are denied a small home and enough wages to provide for them. Barbara Hutton has herself exploited that she pays $650.00 to have one tooth pulled and the girls in her dime stores slave all week for $12 or $14 and must help provide for others out of it. I'll wager to say that the poor class were lucky to have roast pork @ 13¢ per lb on Thanksgiving Day while the rich people in this country probably throwed a lot out in there garbage cans. These so called intelligent rich men including the Congressmen and the Senators better wake up and pass some laws that will aid labor to make a living as they would have never accumulated their vast fortunes had it not been from the hard sweat that honest labor men brought them.

We read with horror of the war in Europe and of the blockade to starve the people into submission and right here in Detroit we have the same kind of a blockade. Do the intelligent men of America think we are going to stand for this much longer. I alone hear a lot of viewpoints and it will be very hard to get our men to fight another war to make more wealth for men that never had to labor and never appreciated where the real source of their wealth derived from. This country was founded on Thanksgiving day to get away from the brutal treatment the British gave them and us real true Americans intend keeping it so. We need men of wealth and men of intelligence but we also need to make labor healthy and self supporting or our nation will soon crumble and it is head on to a good start. Even prisoners will balk at an injustice and We are not prisoners

A true American mother & family
M. Q. L.

## Questions for Reading and Discussion

1. The authors of these letters assumed that the president and other New Dealers would listen to their grievances. Why did they appeal to such high, distant officials? If they did not like their jobs, why didn't they find another place to work or get a better education? Why didn't they ask their employers for better wages, hours, and working conditions?
2. What assumptions did the letter writers make about government? What did they want the government to do?
3. Several letters refer to the American standard of living. What defined that standard? In what ways did the authors of these letters believe they fell short of that standard? How could they achieve it?
4. To what extent had New Deal measures made a difference in their lives?

## DOCUMENT 24-3

# Huey Long Proposes Redistribution of Wealth

*The inadequacy of New Deal reforms to reduce the poverty and suffering of many Americans created support for more drastic measures. Huey Long, U.S. senator from Louisiana, organized the Share Our Wealth Society with the professed goal to guarantee a measure of security and well-being to all Americans. Long's proposals attracted a large following among the many people mired in the lingering Depression and pressured Roosevelt to consider more far-reaching efforts of relief and reform. Long's ideas, expressed in the following speech to a group of supporters in 1935, revealed the widespread perception that, while affluent people remained comfortable, the New Deal did not do enough to protect most Americans from economic misery and insecurity.*

## Speech to Members of the Share Our Wealth Society, 1935

For 20 years I have been in the battle to provide that, so long as America has, or can produce, an abundance of the things which make life comfortable and happy, that none should own so much of the things which he does not need and cannot use as to deprive the balance of the people of a reasonable proportion of the necessities and conveniences of life. The whole line of my political thought has always been that America must face the time when the whole country would shoulder the obligation which it owes to every child born on earth — that is, a fair chance to life, liberty, and happiness.

I had been in the United States Senate only a few days when I began my effort to make the battle for a distribution of wealth among all the people a national Issue for the coming elections. On July 2, 1932, pursuant to a promise made, I heard Franklin Delano Roosevelt, accepting the nomination of the Democratic Party at the Chicago convention for President of the United States, use the following words:

"Throughout the Nation, men and women, forgotten in the political philosophy of the Government for the last years, look to us here for guidance and for a more equitable opportunity to share in the distribution of the national wealth."

It therefore seemed that all we had to do was to elect our candidate and that then my object in public life would be accomplished.

But a few nights before the Presidential election I listened to Mr. Herbert Hoover deliver his speech in Madison Square Garden, and he used these words:

"My conception of America is a land where men and women may walk in ordered liberty, where they may enjoy the advantages of wealth, not concentrated in the hands of a few, but diffused through the lives of all."

So it seems that so popular had become the demand for a redistribution of wealth in America that Mr. Hoover had been compelled to somewhat yield to that for which Mr. Roosevelt had previously declared without reservation.

It is not out of place for me to say that the support which I brought to Mr. Roosevelt to secure his nomination and election as President — and without which it was hardly probable he would ever have been nominated — was on the assurances which I had that he would take the proper stand for the redistribution of wealth in the campaign. He did that much in the campaign; but after his election, what then? I need not tell you the story. We have not time to cry over our disappointments, over promises which others did not keep, and over pledges which were broken.

We have not a moment to lose.

It was after my disappointment over the Roosevelt policy, after he became President, that I saw the light. I soon began to understand that, regardless of what we had been promised, our only chance of securing the fulfillment of such pledges was to organize the men and the women of the United States so that they were a force capable of action, and capable of requiring such a policy from the lawmakers and from the President after they took office. That was the beginning of the Share Our Wealth Society movement.

We now have enough societies and enough members, to say nothing of the well-wishers, who — if they will put their shoulders to the wheel and give us one-half of the time which they do not need for anything else — can force the principles of the Share Our Wealth Society to the fore-front, to where no person participating in national affairs can ignore them further.

We are calling upon people whose souls cannot be cankered by the lure of wealth and corruption. We are calling upon people who have at heart, above their own nefarious possessions, the welfare of this country and of its humanity. We are calling upon them, we are calling upon you, we are calling upon the people of America, upon the men and women who love this country, and who would save their children and their neighbors from calamity and distress, to call in the people whom they know, to acquaint them with the purpose of this society and secure organization and cooperation among everyone willing to lend his hand to this worthy work. Fear of ridicule? Fear of reprisal? Fear of being taken off of the starvation dole? It is too late for our people to have such fears. I have undergone them all. There is nothing under the canopy of heaven which has not been sent to ridicule and embarrass my efforts in this work. And yet, despite such ridicule, face to face in any argument I have yet to see the one of them who dares to gainsay the principle to share our wealth. On the contrary, when their feet are put to the fire, each and every one of them declare that they are in favor of sharing the wealth, and the redistribution of wealth. But then some get suddenly ignorant and say they do not know how to do it. Oh, ye of little faith! God told them how. Apparently they are too lazy in mind or body to want to learn, so long as their ignorance is for the benefit of the 600 ruling families of America who have forged chains of slavery around the wrists and ankles of 125,000,000 free-born citizens. Lincoln freed the black man, but today the white and the black are shackled far worse than any colored person in 1860.

The debt structure alone has condemned the American people to bondage worse than the Egyptians ever forged upon the Israelites. Right now America's debts, public and private, are $262,000,000,000, and nearly all of it has been laid on the shoulders of those who have nothing. It is a debt of more than $2,000 to every man, woman, or child. They can never pay it. They never have paid such debts. No one expects them to pay it. But such is the new form of slavery imposed upon the civilization of America; and the street-corner sports and hired political tricksters, with the newspapers whom they have perverted, undertake to laugh to scorn the efforts of the people to throw off this yoke and bondage; but we were told to do so by the Lord, we were told to do so by the Pilgrim Fathers, we were guaranteed such should be done by our Declaration of Independence and by the Constitution of the United States.

Here is the whole sum and substance of the Share Our Wealth movement:

1.  Every family to be furnished by the Government a homestead allowance, free of debt, of not less than one-third the average family wealth of the country, which means, at the lowest, that every family shall have the reasonable comforts of life up to a value of from $5,000 to $6,000. No person to have a fortune of more than 100 to 300 times the average family fortune, which means that the limit to fortunes is between $1,500,000 and $5,000,000, with annual capital levy taxes imposed on all above $1,000,000.

2.  The yearly income of every family shall not be less than one-third of the average family income, which means, according to the estimates of the statisticians of the United States Government and Wall Street, no family's annual income would be less than from $2,000 to $2,500. No yearly income shall be allowed to any person larger than from 100 to 300 times the size of the average family income, which means that no person would be allowed to earn in any year more than from $600,000 to $1,800,000, all to be subject to present income-tax laws.

3.  To limit or regulate the hours of work to such an extent as to prevent overproduction; the most modern and efficient machinery would be encouraged, so that as much would be produced as possible so as to satisfy all demands of the people, but to also allow the maximum time to the workers for recreation, convenience, education, and luxuries of life.

4.  An old age pension to the persons over 60.

5.  To balance agricultural production with what can be consumed according to the laws of God, which includes the preserving and storage of surplus commodities to be paid for and held by the Government for the emergencies when such are needed. Please bear in mind, however, that when the people of America have had money to buy things they needed, we have never had a surplus of any commodity. This plan of God does not call for destroying any of the things raised to eat or wear, nor does it countenance wholesale destruction of hogs, cattle, or milk.

6.  To pay the veterans of our wars what we owe them and to care for their disabled.

7.  Education and training for all children to be equal in opportunity in all schools, colleges, universities, and other institutions for training in the professions and vocations of life, to be regulated on the capacity of children to learn, and not upon the ability of parents to pay the costs. Training for life's work to be as much universal and thorough for all walks in life as has been the training in the arts of killing.

8.  The raising of revenue and taxes for the support of this program to come from the reduction of swollen fortunes from the top, as well as for the support of public works to give employment whenever there may be any slackening necessary in private enterprise.

### QUESTIONS FOR READING AND DISCUSSION

1.  Why, according to Long, should people with wealth share it with people who needed it? What was the "obligation" of the nation?

2.  According to Long, what was wrong with the New Deal? In what ways were people "shackled far worse" than slaves in 1860?

3.  How would wealth redistribution work, according to Long? How would it differ from existing New Deal programs? How did Long's program differ from "the starvation dole"?

DOCUMENT 24-4

# California Citrus Grower Defends Mexican Farm Workers' Campaign to Organize

*While the New Deal backed the organization of labor unions in major industries, union organization among farm workers failed. But not for lack of trying. Frank Stokes, a citrus grower in California, explained the benefits of organization for growers and criticized them and other Californians for stifling union organization campaigns among Mexican farm workers. Stokes recounted the violence that frequently met attempts to organize unions, disclosing the fear and tension that often pervaded Mexican workers in seemingly peaceful orange groves.*

## Frank Stokes

## *Let the Mexicans Organize, 1936*

California citrus-fruit growers have joined the legions of the exploiters of labor. They have taken over at the same time the whole vicious machinery of vigilantes, strike-breakers, night riders, tear gas, and prejudiced newspapers. This appears strange considering that there was a time when these citrus-fruit growers themselves were so sorely oppressed that they were driven to create one of the first, and certainly one of the greatest, cooperative organizations every formed by tillers of the soil. Because they were being exploited and robbed by brokers and shippers, the California citrus farmers were forced to organize or perish. Their object was to obtain a greater return for their sweat and labor. Yet now they are determined that others shall not be permitted to organize for the same purpose.

Oppression was the father and desperation the mother of the California Fruit Growers' Exchange. It has become a mighty organization with 13,500 grower members. There are in California approximately 309,000 citrus-growing acres valued at close to $618,000,000, and more than 75 per cent of this acreage and value are represented in the exchange. Its headquarters are in the new Sun-Kist building, which it owns, in the city of Los Angeles. All this is the result of banding together of an exploited group of citrus-fruit growers. It is this group which recently crushed ruthlessly an attempt by Mexican workers to organize a union of citrus-fruit pickers.

The Mexican is to agricultural California what the Negro is to the medieval South. His treatment by the vegetable growers of the Imperial Valley is well known. What has happened to him in the San Joaquin has likewise been told. But for a time at least it appeared that the "citrus belt" was different. Then came the strike of the Mexican fruit pickers in Orange County. In its wake came the vigilantes, the night riders, the strike-breakers, the reporters whose job it was to "slant" all the stories in favor of the packers and grove owners. There followed the State Motor Patrol, which for the first time in the history of strike disorders in California set up a portable radio broadcasting station "in a secret place" in the strike area "to direct law-and-order activities." And special deputy badges blossomed as thick as Roosevelt buttons in the recent campaign.

Frank Stokes, "Let the Mexicans Organize," *The Nation* (December 19, 1936), 731–32.

Sheriff Jackson declared bravely: "It was the strikers themselves who drew first blood so from now on we will meet them on that basis." "This is no fight," said he, "between orchardists and pickers. It is a fight between the entire population of Orange County and a bunch of Communists." However, dozens and dozens of non-Communist Mexican fruit pickers were jailed; 116 were arrested en masse while traveling in automobiles along the highway. They were charged with riot and placed under bail of $500 each. Twice their preliminary hearing was delayed on motion of the district attorney. After fifteen days in jail the hearing was finally held — and the state's witnesses were able to identify only one person as having taken part in trouble occurring on the Charles Wagner ranch. Judge Ames of the Superior Court ordered the release of all but the one identified prisoner and severely criticized the authorities for holding the Mexicans in jail for so long a time when they must have known it would not be possible to identify even a small portion of the prisoners.

For weeks during the strike newspaper stories described the brave stand taken by "law-abiding citizens." These stories were adorned with such headlines as "Vigilantes Battle Citrus Strikers in War on Reds." During all this time, so far as I know, only one paper — the Los Angeles *Evening News* — defended the fruit pickers. . . .

These Mexicans were asking for a well-deserved wage increase and free transportation to and from the widely scattered groves; they also asked that tools be furnished by the employers. Finally they asked recognition of their newly formed union. Recognition of the Mexican laboring man's union, his cooperative organization formed in order that he might obtain a little more for his commodity, which is labor — here was the crucial point. The growers and packers agreed to furnish tools; they agreed to furnish transportation to and from the groves. They even agreed to a slight wage increase, which still left the workers underpaid. But recognition of the Mexican workers' union? Never!

I have been an orange grower and a member of the California Fruit Growers' Exchange for twenty years. I have also had connections with other types of ranching less efficiently organized or not organized at all. Only in the citrus business is the producer free of all selling worries. My job is merely to grow the fruit. The exchange picks it, packs it, pools it, according to grade, with the fruit of other members, ships it, sells it, and send me the proceeds. I have often borrowed money from my packing house, secured by my crop, thereby saving interest at the bank. Through the Fruit Growers' Supply Company (owned and operated by the associations with the exchange system) I can buy automobile tires or radios, shotguns or fertilizer, generally at a very substantial discount. I can pay for it at the end of the season.

The Fruit Growers' Supply Company provides other benefits. Because the company owns vast acres of timber and its lumber mill at Susanville, my fruit is shipped in containers furnished at cost. More than one hundred million feet of lumber are required each year for the making of exchange [boxes]. . . . Cooperation even extends to the maintenance of a group of pest-control experts whose services are free to exchange members. In many other ways the citrus-fruit growers of California have profited by cooperation. I irrigate my orchard with water delivered by a non-profit combination of growers. My trees are sprayed or fumigated by a non-profit partnership. Because of cooperation I can sleep through the winter nights or until a voice on the telephone informs me that my thermometers have dropped to the danger point [of freezing the citrus crop].

One would think that California citrus people, at least those belonging to the exchange, would not be averse to organization by others . . . . [M]ore than three-fourths of all citrus growers are steadfast cooperators. If these cooperators had raised their voices to protest against the unjust treatment of the Mexicans, the affair might have ended with honor to us all.

The fact is, however, that Jack Prizer, manager of an exchange packing house in Orange County and a member of the exchange board of directors. . . . was one of those most active in crushing the strike. . . .

I have said that the Mexicans are to agricultural California what the Negro is to the medieval South, exploited and despised. Before the day of the CCC camps Spanish was the language most frequently heard on every mountain fire-line; and those Spanish-speaking people were taken to the fires by force, even though the burning mountains, with their high peaks stopping rain clouds and their dense brush storing water, were vastly more important to white men than to Mexicans. Towns and cities, farms and orchards, valley springs and deep sunk wells, all depend upon those mountains.

Not only in the fields are the Mexican people exploited. Not only as earners but as buyers they are looked upon as legitimate prey — for old washing machines that will not clean clothes, for old automobiles that wheeze and let down, for woolen blankets made of cotton, for last season's shop-worn wearing apparel. Gathered in villages composed of rough board shanties or drifting with the seasons from vegetable fields of the Imperial Valley to the grape vineyards of the San Joaquin, wherever they go it is the same old, pathetic story. Cheap labor!

Usually these people are patient and yielding. But occasionally a leader appears — he is always said to be a Communist — and then they rise up in their righteous wrath and strike. They struck in the Imperial Valley and they lost. They struck in the glorious land north of the Tehachapi — and again they lost. They lost because of tear-gas bombs, special deputies, and unfriendly newspapers. Lastly, they struck in Orange County. And once more they have lost.

### QUESTIONS FOR READING AND DISCUSSION

1. According to Frank Stokes, how did citrus growers benefit from organization and cooperation?
2. Why did most growers oppose the Mexican farm workers' efforts to organize? Did they intend to deny Mexican farm laborers the benefits they themselves enjoyed from organization? Why or why not?
3. Why did Mexican farm laborers continue to work, even when strikes failed?
4. What did Stokes mean by comparing Mexican workers to "the Negro" in the "medieval South"?
5. How might a Mexican farm worker have responded to the arguments of Stokes? How might other citrus growers have responded?

## DOCUMENT 24-5

# *Conservatives Criticize the New Deal*

*New Deal programs and goals outraged many conservative Americans. Herbert Hoover, often blamed for neglecting the suffering of poor Americans during his presidency, bitterly accused the New Deal of violating fundamental American ideals of liberty. Hoover's speech during the presidential campaign of 1936, excerpted here, expressed the deeply held beliefs of many conservatives that the New Deal undermined rather than exemplified the promise of America. The following letter to Eleanor Roosevelt from Minnie A. Hardin, a taxpayer from Columbus, Indiana, detailed conservatives' objections to the consequences of New Deal programs for struggling taxpayers and for those who received federal help. Both Hoover and Hardin disclosed assumptions about individuals and government common among the New Deal's conservative critics.*

# Herbert Hoover
## *Anti-New Deal Campaign Speech,* 1936

Through four years of experience this New Deal attack upon free institutions has emerged as the transcendent issue in America.

All the men who are seeking for mastery in the world today are using the same weapons. They sing the same songs. They all promise the joys of Elysium without effort.

But their philosophy is founded on the coercion and compulsory organization of men. True liberal government is founded on the emancipation of men. This is the issue upon which men are imprisoned and dying in Europe right now.

Freedom does not die from frontal attack. It dies because men in power no longer believe in a system based upon liberty.

I gave the warning against this philosophy of government four years ago from a heart heavy with anxiety for the future of our country. It was born from many years experience of the forces moving in the world which would weaken the vitality of American freedom. It grew in four years of battle as President to uphold the banner of free men.

And that warning was based on sure ground from my knowledge of the ideas that Mr. Roosevelt and his bosom colleagues had covertly embraced despite the Democratic platform.

Those ideas were not new. Most of them had been urged upon me.

During my four years powerful groups thundered at the White House with these same ideas. Some were honest, some promising votes, most of them threatening reprisals, and all of them yelling "reactionary" at us.

I rejected the notion of great trade monopolies and price-fixing through codes. That could only stifle the little business man by regimenting him under the big brother. That idea was born of certain American Big Business and grew up to be the NRA.

I rejected the schemes of "economic planning" to regiment and coerce the farmer. That was born of a Roman despot 1,400 years ago and grew up into the AAA.

I refused national plans to put the government into business in competition with its citizens. That was born of Karl Marx.

I vetoed the idea of recovery through stupendous spending to prime the pump. That was born of a British professor.

I threw out attempts to centralize relief in Washington for politics and social experimentation. I defeated other plans to invade States' rights, to centralize power in Washington. Those ideas were born of American radicals.

*New York Times,* October 31, 1936; Eleanor Roosevelt Papers, Series 190, Miscellaneous, 1937, Franklin D. Roosevelt Library.

I stopped attempts at currency inflation and repudiation of government obligation. That was robbery of insurance policy holders, savings bank depositors and wage-earners. That was born of the early Brain Trusters.

I rejected all these things because they would not only delay recovery but because I knew that in the end they would shackle free men.

Rejecting these ideas we Republicans had erected agencies of government which did start our country to prosperity without the loss of a single atom of American freedom.

Our people did not recognize the gravity of the issue when I stated it four years ago. That is no wonder, for the day Mr. Roosevelt was elected recovery was in progress, the Constitution was untrampled, the integrity of the government and the institutions of freedom were intact.

It was not until after the election that the people began to awake. Then the realization of intended tinkering with the currency drove bank depositors into the panic that greeted Mr. Roosevelt's inauguration.

Recovery was set back for two years, and hysteria was used as the bridge to reach the goal of personal government.

I am proud to have carried the banner of free men to the last hour of the term my countrymen entrusted it to me. It matters nothing in the history of a race what happens to those who in their time have carried the banner of free men. What matters is that the battle shall go on.

The people know now the aims of this New Deal philosophy of government.

We propose instead leadership and authority in government within the moral and economic framework of the American System.

We propose to hold to the Constitutional safeguards of free men.

We propose to relieve men from fear, coercion and spite that are inevitable in personal government.

We propose to demobilize and decentralize all this spending upon which vast personal power is being built.

We propose to amend the tax laws so as not to defeat free men and free enterprise.

We propose to turn the whole direction of this country toward liberty, not away from it.

The New Dealers say that all this that we propose is a worn-out system; that this machine age requires new measures for which we must sacrifice some part of the freedom of men. Men have lost their way with a confused idea that governments should run machines.

Man-made machines cannot be of more worth than men themselves. Free men made these machines. Only free spirits can master them to their proper use.

The relation of our government with all these questions is complicated and difficult. They rise into the very highest ranges of economics, statesmanship and morals.

And do not mistake. Free government is the most difficult of all government. But it is everlastingly true that the plain people will make fewer mistakes than any group of men no matter how powerful. But free government implies vigilant thinking and courageous living and self-reliance in a people.

Let me say to you that any measure which breaks our dikes of freedom will flood the land with misery.

# Minnie Hardin
## *Letter to Eleanor Roosevelt,* December 14, 1937

Mrs. Roosevelt:

I suppose from your point ōf view the work relief, old age pensions, slum clearance and all the rest seems like a perfect remedy for all the ills of this country, but I would like for you to see the results, as the other half see them.

We have always had a shiftless, never-do-well class of people whose one and only aim in life is to live without work. I have been rubbing elbows with this class for nearly sixty years and have tried to help some of the most promising and have seen others try to help them, but it can't be done. We cannot help those who will not try to help themselves and if they do try, a square deal is all they need, and by the way that is all this country needs or ever has needed: a square deal for all and then, let each paddle their own canoe, or sink.

There has never been any necessity for any one who is able to work, being on relief in this locality, but there have been many eating the bread of charity and they have lived better than ever before. I have had taxpayers tell me that their children came from school and asked why they couldn't have nice lunches like the children on relief. The women and children around here have had to work at the fields to help save the crops and several women fainted while at work and at the same time we couldn't go up or down the road without stumbling over some of the reliefers, moping around carrying dirt from one side of the road to the other and back again, or else asleep. I live alone on a farm and have not raised any crops for the last two years as there was no help to be had. I am feeding the stock and have been cutting the wood to keep my home fires burning. There are several reliefers around here now who have been kicked off relief but they refuse to work unless they can get relief hours and wages, but they are so worthless no one can afford to hire them.

As for the clearance of the real slums, it can't be done as long as their inhabitants are allowed to reproduce their kind. I would like for you to see what a family of that class can do to a decent house in a short time. Such a family moved into an almost new, neat, four-room house near here last winter. They even cut down some of the shade trees for fuel, after they had burned everything they could pry loose. There were two big idle boys in the family and they could get all the fuel they wanted, just for the cutting, but the shade trees were closer and it was taking a great amount of fuel, for they had broken out several windows and they had but very little bedding. There were two women there all the time and three part of the time and there was enough good clothing tramped in the mud around the yard to have made all the bedclothes they needed. It was clothing that had been given them and they had worn it until it was too filthy to wear any longer without washing, so they threw it out and begged more. I will not try to describe their filth for you would not believe me. They paid no rent while there and left between two suns owing everyone from whom they could get a nickels worth of anything. They are just a fair sample of the class of people on whom so much of our hard earned tax money is being squandered and on whom so much sympathy is being wasted.

As for the old people on beggars' allowances: the taxpayers have provided homes for all the old people who never liked to work, where they will be neither cold nor hungry: much better homes than most of them have ever tried to provide for themselves. They have lived many years through the most prosperous times of our country and had an opportunity to prepare for old age, but they spent their lives in idleness or worse and now they expect those who have worked like slaves, to provide a living for them and all their worthless descendants. Some of them are asking for from thirty to sixty dollars a month when I have known them to live on a dollar a week rather than go to work. There is many a little child doing without butter on its bread, so that some old sot can have his booze and tobacco: some old sot who spent his working years loafing around pool rooms and saloons, boasting that the world owed him a living.

Even the child welfare has become a racket. The parents of large families are getting divorces, so that the mothers and children can qualify for aid. The children have to join the ranks of the "unemployed" as they grow up, for no child that has been raised on charity in this community has ever amounted to anything.

You people who have plenty of this worlds goods and whose money comes easy, have no idea of the heart-breaking toil and self-denial which is the lot of the working people who are trying to make an honest living, and then to have to shoulder all these unjust burdens seems like the last straw. During the worst of the depression many of the farmers had to deny their families butter, eggs, meat, etc. and sell it to pay their taxes and then had to stand by and see the dead-beats carry it home to their families by the arm load, and they knew their tax money was helping pay for it. One woman saw a man carry out eight pounds of butter at one time. The crookedness, selfishness, greed and graft of the crooked politicians is making one gigantic racket out of the new deal, and it is making this a nation of dead-beats and beggars and if it continues the people who will work will soon be nothing but slaves for the pampered poverty rats and I am afraid these human parasites are going to become a menace to the country unless they are disfranchised. No one should have the right to vote theirself a living at the expense of the taxpayers. They learned their strength at the last election and also learned that they can get just about what they want by "voting right." They have had a taste of their coveted life of idleness, and at the rate they are increasing, they will soon control the country. The twentieth child arrived in the home of one chronic reliefer near here some time ago.

Is it any wonder the taxpayers are discouraged by all this penalizing of thrift and industry to reward shiftlessness, or that the whole country is on the brink of chaos?

### QUESTIONS FOR READING AND DISCUSSION

1. According to Hoover and Hardin, how did the New Deal "weaken the vitality of American freedom" and "shackle free men"?

2. What did Hoover believe were the most important sources of New Deal programs? How did Republican ideals differ from the New Deal, according to Hoover? What did Hoover believe was the proper relationship between individuals and the government?

3. What contrasts did Hardin note between her life and the lives of people who benefitted from the New Deal? How did her notion of a "square deal" differ from the New Deal?

4. What solutions did Hardin propose to the problems of poverty? Why were "the people who . . . work . . . nothing but slaves for the pampered poverty rats"? What did Hardin believe the government should do about poor people?

COMPARATIVE QUESTIONS_____

1. In what ways did working people's views of government, as expressed in their letters and in the Mexican farm workers' attempts to organize a union, differ from those expressed by Franklin Roosevelt in his speech?

2. What might Republican opponents of the New Deal have said about Huey Long's plans? To what extent was Long a departure from the New Deal or merely an extension of it? How might a New Dealer criticize Long's proposals? What might Long have said about the Mexican farm workers' attempts to unionize?

3. How might the working people who wrote to New Dealers and the Mexican farm laborers in California have responded to Republican critics of the New Deal that they were "human parasites" and "pampered poverty rats"?

4. The documents in this chapter express conflicting views about the relationship between individual freedom and government action. To what extent did the New Deal alter that relationship, according to these authors?

# CHAPTER 25

# THE SECOND WORLD WAR
## 1939–1945

Nothing in the previous history of the world compared with the conflagration of World War II. The entire globe became engulfed by fighting, preparing to fight, or supplying combatants. The high stakes of the conflict were made clear by the attack on Pearl Harbor and reports of Nazi anti-Semitism. Nearly all Americans enlisted in the war effort, whether or not they wore a uniform. The following documents illustrate some of the experiences, at home and overseas, shared by millions of Americans during World War II and contemplate the long-term consequences of those experiences.

## DOCUMENT 25-1

## *President Franklin D. Roosevelt Requests Declaration of War on Japan*

*The Japanese surprise attack on Pearl Harbor catapulted the United States into World War II. The attack erased hesitations many Americans had felt about getting entangled in another foreign war. Although the war in Europe had been under way since 1939 and the United States had aided the Allies, war was not declared on Germany until, after Pearl Harbor, Hitler declared war on the United States. President Roosevelt's speech to Congress on December 8, 1941, communicated the sense of crisis and resolve felt by most Americans on the day after Pearl Harbor.*

### *Speech to Congress,* December 8, 1941

Yesterday, December 7, 1941 — a date which will live in infamy — the United States of America was suddenly and deliberately attacked by naval and air forces of the Empire of Japan.

The United States was at peace with that Nation and, at the solicitation of Japan, was still in conversation with its Government and its Emperor looking toward the maintenance of peace in the Pacific. Indeed, one hour after Japanese

---

*Congressional Record*, 77th Cong., 1st sess., vol. 87, pt. 9, 9519–20 (Washington, D.C.: U.S. Government Printing Office, 1941).

air squadrons had commenced bombing in Oahu, the Japanese Ambassador to the United States and his colleague delivered to the Secretary of State a formal reply to a recent American message. While this reply stated that it seemed useless to continue the existing diplomatic negotiations, it contained no threat or hint of war or armed attack.

It will be recorded that the distance of Hawaii from Japan makes it obvious that the attack was deliberately planned many days or even weeks ago. During the intervening time the Japanese Government has deliberately sought to deceive the United States by false statements and expressions of hope for continued peace.

The attack yesterday on the Hawaiian Islands has caused severe damage to American naval and military forces. Very many American lives have been lost. In addition American ships have been reported torpedoed on the high seas between San Francisco and Honolulu.

Yesterday the Japanese Government also launched an attack against Malaya.

Last night Japanese forces attacked Hong Kong.

Last night Japanese forces attacked Guam.

Last night Japanese forces attacked the Philippine Islands.

Last night the Japanese attacked Wake Island.

This morning the Japanese attacked Midway Island.

Japan has, therefore, undertaken a surprise offensive extending throughout the Pacific area. The facts of yesterday speak for themselves. The people of the United States have already formed their opinions and well understand the implications to the very life and safety of our Nation.

As Commander in Chief of the Army and Navy I have directed that all measures be taken for our defense.

Always will we remember the character of the onslaught against us.

No matter how long it may take us to overcome this premeditated invasion, the American people in their righteous might will win through to absolute victory.

I believe I interpret the will of the Congress and of the people when I assert that we will not only defend ourselves to the uttermost but will make very certain that this form of treachery shall never endanger us again.

Hostilities exist. There is no blinking at the fact that our people, our territory, and our interests are in grave danger.

With confidence in our armed forces — with the unbounded determination of our people — we will gain the inevitable triumph — so help us God.

I ask that the Congress declare that since the unprovoked and dastardly attack by Japan on Sunday, December 7, a state of war has existed between the United States and the Japanese Empire.

## QUESTIONS FOR READING AND DISCUSSION

1. Why did Roosevelt call the attack on Pearl Harbor a "a date that will live in infamy"? To what extent were "our people, our territory, and our interests . . . in grave danger"?

2. Where else did Japanese forces attack? Why?

3. Do you think Roosevelt's speech would have been effective in enlisting Americans' support for the war against Japan? Why or why not?

4. In this speech, Roosevelt made no mention of Germany and the war in Europe. Why? To what extent did Germany threaten American people, territory, and interests?

## DOCUMENT 25-2

# A Japanese American Woman Recalls Pearl Harbor

*The attack on Pearl Harbor inaugurated a wave of anti-Japanese sentiment and activity that culminated in the internment of citizens of Japanese ancestry in camps scattered throughout the West. Monica Sone, a native of Seattle and student at the University of Washington, was first interned along with her family at Camp Harmony in Puyallup, Washington, and later moved to Camp Minidoka in Idaho. Sone's memoir, the source of the following excerpt, reveals the emotions that engulfed her and her family members as the nation mobilized for war against Japan.*

## Monica Sone

## *Nisei Daughter,* 1953

On a peaceful Sunday Morning, December 7, 1941, Henry, Sumi, and I were at choir rehearsal singing ourselves hoarse in preparation for the annual Christmas recital of Handel's "Messiah." Suddenly Chuck Mizuno, a young University of Washington student, burst into the chapel, gasping as if he had sprinted all the way up the stairs.

"Listen, everybody!" he shouted. "Japan just bombed Pearl Harbor . . . in Hawaii. It's war!"

The terrible words hit like a blockbuster, paralyzing us. . . . I felt as if a fist had smashed my pleasant little existence, breaking it into jigsaw puzzle pieces. An old wound opened up again, and I found myself shrinking inwardly from my Japanese blood, the blood of an enemy. I knew instinctively that the fact that I was an American by birthright was not going to help me escape the consequences of this unhappy war.

One girl mumbled over and over again, "It can't be, God, it can't be!" Someone else was saying, "What a spot to be in! Do you think we'll be considered Japanese or Americans?"

A boy replied quietly, "We'll be Japs, same as always. But our parents are enemy aliens now, you know."

A shocked silence followed. Henry came for Sumi and me. "Come on, let's go home," he said. . . .

Mother was sitting limp in the huge armchair as if she had collapsed there, listening dazedly to the turbulent radio. Her face was frozen still, and the only words she could utter were, "Komatta neh, komatta neh. How dreadful, how dreadful.". . .

With every fiber of my being I resented this war. I felt as if I were on fire. "Mama, they should never have done it," I cried. "Why did they do it? Why? Why?"

Mother's face turned paper white. "What do you know about it? Right or wrong, the Japanese have been chafing with resentment for years. It was bound to happen, one time or another. You're young, Ka-chan, you know very little about the ways of nations. . . . "

Discussion of politics, especially Japan versus America, had become taboo in our family for it sent tempers skyrocketing. Henry and I used to criticize Japan's aggressions in China and Manchuria while Father and Mother condemned Great

Monica Sone, *Nisei Daughter* (Boston: Little Brown & Co., 1953).

Britain and America's superior attitude toward Asiatics and their interference with Japan's economic growth. During these arguments, we had eyed each other like strangers, parents against children. . . .

Just then the shrill peel of the telephone cut off the possibility of a family argument. When I answered, a young girl's voice fluttered through breathily, "Hello, this is Taeko Tanabe. . . . "

The next day we learned that Taeko was trying desperately to locate her mother because FBI agents had swept into their home and arrested Mr. Tanabe, a newspaper editor. The FBI had permitted Taeko to try to locate her mother before they took Mr. Tanabe away while they searched the house for contraband and subversive material, but she was not to let anyone else know what was happening. . . .

We were shocked to read Attorney General Biddle's announcement that 736 Japanese had been picked up in the United States and Hawaii. Then Mrs. Tanabe called Mother about her husband's arrest, and she said at least a hundred others had been taken from our community. Messrs. Okayama, Higashi, Sughira, Mori, Okada — we knew them all.

"But why were they arrested, Papa? They weren't spies, were they?"

Father replied almost curtly, "Of course not! They were probably taken for questioning."

The pressure of war moved in on our little community. The Chinese consul announced that all the Chinese would carry identification cards and wear "China" badges to distinguish them from the Japanese. Then I really felt left standing out in the cold. The government ordered the bank funds of all Japanese nationals frozen. Father could no longer handle financial transactions through his bank accounts, but Henry, fortunately, was of legal age so that business could be negotiated in his name.

In the afternoon President Roosevelt's formal declaration of war against Japan was broadcast throughout the nation. In grave, measured words, he described the attack on Pearl Harbor as shameful, infamous.

I writhed involuntarily. I could no more have escaped the stab of self-consciousness than I could have changed my Oriental features. . . .

It made me positively hivey the way the FBI agents continued their raids into Japanese homes and business places and marched the Issei men away into the old red brick immigration building, systematically and efficiently, as if they were stocking a cellarful of choice bottles of wine. At first we noted that the men arrested were those who had been prominent in community affairs, like Mr. Kato, many times president of the Seattle Japanese Chamber of Commerce, and Mr. Ohashi, the principal of our Japanese language school, or individuals whose business was directly connected with firms in Japan; but as time went on, it became less and less apparent why the others were included in these raids.

We wondered when Father's time would come. We expected momentarily to hear strange footsteps on the porch and the sudden demanding ring of the front doorbell. . . . Once when our doorbell rang after curfew hour, I completely lost my Oriental stoicism which I had believed would serve me well under the most trying circumstances. . . .

Gradually we became uncomfortable with our Japanese books, magazines, wall scrolls, and knickknacks. When Father's hotel friends, Messrs. Sakaguchi, Horiuchi, Nishibue, and a few others vanished, and their wives called Mother weeping and warning her again about having too many Japanese objects around the house, we finally decided to get rid of some of ours. We knew it was impossible to destroy everything. The FBI would certainly think it strange if they found us sitting in a bare house, totally purged of things Japanese. But it was as if we could no longer stand the tension of waiting, and we just had to do something against the black day. We worked all night, feverishly combing through bookshelves, closets, drawers, and furtively creeping down to the basement furnace for the burning. I gathered together my well-worn Japanese language schoolbooks which I had been saving over a period of ten years with the thought that they might come in handy when I wanted to teach Japanese to my own children. I threw them into the fire and watched them flame and shrivel into black ashes. . . .

Mrs. Matsui kept assuring us that the FBI would get around to us yet. It was just a matter of time and the least Mother could do for Father was to pack a suitcase for him. . . . So Mother dutifully packed a suitcase for Father with toilet articles, warm flannel pajamas, and extra clothes, and placed it in the front hall by the door. It was a personal affront, the way it stood there so frank and unabashedly. Henry and I said that it was practically a confession that Papa was a spy, "So please help yourself to him, Mr. FBI, and God speed you.". . .

We had a family conference to discuss the possibility of Father and Mother's internment. Henry was in graduate school and I was beginning my second year at the university. We agreed to drop out should they be taken and we would manage the hotel during our parents' absence. Every weekend Henry and I accompanied Father to the hotel and learned how to keep the hotel books, how to open the office safe, and what kind of linen, paper towels, and soap to order.

Then a new menace appeared on the scene. Cries began to sound up and down the coast that everyone of Japanese ancestry should be taken into custody. For years the professional guardians of the Golden West had wanted to rid their land of the Yellow Peril, and the war provided an opportunity for them to push their program through. As the chain of Pacific islands fell to the Japanese, patriots shrieked for protection from us. A Californian sounded the alarm: "The Japanese are dangerous and they must leave. Remember the destruction and the sabotage perpetrated at Pearl Harbor. Notice how they have infiltrated into the harbor towns and taken our best land.". . .

In February, Executive Order No. 9066 came out, authorizing the War Department to remove the Japanese from such military areas as it saw fit, aliens and citizens alike. Even if a person had a fraction of Japanese blood in him, he must leave on demand.

A pall of gloom settled upon our home. We couldn't believe that the government meant that the Japanese-Americans must go, too. We had heard the clamoring of superpatriots who insisted loudly, "Throw the whole kaboodle out. A Jap's a Jap, no matter how you slice him. You can't make an American out of little Jap junior just by handing him an American birth certificate." But we had dismissed these remarks as just hot blasts of air from an overheated patriot. We were quite sure that our rights as American citizens would not be violated, and we would not be marched out of our homes on the same basis as enemy aliens.

In anger, Henry and I read and reread the Executive Order. Henry crumpled the newspaper in his hand and threw it against the wall. "Doesn't my citizenship mean a single blessed thing to anyone? Why doesn't somebody make up my mind for me. First they want me in the army. Now they're going to slap an alien 4-C on me because of my ancestry. What the hell!"

Once more I felt like a despised, pathetic two-headed freak, a Japanese and an American, neither of which seemed to be doing me any good. The Nisei leaders in the community rose above their personal feelings and stated that they would cooperate and comply with the decision of the government as their sacrifice in keeping with the country's war effort, thus proving themselves loyal American citizens. I was too jealous of my recently acquired voting privilege to be gracious about giving in, and I felt most uncooperative. . . .

Events moved rapidly. General DeWitt marked off western Washington, Oregon, and all of California, and the southern half of Arizona as Military Area No. 1, hallowed ground from which we must remove ourselves as rapidly as possible. Unfortunately we could not simply vanish into thin air, and we had no place to go. We had no relatives in the east we could move in on. All our relatives were sitting with us in the forbidden area, themselves wondering where to go. The neighboring states in the line of exit for the Japanese protested violently at the prospect of any mass invasion. They said, very sensibly, that if the coast didn't want the Japanese hanging around, they didn't either. A few hardy families in the community liquidated their property, tied suitcases all around their cars, and sallied eastward. They were greeted by signs in front of store windows, "Open season for Japs!" and "We kill rats and Japs here.". . .

General DeWitt must have finally realized that if he insisted on voluntary mass evacuation, hundreds and thousands of us would have wandered back and forth, clogging the highways and pitching tents along the roadside, eating and sleeping in colossal disorder. He suddenly called a halt to voluntary movement, although most of the Japanese were not budging an inch. He issued a new order, stating that no Japanese could leave the city, under penalty of arrest. The command had hatched another plan, a better one. The army would move us out as only the army could do it, and march us in neat, orderly fashion into assembly centers. We would stay in these centers only until permanent camps were set up inland to isolate us.

The orders were simple:

Dispose of your homes and property. Wind up your business. Register the family. One seabag of bedding, two suitcases of clothing allowed per person. People in District #1 must report at 8th and Lane Street, 8 P.M. on April 28.

I wanted no part of this new order. I had read in the paper that the Japanese from the state of Washington would be taken to a camp in Puyallup, on the state fairgrounds. The article apologetically assured the public that the camp would be temporary and that the Japanese would be removed from the fairgrounds and parking lots in time for the opening of the annual State Fair. . . .

One evening Father told us that he would lose the management of the hotel unless he could find someone to operate it for the duration. . . .

Sumi asked, "What happens if we can't find anyone?"

"I lose my business and my livelihood. I'll be saying good-bye to a lifetime of labor and all the hopes and plans I had for the family."

We sagged. . . .

We listened to Father wide-eyed and wistful. It had been a wonderful, wonderful dream.

## QUESTIONS FOR READING AND DISCUSSION

1. Why were Sone and her friends so pessimistic about their fate on learning about Pearl Harbor? How did they and other Americans answer the question, "Do you think we'll be considered Japanese or Americans?"

2. How did Monica's attitudes toward Japan and "things Japanese" change, if at all? Did her attitudes toward America change? If so, how and why?

3. What was the significance of what Sone called the "professional guardians of the Golden West [who] had wanted to rid their land of the Yellow Peril"?
4. How did the internment order affect the Sone family?
5. How might government officials have answered Henry Sone's question, "Doesn't my citizenship mean a single blessed thing to anyone?"

## DOCUMENT 25-3

# The Holocaust:
# A Journalist Reports on Nazi Massacres of Jews

*Nazi anti-Semitism was well known in the United States because Adolf Hitler had sponsored persecution of German Jews for more than a decade. But during World War II, many Americans and others among the Allied powers considered reports of Nazi policies of systematic annihilation of Europe's Jews utterly incredible. American journalist Varian Fry, who had reported on the rise of the Nazis in Germany during the 1930s, helped many Jews escape from occupied France in the early 1940s. Fry published "The Massacre of the Jews," excerpted here, in a major American magazine in December 1942. Fry outlined the horrific dimensions of Nazi atrocities and proposed possible responses by the United States and its allies. His article documents the widespread disbelief about the ongoing Holocaust and the reluctance of Allied governments to divert attention and resources from the all-consuming military conflict.*

## Varian Fry
### The Massacre of the Jews, December 21, 1942

There are some things so horrible that decent men and women find them impossible to believe, so monstrous that the civilized world recoils incredulous before them. The recent reports of the systematic extermination of the Jews in Nazi Europe are of this order.

We are accustomed to horrors in the historical past and accept them as a matter of course. The persecution of the Jews in Egypt and the Roman Empire, the slaughters of Genghis Khan, the religious mania which swept Europe in the fifteenth and sixteenth centuries, the Indian massacres in America, and the equally brutal retaliations of the white men — all these we credit without question, as phenomena of ages less enlightened than our own. When such things occur in our own times, like the Armenian massacres, we put them down to the account of still half-barbarous peoples. But that such things could be done by contemporary western Europeans, heirs of the humanist tradition, seems hardly possible.

Our skepticism has been fortified by our experience with "atrocity stories" during the last war. We were treated, during that war, to many accounts of German atrocities. We were told of the rape of nuns, the forced prostitution of young Belgian girls, of German soldiers spearing infants on their bayonets, or deliberately and wantonly cutting off their hands. Later, when the bitterness of war had

Varian Fry, "The Massacre of the Jews," *New Republic* (December 21, 1942), 816–19.

subsided, and Allied investigators were able to interview the populations of the formerly occupied countries, and scholars were let loose on the documents, most of these atrocities were found to have been invented. The natural reaction was to label all atrocity stories "propaganda" and refuse to believe them.

That habit of thought has lasted down to the present day. The Nazis have given us many reasons to change our thinking habits since they assumed power, but we have been slow to learn the new lesson. I remember how skeptical I was myself the first time a Nazi official told me that Hitler and Goebbels were bent on the physical annihilation of the Jews. On July 15, 1935, the S.A.[1] staged its first pogrom in Berlin. I was in Berlin at the time and witnessed the whole thing. I saw the S.A. men, unmistakable despite their mufti [civilian clothes], throwing chairs and tables through the plate-glass windows of Jewish-owned cafés, dragging Jewish men and women out of buses and chasing them up the streets, or knocking them down and kicking them in the face and belly as they lay prostrate on the sidewalk. And I heard them chanting their terrible song:

Wenn Judenblut vom Messer spritzt,
Dann geht es nochmal so gut!

[When Jewish blood spurts from the knife,
Then everything will be fine again.]

The next day, in a state of high indignation, I went to see "Putzi" Hanfstaengl, then chief of the Foreign Press Division of the Propaganda Ministry. On my way to his office, I learned that one of the victims of the previous night's bestiality had already died of his injuries. Yet, when Hanfstaengl told me, in his cultured Harvard accent, that the "radicals" among the Nazi Party leaders intended to "solve" the "Jewish problem" by the physical extermination of the Jews, I only half believed him. It was not much more than a year after the Blood Bath of June 30, 1934; yet even then I could not believe that there were men in positions of power and authority in western Europe in the twentieth century who could seriously entertain such a monstrous idea.

I learned better in November 1938, when the Nazi leaders openly encouraged the burning of synagogues, the pillage of Jewish homes, and the murder of their inhabitants.

One reason the Western world failed to rouse itself more promptly to the Nazi menace was surely this tendency to dismiss as impossible fantasy the many warnings the Nazis themselves gave us. We made the terrible mistake of judging the Nazis by our own standards, failing even after the war had begun to realize how completely they had renounced, if indeed they had ever espoused, those standards. Even today, after more than three years of the Nazi kind of war in Europe, and more than one year of direct experience with it ourselves, there are still far too many among us who do not understand the nature of the enemy — an enemy who will stop at literally nothing to achieve his ends. And his ends are the enslavement or annihilation not only of the Jews but, after them, of all the non-German peoples of Europe and, if possible, the entire world.

---

[1]**S.A.:** Sturm Abteilung, paramilitary organization of Nazi partisans.

The program is already far advanced. According to a report to the President by leaders of American Jewish groups, nearly 2,000,000 European Jews have already been slain since the war began, and the remaining 5,000,000 now living under Nazi control are scheduled to be destroyed as soon as Hitler's blond butchers can get around to them. Of the 275,000 Jews who were living in Germany and Austria at the outbreak of the war, only 52,000 to 55,000 remain. The 170,000 Jews in Czechoslovakia have been reduced to 35,000. The figures for Poland, where the Nazi program has been pushed very rapidly, are uncertain. There were 3,300,000 Jews in Poland at the beginning of the war, but some 500,000 fled to Russia, leaving approximately 2,800,000 behind. By the beginning of the summer of 1942, this number had already been reduced to 2,200,000, and deportations and massacres since that time have been on an ever increasing scale. In the ghetto of Warsaw, in which 550,000 Jews once dwelt, there are today fewer than 50,000. In the city of Riga, Latvia, 8,000 Jews were killed in a single night. A week later 16,000 more were led into a woods, stripped, and machine-gunned.

It is not merely central and eastern Europe which are being "purged," or rendered "Judenrein," as the Nazis like to say. The Netherlands has already given up 60,000 of its 180,000 Jews. Of the 85,000 who once lived in Belgium, only 8,000 remain today, while of the 340,000 Jews of France, more than 65,000 have been deported. Even Norway has begun to ship her Jewish citizens eastward to the Nazi slaughter houses and starvation pens.

The methods employed by the Nazis are many. There is starvation: Jews all over Europe are kept on rations often only one-third or one-fourth what is allowed to non-Jews. Slow death is the inevitable consequence. There is deportation: Jews by the hundreds of thousands have been packed into cattle cars, without food, water, or sanitary conveniences of any sort, and shipped the whole breadth of Europe. When the cars arrive at their destination, about a third of the passengers are already dead. There are the extermination centers, where Jews are destroyed by poison gas or electricity. There are specially constructed trucks, in which Jews are asphyxiated by carbon monoxide from the exhausts, on their way to burial trenches. There are the mines, in which they are worked to death, or poisoned by fumes of metals. There is burning alive, in crematoria, or buildings deliberately set on fire. There is the method of injecting air-bubbles into the blood stream: it is cheap, clean, and efficient, producing clots, embolisms, and death within a few hours. And there is the good old-fashioned system of standing the victims up, very often naked, and machine-gunning them, preferably beside the graves they themselves have been forced to dig. It saves time, labor, and transportation. . . .

Letters, reports, cables all fit together. They add up to the most appalling picture of mass murder in all human history. Nor is it only the Jews who are threatened. Polish authorities assert that many hundreds of thousands of non-Jewish Poles have been slain with equal callousness, and soberly warn that the entire Polish people may be wiped out before this war is over. The decimation of the Greek people is a matter of record. The Nazis are evidently quite indifferent to it, if they do not actually welcome it. Thousands of French will die of hunger and cold this winter, and thousands more will never be born, either because the fathers who might have begotten them are being held in Nazi prison camps, or because the mothers are too undernourished to carry them. The same thing is true of many other countries of Europe. And by their executions of "hostages" the Nazis are systematically destroying the potential leaders of democratic movements in all the countries they have overrun.

We must face the terrible truth. Even though Hitler loses this war, he may win it anyway, at least as far as Europe is concerned. There are reports, apparently trustworthy, that the Nazis and the German army are prepared for eventual retreat, and that their plans call for the extermination of every living thing and the destruction of all physical property in the areas they may be forced to evacuate. When we remember that, even after the war of 1914–18 was hopelessly lost and the German army was retreating in confusion on the Western Front, it still found time, and the will, wantonly to destroy the factories and flood the mines in its path, we may well believe that this time it will be even more thorough, go even more berserk.

If this happens, we shall be confronted with the most frightful dilemma imaginable. Every man, woman, and child in Europe will become a hostage, a means of blackmail. If we continue the war, they will die. Yet if we do not continue the war, the Nazis will have won all they can then hope to win — time. Time to regroup their forces, divide ours and strike again.

Our only course then will be to overwhelm them so rapidly that they will not be able to carry out their threats. For that we shall need all the strength we can possibly muster, and all the courage. The Nazis will certainly hope to cut off our allies one by one by threatening the total annihilation of their peoples if they continue to oppose them. We and our allies must be prepared to face the challenge unflinchingly.

Meanwhile, there are some things which can be done now, slight as the chances are that they will have much effect in deterring Hitler and his followers from their homicidal mania. President Roosevelt could and should speak out again against these monstrous events. A stern warning from him will have no effect on Hitler, but it may impress some Germans like the officer who helped the Jew from Brussels to escape. A similar warning from Churchill might help, too. A joint declaration, couched in the most solemn terms, by the Allied governments, of the retribution to come might be of some avail. Tribunals should be set up now to begin to amass the facts. Diplomatic warnings, conveyed through neutral channels, to the governments of Hungary, Bulgaria, and Rumania might save at least some of the 700,000 to 900,000 Jews still within their borders. The Christian churches might also help, at least in countries like France, Holland, Belgium, Norway, the Pope by threatening with excommunication all Catholics who in any way participate in these frightful crimes, the Protestant leaders by exhorting their fellow communicants to resist to the utmost the Nazis' fiendish designs. We and our allies should perhaps reconsider our policy of total blockade of the European continent and examine the possibilities of extending the feeding of Greece to other occupied countries under neutral supervision. Since one of the excuses the Nazis now offer for destroying the Jews and Poles is that there is not enough food to go around, we might at least remove the grounds for the excuse by offering to feed the populations of the occupied countries, given proper guarantees that the food will not fall into the hands of the enemy.

If we do any or all of these things, we should broadcast the news of them day and night to every country of Europe, in every European language. There is a report, which I have not been able to verify, that the OWI [Office of War Information] has banned mention of the massacres in its shortwave broadcasts. If this is true, it is a sadly mistaken policy. We have nothing to gain by "appeasing" the anti-Semites and the murderers. We have much to gain by using the facts to create resistance and eventually rebellion. The fact that the Nazis do not commit their massacres in western Europe, but transport their victims to the East before destroying them, is certain proof that they fear the effect on the local populations of the news of their crimes.

Finally, and it is a little thing, but at the same time a big thing, we can offer asylum now, without delay or red tape, to those few fortunate enough to escape from the Aryan paradise. We can do this without any risk to ourselves, because we can intern the refugees on arrival, and examine them at leisure before releasing them. If there is the slightest doubt about any of them, we can keep them interned for the duration of the war. Despite the fact that the urgency of the situation has never been greater, immigration into the United States in the year 1942 will have been less than ten percent of what it has been in "normal" years before Hitler, when some of the largest quotas were not filled. There have been bureaucratic delays in visa procedure which have literally condemned to death many stalwart democrats. These delays have caused an understandable bitterness among Jews and non-Jews in Europe, who have looked to us for help which did not come.

My Marseilles correspondent, who is neither a Jew nor a candidate for a visa, writes that, "in spite of the Nazi pressure, which she feels more than any other neutral, and in spite too of the reactionary tendencies of her middle class, the little country of Switzerland will [by accepting 9,000 refugees from Nazi terror since July] have contributed more to the cause of humanity than the great and wealthy United States, its loud declamations about the rights of the people and the defense of liberty notwithstanding."

This is a challenge which we cannot, must not, ignore.

### QUESTIONS FOR READING AND DISCUSSION

1. According to Fry, why did many people find it difficult to believe reports of the massacre of Europe's Jews?
2. What significance did he attribute to the "heirs of the humanist tradition"? What was the Nazis' view of the "Jewish problem"? Why was it a "problem"? In what sense did Americans judge the Nazis "by our own standards"?
3. What responsibilities did Fry believe the United States had to aid the victims of Nazi atrocities? What might realistically be done to oppose the massacres?
4. To what extent did the U.S. government respond to appeals such as Fry's? What accounted for government policies?

## DOCUMENT 25-4

# *Soldiers Send Messages Home*

*At home, Americans built a war economy. Thousands of tanks, airplanes, and ships came off American assembly lines. Millions of uniforms, bombs, and bullets funneled from civilian plants into military warehouses. Vital and compelling as all this military production was, probably no domestic activity was more important to Americans on the home front than the post office. Letters from loved ones in uniform overseas —"V mail" — were treasured. News of the war was always welcome, but news that the soldier was still alive was even better. The following correspondence illustrates what home-front Americans learned when they opened V mail.*

## Sergeant Irving Strobing

### *Radio Address from Corregidor, Philippines,* May 5 or 6, 1942

They are not yet near. We are waiting for God only knows what. How about a chocolate soda? Not many. Not here yet. Lots of heavy fighting going on. We've only got about one hour, twenty minutes before. . . . We may have to give up by noon. We don't know yet. They are throwing men and shells at us and we may not be able to stand it. They have been shelling us faster than you can count. . . .

We've got about fifty-five minutes and I feel sick at my stomach. I am really low down. They are around us now smashing rifles. They bring in the wounded every minute. We will be waiting for you guys to help. This is the only thing I guess that can be done. General Wainwright is a right guy and we are willing to go on for him, but shells are dropping all night, faster than hell. Damage terrific. Too much for guys to take.

Enemy heavy cross-shelling and bombing. They have got us all around and from skies. From here it looks like firing ceased on both sides. Men here all feeling bad, because of terrific nervous strain of the siege. Corregidor used to be a nice place, but it's haunted now. Withstood a terrific pounding. Just made broadcast to Manila to arrange meeting for surrender. Talk made by General Beebe. I can't say much.

I can hardly think. Can't think at all. Say, I have sixty pesos you can have for this weekend. The jig is up. Everyone is bawling like a baby. They are piling dead and wounded in our tunnel. Arms weak from pounding [radio] key long hours, no rest, short rations. Tired. I know now how a mouse feels. Caught in a trap waiting for guys to come along finish it. Got a treat. Can pineapple. Opening it with a Signal Corps knife.

My name Irving Strobing. Get this to my mother. Mrs. Minnie Strobing, 605 Barbey Street, Brooklyn, New York. They are to get along O.K. Get in touch with them soon as possible. Message, My love to Pa, Joe, Sue, Mac, Carrie, Joy and Paul. Also to all family and friends. God bless 'em all, hope they be here when I come home. Tell Joe wherever he is to give 'em hell for us. My love to all. God bless you and keep you. Love.

Sign my name and tell Mother how you heard from me. Stand by. . . . Strobing

## John Conroy

### *Letter,* December 24, 1942

Mare Island Naval Hospital, San Francisco

Dear Mother and Dad:

. . .You keep asking so I'll tell you. I have been shell-shocked and bomb-shocked. My memory is very dim regarding my civilian days. They feel that sudden shock in action now would affect my sanity. All the boys back here have received the same diagnosis. Injury to my back helps to make further combat

Annette Tapert, ed., *Lines of Battle: Letters from American Servicemen, 1941–1945* (New York: Times Books, 1987), 20–286.

service for me impossible. It's so very difficult for me to explain, to say the things I want to, my thoughts are so disconnected.

Of course I'm not insane. But I've been living the life of a savage and haven't quite got used to a world of laws and new responsibilities. So many of my platoon were wiped out, my old Parris Island buddies, that it's hard to sleep without seeing them die all over again. Our living conditions on Guadalcanal had been so bad — little food or hope — fighting and dying each day — four hours sleep out of 72 — the medicos here optimistically say I'll pay for it the rest of my life. My bayonet and shrapnel cuts are all healed up, however. Most of us will be fairly well in six months, but none of us will be completely cured for years. My back is in bad condition. I can't stand or walk much. The sudden beat of a drum or any sharp, resonant noise has a nerve-ripping effect on us.

Ah, well, let's not think, but just be happy that we'll all be together soon.

Loads and loads of love,
John

## Allen Spach
### *Letter,* February 1943

[February 1943]

Dear Dad,
I think you will find this letter quite different than the others which you've received from me. My health is well as could be expected as most of us boys in the original outfit that left the States together about [CENSORED] of us are still here. The other are replacements. The missing have either been killed, wounded or from other various sources mainly malaria fever.

On May 16 '42 we left New River N.C., and went to the docks at Norfolk. On the 20th at midnight we hit the high seas with 7,000 marines aboard the U.S.S. Wakefield. We went down through the Panama Canal and past Cuba. On the 29th we crossed the international date line. . . . Was continually harassed by submarines as we had no convoy whatsoever.

We landed in New Zealand 28 days later and they were wonderful to us as we were the first Americans to arrive there. We lived aboard ship at the dock for about a month loading equipment on incoming ships getting ready for "The Day." After working day and night we left and went to one of the Fiji Islands for four days. I was aboard the U.S.S. Fuller picked up in New Zealand. In our convoy were about 100 ships including 3 aircraft carriers and the battleship, North Carolina. We also had air protection from Flying Fortresses coming from Australia. On August 6 we had our last dinner aboard ship and they gave us all we wanted with ice cream and a pack of cigarettes. Just like a man doomed for the electric chair he got any kind of food for this last meal. That was our last for a while. Each one of us received a letter from our commanding officer, the last sentence reading Good Luck, God Bless You and to hell with the japs. On the morning of the 7th I went over the side with the first wave of troops as Rifle Grenadier, just another chicken in the infantry. With naval bombardment and supreme control of the air we hit the beach at 9.47. All hell broke loose. Two days later our ships left taking our aircraft with them, never to have any sea and air protection for the next two [CENSORED]. In the meantime the Japanese navy and air force took the advantage and gave us hell from sea and air. I won't say what the ground troops had to offer us yet. I can say we never once retreated but kept rushing forward taking the airport first thing.

Left to do or die we fought hard with one purpose in mind to do, kill every slant eyed bastard within range of rifle fire or the bayonet which was the only thing left to stop their charge. We were on the front lines 110 days before we could drop back for a shave, wash up. Don't many people know it but we were the first allied troops to be on the lines that long, either in this war or the last. We have had to face artillery both naval and field, mortar bombings sometimes three or four times a day, also at night, flame throwers, hand grenades, tanks, booby traps, land mines, everything I guess except gas. The most common headache caused by machine gun fire, snipers, rifle fire, and facing sabers, bayonet fighting, the last most feared by all. A war in five offensive drives and also in defense of our own lines. I've had buddies shot down on both sides of me, my closest calls being a shot put through the top of my helmet by a sniper. Once I had to swim a river when we were trapped by the enemy.

With no supplies coming in we had to eat coconuts, captured rice, crab meat, fish heads. We also smoked their dopey cigarettes. We also captured a warehouse full of good Saba Beer, made in Tokyo. Didn't shave or have hair cut for nearly four months, looked rather funny too. Wore Jap clothing such as underwear, socks, shoes. Had plenty of thrills watching our boys in the air planes dog fighting after they sent us some planes to go on the newly finished field that they had built. . . . What few of the old fellows here are scarred by various wounds and 90% have malaria. I've been down with it several times but I dose heavy with quinine till I feel drunk. . . . We want to come home for a while before seeing action again which is in the very near future, but they won't do it even though the doctors want us to. We were continually bombed and strafed but took it pretty good. The average age of the boys was 21 and were around 18 to 20. When we were finally relieved by the army who were all larger and older they were surprised to find us kids who had done such a good job. My best buddie at the time was caught in the face by a full blast of machine gun fire and when the hole we were laying in became swamped by flies gathering about him and being already dead, I had to roll him out of the small hole on top of the open ground and the dirty SOBs kept shooting him full of holes. Well anyway God spared my life and I am thankful for it. I know that your and dear Mama's prayers helped bring me safely through the long months of it. I hope that you will forgive me of my misdoings as it had to take this war to bring me to my senses. Only then did I realize how much you both had done for me and Dear God, maybe I can come through the next to see you and my friends again. . . .

God bless the whole world and I'm looking forward to the days when Italy and Germany are licked so that the whole might of the allied nations can be thrown in to crush Japan and the swines that are her sons, fighting to rule the white race. I heard an English speaking Nip say that if he didn't die fighting, that is if he didn't win or if he was captured and later came to Japan, he would be put in prison for 17 years and that all his property would be taken over by the government. That's his point of view. Where ever we go us boys will do our best always till the end when we don't have the strength to press a trigger.

Love always,
Your son,
Allen

# James McMahon
## *Letter,* March 10, 1944

March 10, 1944

My Dear Parents:

This letter will introduce my best buddy Bill Nelson. I was on Captain De-Mont's crew with him. . . .

10.18.43. My first raid was a diversion over the North Sea. We had no fighter escort and got lost and ended up over Holland (Friesian Islands). I saw my first enemy fighters, four ME-109s, and they shot down a B-24. It went into a dive and no one got out. The next raid was Wilhelmshaven on Nov. 3rd (1943). The sky was overcast, but we bombed anyway and did a good job. I only saw one other B-24 go down. My next raid was Bremen on November 13th. About 10 minutes from the target I noticed our waist gunner was unconscious and appeared to be dying (which he was). Immediately Captain DeMont dropped down to 5,000 feet and headed for home. The waist gunner (Erderly) was dying from lack of oxygen and frostbite (57 below). On the way home he came to and when we landed he went into the hospital. That day Freddie's ship and two others from our squadron went down. One of the waist gunners on his crew is safe but we believe all others are dead. It was over the North Sea they went down and you can't live more than 10 minutes in that water.

Well, my next raid was Kjeller, Norway, November 18th. It was cold as hell and Bill will go more into detail for you. No flack but coming out we were about 50 miles from land and the Jerry fighters jumped us. There was about 25 or 30 (maybe more) twin engine jobs. . . . Well, Bill got the first one, and then things popped. Our tail gunner Ray Russell got the next one and then (I was on the right waist gun) one popped up out of a cloud and tried to draw a bead on us. I shot his left engine off and killed the pilot and it went down in flames, its wing falling off. Bill in the meantime is having a party for himself. I looks over to see how he's going and he is firing so long at one of the bastards that his bullets are coming out red hot. He kills the pilot of this one and shoots the left wing off, and down goes number four in flames. In the meantime 12 B-24s get shot down, but then the fighters leave us and we pat each other on the back. Boy what a day. Man did we have fun. Well on my next raid, Kiel Dec. 13th, I was engineer riding the top turret. The flack was bad, but again the cloud cover was with us and we didn't get any holes. . . .

Dec. 31st. St. Angeley. Again I went to Kiel. This time as a waist gunner. My ship was in the low element flying in "Coffin Corner." The weather was perfect over the target and we didn't even see any flack till we opened our bomb bay doors. Then all hell broke loose. The sky turned black with flack. Our control cables were shot out on the left hand side, and our 4 engine was also shot out. The top turret got about 20 holes in it, and also the nose turret. The bombardier was hit in the throat (he recovered). All at once I was knocked down as something hit me in the back. A piece of flack was sticking out of my jacket. I was so scared by now that I could hardly stand up and I couldn't see as the sweat was running into my eyes. The temperature was 45 below too. Well, we went into a crazy spin and I was halfway out of the window when he pulled it out and we headed for home. We almost didn't make it. The fighters stayed a way out and didn't attack us. After this raid my nerves were so shot I could hardly write. We were under artillery (flack) fire for 12 minutes that time. It is the most terrible experience you can have. It is just like going "over the top" into an artillery barrage. I saw 2 ships blow up this day, and one go down by fighters. It makes a guy so damned mad and you can't do anything about it. . . .

2,20,44. Well my next raid was Gotha. It's a wonderful trip. I was in the nose turret and I didn't even see a burst of flack. This raid is a milk run. Too bad they can't all be like that. Well now comes the next one. This one will slay you.

BERLIN! on the 6th March. I was in the tail turret and we were high element and "coffin corner." The sky was perfect, no clouds, which meant the fighters were going to come up and the flack would be accurate. On this raid I should have been as nervous as hell, but I thought of Thom, Henn, Fred, and all the fellows I had seen go down. I figured if I came back, O.K., but if I went down it would be for Thom. Gee I felt glad. Well, all the way in to the target the flack was bad, and the Jerry fighters sure played hell. Our fighters sure gave them hell too. Well I didn't get any more shots at fighters till the target. I saw one FW-190 shoot down one of our planes which went into a dive and went straight down. Then all hell broke loose. The flack was terrible and the fighters everywhere. The group right behind us was catching hell with fighters (FW-190s) and I got in about 10 squirts at them. We kept flying through the flack and made two runs on the target which took about 20 minutes. All this time I can see Berlin, and man there are 24's and 17's all over the place. I see our bombs hit smack on the target and my heart bleeds for those damned Krauts down there. Well after that for 100 miles I can see the fires and smoke. It looks like all Berlin is on fire. Boy do I feel good. I'm laughing like hell for some reason. I guess it is because I am still there. Well after I get back to base (after squirting those Jerry fighters all the way home) I go to sleep and dream of Thom. All the time over the target I was thinking about him and Dad and Mom and Sis and . . . [e]verything was going through my mind at once. I sure feel good, 'cause we knocked the hell out of them. We didn't even get a scratch on the plane either. And that sure is something for the books. By the time you get this letter, I will probably have 5 or 6 more raids in, but I will explain them to you myself. I want you to promise that you will not tell about anything in this letter. Except maybe that I've been to Berlin. I am sure proud of my record. 9 times over the target and 7 times deep into Germany.

I want you to know that if anything ever happens to me that I think I have the most wonderful and courageous parents in the world, and the most beautiful and wonderful sister on this earth. I am proud of you all and my brother Thom. . . . God Bless you all and keep you safe. I'll come back. I can't say I know I will, but I have as good a chance as anyone. Give my pal Bill the best you've got, 'cause he's the best the E.T.O. [European Theater of Operations] has. Let Joe take him down to Eddie's and give him plenty Scotch. He was raised on the stuff. God bless you. I hope this letter gives you an idea of what Bill and I have been through. So long. Hope I see you soon.

Your loving son,
Jimmie

# David Mark Olds
## *Letter,* July 12, 1945

Rosenheim
July 12, 1945

Dear family:

. . . Dad, you ask for my opinion and reactions and those of the GI in general about several things. . . . For one thing everybody is mostly concerned with getting his own skin back to the States and home, regardless of what he leaves here and in what condition it is. I think this is a pretty universal feeling anyway — leave it to the next fellow or the politicians to worry about the world. I wanna go home and get some small measure of happiness out of life. There are many of us who feel that not much good will be done with all these noble efforts. First of all, the death of President Roosevelt was almost a mortal blow. Second the regrowth of national selfishness which we can plainly see in France, where we are no longer the saviors but annoying foreigners who interfere with their life. Thirdly, the turmoil in England, and finally the pathetic shortsightedness of those who keep hinting at and whooping up talk of war with Russia. Everywhere we hear how terrible the occupying Russian forces are, how barbaric, how savage, how primitive, etc. etc., and I blush to say, many who say this are wearing the American uniform, men who should realize that without Russia's help we would have surely been beaten. . . . [S]ooner or later . . . the disarming friendliness and cleverness of the Germans will make us doubt if they are so bad. "After all they are a civilized nation, they have great men, etc. etc." My own solution . . . would have a very liberal policy of passes so that men could get out of this accursed country say once a month or so, to breathe the freer air of the Allied countries. Let them change the occupying personnel every six months or so. Let the German PWs be kept in the Army and used as labor of all kinds, farm, factory, etc., instead of discharging them here while we poor bastards have to sit and sweat in the Army in a foreign hated land. I would crush every vestige of military or industrial might in Germany. Let them be a pauper nation. They deserve it. Let the Russians take over, they have shown how to handle them — be rough with them. Of course some innocent and some helpless will suffer — too bad — in the Army you learn callousness. It is impossible I know, but I would love to personally shoot all young Hitlerites, say between the ages of 10 and 30, and have a rigidly supervised program of education for the young. I don't know if that gives you any better idea of how I feel. . . .

You also asked about the concentration camps and the mass grave victims. It is hard for me to convey all of it to you. You drive through the surrounding towns where there are happy little children at play, and people going about their business, looking like any townspeople the world over, yet within two miles of them, its charged fences harsh against the plains, its chimneys belching smoke from cremating ovens — within two miles is a concentration camp whose very existence is such a horrible thought that a man may doubt that any good can exist in the same world, let alone area, with them. The humans who, though long dead, are yet physically alive with their stick like limbs and vacant faces are so terrible a blasphemy on civilization — yet the German civilians nearby either pretend not to realize them, or what is worse, see no wrong. God, how can people be like that. The concentration camp is even worse when it is empty, and just stands there, a mute testimonial to a brutality beyond comprehension. The gas chambers, as neat and as clean as shower rooms, the cremating ovens where the odor of human flesh is yet ingrained in the bricks, the pitiful barracks and grounds enclosed by the deadly barbed wire and guarded walls. I have seen soldiers get sick standing in the empty desolate chambers, thinking of the horror the walls have seen.

The mass graves and reburials are, for brutality, even worse. Is your stomach strong? Let me tell you about Volarv. The SS troopers and the civilians of the town, including some women, when the Germans were falling back in April, rounded up some 200 Jews with about 50 women in the lot. The men were emasculated, disembowelled and shot. The women were killed very simply. A bayonet was run into their reproductive organs and into their bowels. Pretty, isn't it. When they were being dug up from the ditch where they had been thrown, placed in rude but honorable wooden coffins, and being reburied in plots dug by German civilians and soldiers, American officers and men called all the people out of the town to witness the burial, to see the bodies, to touch the bodies, to have that memory printed on their minds of what a horrible thing they had done, only few of them showed either remorse or sickness. They stood there, hard and sullen-faced, muttering and obstinate. They would turn away and be forced to turn back and look. These same people would have cried in anguish had this been done to their own, to Germans, but what if it happened to inferior people, to Jews, and Russians, and Poles? A shrug of the shoulders, too bad, it had to be done. And yet how quickly these things can be forgotten here. . . . I want to get out of this country while I still hate it. Forgive me if this picture seems too pessimistic — I have been here longer than I want to, and it is all getting on my nerves.

Love,
David

#### QUESTIONS FOR READING AND DISCUSSION

1. How did the war affect these soldiers? Did it change their attitudes toward themselves, their families, and the meaning of the war?
2. What did these soldiers think about their fellow soldiers and their enemy?
3. How might reading these and other such letters from Americans in the service have influenced the views of people on the home front? To what degree did these private letters reinforce or qualify official, public accounts of the war?

## DOCUMENT 25-5

# *The War Between the Sexes*

*Wartime mobilization gave jobs to millions of women, and along with work came wages and relative freedom from old dependencies of family and domestic confinement. The dramatic social changes on the home front caused many Americans to fear that traditional gender relations were in disarray and must be restored. A San Francisco journalist, Willard Waller, argued that the returning soldiers' next war would be against the women who had taken their jobs and now wanted freedom and equality. Waller's article, excerpted below, expressed concerns common among many Americans that wartime changes at home were undermining the world they believed the war was being fought to save.*

# Willard Waller
## The Coming War on Women, 1945

When our soldiers get through fighting Germans and Japs, they will have to fight their own women. For the next war is the war of the sexes. Founded upon the oldest antagonism in the world, this ancient conflict sometimes smoulders but it never dies. It is not a savage war but a very important one, because our future depends upon its outcome.

During the war years, American women have forged steadily ahead in industry, politics and education, but the soldiers probably will put an end to all that when they return. Several soldiers, wounded on widely separated war fronts, recently spoke their opinions about women working after the war, in no uncertain terms. They, speaking for themselves, said women's place is in the home.

Tech. Sgt. John A. Price, who was wounded in the European theater, is married and has a little girl. "After the war," he says, "women will be needed in the home. They're needed to rear children to become good citizens. Our civilization needs homes, and the woman is the foundation of a good home."

Now convalescing . . . is Cpl. Fred Bienstock, who says: "I'm married. My wife's working now, but we want to start a family as soon as possible. You can't have a family when the wife is working. I want her to quit, and let me do the supporting. Anyway, there aren't going to be too many jobs and the men ought to get'em. And something else: If a woman isn't married, she certainly isn't going to be unless she quits her job — or is willing to quit."

Wounded in the Middle East, Cpl. Otto Makovy declared, "I'm not married. But when I am, I'll insist on doing all the supporting and my wife's staying home. That's a woman's place. Another thing it seems to me that we won't have to worry so much about juvenile delinquency if there's somebody in the home looking after the kids. . . . "

Always the two halves of the human race have struggled for supremacy. Especially in the period following a major war are men and women at loggerheads. War brings a temporary revolution in the relations of the two sexes. One might say the women get out of hand. This happened in World War I, and, before that, in our Civil and Revolutionary Wars. But after this war the women will probably put up a stronger fight for supremacy because this war's changes have merely climaxed generations of feministic progress.

### Three Phases

The battles in the coming war on women will be three: the battle for jobs, the battle of the birth rate, and the battle of personal ascendancy. But may God help the men, the women and the United States of America if the men lose. At least for the next generation, the patriarchal family must be restored and strengthened. Women must bear and rear children; husbands must support them.

First will come the battle of jobs. Because we must have jobs for returning veterans as well as for millions of displaced war workers, many millions of women are certain to be forced out of industry. We hear a lot of easy talk about 60,000,000 postwar jobs, but such a figure is more a possibility than a probability.

Willard Waller, "The Coming War on Women," *San Francisco Chronicle This Week Magazine*, February 18, 1945.

Even today, at the peak of our war effort, we have, as of August, 1944, somewhat less than 54,000,000 employed in civilian pursuits. . . . Even if, by some miracle, there are 60,000,000 jobs, there will be a great surplus of labor when the veterans return. That means there will be some millions of men, with families, tramping the streets and looking for jobs. This group will exert pressure on the jobs of 18,460,000 women now employed. Many of these women, of course, will marry or return to already established homes.

If we are intelligent, we can make use of the postwar displacement of women by men to put more men in certain fields where they are now lacking. More men are needed in the teaching profession, which has become increasingly feminized since women got their first real foothold during the Civil War. The public schools could absorb at least 250,000 men. Other fields, such as social work, would also be better for a strong infusion of masculinity.

However the affair is managed, millions of women must give up their jobs. There is other work for them to do, woman's work. Here will arise the second battle, that of the birth rate. For our nation must have more babies or become a second-rate power. Estimates of the populations of 1970, based upon prewar birth rates, show the future strength of nations in the clearest possible perspective. In 1970 Russia may have 250,000,000 people, possibly many more. Japan, unless checked, may have 100,000,000. India's youthful population may reach 500,000,000.

In 1970 the United States may have a rapidly aging population of about 160,000,000. It may have difficulty in keeping its position as a major power. Russia may have twice as many men of military age, and twice as many women to propagate the next generation. Other nations encourage reproduction by every device that the ingenuity of lawmakers can invent, but our country, unable to face the facts of life, continues to give every advantage and preferment to the unmarried and the childless.

If we are to have an adequate birth rate, we must hear less talk about women's rights and more about their duty to the race. The plain fact is, women do not produce children under the conditions of freedom and equality that have existed in the United States since the last war. The birth rate among the educated, emancipated women is very low indeed, since few women manage to compete with men and, at the same time, produce their due number of children. Usually the career of a brilliant woman is bought at the cost of an empty nursery. The price is too high, even if the contribution is great.

### Threat to the Nation

The facts behind these statements? Consider the birth rate among college-educated women, who have failed for generations to produce enough children to maintain their own numbers. Or consider a small sample of 100 married women listed in "Who's Who." Sixty-nine of these distinguished women are childless; the other 31 have borne a total of 70 children; only eight members of the group have contributed three or more members to the next generation. To keep up their proportion these women should have borne 300 children, instead of 70.

The failure of able women to reproduce is a serious threat to the nation, because both the quantity and quality of the population are important. If the reproduction of people with superior capacities stops but a single generation, the race can never be the same again. We cannot afford sex equality if it entails biological degeneration. Therefore, we must exert pressure, offer every inducement to favor reproduction, especially of the fit.

Now surely some old-fashioned feminist will say that a woman is the mistress of her own body; the nation has no right to force her to bear children. Well, a man is the master of his body too, but hardly anyone questions the right of the nation to force him to expose his body to the risks of war. A woman's ownership of her body should be subordinate to her obligation as the trustee of the race.

There is yet a third battle, that of personal ascendancy. In vulgar language, men and women must fight it out to see who is going to wear the pants. Here men should gain at least a partial victory. Both men and women will be happier so, for even women are rarely wholehearted feminists. But whether the women like it or not they will have to give some ground. Men are certain to gain some victories, if only because they are so few and women like living alone even less than men. And young men who have fought a war are not likely to accept petticoat domination.

It will be better for the men, and the women too, if the men do not go down in defeat. For nobody loves a henpecked man, not even the woman who henpecks him. To illustrate, let me tell about a really henpecked man who I once knew. Shortly after his marriage, his wife forced him to give up smoking. Occasionally he would visit his bachelor friends, and sometimes smoke a cigarette, After such a spree he would carefully gargle with a deodorizing mouthwash. "Juanita would give me hell," he explained, "if she smelled smoke on my breath." On his rare evening away from home he played cribbage, but his wife always scolded him if he lost. One evening he played with Jones and lost a dollar. He gave Jones a dollar and a half. His conversation with his wife was as follows: "Well, where have you been?" "Uh — playing cribbage with Jones." "And how much did you lose this time?" "Jones owes me fifty cents." The moral of that story is: Nobody feels sorry for such a poor devil, but is contemptuous of him, resents him as a poor example of his sex. His wife resents him most of all. A man living with a modern woman faces hard choices.

It is not so easy, as once it was, to kill the cat on the first day, but it is necessary to keep on trying. The woman of today is so constituted that she cannot help trying to dominate her husband, and if she fails she will resent that, but if she succeeds she will be forever embittered. Therefore a husband will do just as well to give up trying to please his wife in all things and be content with pleasing himself in many matters.

In the struggle for domination, the simplest, most straightforward methods are probably best for the man. A man should not try to convince his wife that he is more intelligent than she is, because very likely that is not true. It is better just to tell her plainly that he is going to be the boss, and then she will be very angry and will threaten to leave him and will love him to distraction.

And that is why the men must win the postwar battle of the sexes. They cannot afford defeat; the women cannot afford victory.

## QUESTIONS FOR READING AND DISCUSSION

1. According to Willard Waller, what was the proper role for women during the war? Why did war bring about what he called "a temporary revolution in the relations of the two sexes"?

2. In what ways, according to Waller, would the battle of the sexes be fought? To what extent would wartime experiences of men and women influence the battle of the sexes Waller predicted?

3. What did Waller mean by women's "duty to the race"? What race did he have in mind? Why did he believe "women cannot afford victory" in the battle of the sexes?

4. What assumptions did Waller make about men and their duties? Do you think soldiers, such as the ones he quoted, shared his views? Why or why not?

5. Do you think wartime experiences had similar meanings for American men and women? Why or why not? Did Waller misinterpret or overlook these meanings?

## COMPARATIVE QUESTIONS

1. How did the experience of the Sone family compare with the policies of the governments the United States fought against?

2. To what extent did soldiers' letters home contain evidence of the meaning of official wartime goals in their own daily experiences? How did the letters' concerns about the home front compare to the fears expressed by Willard Waller?

3. In what ways did the war intensify racial and gender identities and stereotyping, according to the documents in this chapter?

4. Judging from the documents in this chapter, was World War II a just war? Why or why not?

# CHAPTER 26

# COLD WAR POLITICS IN THE TRUMAN YEARS
## 1945–1953

After World War II, the United States and the Soviet Union — former allies — squared off as antagonists. Their confrontation escalated to a cold war within months after the surrender of Germany and Japan. The cold war shaped American foreign and domestic policy for nearly half a century. American policymakers maneuvered to maintain military strength in order to contain Soviet influence in the world, while many politicians worried about internal subversion by Communist agents or dupes. GIs returning from Europe or the Pacific found a home front transformed by American power and prosperity, which the Korean War soon tested. The following documents reveal the crosscurrents of victory and continued warfare, of confidence and anxiety, and of possibilities and threats that characterized the Truman years.

## DOCUMENT 26-1
## *General Marshall Summarizes the Lessons of World War II*

*In November 1945, General George C. Marshall, one of the nation's most distinguished military leaders, outlined the lessons of World War II. Marshall argued that America could no longer afford to be ill-prepared for the next major conflict. The nature of modern warfare required careful military planning if the Allies' hard-won victory was to make possible a lasting peace. Marshall outlined an influential plan to make military readiness a major feature of postwar American society. Marshall's plan, in the report excerpted here, expressed both the immense sacrifices that brought victory in World War II and the persistent fear that, in a dangerous world, only systematic military preparedness for the entire society could reduce the need for future sacrifices.*

## *For the Common Defense,* 1945

To fulfill its responsibility for protecting this nation against foreign enemies, the Army must project its planning beyond the immediate future. In this connection I feel that I have a duty, a responsibility, to present publicly at this time my conception, from a military point of view, of what is required to prevent another international catastrophe.

For years men have been concerned with individual security. Modern nations have given considerable study and effort to the establishment of social security systems for those unable or unwise enough to provide for themselves. But effective insurance against the disasters which have slaughtered millions of people and leveled their homes is long overdue.

We finish each bloody war with a feeling of acute revulsion against this savage form of human behavior, and yet on each occasion we confuse military preparedness with the causes of war and then drift almost deliberately into another catastrophe. This error of judgment was defined long ago by [George] Washington. He proposed to endow this nation at the outset with a policy which should have been a reasonable guarantee of our security for centuries. The cost of refusing his guidance is recorded in the sacrifice of life and in the accumulation of mountainous debts. We have continued [being] impractical. We have ignored the hard realities of world affairs. We have been purely idealistic.

We must start, I think, with a correction of the tragic misunderstanding that a security policy is a war policy. War has been defined by a people who have thought a lot about it — the Germans. They have started most of the recent ones. The German soldier-philosopher Clausewitz described war as a special violent form of political action. Frederic of Prussia, who left Germany the belligerent legacy which has now destroyed her, viewed war as a device to enforce his will whether he was right or wrong. He held that with an invincible offensive military force he could win any political argument. This is the doctrine [Adolf] Hitler carried to the verge of complete success. It is the doctrine of Japan. It is a criminal doctrine, and like other forms of crime, it has cropped up again and again since man began to live with his neighbors in communities and nations. There has long been an effort to outlaw war for exactly the same reason that man has outlawed murder. But the law prohibiting murder does not of itself prevent murder. It must be enforced. The enforcing power, however, must be maintained on a strictly democratic basis. There must not be a large standing army subject to the behest of a group of schemers. The citizen-soldier is the guarantee against such a misuse of power.

In order to establish an international system for preventing wars, peace-loving peoples of the world are demonstrating an eagerness to send their representatives to such conferences as those at Dumbarton Oaks and San Francisco[1] with the fervent hope that they may find a practical solution. Yet, until it is proved that such a solution has been found to prevent wars, a rich nation which lays down its arms as we have done after every war in our history, will court disaster.

---

General George C. Marshall, "For the Common Defense: Biennial Report of the Chief of Staff, July 1, 1943 to June 30, 1945," *The War Reports* (Philadelphia: J. B. Lippincott, 1947), 289–96.

[1]These conferences built the foundation of what became the United Nations.

The existence of the complex and fearful instruments of destruction now available make this a simple truth which is, in my opinion, undebatable.

So far as their ability to defend themselves and their institutions was concerned, the great democracies were sick nations when Hitler openly massed his forces to impose his will on the world. As sick as any was the United States of America. We had no field army. There were the bare skeletons of three and one-half divisions scattered in small pieces over the entire United States. It was impossible to train even these few combat troops as divisions because motor transportation and other facilities were lacking and funds for adequate maneuvers were not appropriated. The air forces consisted of a few partially equipped squadrons serving continental United States, Panama, Hawaii, and the Philippines; their planes were largely obsolescent and could hardly have survived a single day of modern aerial combat. We lacked modern arms and equipment. When President Roosevelt proclaimed, on 8 September 1939, that a limited emergency existed for the United States we were, in terms of available strength, not even a third-rate military power. Some collegians had been informing the world and evidently convincing the Japanese that the young men of America would refuse to fight in defense of their country.

The German armies swept over Europe at the very moment we sought to avoid war by assuring ourselves that there could be no war. The security of the United States of America was saved by sea distances, by Allies, and by the errors of a prepared enemy. For probably the last time in the history of warfare those ocean distances were a vital factor in our defense. We may elect again to depend on others and the whim and error of potential enemies, but if we do we will be carrying the treasure and freedom of this great Nation in a paper bag.

Returning from France after the last war, with General Pershing, I participated in his endeavors to persuade the nation to establish and maintain a sound defense policy. Had his recommendations been accepted, they might have saved this country the hundreds of billions of dollars and the more than a million casualties it has cost us again to restore the peace. We might even have been spared this present world tragedy. General Pershing was asked against whom do we prepare. Obviously that question could not be answered specifically until nearly 20 years later when Adolf Hitler led the replenished armies of defeated Germany back into world conflict. Even as late as 1940 I was asked very much the same question before a committee of Congress. Not even then could I say definitely exactly where we might have to fight, but I did recall that in past wars the United States forces had fought in Latin America, in France, in Belgium, in Germany, in Russia, in Siberia, in Africa, in the Philippines, and in China, but I did not anticipate that in the near future American soldiers would fight in the heart of Burma and in the islands of the vast Pacific, and would be garrisoning areas across the entire land and water masses of the earth. From this lesson there is no alternative but that this nation must be prepared to defend its interest against any nation or combination of nations which might sometime feel powerful enough to attempt the settlement of political arguments or gain resources or territory by force of arms.

Twice in recent history the factories and farms and people of the United States have foiled aggressor nations; conspirators against the peace would not give us a third opportunity.

Between Germany and America in 1914 and again in 1939 stood Great Britain and the U.S.S.R., France, Poland, and the other countries of Europe. Because the technique of destruction had not progressed to its present peak, these nations had to be eliminated and the Atlantic Ocean crossed by ships before our factories could be brought within the range of the enemy guns. At the close of the German war in Europe they were just on the outer fringes of the range of fire from an enemy in Europe. [Hermann] Goering stated after his capture that it was a certainty the eastern American cities would have been under rocket bombardment had Germany remained undefeated for two more years. The first attacks would have started much sooner. The technique of war has brought the United States, its homes and factories into the front line of world conflict. They escaped destructive bombardment in the second World War. They would not in a third.

It no longer appears practical to continue what we once conceived as hemispheric defense as a satisfactory basis for our security. We are now concerned with the peace of the entire world. And the peace can only be maintained by the strong.

What then must we do to remain strong and still not bankrupt ourselves on military expenditures to maintain a prohibitively expensive professional army even if one could be recruited? President Washington answered that question in recommendations to the first Congress to convene under the United States Constitution. He proposed a program for the peacetime training of a citizen army. At that time the conception of a large professional Regular Army was considered dangerous to the liberties of the Nation. It is still so today. But the determining factor in solving this problem will inevitably be the relation between the maintenance of military power and the cost in annual appropriations. No system, even if actually adopted in the near future, can survive the political pressure to reduce the military budget if the costs are high — and professional armies are very costly.

There is now another disadvantage to a large professional standing army. Wars in the twentieth century are fought with the total resources, economic, scientific, and human of entire nations. Every specialized field of human knowledge is employed. Modern war requires the skills and knowledge of the individuals of a nation.

Obviously we cannot all put on uniforms and stand ready to repel invasion. The greatest energy in peacetime of any successful nation must be devoted to productive and gainful labor. But all Americans can, in the next generations, prepare themselves to serve their country in maintaining the peace or against the tragic hour when peace is broken, if such a misfortune again overtakes us. This is what is meant by Universal Military *Training*. It is not universal military *service* — the actual induction of men into the combatant forces. Such forces would be composed during peacetime of volunteers. The trainees would be in separate organizations maintained for training purposes only. Once trained, young men would be freed from further connection with the Army unless they chose, as they now may, to enroll in the National Guard or an organized reserve unit, or to volunteer for service in the small professional army. When the Nation is in jeopardy they could be called, just as men are now called, by a committee of local neighbors, in an order of priority and under such conditions as directed at that time by the Congress. . . .

Out of our entire military mobilization of 14,000,000 men, the number of infantry troops was less than 1,500,000 Army and Marine.

The remainder of our armed forces, sea, air, and ground, was largely fighting a war of machinery. Counting those engaged in war production there were probably 75,000,000 to 80,000,000 Americans directly involved in prosecution of the war. To technological warfare we devoted 98 percent of our entire effort.

Nor is it proposed now to abandon this formula which has been so amazingly successful. The harnessing of the basic power of the universe will further spur our efforts to use brain for brawn in safeguarding the United States of America.

However, technology does not eliminate the need for men in war. The air forces, which were the highest developed technologically of any of our armed forces in this war, required millions of men to do their job. Every B-29 that winged over Japan was dependent on the efforts of 12 officers and 73 men in the immediate combat area alone.

The number of men that were involved in the delivery of the atomic bomb on Hiroshima was tremendous. First we had to have the base in the Marianas from which the plane took off. This first required preliminary operations across the vast Pacific, thousands of ships, millions of tons of supply, the heroic efforts of hundreds of thousands of men. Further, we needed the B-20's and their fighter escort which gave us control of the air over Japan. This was the result of thousands of hours of training and preparation in the U.S., and the energies of hundreds of thousands of men.

The effect of technology on the military structure is identical to its effect on the national economy. Just as the automobile replaced the horse and made work for millions of Americans, the atomic explosives will require the services of millions of men if we are compelled to employ them in fighting our battles.

This war has made it clear that the security of the Nation, when challenged by an armed enemy, requires the services of virtually all able-bodied male citizens within the effective military age group.

#### QUESTIONS FOR READING AND DISCUSSION

1. Why was the United States "sick," unprepared for World War II, according to Marshall? What did Marshall mean by saying that Americans "have been purely idealistic"?
2. How did modern warfare require different methods and different preparations and bring American "homes and factories into the front lines of world conflict"?
3. What did Marshall believe were the advantages and disadvantages of universal military training? What were the social and economic implications of using "brain for brawn" to safeguard the United States?
4. What assumptions was Marshall arguing against? What did he perceive as the principal dangers confronting postwar American society?

## DOCUMENT 26-2

# *George F. Kennan Outlines Containment*

*For American policymakers, no problem loomed larger in the postwar world than relations with the Soviet Union. Soviet armies had been decisive in the defeat of Nazi Germany and currently occupied most of Eastern Europe. Soviet leaders were Communists who professed their hatred of capitalism and the political institutions of the United States and other Western democracies. George F. Kennan, a diplomat in the U.S. Embassy in Moscow, sent a long, secret telegram to the State Department early in 1946 that was the embryo of what became the American policy of containment. Excerpts from that telegram follow.*

# *The Long Telegram,* February 22, 1946

... BASIC FEATURES OF POST-WAR SOVIET OUTLOOK, AS PUT FORWARD BY OFFICIAL PROPAGANDA MACHINE, ARE AS FOLLOWS:

(A) USSR still lives in antagonistic "capitalist encirclement" with which in the long run there can be no permanent peaceful coexistence. . . .

(B) Capitalist world is beset with internal conflicts, inherent in nature of capitalist society. . . .

(C) Internal conflicts of capitalism inevitably generate wars. . . .

(D) Intervention against USSR, while it would be disastrous to those who undertook it, would cause renewed delay in progress of Soviet socialism and must therefore be forestalled at all costs.

(E) Conflicts between capitalist states, though likewise fraught with danger for USSR, nevertheless hold out great possibilities for advancement of socialist cause, particularly if USSR remains militarily powerful, ideologically monolithic and faithful to its present brilliant leadership. . . .

So much for premises. To what deductions do they lead from standpoint of Soviet policy? To following:

(A) Everything must be done to advance relative strength of USSR as factor in international society. Conversely, no opportunity must be missed to reduce strength and influence, collectively as well as individually, of capitalist powers.

(B) Soviet efforts, and those of Russia's friends abroad, must be directed toward deepening and exploiting of differences and conflicts between capitalist powers. . . .

(C) "Democratic-progressive" elements abroad are to be utilized to maximum to bring pressure to bear on capitalist governments along lines agreeable to Soviet interests. . . .

Before examining ramifications of this party line in practice there are certain aspects of it to which I wish to draw attention.

First, it does not represent natural outlook of Russian people. Latter are, by and large, friendly to outside world, eager for experience of it, eager to measure against it talents they are conscious of possessing, eager above all to live in peace and enjoy fruits of their own labor. Party line only represents thesis which official propaganda machine puts forward with great skill and persistence to a public often remarkably resistant in the stronghold of its innermost thoughts. But party line is binding for outlook and conduct of people who make up apparatus of power-party, secret police and government — and it is exclusively with these that we have to deal.

Second, please note that premises on which this party line is based are for most part simply not true. Experience has shown that peaceful and mutually profitable coexistence of capitalist and socialist states is entirely possible. Basic internal conflicts in advanced countries are no longer primarily those arising out

*Foreign Relations of the United States,* 1946, vol. 6 (Washington, D.C.: U.S. Government Printing Office).

of capitalist ownership of means of production, but are ones arising from advanced urbanism and industrialism as such, which Russia has thus far been spared not by socialism but only by her own backwardness. . . .

At bottom of Kremlin's neurotic view of world affairs is traditional and instinctive Russian sense of insecurity. Originally, this was insecurity of a peaceful agricultural people trying to live on vast exposed plain in neighborhood of fierce nomadic peoples. To this was added, as Russia came into contact with economically advanced west, fear of more competent, more powerful, more highly organized societies in that area. But this latter type of insecurity was one which afflicted rather Russian rulers than Russian people; for Russian rulers have invariably sensed that their rule was relatively archaic in form, fragile and artificial in its psychological foundation, unable to stand comparison or contact with political systems of western countries. For this reason they have always feared foreign penetration, feared direct contact between western world and their own, feared what would happen if Russians learned truth about world without or if foreigners learned truth about world within. And they have learned to seek security only in patient but deadly struggle for total destruction of rival power, never in compacts and compromises with it. . . .

This thesis provides justification for that increase of military and police power of Russian state, for that isolation of Russian population from outside world, and for that fluid and constant pressure to extend limits of Russian police power which are together the natural and instinctive urges of Russian rulers. Basically this is only the steady advance of uneasy Russian nationalism, a centuries old movement in which conceptions of offense and defense are inextricably confused. But in new guise of international Marxism, with its honeyed promises to a desperate and war torn outside world, it is more dangerous and insidious than ever before. . . .

In summary, we have here a political force committed fanatically to the belief that with US there can be no permanent modus vivendi, that it is desirable and necessary that the internal harmony of our society be disrupted, our traditional way of life be destroyed, the international authority of our state be broken, if Soviet power is to be secure. This political force has complete power of disposition over energies of one of world's greatest peoples and resources of world's richest national territory, and is borne along by deep and powerful currents of Russian nationalism. In addition, it has an elaborate and far flung apparatus for exertion of its influence in other countries, an apparatus of amazing flexibility and versatility, managed by people whose experience and skill in underground methods are presumably without parallel in history. Finally, it is seemingly inaccessible to considerations of reality in its basic reactions. For it, the vast fund of objective fact about human society is not, as with us, the measure against which outlook is constantly being tested and re-formed, but a grab bag from which individual items are selected arbitrarily and tendenciously to bolster an outlook already preconceived. This is admittedly not a pleasant picture. Problem of how to cope with this force is undoubtedly greatest task our diplomacy has ever faced and probably greatest it will ever have to face. . . . It should be approached with same thoroughness and care as solution of major strategic problem in war, and if necessary, with no smaller outlay in planning effort. I cannot attempt to suggest all answers here. But I would like to record my conviction that problem is within our power to solve — and that without recourse to any general military conflict.

And in support of this conviction there are certain observations of a more encouraging nature I should like to make:

(One) Soviet power, unlike that of Hitlerite Germany, is neither schematic nor adventuristic. It does not work by fixed plans. It does not take unnecessary risks. Impervious to logic of reason, and it is highly sensitive to logic of force. For this reason it can easily withdraw — and usually does — when strong resistance is encountered at any point. Thus, if the adversary has sufficient force and makes clear his readiness to use it, he rarely has to do so. . . .

(Two) Gauged against western world as a whole, Soviets are still by far the weaker force. Thus, their success will really depend on degree of cohesion, firmness and vigor which western world can muster. And this is factor which it is within our power to influence.

(Three) Success of Soviet system, as form of internal power, is not yet finally proven. It has yet to be demonstrated that it can survive supreme test of successive transfer of power from one individual or group to another. Lenin's death was first such transfer, and its effects wracked Soviet state for 15 years after. Stalin's death or retirement will be second. But even this will not be final test. Soviet internal system will now be subjected, by virtue of recent territorial expansions, to series of additional strains which once proved severe tax on Tsardom. We here are convinced that never since termination of civil war have mass of Russian people, been emotionally farther removed from doctrines of communist party than they are today. In Russia, party has now become a great and — for the moment — highly successful apparatus of dictatorial administration, but it has ceased to be a source of emotional inspiration. Thus, internal soundness and permanence of movement need not yet be regarded as assured.

(Four) All Soviet propaganda beyond Soviet security sphere is basically negative and destructive. It should therefore be relatively easy to combat it by any intelligent and really constructive program.

For these reasons I think we may approach calmly and with good heart problem of how to deal with Russia. As to how this approach should be made, I only wish to advance, by way of conclusion, following comments:

(One) Our first step must be to apprehend, and recognize for what it is, the nature of the movement with which we are dealing. We must study it with same courage, detachment, objectivity, and same determination not to be emotionally provoked or unseated by it, with which doctor studies unruly and unreasonable individual.

(Two) We must see that our public is educated to realities of Russian situation. I cannot over-emphasize importance of this. Press cannot do this alone. It must be done mainly by government, which is necessarily more experienced and better informed on practical problems involved. . . . I am convinced that there would be far less hysterical anti-Sovietism in our country today if realities of this situation were better understood by our people. There is nothing as dangerous or as terrifying as the unknown. It may also be argued that to reveal more information on our difficulties with Russia would reflect unfavorably on Russian American relations. I feel that if there is any real risk here involved, it is one which we should have courage to face, and sooner the better. But I cannot see what we would be risking. Our stake in this country, even coming on heels of tremendous demonstrations of our friendship for Russian people, is remarkably small. We have here no investments to guard, no actual trade to lose, virtually no citizens to protect, few cultural contacts to preserve. Our only stake lies in what we hope rather than what we have; and I am convinced we have better chance of realizing those hopes if our public is enlightened and if our dealings with Russians are placed entirely on realistic and matter of fact basis.

(Three) Much depends on health and vigor of our own society. World communism is like malignant parasite which feeds only on diseased tissue. This is point at which domestic and foreign policies meet. Every courageous and incisive measure to solve internal problems of our own society, to improve self-confidence, discipline, morale and community spirit of our own people, is a diplomatic victory over Moscow worth a thousand diplomatic notes and joint communiqués. If we cannot abandon fatalism and indifference in face of deficiencies of our own society, Moscow will profit. . . .

(Four) We must formulate and put forward for other nations a much more positive and constructive picture of sort of world we would like to see than we have put forward in past. It is not enough to urge people to develop political processes similar to our own. Many foreign peoples, in Europe at least, are tired and frightened by experiences of past, and are less interested in abstract freedom than in security. They are seeking guidance rather than responsibilities. We should be better able than Russians to give them this. And unless we do, Russians certainly will.

(Five) Finally we must have courage and self-confidence to cling to our own methods and conceptions of human society. After all, the greatest danger that can befall us in coping with this problem of Soviet Communism, is that we shall allow ourselves to become like those with whom we are coping.

## QUESTIONS FOR READING AND DISCUSSION

1. According to Kennan, why did the official Soviet view of the United States emphasize that "there can be no permanent modus vivendi"?

2. What policies were the leaders of the Soviet Union likely to follow? Did the Russian people share their leaders' perspectives?

3. What policies did Kennan recommend that the United States adopt toward the Soviets? What did the United States have to fear from the Russians?

4. How did Kennan recommend that the U.S. government build support for its policy toward the Soviets? Why did he warn that "the greatest danger that can befall us in coping with . . . Soviet Communism, is that we shall allow ourselves to become like those with whom we are coping"?

## DOCUMENT 26-3

# *Cold War Blueprint*

*In 1950, the National Security Council advised President Truman in a top-secret memorandum titled NSC-68 that "the survival of the free world is at stake" in the cold war between the United States and the Soviet Union. NSC-68 provided a blueprint for American foreign policy in the cold war, complete with moral and political justifications for understanding "that the cold war is in fact a real war." The proposals and reasoning of NSC-68 governed American policy during the cold war, outlining the framework for what some scholars have termed "the national security state."*

## NSC-68: U.S. Objectives and Programs for National Security, 1950

Within the past thirty-five years the world has experienced two global wars of tremendous violence. It has witnessed two revolutions — the Russian and the Chinese — of extreme scope and intensity. It has also seen the collapse of five empires — the Ottoman, the Austro-Hungarian, German, Italian, and Japanese — and the drastic decline of two major imperial systems, the British and the French. During the span of one generation, the international distribution of power has been fundamentally altered. . . .

Two complex sets of factors have now basically altered this historic distribution of power. First, the defeat of Germany and Japan and the decline of the British and French Empires have interacted with the development of the United States and the Soviet Union in such a way that power increasingly gravitated to these two centers. Second, the Soviet Union, unlike previous aspirants to hegemony, is animated by a new fanatic faith, antithetical to our own, and seeks to impose its absolute authority over the rest of the world. Conflict has, therefore, become endemic and is waged, on the part of the Soviet Union, by violent or non-violent methods in accordance with the dictates of expediency. With the development of increasingly terrifying weapons of mass destruction, every individual faces the ever-present possibility of annihilation should the conflict enter the phase of total war.

On the one hand, the people of the world yearn for relief from the anxiety arising from the risk of atomic war. On the other hand, any substantial further extension of the area under the domination of the Kremlin[1] would raise the possibility that no coalition adequate to confront the Kremlin with greater strength could be assembled. It is in this context that this Republic and its citizens in the ascendancy of their strength stand in their deepest peril.

The issues that face us are momentous, involving the fulfillment or destruction not only of this Republic but of civilization itself. They are issues which will not await our deliberations. With conscience and resolution this Government and the people it represents must now take new and fateful decisions. . . .

The Kremlin regards the United States as the only major threat. . . . The implacable purpose of the slave state to eliminate the challenge of freedom has placed the two great powers at opposite poles. It is this fact which gives the present polarization of power the quality of crisis.

The free society values the individual as an end in himself, requiring of him only that measure of self-discipline and self-restraint which make the rights of each individual compatible with the rights of every other individual. The freedom of the individual has as its counterpart, therefore, the negative responsibility of the individual not to exercise his freedom in ways inconsistent with the freedom of other individuals and the positive responsibility to make constructive use of his freedom in the building of a just society.

From this idea of freedom with responsibility derives the marvelous diversity, the deep tolerance, the lawfulness of the free society. This is the explanation of the strength of free men. It constitutes the integrity and the vitality of a free and democratic system. The free society attempts to create and maintain an environment in

---

U.S. Department of State, *Foreign Relations of the United States: 1950*, vol. I.
[1]**Kremlin:** The government headquarters of the Soviet Union in Moscow.

which every individual has the opportunity to realize his creative powers. It also explains why the free society tolerates those within it who would use their freedom to destroy it. By the same token, in relations between nations, the prime reliance of the free society is on the strength and appeal of its idea, and it feels no compulsion sooner or later to bring all societies into conformity with it. . . .

The idea of freedom is the most contagious idea in history, more contagious than the idea of submission to authority. For the breadth of freedom cannot be tolerated in a society which has come under the domination of an individual or group of individuals with a will to absolute power. Where the despot holds absolute power. . . . all other wills must be subjugated in an act of willing submission, a degradation willed by the individual upon himself under the compulsion of a perverted faith. It is the first article of this faith that he finds and can only find the meaning of his existence in serving the ends of the system. The system becomes God, and submission to the will of God becomes submission to the will of the system. . . .

The same compulsion which demands total power over all men within the Soviet state without a single exception, demands total power over all Communist Parties and all states under Soviet domination. . . . By the same token the "peace policy" of the Soviet Union, described at a Party Congress as "a more advantageous form of fighting capitalism," is a device to divide and immobilize the non-Communist world, and the peace the Soviet Union seeks is the peace of total conformity to Soviet policy.

The antipathy of slavery to freedom explains the iron curtain, the isolation, the autarchy of the society whose end is absolute power. The existence and persistence of the idea of freedom is a permanent and continuous threat to the foundation of the slave society; and it therefore regards as intolerable the long continued existence of freedom in the world. What is new, what makes the continuing crisis, is the polarization of power which now inescapably confronts the slave society with the free.

The assault on free institutions is world-wide now, and in the context of the present polarization of power a defeat of free institutions anywhere is a defeat everywhere. . . .

Thus unwillingly our free society finds itself mortally challenged by the Soviet system. No other value system is so wholly irreconcilable with ours, so implacable in its purpose to destroy ours, so capable of turning to its own uses the most dangerous and divisive trends in our own society, no other so skillfully and powerfully evokes the elements of irrationality in human nature everywhere, and no other has the support of a great and growing center of military power. . . .

A more rapid build-up of political, economic, and military strength and thereby of confidence in the free world. . . . is the only course which is consistent with progress toward achieving our fundamental purpose. The frustration of the Kremlin design requires the free world to develop a successfully functioning political and economic system and a vigorous political offensive against the Soviet Union. These, in turn, require an adequate military shield under which they can develop. It is necessary to have the military power to deter, if possible, Soviet expansion, and to defeat, if necessary, aggressive Soviet or Soviet-directed actions of a limited or total character. The potential strength of the free world is great; its ability to develop these military capabilities and its will to resist Soviet expansion will be determined by the wisdom and will with which it undertakes to meet its political and economic problems.

1.  Military aspects. . . . The history of war . . . indicates that a favorable decision can only be achieved through offensive action. Even a defensive strategy, if it is to be successful, calls not only for defensive forces to hold vital positions while mobilizing and preparing for the offensive, but also for offensive forces to attack the enemy and keep him off balance. . . .

In the broadest terms, the ability to perform these tasks requires a build-up of military strength by the United States and its allies to a point at which the combined strength will be superior for at least these tasks, both initially and throughout a war, to the forces that can be brought to bear by the Soviet Union and its satellites. In specific terms, . . . [we must] provide an adequate defense against air attack on the United States and Canada and an adequate defense against air and surface attack on the United Kingdom and Western Europe, Alaska, the Western Pacific, Africa, and the Near and Middle East, and on the long lines of communication to these areas. Furthermore, it is mandatory that in building up our strength, we enlarge upon our technical superiority by an accelerated exploitation of the scientific potential of the United States and our allies.

Forces of this size and character are necessary not only for protection against disaster but also to support our foreign policy. . . . [I]t is clear that a substantial and rapid building up of strength in the free world is necessary to support a firm policy intended to check and to roll back the Kremlin's drive for world domination. . . .

2.  Political and economic aspects. The immediate objectives . . . are a renewed initiative in the cold war and a situation to which the Kremlin would find it expedient to accommodate itself, first by relaxing tensions and pressures and then by gradual withdrawal. The United States cannot alone provide the resources required for such a build-up of strength. The other free countries must carry their part of the burden, but their ability and determination to do it will depend on the action the United States takes to develop its own strength and on the adequacy of its foreign political and economic policies. . . .

At the same time, we should take dynamic steps to reduce the power and influence of the Kremlin inside the Soviet Union and other areas under its control. The objective would be the establishment of friendly regimes not under Kremlin domination. Such action is essential to engage the Kremlin's attention, keep it off balance, and force an increased expenditure of Soviet resources in counteraction. In other words, it would be the current Soviet cold war technique used against the Soviet Union.

A program for rapidly building up strength and improving political and economic conditions will place heavy demands on our courage and intelligence; it will be costly; it will be dangerous. But half-measures will be more costly and more dangerous, for they will be inadequate to prevent and may actually invite war. Budgetary considerations will need to be subordinated to the stark fact that our very independence as a nation may be at stake. . . .

The threat to the free world involved in the development of the Soviet Union's atomic and other capabilities will rise steadily and rather rapidly. For the time being, the United States possesses a marked atomic superiority over the Soviet Union which, together with the potential capabilities of the United States and other free countries in other forces and weapons, inhibits aggressive Soviet action. This provides an opportunity for the United States, in cooperation with other free countries, to launch a build-up of strength which will support a firm policy directed to the frustration of the Kremlin design. . . .

In particular, the United States now faces the contingency that within the next four or five years the Soviet Union will possess the military capability of delivering a surprise atomic attack of such weight that the United States must have substantially increased general air, ground, and sea strength, atomic capabilities, and air and civilian defenses to deter war and to provide reasonable assurance, in the event of war, that it could survive the initial blow and go on to the eventual attainment of its objectives. In return, this contingency requires the intensification of our efforts in the fields of intelligence and research and development. . . .

The whole success of the proposed program hangs ultimately on recognition by this Government, the American people, and all free peoples, that the cold war is in fact a real war in which the survival of the free world is at stake.

QUESTIONS FOR READING AND DISCUSSION

1. According to NSC-68, how had the distribution of international power been altered and why was the present situation a "crisis"? What made "the cold war . . . in fact a real war"?
2. Why did the "free society" find itself "mortally challenged by the Soviet system"? Why was the Soviet Union different from, for example, American enemies in World War II, Germany, and Japan?
3. Why was "a defeat of free institutions anywhere . . . a defeat everywhere"?
4. To what extent did the proposed plan employ "the current Soviet cold war technique used against the Soviet Union" itself?
5. In what ways were slavery and freedom "at stake"?

DOCUMENT 26-4

# Senator Joseph McCarthy Hunts Communists

*The cold war was fought at home as well as overseas. The notion that Soviet spies had infiltrated the U.S. government as well as labor unions, universities, and the entertainment industry appealed to many Americans. Joseph R. McCarthy, a Republican senator from Wisconsin, intensified the search for secret Communists with his speech in Wheeling, West Virginia, in February 1950. In this speech, McCarthy charged that the State Department employed more than two hundred Communists, but in the version of the speech he entered in the* Congressional Record, *excerpted here, he reduced the number to fifty-seven. McCarthy's speech illustrates the tendency of many politicians during the cold war to label their political opponents Communists or Communist sympathizers.*

## Speech Delivered in Wheeling, West Virginia, February 9, 1950

Today we are engaged in a final, all-out battle between communistic atheism and Christianity. The modern champions of communism have selected this as the time. And, ladies and gentlemen, the chips are down — they are truly down. . . .

---

*Congressional Record*, Senate, 81st Cong., 2d sess., 1950 (Washington, D.C.: U.S. Government Printing Office).

Ladies and gentlemen, can there be anyone here tonight who is so blind as to say that the war is not on? Can there be anyone who fails to realize that the Communist world has said, "The time is now" that this is the time for the showdown between the democratic Christian world and the Communist atheistic world?

Unless we face this fact, we shall pay the price that must be paid by those who wait too long.

Six years ago, at the time of the first conference to map out the peace — Dumbarton Oaks — there was within the Soviet orbit 180,000,000 people. Lined up on the antitotalitarian side there were in the world at that time roughly 1,625,000,000 people. Today, only 6 years later, there are 800,000,000 people under the absolute domination of Soviet Russia — an increase of over 400 percent. On our side, the figure has shrunk to around 500,000,000. In other words, in less than 6 years the odds have changed from 9 to 1 in our favor to 8 to 5 against us. This indicates the swiftness of the tempo of Communist victories and American defeats in the cold war. As one of our outstanding historical figures once said, "When a great democracy is destroyed, it will not be because of enemies from without, but rather because of enemies from within."

The truth of this statement is becoming terrifyingly clear as we see this country each day losing on every front.

At war's end we were physically the strongest nation on earth and, at least potentially, the most powerful intellectually and morally. Ours could have been the honor of being a beacon in the desert of destruction, a shining living proof that civilization was not yet ready to destroy itself. Unfortunately, we have failed miserably and tragically to arise to the opportunity.

The reason why we find ourselves in a position of impotency is not because our only powerful potential enemy has sent men to invade our shores, but rather because of the traitorous actions of those who have been treated so well by this Nation. It has not been the less fortunate or members of minority groups who have been selling this Nation out, but rather those who have had all the benefits that the wealthiest nation on earth has had to offer — the finest homes, the finest college education, and the finest jobs in Government we can give.

This is glaringly true in the State Department. There the bright young men who are born with silver spoons in their mouths are the ones who have been worst.

Now I know it is very easy for anyone to condemn a particular bureau or department in general terms. Therefore, I would like to cite one rather unusual case — the case of a man who has done much to shape our foreign policy.

When Chiang Kai-shek was fighting our war, the State Department had in China a young man named John S. Service. His task, obviously, was not to work for the communization of China. Strangely, however, he sent official reports back to the State Department urging that we torpedo our ally Chiang Kai-shek and stating, in effect, that communism was the best hope of China.

Later, this man — John Service — was picked up by the Federal Bureau of Investigation for turning over to the Communists secret State Department information. Strangely, however, he was never prosecuted. However, Joseph Grew, the Under Secretary of State, who insisted on his prosecution, was forced to resign. Two days after Grew's successor, Dean Acheson, took over as Under Secretary of State, this man — John Service — who had been picked up by the FBI and who had previously urged that communism was the best hope of China, was not only reinstated in the State Department but promoted. And finally, under Acheson, placed in charge of all placements and promotions.

Today, ladies and gentlemen, this man Service is on his way to represent the State Department and Acheson in Calcutta — by far and away the most important listening post in the Far East. . . .

This, ladies and gentlemen, gives you somewhat of a picture of the type of individuals who have been helping to shape our foreign policy. In my opinion the State Department, which is one of the most important government departments, is thoroughly infested with Communists.

I have in my hand 57 cases of individuals who would appear to be either card carrying members or certainly loyal to the Communist Party, but who nevertheless are still helping to shape our foreign policy.

One thing to remember in discussing the Communists in our government is that we are not dealing with spies who get 30 pieces of silver to steal the blueprints of a new weapon. We are dealing with a far more sinister type of activity because it permits the enemy to guide and shape our policy. . . .

The FBI, I may add, has done an outstanding job, as all persons in Washington, Democrats and Republicans alike, agree. If [FBI director] J. Edgar Hoover had a free hand, we would not be plagued by Hisses . . . in high positions of power in the State Department. The FBI has only power to investigate. . . .

This brings us down to the case of one Alger Hiss who is important not as an individual any more, but rather because he is so representative of a group in the State Department. It is unnecessary to go over the sordid events showing how he sold out the Nation which had given him so much. Those are rather fresh in all of our minds.

However, it should be remembered that the facts in regard to his connection with this international Communist spy ring were made known to the then Under Secretary of State Berle 3 days after Hitler and Stalin signed the Russo-German alliance pact. At that time one Whittaker Chambers — who was also part of the spy ring — apparently decided that with Russia on Hitler's side, he could no longer betray our Nation to Russia. He gave Under Secretary of State Berle — and this is all a matter of record — practically all, if not more, of the facts upon which Hiss' conviction was based.

Under Secretary Berle promptly contacted Dean Acheson and received word in return that Acheson (and I quote) "could vouch for Hiss absolutely" — at which time the matter was dropped. And this, you understand, was at a time when Russia was an ally of Germany. This condition existed while Russia and Germany were invading and dismembering Poland, and while the Communist groups here were screaming "warmonger" at the United States for their support of the allied nations.

Again in 1943, the FBI had occasion to investigate the facts surrounding Hiss' contacts with the Russian spy ring. But even after that FBI report was submitted, nothing was done.

Then, late in 1948 — on August 5 — when the Un-American Activities Committee called Alger Hiss to give an accounting, President Truman at once issued a Presidential directive ordering all Government agencies to refuse to turn over any information whatsoever in regard to the Communist activities of any Government employee to a congressional committee.

Incidentally, even after Hiss was convicted — . . . it is interesting to note that the President still labeled the exposé of Hiss as a "red herring."

If time permitted, it might be well to go into detail about the fact that Hiss was Roosevelt's chief adviser at Yalta when Roosevelt was admittedly in ill health and tired physically and mentally . . . and when, according to the Secretary of State, Hiss and Gromyko drafted the report on the conference. . . .

According to the then Secretary of State Stettinius, here are some of the things that Hiss helped to decide at Yalta. (1) The establishment of a European High Commission; (2) the treatment of Germany — this you will recall was the conference at which it was decided that we would occupy Berlin with Russia occupying an area completely circling the city, which, as you know, resulted in the Berlin airlift which cost 31 American lives; (3) the Polish question; (4) the relationship between UNRRA [United Nations Relief and Rehabilitation Administration] and the Soviet; (5) the rights of Americans on control commissions of Rumania, Bulgaria, and Hungary; (6) Iran; (7) China — here's where we gave away Manchuria; (8) Turkish Straits question; (9) international trusteeships; (10) Korea.

Of the results of this conference, Arthur Bliss Lane of the State Department had this to say: "As I glanced over the document, I could not believe my eyes. To me, almost every line spoke of a surrender to Stalin."

As you hear this story of high treason, I know that you are saying to yourself, "Well, why doesn't the Congress do something about it?" Actually, ladies and gentlemen, one of the important reasons for the graft, the corruption, the dishonesty, the disloyalty, the treason in high Government positions — one of the most important reasons why this continues is a lack of moral uprising on the part of the 140,000,000 American people. In the light of history, however, this is not hard to explain.

It is the result of an emotional hang-over and a temporary moral lapse which follows every war. It is the apathy to evil which people who have been subjected to the tremendous evils of war feel. As the people of the world see mass murder, the destruction of defenseless and innocent people, and all of the crime and lack of morals which go with war, they become numb and apathetic. It has always been thus after war.

However, the morals of our people have not been destroyed. They still exist. This cloak of numbness and apathy has only needed a spark to rekindle them. Happily, this spark has finally been supplied.

As you know, very recently the Secretary of State proclaimed his loyalty to a man guilty of what has always been considered as the most abominable of all crimes — of being a traitor to the people who gave him a position of great trust. The Secretary of State in attempting to justify his continued devotion to the man who sold out the Christian world to the atheistic world, referred to Christ's Sermon on the Mount as a justification and reason therefor, and the reaction of the American people to this would have made the heart of Abraham Lincoln happy.

When this pompous diplomat in striped pants, with a phony British accent, proclaimed to the American people that Christ on the Mount endorsed communism, high treason, and betrayal of a sacred trust, the blasphemy was so great that it awakened the dormant indignation of the American people.

He has lighted the spark which is resulting in a moral uprising and will end only when the whole sorry mess of twisted, warped thinkers are swept from the national scene so that we may have a new birth of national honesty and decency in Government.

1. According to McCarthy, what was the evidence that the United States was losing the cold war? Why had the United States failed to maintain the strong position it had at the end of World War II?

2. Who, according to McCarthy, had "been selling the nation out"? To what extent did McCarthy express insecurities and resentments about class differences?

3. What should Americans do, according to McCarthy, now that they were "engaged in a final, all-out battle between communistic atheism and Christianity"?

4. To what extent did McCarthy's criticisms differ from the goals of the government's cold war policies? What goals motivated McCarthy? Why?

## DOCUMENT 26-5

# A POW in Korea

*During the fierce battles of the Korean War, many Americans were captured and taken to prisoner-of-war camps. In the camps, POWs often received political indoctrination. Nick Tosques spent two and a half years in a POW camp, as he recalled in an interview excerpted here. Tosques's experiences reveal that cold war battlefields extended from combat zones to beliefs.*

## Nick Tosques

### Oral History

I was sent straight over to Korea. . . . The 555th, they called it the Triple Nickles, had just been hit hard. They'd been overrun and lost a lot of men and a lot of their guns. . . .

At that time, early September of 1950, they were still fighting in the Pusan perimeter. There were fire missions every day, and I had to learn real fast. . . .

I learned how to load the gun, I learned how to fire it, and I learned everything fast, because if you didn't, you didn't survive. The North Koreans kept punching holes in our line, and many times we'd have to fire at point-blank range. . . . [A]fter the breakout from the Pusan perimeter we went up with them almost to the Yalu River.

Up at the Yalu the word was, "You'll be having your Christmas dinner in Japan, and then it's back home to the States."

Next thing we knew, we were back below the 38th parallel. And the only people going home were the guys with serious wounds. The Chinese had come into the war, and Christ did we take a beating. I never saw so much stuff go up in smoke during that retreat. Tons and tons of C rations, ammunition, equipment, gasoline. Anything we couldn't carry back with us we burned.

After a couple of months we were back on the offensive. In April of 1951 I got picked to go on ten days R [rest] and R [relaxation] in Tokyo. . . .

Rudy Tomedi, *No Bugles, No Drums: An Oral History of the Korean War* (New York: John Wiley & Sons, 1993), 224–34.

I'm supposed to go home in two weeks. A couple days later the Chinese started their spring offensive. They decided they were going to push us back below the 38th parallel again.

I was still thinking, Well, I'm going home.

All we were doing now was firing and firing and firing. Day and night. In shifts. But we couldn't stop them.

On the afternoon of the twenty-fifth of April our CO [commanding officer] came out to the gun positions and said, "Pack up and leave. We're getting the hell out of here."

Up ahead we could see the guys . . . leaving their positions. They were jumping on trucks and heading back toward us. We hitched up our guns and jumped on our own trucks and joined them on the road, but I don't think we went more than a mile when we ran into a roadblock. The Chinese had gotten in behind us and knocked out an American tank and put it across the road. Both sides of the road dropped off into rice paddies, so when we came to the roadblock we had to stop. And as soon as we stopped the Chinese opened up from the hills all around us.

Machine-gun fire. Mortar fire. Rifle fire. It poured in on us like rain. We unhooked our guns, swung them around, and fired pointblank open the breech block, aim down the barrel, ram the shell in, and fire. And hope you hit something.

Some of the Chinese moved in close enough to throw hand grenades. There were explosions going off all around my gun. Somebody yelled, "Nick, look up!" I looked up and I saw the grenade coming, and the last thing I remember is taking a flying leap.

Next thing I knew, it was night. I don't know how long I was out, but it had been daytime when I jumped away from that grenade. I remember pinching myself. I thought I might be dreaming. All around me are dead and wounded men. The trucks are on fire. I didn't know which way to go, so finally I got up. . . .

Up the road a little ways I ran into three or four guys. . . . They were huddled together along the road. . . . But no matter which way we tried to go, we would hear Chinese talking. Out in the dark ahead of us and all around us.

So finally I said, "Look, get rid of your rifles, lie down, and play dead."

But what the Chinese did was go around and stick all the bodies with bayonets. Not to kill the wounded, but to see if anybody was still alive. They knew that someday there was going to be peace talks, and they wanted as many prisoners as they could get. . . .

It wasn't until daybreak that I realized the fix I was in. It didn't sink in right away that I was a prisoner. . . .

On the first day they brought in an officer who spoke English, and the interrogations started. During basic training every soldier is told: If you're captured, you give only your name, rank, and serial number. But you can say that for only so long. You see some of the other guys getting hit in the back or the kidneys with a rifle butt, and hit hard, and you start thinking about what else you can say without really telling them anything.

This Chinese officer asked me, "What outfit?" I didn't tell him. But when he said, "Those trucks, and those big guns, were you with them?" I said, "Yeah."

Only that. "Yeah."

Then he asked me where I was from. I said Washington. I didn't say Washington D.C., or Washington State. Just Washington.

He didn't press me. I saw that if I just gave him an answer, he'd move on. It didn't have to be an exact answer, just so it looked like I was cooperating. There were a lot of interrogation sessions, but I don't think anybody actually told them very much.

Over the next couple of days other prisoners were brought in, and when we got to be a fairly large group they told us we were going north to a POW camp. . . .

The march north lasted around sixty days. I was captured on the twenty-fifth of April and it was toward the end of June when we got to . . . North Korea. . . .

Camp . . . turned out to be just a collection of old Korean mud huts and a few wooden buildings. There was no fence. After we were there a few days, during one of the lecture sessions when they would ask if there were any questions, somebody asked about that.

"Why isn't there a fence? Where's the barbed wire?" And the interpreter said, "We don't need barbed wire. Your faces are the barbed wire."

The first thing they did was break us up into small groups. Ten men were put into each little room. Not in each hut, but in each room. The rooms were about the size of a large closet. You couldn't move without touching somebody.

They took our clothes and gave us thin blue uniforms. We were all filthy, nobody had had a bath for two months, but we were not allowed to bathe. Everybody had body lice. They were in your hair, in your clothes, all over your body, and there was only one way to kill them: one at a time, between your thumbnails.

Right away the interrogations started. They interrogated us every day, and also at night. They'd take us out in groups, sometimes at two or three in the morning. You never knew when they were coming for you.

They found out, though not from me, that I was from Washington D.C., and then I was interrogated something awful. Hour after hour. What street is the White House on? Where is this building located? Where is that building located? Like it was a big military secret. You could get it from a guidebook, what they were asking. But I couldn't remember where everything was. I'd never paid that much attention to the streets these buildings were on. And when I couldn't answer, *whap*, I'd get hit with a rubber hose on the back of the neck.

Pretty soon I was telling them anything, just to keep from getting hit. That building's here, that other building's there. What the hell, how are they going to know? Well, somehow they found out I was making the stuff up. Whap. The rubber hose again. I guess it never occurred to them that I was telling the truth when I said I couldn't remember. I was from Washington D.C., and in their minds everybody from Washington was supposed to know where all the government buildings were. And also what the government was doing.

Then there were the lectures. We were given lectures every day. "You're capitalists. Your government lies to you. The rich people don't care about you, that's why they sent you over here to die. Your government makes war to oppress the Korean people." That kind of baloney.

We had to learn about communism. The only way to live. The only way to go. How under communism everyone is equal. We had to listen to that stuff every single day. . . .

The mornings were for hard labor. We'd be marched up into the hills to chop wood for them. All the huts were heated with firewood. We had to cut down the wood, chop it into sticks, and carry these big bundles of sticks down to the camp.

The afternoon was study time. We'd study about how Mao Tse-tung and his bunch got rid of Chiang Kai-shek and all the capitalists in China. How capitalism was no good. How the working man was exploited. How communism was the only way to go. And we had guys who turned. Who fell for that baloney. Not right away. But it was pounded and pounded and pounded into us. Every day. Every day. Capitalism no, communism yes.

Like most of the others, I went along with it. Yeah, yeah, yeah. You're right. You're right. But in the back of our minds all we're thinking about is home. About getting back, going to work, and buying what the hell we wanted.

After each study session we'd be sent back to our huts to discuss communism, but what we'd do, we'd put one guy on watch and then we'd talk about anything but communism. What kind of work did you do at home? What kind of car did you drive? Did you have any girlfriends?

But you couldn't completely ignore the lessons, because in the mass study sessions they would ask what you learned. What are you studying? Do you know how your government lies to you? That your Harry Truman lies. That he will never get you home.

There were times when I did lose hope of ever getting back. After a few months in the camp they told us that peace talks were starting. But nothing happened. . . .

After that happens three or four times, what are you going to believe? Months go by, a year, two years, and we're still there. Some guys didn't even believe there were any talks, that the Chinese were just playing with our minds.

A lot of guys got very depressed. A few even committed suicide. It got to be too much for them. They finally lost hope permanently, and when that happened you were a goner. . . .

I remember the first time they told us the war was over. We didn't believe it. They had to keep repeating it, because by this time we didn't trust anything they said.

### QUESTIONS FOR READING AND DISCUSSION

1. How was Tosques captured, and where was he taken?
2. What did his Chinese interrogators want to know? What did the interrogators hope to achieve by brainwashing POWs?
3. Tosques reported that when he and other POWs were told the war was over, "We didn't believe it." Why? Did Tosques's experience show that brainwashing worked?

### COMPARATIVE QUESTIONS

1. How did George F. Kennan's views of Communists differ from those in NSC-68? How did they compare to Joseph R. McCarthy's? How did Kennan's views of the internal dangers of the cold war differ from McCarthy's and those of NSC-68?
2. To what degree was General Marshall's plan for military readiness consistent with Kennan's proposal for confronting the Soviet threat? Did Marshall perceive the Soviet Union as the major danger facing the United States, as Kennan and NSC-68 did?
3. Did Tosques's POW experiences bear out McCarthy's, Kennan's, and NSC-68's views about the threat of communism?
4. To what extent were the views of the individuals in these documents shaped by what they perceived as the lessons of World War II? What were those lessons, according to the documents in this chapter?

# CHAPTER 27

# THE POLITICS AND CULTURE OF ABUNDANCE
## 1952–1960

D uring the 1950s, Americans bought homes, refrigerators, cars, television sets, and other goods at an unprecedented pace. People could not seem to get enough of anything. Many worried that prosperity had a dark side that threatened to undermine traditional values, while the cold war caused government officials to make civil defense plans for a possible nuclear Armageddon, thereby spreading public anxiety. In the cold war climate, raising questions about the role of women, the justice of segregation, or the cold war itself seemed subversive to many people. The numerous achievements of the nation during the 1950s seemed to be creating new, unsettling problems. The documents that follow illustrate Americans' often conflicting faith in both the new and the tried and true.

## DOCUMENT 27-1

### *Edith M. Stern Attacks the Domestic Bondage of Women*

*The prosperity of the 1950s made it possible for a home to be a castle in new ways, and most Americans assumed that each castle would have its queen. Edith Stern, a college-educated writer living in Washington, D.C., ridiculed the assumption that women lived queenly lives of domestic bliss. Men, industrial workers, and even slaves had advantages housewives lacked, Stern declared. Stern's description of household bondage, written for a magazine in 1949 and excerpted here, expressed the frustrations and the aspirations of many American women and raised questions about why such bondage existed and how it might be changed.*

### *Women Are Household Slaves,* 1949

HELP WANTED: DOMESTIC: FEMALE. All cooking, cleaning, laundering, sewing, meal planning, shopping, weekday chauffeuring, social secretarial

---

Edith M. Stern, "Women Are Household Slaves," *American Mercury* 68 (January 1949), 71–76.

_rvice, and complete care of three children. Salary at employer's option. Time off if possible.

No one in her right senses would apply for such a job. No one in his right senses, even a desperate widower, would place such an advertisement. Yet it correctly describes the average wife and mother's situation, in which most women remain for love, but many because they have no way out.

A nauseating amount of bilge is constantly being spilled all over the public press about the easy, pampered existence of the American woman. Actually, the run of the mill, not gainfully employed female who is blessed with a husband and from two to four children leads a kind of life that theoretically became passé with the Emancipation Proclamation. Its confinement makes her baby's play pen seem like the great open spaces. Its hours — at least fourteen a day, seven days a week — make the well known sunup to sundown toil of sharecroppers appear, in comparison, like a union standard. Beside the repetitious, heterogeneous mass of chores endlessly bedeviling the housewife, an executive's memorandum of unfinished business is a virgin sheet.

Housewifery is a complex of housekeeping, household management, housework and childcare. Some of its elements, such as budgeting, dietetics, and above all, the proper upbringing of children, involve the higher brain centers; indeed, home economics has quite as respectable an academic status as engineering, and its own laboratories, dissertations and hierarchy of degrees. Other of its facets, and those the most persistent and time-consuming, can be capably handled by an eight-year-old child. The role of the housewife is, therefore, analogous to that of the president of a corporation who would not only determine policies and make over-all plans but also spend the major part of his time and energy in such activities as sweeping the plant and oiling machines.

Industry, of course, is too thrifty of the capacities of its personnel to waste them in such fashion. Likewise, organized labor and government afford workers certain standardized legal or customary protections. But in terms of enlightened labor practice, the housewife stands out blackly as the Forgotten Worker.

She is covered by no minimum wage law; indeed, she gets no wages at all. Like the bondservant of another day, or the slave, she receives maintenance; but anything beyond that, whether in the form of a regular "allowance" or sporadic largesse, is ruggedly individualistic. . . .

No state or county health and sanitation inspectors invade the privacy of the home, as they do that of the factory; hence kitchens and domestic dwellings may be ill-ventilated, unsanitary and hazardous without penalty. That many more accidents occur in homes than in industry is no coincidence. Furthermore, when a disability is incurred, such as a bone broken in a fall off a ladder or legs scalded by the overturning of a kettle of boiling water, no beneficent legislation provides for the housewife's compensation.

Rest periods are irregular, about ten to fifteen minutes each, a few times during the long day; night work is frequent and unpredictably occasioned by a wide variety of factors such as the mending basket, the gang gathering for a party, a sick child, or even more pressing, a sick husband. The right to a vacation, thoroughly accepted in business and industry, is non-existent in the domestic sphere. When families go to beach bungalows or shacks in the woods Mom continues on almost the same old treadmill; there are still little garments to be buttoned and unbuttoned, three meals a day to prepare, beds to be made and dishes to be washed. Even on jolly whole-family motor trips with the blessings of life in tourist camps or hotels, she still has the job considered full time by paid nurses and governesses.

Though progressive employers make some sort of provision for advancement, the housewife's opportunities for advancement are nil; the nature and scope of her job, the routines of keeping a family fed, clothed and housed remain always the same. If the male upon whom her scale of living depends prospers, about all to which she can look forward is a larger house — and more work. Once, under such circumstances, there would have been less, thanks to servants. Currently, however, the jewel of a general houseworker is virtually extinct and even the specialists who smooth life for the wealthy are rarities.

Industry has a kind of tenderness toward its women workers that is totally lacking towards women workers in the home. Let a plant employee be known to be pregnant, and management and foremen, who want to experience no guilt feelings toward unborn innocents, hasten to prevent her doing any kind of work that might be a strain upon her. In the home, however, now as for centuries, a "normal" amount of housework is considered "healthy" — not to mention, since no man wants to do it, unavoidable. There may be a few proscriptions against undue stretching and heavy lifting, but otherwise, pregnant or not, the housewife carries on, turning mattresses, lugging the vacuum cleaner up and down stairs, carrying winter overcoats to the attic in summer and down from it in the fall, scrubbing kitchen and bathroom floors, washing woodwork if that is indicated by the season, and on her feet most of the time performing other such little chores beside which sitting at an assembly line or punching a typewriter are positively restful.

Despite all this, a good many arguments about the joys of housewifery have been advanced, largely by those who have never had to work at it. One much stressed point is that satisfaction every good woman feels in creating a home for her dear ones. Well, probably every good woman does feel it, perhaps because she has had it so drummed into her that if she does not, she is not a good woman; but that satisfaction has very little to do with housewifery and housework. It is derived from intangibles, such as the desirable wife-husband and mother-child relationships she manages to effect, the permeating general home atmosphere of joviality or hospitality or serenity or culture to which she is the key, or the warmth and security she gives to the home by way of her personality, not her broom, stove or dishpan. For a woman to get a rewarding sense of total creation by way of the multiple, monotonous chores that are her daily lot would be as irrational as for an assembly line worker to rejoice that he had created an automobile because he tightens a bolt. It is difficult to see how clearing up after meals three times a day and making out marketing lists (three lemons, two packages of soap powder, a can of soup), getting at the fuzz in the radiators with the hard rubber appliance of the vacuum cleaner, emptying wastebaskets and washing bathroom floors day after day, week after week, year after year, add up to a sum total of anything except minutiae that laid end to end reach nowhere.

According to another line of reasoning, the housewife has the advantage of being "her own boss" and unlike the gainfully employed worker can arrange her own schedules. This is pure balderdash. . . . If there is anything more inexorable than children's needs, from an infant's yowls of hunger and Junior's shrieks that he has just fallen down the stairs to the subtler need of an adolescent for a good listener during one of his or her frequent emotional crises, it is only the pressure of Dad's demand for supper as soon as he gets home. . . . What is more, not her own preferences as to hours, but those set by her husband's office or plant, by the schools, by pediatricians and dentists, and the children's homework establish when the housewife rises, when she goes forth, and when she cannot get to bed.

Something else makes a mockery of self-determined routines; interruptions from the outside world. Unprotected by butler or doorman, the housewife is at the mercy of peddlers, plain or fancy Fuller brush; odd-job seekers; gas and electric company men who come to read meters; the Salvation Army in quest of newspapers; school children hawking seeds or tickets or chances; and repair men suggesting that the roof is in a hazardous condition or household machinery needs overhauling. Unblessed with a secretary, she answers telephone calls from insurance and real estate agents who "didn't want to bother your husband at his office.". . . All such invasions have a common denominator: the assumption that the housewife's time, like that of all slave labor, has no value.

In addition to what housewifery has in common with slavery, there are factors making it even less enviable as a way of life. The jolly gatherings of darkies with their banjos in the Good Old Days Befoh de Wah may be as mythical as the joys of housewifery, but at any rate we can be sure that slaves were not deprived of social intercourse throughout their hours of toil; field hands worked in gangs, house servants in teams. The housewife, however, carries through each complex operation of cooking, cleaning, tidying and laundering solo; almost uniquely among workers since the Industrial Revolution, she does not benefit by division of labor. Lunch time, ordinarily a pleasant break in the working day, for her brings no pleasant sociability with the girls in the cafeteria, the hired men in the shade of the haystack, or even the rest of the household staff in the servants' dining room. From the time her husband departs for work until he returns, except for an occasional chat across the back fence or a trek to market with some other woman as childbound, housebound, and limited in horizons as herself, she lacks adult company; and even to the most passionately maternal, unbroken hours of childish prattle are no substitute for the conversation of one's peers, whether that be on a high philosophical plane or on the lower level of neighborhood gossip. The Woman's Club, happy hunting ground of matrons in their forties, is perhaps a reaction against this enforced solitude during earlier married life.

Something else enjoyed by slaves, but not by housewives, was work in some measure appropriate to their qualifications. The more intelligent were selected as house servants; the huskier as field hands. Such crude vocational placement has been highly refined in industry, with its battery of intelligence and aptitude tests, personnel directors and employment counselors. Nothing of the kind is even attempted for unpaid domestic workers. When a man marries and has children, it is assumed that he will do the best work along lines in which he has been trained or is at least interested. When a woman marries and has children, it is assumed that she will take to housewifery. But whether she takes to it or not, she does it.

Such regimentation, for professional or potentially professional women, is costly both for the individual and society. For the individual, it brings about conflicts and frustrations. The practice of housewifery gives the lie to the theory of almost every objective of higher education. The educated individual should have a community, a national, a world viewpoint; but that is pretty difficult to get and hold when you are continually involved with cleaning toilets, ironing shirts, peeling potatoes, darning socks and minding children. The educated should read widely; but reading requires time and concentration and besides, the conscientious housewife has her own five-foot shelf of recipes and books on child psychology to occupy her. Most frustrating of all, education leads one to believe that a project attempted should be systematically carried through to completion. In housewifery there is inevitable hopping from one unrelated, unfinished task to another; start the dinner — get at the mending — collect the baby — take down the laundry — finish the dinner is about the maximum height of efficiency. This innate incoherence of housewifery is like a mental patient's flight of ideas; nothing leads quite logically from one thing to another; and the woman schooled like her husband to think generally and in sequence, has a bad time of it intellectually and emotionally as a result.

Perhaps even more deplorable is the loss to society when graduate nurses, trained teachers, lawyers, physicians, artists and other gifted women are unable to utilize their prolonged and expensive educations for the common good. Buried in the homemade cakes the family loves, lost among the stitches of patches, sunk in the suds of the week's wash, are incalculable skilled services.

But just as slaves were in the service of individual masters, not of the community or state or nation in general, so are housewives bound to the service of individual families. That it devolves upon a mother to tend her children during helpless infancy and childhood — or at any rate, to see that they are tended by someone — is undeniable. But only a psychology of slavery can put women at the service of grown men. Ironically, the very gentlemen scrupulous about opening a door for a lady, carrying her packages, or helping her up onto a curb, take it for granted that at mealtime, all their lives long, ladies should carry their food to them and never sit through a meal while they never get up. A wife, when she picks up the soiled clothing her husband has strewn on the floor, lugs his garments to the tailor, makes his twin bed, or sews on his buttons, acts as an unpaid body-servant. If love is the justification for this role, so was love a justification for antebellum Mammies. Free individuals, in a democracy, perform personal services for themselves or, if they have the cash, pay other free individuals to wait on them. It is neither freedom nor democracy when such service is based on color or sex.

As long as the institution of housewifery in its present form persists, both ideologically and practically it blocks any true liberation of women. The vote, the opportunity for economic independence, and the right to smoke cigarettes are all equally superficial veneers over a deep-rooted, ages-old concept of keeping woman in her place. Unfortunately, however, housewives not only are unorganized, but also, doubtless because of the very nature of their brain-dribbling, spirit-stifling vocation, conservative. There is therefore little prospect of a Housewives' Rebellion. There is even less, in the light of men's comfortable setup under the present system, of a male-inspired movement for Abolition!

## QUESTIONS FOR READING AND DISCUSSION

1. Why did housewives accept their chores and confinements, according to Stern? How did their experiences differ from the "nauseating . . . bilge" in the press?

2. To what extent was "the housewife . . . the Forgotten Worker"? Why were housewives different from industrial workers?

3. Why did Stern believe housewives were comparable to slaves? Did her comparison fail to mention important differences between housewives and workers or slaves?

4. In what ways did housewifery block "any true liberation of women"? How could women liberate themselves from housewifery? Why did Stern believe that there was "little prospect of a Housewives' Rebellion"?

5. How might a woman who worked in a factory have responded to Stern's arguments? What might an African American woman who worked as a domestic servant in a white household have said about Stern's statements?

## DOCUMENT 27-2

# *Allen Ginsberg Ridicules American Hypocrisy and Complacency*

*The complacency of the 1950s that many Americans embraced stultified others. In his poem "America," Beat poet Allen Ginsberg expressed rage at the hypocrisy, blindness, and greed of the 1950s. Ginsberg's poem, written in Berkeley, California, on January 17, 1956, put into words the undercurrent of dissatisfaction that spread far beyond the Beats.*

### *America,* January 17, 1956

America I've given you all and now I'm nothing.
America two dollars and twentyseven cents January 17, 1956.
I can't stand my own mind.
America when will we end the human war?
Go fuck yourself with your atom bomb.
I don't feel good don't bother me.
I won't write my poem till I'm in my right mind.
America when will you be angelic?
When will you take off your clothes?
When will you look at yourself through the grave?
When will you be worthy of your million Trotskyites?
America why are your libraries full of tears?
America when will you send your eggs to India?
I'm sick of your insane demands.
When can I go into the supermarket and buy what I need with my good looks?
America after all it is you and I who are perfect not the next world.
Your machinery is too much for me.
You made me want to be a saint.
There must be some other way to settle this argument.
Burroughs is in Tangiers I don't think he'll come back it's sinister.
Are you being sinister or is this some form of practical joke?
I'm trying to come to the point.
I refuse to give up my obsession.
America stop pushing I know what I'm doing.
America the plum blossoms are falling.
I haven't read the newspapers for months, everyday somebody goes on trial
     for murder.
America I feel sentimental about the Wobblies.

Allen Ginsberg, "America," in *Collected Poems, 1947–1980* (New York: Harper & Row, 1984), 146–48.

America I used to be a communist when I was a kid I'm not sorry.
I smoke marijuana every chance I get.
I sit in my house for days on end and stare at the roses in the closet.
When I go to Chinatown I get drunk and never get laid.
My mind is made up there's going to be trouble.
You should have seen me reading Marx.
My psychoanalyst thinks I'm perfectly right.
I won't say the Lord's Prayer.
I have mystical visions and cosmic vibrations.
America I still haven't told you what you did to Uncle Max after he came
     over from Russia.
I'm addressing you.
Are you going to let your emotional life be run by Time Magazine?
I'm obsessed by Time Magazine.
I read it every week.
Its cover stares at me every time I slink past the corner candystore.
I read it in the basement of the Berkeley Public Library.
It's always telling me about responsibility. Businessmen are serious.
     Movie producers are serious. Everybody's serious but me.
It occurs to me that I am America.
I am talking to myself again.

Asia is rising against me.
I haven't got a chinaman's chance.
I'd better consider my national resources.
My national resources consist of two joints of marijuana millions of genitals
     an unpublishable private literature that jetplanes 1400 miles an hour and
     twentyfive-thousand mental institutions.
I say nothing about my prisons nor the millions of underprivileged who live
     in my flowerpots under the light of five hundred suns.
I have abolished the whorehouses of France, Tangiers is the next to go.
My ambition is to be President despite the fact that I'm a Catholic.

America how can I write a holy litany in your silly mood?
I will continue like Henry Ford my strophes are as individual as his automo-
     biles more so they're all different sexes.
America I will sell you strophes $2500 apiece $500 down on your old strophe
America free Tom Mooney
America save the Spanish Loyalists
America Sacco & Vanzetti must not die
America I am the Scottsboro boys.
America when I was seven momma took me to Communist Cell meetings
     they sold us garbanzos a handful per ticket a ticket costs a nickel and the
     speeches were free everybody was angelic and sentimental about the
     workers it was all so sincere you have no idea what a good thing the party
     was in 1935 Scott Nearing was a grand old man a real mensch Mother
     Bloor the Silk-strikers' Ewig-Weibliche made me cry I once saw the
     Yiddish orator Israel Amter plain. Everybody must have been a spy.
America you don't really want to go to war.
America it's them bad Russians.

Them Russians them Russians and them Chinamen. And them Russians.
The Russia wants to eat us alive. The Russia's power mad. She wants to take
  our cars from out our garages.
Her wants to grab Chicago. Her needs a Red Reader's Digest. Her wants our
  auto plants in Siberia. Him big bureaucracy running our fillingstations.
That no good. Ugh. Him make Indians learn read. Him need big black nig-
  gers. Hah. Her make us all work sixteen hours a day. Help.
America this is quite serious.
America this is the impression I get from looking in the television set.
America is this correct?
I'd better get right down to the job.
It's true I don't want to join the Army or turn lathes in precision parts facto-
  ries, I'm nearsighted and psychopathic anyway.
America I'm putting my queer shoulder to the wheel.

QUESTIONS FOR READING AND DISCUSSION

1. What did Ginsberg criticize about America? How, according to the poet, did
   *Time* magazine run America's emotional life? Why did that matter?

2. What did Ginsberg identify as the nation's resources? What affection did he
   express for America? What was the significance of his statement, "It occurs to
   me that I am America"?

3. What impressions did television give about Americans, Russians, and Chinese? What was wrong with those impressions, according to Ginsberg?

4. Ginsberg repeatedly invokes historical events in this poem. Why were those
   events important to him and to America?

5. How was Ginsberg going to "get right down to the job"? What was "the job"?

DOCUMENT 27-3

# Rosa Parks Says "No": A Memoir

*Racial segregation was the rule rather than the exception during the 1950s in the south-*
*ern states, where the great majority of black Americans lived. Outside the South, Jim*
*Crow laws were less common, but racial prejudice and discrimination were widespread.*
*In Montgomery, Alabama, on December 1, 1955, Rosa Parks refused to leave her seat in a*
*segregated bus, setting off what became a full-scale, nationwide assault on Jim Crow laws.*
*Parks described her experience in her memoir, excerpted here.*

## My Story

I don't think any segregation law angered black people in Montgomery more
than bus segregation. . . . Here it was, half a century after the first segregation
law, and there were 50,000 African Americans in Montgomery. More of us rode
the buses than Caucasians did, because more whites could afford cars. It was very

Rosa Parks, *Rosa Parks: My Story* (New York: Dial Books, 1992), 108–25.

humiliating having to suffer the indignity of riding segregated buses twice a day, five days a week, to go downtown and work for white people.

There were incidents all the time. Mrs. [Virginia] Durr [a white woman] says that I would tell her about them time and time again. Mr. [E. D.] Nixon [a black community leader] used to try to negotiate some small changes. I know Mr. Nixon said that at some point he went to the bus company about black people having to pay at the front door and then go around to the back door to enter. They told him, "Your folks started it. They do it because they want to."

Another time he went to see about extending the route of the Day Street bus. Black people in a little community on the other side of the Day Street Bridge had to walk across the bridge, about half a mile, to get to the bus. Mr. Nixon went down to the bus company to protest. He was always going down to the bus company to protest; sometimes he went by himself, sometimes he took someone with him. He himself did not ride the buses — he had his own car; but he was acting on behalf of the community. The bus company told him that as long as the people were willing to walk the half mile and then pay to ride the rest of the way downtown, they had no need to extend the bus line.

Jo Ann Robinson [a black woman] was an English professor at Alabama State College. Back in 1946 she had helped found the Women's Political Council. Over the years she'd had her share of run-ins with bus drivers, but at first she couldn't get the other women in the Council to get indignant. She was from Cleveland, Ohio, and most of them were natives of Montgomery. When she complained about the rudeness of the bus drivers, they said that was a fact of life in Montgomery. She had often brought protests to the bus company on behalf of the Women's Political Council. Finally she managed to get the company to agree that the buses would stop at every corner in black neighborhoods, just as they did in the white neighborhoods. But this was a very small victory.

What galled her, and many more of us, was that blacks were over sixty-six percent of the riders. It was unfair to segregate us. But neither the bus company nor the mayor nor the city commissioners would listen. I remember having discussions about how a boycott of the city buses would really hurt the bus company in its pocketbook. But I also remember asking a few people if they would be willing to stay off the buses to make things better for us, and them saying that they had too far to go to work. So it didn't seem as if there would be much support for a boycott. The Montgomery NAACP was beginning to think about filing suit against the city of Montgomery over bus segregation. But they had to have the right plaintiff and a strong case. The best plaintiff would be a woman, because a woman would get more sympathy than a man. And the woman would have to be above reproach, have a good reputation, and have done nothing wrong but refuse to give up her seat. . . .

I was in on the discussions about the possible court cases. But that is not why I refused to give up my bus seat to a white man on Thursday, December 1, 1955. I did not intend to get arrested. If I had been paying attention, I wouldn't even have gotten on that bus.

I was very busy at that particular time. I was getting an NAACP workshop together for the 3rd and 4th of December, and I was trying to get the consent of Mr. H. Council Trenholm at Alabama State to have the Saturday meeting at the college. He did give permission, but I had a hard time getting to him to get permission to use the building. I was also getting the notices in the mail for the election of officers of the Senior Branch of the NAACP, which would be the next week.

When I got off from work that evening of December 1, I went to Court Square as usual to catch the Cleveland Avenue bus home. I didn't look to see who was driving when I got on, and by the time I recognized him, I had already paid my fare. It was the same driver who had put me off the bus back in 1943, twelve years earlier. He was still tall and heavy, with red, rough-looking skin. And he was still mean-looking. I didn't know if he had been on that route before — they switched the drivers around sometimes. I do know that most of the time if I saw him on a bus, I wouldn't get on it.

I saw a vacant seat in the middle section of the bus and took it. I didn't even question why there was a vacant seat even though there were quite a few people standing in the back. If I had thought about it at all, I would probably have figured maybe someone saw me get on and did not take the seat but left it vacant for me. There was a man sitting next to the window and two women across the aisle.

The next stop was the Empire Theater, and some whites got on. They filled up the white seats, and one man was left standing. The driver looked back and noticed the man standing. Then he looked back at us. He said, "Let me have those front seats," because they were the front seats of the black section. Didn't anybody move. We just sat right where we were, the four of us. Then he spoke a second time: "Y'all better make it light on yourselves and let me have those seats."

The man in the window seat next to me stood up, and I moved to let him pass by me, and then I looked across the aisle and saw that the two women were also standing. I moved over to the window seat. I could not see how standing up was going to "make it light" for me. The more we gave in and complied, the worse they treated us.

I thought back to the time when I used to sit up all night and didn't sleep, and my grandfather would have his gun right by the fireplace, or if he had his one-horse wagon going anywhere, he always had his gun in the back of the wagon. People always say that I didn't give up my seat because I was tired, but that isn't true. I was not tired physically, or no more tired than I usually was at the end of a working day. I was not old, although some people have an image of me as being old then. I was forty-two. No, the only tired I was, was tired of giving in.

The driver of the bus saw me still sitting there, and he asked was I going to stand up. I said, "No." He said, "Well, I'm going to have you arrested." Then I said, "You may do that." These were the only words we said to each other. I didn't even know his name, which was James Blake, until we were in court together. He got out of the bus and stayed outside for a few minutes, waiting for the police.

As I sat there, I tried not to think about what might happen. I knew that anything was possible. I could be manhandled or beaten. I could be arrested. People have asked me if it occurred to me then that I could be the test case the NAACP had been looking for. I did not think about that at all. In fact if I had let myself think too deeply about what might happen to me, I might have gotten off the bus. But I chose to remain.

Meanwhile there were people getting off the bus and asking for transfers, so that began to loosen up the crowd, especially in the back of the bus. Not everyone got off, but everybody was very quiet. What conversation there was, was in low tones; no one was talking out loud. It would have been quite interesting to have seen the whole bus empty out. Or if the other three had stayed where they were, because if they'd had to arrest four of us instead of one, then that would have given me a little support. But it didn't matter. I never thought hard of them at all and never even bothered to criticize them.

Eventually two policemen came. They got on the bus, and one of them asked me why I didn't stand up. I asked him, "Why do you all push us around?" He said to me, and I quote him exactly, "I don't know, but the law is the law and you're under arrest." One policeman picked up my purse, and the second one picked up my shopping bag and escorted me to the squad car. . . .

I wasn't frightened at the jail. I was more resigned than anything else. I don't recall being real angry, not enough to have an argument. I was just prepared to accept whatever I had to face. I asked again if I could make a telephone call. I was ignored. . . .

I called home. My husband [Parks] and mother were both there. She answered the telephone. I said, "I'm in jail. See if Parks will come down here and get me out."

She wanted to know, "Did they beat you?"

I said, "No, I wasn't beaten, but I am in jail."

She handed him the telephone, and I said, "Parks, will you come get me out of jail?"

He said, "I'll be there in a few minutes." He didn't have a car, so I knew it would be longer. . . .

[T]he word was already out about my arrest. Mr. Nixon had been notified by his wife, who was told by a neighbor Bertha Butler, who had seen me escorted off the bus. Mr. Nixon called the jail to find out what the charge was, but they wouldn't tell him. Then he had tried to reach Fred Gray, one of the two black lawyers in Montgomery, but he wasn't home. So finally Mr. Nixon called Clifford Durr, the white lawyer who was Mrs. Virginia Durr's husband. Mr. Durr called the jail and found out that I'd been arrested under the segregation laws. He also found out what the bail was. . . .

Mrs. Durr was the first person I saw as I came through the iron mesh door with matrons on either side of me. There were tears in her eyes, and she seemed shaken, probably wondering what they had done to me. As soon as they released me, she put her arms around me, and hugged and kissed me as if we were sisters.

I was real glad to see Mr. Nixon and Attorney Durr too. We went to the desk, where I picked up my personal belongings and was given a trial date. Mr. Nixon asked that the date be the following Monday, December 5, 1955, explaining that he was a Pullman porter and would be out of Montgomery until then. We left without very much conversation, but it was an emotional moment. I didn't realize how much being in jail had upset me until I got out. . . .

Everyone was angry about what had happened to me and talking about how it should never happen again. I knew that I would never, never ride another segregated bus, even if I had to walk to work. But it still had not occurred to me that mine could be a test case against the segregated buses.

Then Mr. Nixon asked if I would be willing to make my case a test case against segregation. I told him I'd have to talk with my mother and husband. Parks was pretty angry. He thought it would be . . . difficult to get people to support me as a test case. . . . We discussed and debated the question for a while. In the end Parks and my mother supported the idea. They were against segregation and were willing to fight it. And I had worked on enough cases to know that a ruling could not be made without a plaintiff. So I agreed to be the plaintiff.

Mr. Nixon was happy as could be when I told him yes. I don't recall exactly what he said, but according to him, he said, "My God, look what segregation has put in my hands." What he meant by that was that I was a perfect plaintiff. "Rosa

Parks worked with me for twelve years prior to this," he would tell reporters later. "She was secretary for everything I had going — the Brotherhood of Sleeping Car Porters, NAACP, Alabama Voters' League, all of those things. I knew she'd stand on her feet. She was honest, she was clean, she had integrity. The press couldn't go out and dig up something she did last year, or last month, or five years ago. They couldn't hang nothing like that on Rosa Parks."

I had no police record, I'd worked all my life, I wasn't pregnant with an illegitimate child. The white people couldn't point to me and say that there was anything I had done to deserve such treatment except to be born black.

QUESTIONS FOR READING AND DISCUSSION

1. What did Rosa Parks think about segregation?
2. In what ways did she and other African Americans in Montgomery protest segregation?
3. Why did the bus company and city officials oppose attempts to desegregate buses? To what extent were whites united in favor of segregation?
4. Why was Mr. Nixon "as happy as he could be"? Why was Rosa Parks's husband "pretty angry"?

DOCUMENT 27-4

## Civil Defense in the Nuclear Shadow

*During the cold war, Americans lived in the shadow of a possible Soviet nuclear attack on the United States. Civil defense agencies recommended that Americans prepare for nuclear warfare. As the North Dakota survival guide excerpted below suggests, individual citizens needed to be "self-reliant" since an attack would destroy virtually everything at the blast site and would spread dangerous radioactive fallout for many miles. Such plans, which existed in all states, encouraged individual Americans to get ready for nuclear war, bringing cold war hostility into the daily lives of ordinary citizens.*

### North Dakota Civil Defense Agency
### *How You Will Survive*, 1960

#### *Yes, We Can Be Attacked*

Long range jet bombers are presently in the hands of many nations, friendly and hostile. The intercontinental missile that can be sent almost anywhere in the world is being rapidly developed. Both the jet bombers and the missiles will be able to bring deadly weapons down on the United States. Military planners admit that even the best defense system will not be able to stop all enemy planes or missiles.

The weapon most likely to be used in an all out war is the hydrogen bomb which now has 1000 times the explosive force of the atomic bombs dropped on Japan in World War II. The North Dakota Survival Plan [also] anticipates the use of bacteriological and chemical mixtures to further cripple the nation.

---

North Dakota Civil Defense Agency, *The North Dakota Plan: How You Will Survive* (Bismarck, ND: 1960).

## Heat

Since the hydrogen bomb is expected to be the most dangerous weapon, we must know what this bomb can do. Its explosions will generate heat that comes close to that actually on the sun. With an expected temperature of several million degrees Fahrenheit at the point of the blast, the heat will melt metal and destroy all life within the immediate area.

## Blast

The concussion created by the explosion will turn skyscrapers into shambles. Humans or animals caught in the immediate area will die from rupture of lungs and blood vessels due to the sudden changes in pressure.

## Radioactivity

The explosion of a hydrogen bomb will create deadly rays which can pass through flesh and destroy it. The radiation intensity from residual fallout will be so great near the target that people won't be able to live there for days, weeks, months, and possibly years. As the bomb bursts, it will throw radioactive particles into the air where the winds will pick them up and spread them throughout the country. As a result, the effects of hydrogen warfare can reach several hundred miles from the target.

## Targets

North Dakota is presumed to have four possible targets which the enemy may strike. They are the air force bases at Minot and Grand Forks, Hector Airport in Fargo and the State Capitol in Bismarck.

The largest hydrogen bomb presently anticipated in our plans is equal to 20 million tons of TNT. This would create damage 20 miles from the point of explosion, creating a damage area 40 miles across. Destruction would be absolute at the burst site but would gradually diminish outward. . . .

## The Plan of Defense

### Interception

The major portion of the American defense system is military. This includes mobilization of the armed forces for repelling an attack and proceeding to defeat the enemy. We can expect rapid interception of enemy planes but even the best of the military planners concede that some enemy planes are bound to get through.

### Warning

As soon as enemy planes are sighted or enemy action is definite, the national warning point at Colorado Springs, Colorado, will relay the warning to four points in North Dakota. . . .

### Warning Point

As soon as the warning point receives the alert, it will send the alert to the entire State Civil Defense organization through the police radio system. On this system are the highway patrolmen, the state game wardens, all sheriffs and city police departments. The state [warning] points as well as the local points will immediately warn the Civil Defense organizations, the governing official and civilians.

## You Will Be Alerted!

Every city and county will have a warning system to reach the public. . . . The system must be finely developed in the four target areas as evacuation or shelter are the only practical defenses against hydrogen weapons. Alert systems are necessary outside of the target areas since radioactivity may endanger lives and the Civil Defense forces must be mobilized to help meet the demands for housing and supplies. In target areas, a steady siren blast will mean evacuate; a wailing sound will mean to take cover. . . .

### *Evacuation*

### Government

One of the most critical responsibilities during an attack is the preservation of our government — and law and order. Since we know that destruction of democracy is one of the objectives of communism, we can be assured that they shall seek to destroy our organized society. All officials of government in each target area must evacuate as a group and re-establish themselves at a new site.

### Civil Defense

Local Civil Defense organizations will have the responsibility of supervising the evacuation of equipment and supplies from the target areas. This will include rescue trucks, fire trucks, radio equipment, foodstuffs, heavy equipment, and a mass of usable items that will be needed for recovery.

### Civilians

The people must be prepared to leave the target areas as well as stand by for possible movement out of fallout patterns. Civilians must take all supplies possible so they can maintain themselves until they can be taken care of outside of the target areas.

### *You Must Follow Traffic*

We can expect congested traffic in a full-scale evacuation of the target areas. Everyone must be prepared to follow the emergency traffic rules:

1. Know your evacuation plan. Each city has one.
2. Outbound highways will be for one direction only — OUT.
3. Follow directions given by police and auxiliary police.
4. Do not try to travel into a possible target area when an alert has been given.

### *You Will Be Assigned Shelter*

Evacuees coming from the target areas will be cared for in the outlying areas, with Civil Defense organizations in the "support" area being responsible for housing and feeding. In most cases, housing will be in private homes and farms. Evacuees will remain in private dwellings until the alert is over or the economy can be rebuilt.

### *You Must Be Self-Reliant*

### Provide Your Own Travel

Every family should arrange for its own travel. Vehicles should always be kept in good running condition. The tank should always be half full of gasoline. A reserve supply should be kept in the trunk for emergencies. Every family should make arrangements for travel under all circumstances. In addition to providing its own transportation, families should pick up others who may be stranded.

### Provide Your Own Needs for Seven Days
In the initial attack, you will be unable to depend on others. So be prepared to survive by yourself for one week.

1. Stock basic food for immediate packing.
2. Take a good supply of fresh, clean water.
3. Take blankets and clothing for cold weather.

### Shelter in Target Area
If you are caught in the target area when the "Take Cover" signal (a wailing signal on the siren) is given, you must get into the deepest possible location. Perhaps the handiest will be your house basement. Shut off all power, gas and water lines leading into your house.

### Shelter Yourself from Fallout
Once in the reception area, your main concern will be radiation from fallout. Fallout is the radioactive particles falling from the sky which can be fatal if you are exposed over [a] period of time. Fallout will be carried by the wind in an oval pattern away from the target. The Civil Defense organization will attempt to constantly monitor the fallout intensity so you can be alerted when it becomes critical.

### Root Cellars
In the rural parts of North Dakota, farmers and residents of smaller communities have built root cellars to store foodstuffs and as shelter from tornadoes. Whether constructed of concrete or sod, these root cellars are excellent protection against heavy radioactivity. The ideal covering is two or three feet of sod or concrete. Such a shelter should be equipped for two weeks and should have carefully controlled ventilation.

### Basements and Interiors
If a root cellar is not available, the next best shelter is the home itself, and more particularly the basement, if you have one. An ordinary house without [a] basement probably would cut the radiation in half, if you stay on the first floor near the center of the house. Staying in a house basement will reduce your exposure to about 1/10 the outside exposure rate. If you should elect to build a shelter in a corner of your basement, you may reduce the exposure to 1/500 or more. The State Civil Defense Office . . . has plans and specifications for several types of fallout shelters. These plans are designed to aid the homeowner who desires to build his own shelter at a minimum cost and graduate in scale to a more expensive shelter located underground adjacent to the home.

### Shelter Supplies
Whether you evacuate or take shelter in an emergency, one of the basic necessities is an adequate food supply for your family. You should assemble a two-week food supply in your home shelter area, and a three-day evacuation survival kit in your family automobile. . . .

## Shelter Livestock

If you have livestock of any kind, you should get it under cover. A barn or cattleshed will prevent material damage to your animals. If you have no enclosed area for them, even a roof shelter will help prevent the particles from settling on their bodies. You should also get their feed under cover.

## Cleaning the Contaminated

As soon as possible, the people who have been in radioactive areas must wash thoroughly in purified water to wash off any particles that may have fallen on them. Everything exposed should also be washed in clean water, such as clothing, blankets, and household goods. Radioactivity cannot be cleansed but it can be washed away with the particles emitting it . . . .

QUESTIONS FOR READING AND DISCUSSION

1. What assumptions about nuclear attack guide the North Dakota survival plan? What will happen to ordinary citizens in the event of an attack?
2. Given the power of nuclear weapons, how could citizens be self-reliant? Did the North Dakota plan consider survival likely within the "target areas"? How and why?
3. Does the North Dakota plan encourage citizens to be fearful? Optimistic? Why or why not? Do you consider the North Dakota plan a credible way to survive a nuclear attack? Why or why not?
4. What political messages did the North Dakota plan convey? Did such plans make citizens safer? Did they have any influence on attitudes about the cold war?

## DOCUMENT 27-5

# President Dwight D. Eisenhower
# Warns about the Military-Industrial Complex

*After eight years as president and a lifetime of service at the highest levels of the U.S. military, Dwight D. Eisenhower delivered his farewell address on nationwide television. In his address, excerpted here, Eisenhower surveyed American achievements during the 1950s and identified threats posed by those achievements. His assessment suggests the qualms that, for many Americans, mingled with confidence about the future.*

## Farewell Address, January 1961

This evening I come to you with a message of leave-taking and farewell, and to share a few final thoughts with you, my countrymen. . . .

We now stand ten years past the midpoint of a century that has witnessed four major wars among great nations. Three of these involved our own country. Despite these holocausts America is today the strongest, the most influential and most productive nation in the world. Understandably proud of this pre-eminence, we yet realize that America's leadership and prestige depend, not merely upon

*Public Papers of the Presidents of the United States: Dwight D. Eisenhower, 1960–61* (1961).

our unmatched material progress, riches and military strength, but on how we use our power in the interests of world peace and human betterment.

Throughout America's adventure in free government, our basic purposes have been to keep the peace; to foster progress in human achievement, and to enhance liberty, dignity and integrity among people and among nations. To strive for less would be unworthy of a free and religious people. Any failure traceable to arrogance, or for lack of comprehension or readiness to sacrifice would inflict upon us grievous hurt both at home and abroad.

Progress toward these noble goals is persistently threatened by the conflict now engulfing the world. It commands our whole attention, absorbs our very beings. We face a hostile ideology global in scope, atheistic in character, ruthless in purpose, and insidious in method. Unhappily the danger it poses promises to be of indefinite duration. To meet it successfully, there is called for, not so much the emotional and transitory sacrifices of crisis, but rather those which enable us to carry forward steadily, surely, and without complaint the burdens of a prolonged and complex struggle — with liberty the stake. Only thus shall we remain, despite every provocation, on our charted course toward permanent peace and human betterment.

Crises there will continue to be. In meeting them, whether foreign or domestic, great or small, there is a recurring temptation to feel that some spectacular and costly action could become the miraculous solution to all current difficulties. A huge increase in newer elements of our defense; development of unrealistic programs to cure every ill in agriculture; a dramatic expansion in basic and applied research — these and many other possibilities, each possibly promising in itself, may be suggested as the only way to the road we wish to travel.

But each proposal must be weighed in the light of a broader consideration: the need to maintain balance in and among national programs — balance between the private and the public economy, balance between cost and hoped for advantage — balance between the clearly necessary and the comfortably desirable; balance between our essential requirements as a nation and the duties imposed by the nation upon the individual; balance between actions of the moment and the national welfare of the future. Good judgment seeks balance and progress; lack of it eventually finds imbalance and frustration.

The record of many decades stands as proof that our people and their government have, in the main, understood these truths and have responded to them well, in the face of stress and threat. But threats, new in kind or degree, constantly arise. I mention two only.

A vital element in keeping the peace is our military establishment. Our arms must be mighty, ready for instant action, so that no potential aggressor may be tempted to risk his own destruction.

Our military organization today bears little relation to that known by any of my predecessors in peacetime, or indeed by the fighting men of World War II or Korea. Until the latest of our world conflicts, the United States had no armaments industry. American makers of plowshares could, with time and as required, make swords as well. But now we can no longer risk emergency improvisation of national defense; we have been compelled to create a permanent armaments industry of vast proportions. Added to this, three and a half million men and women are directly engaged in the defense establishment. We annually spend on military security more than the net income of all United States corporations.

This conjunction of an immense military establishment and a large arms industry is new in the American experience. The total influence — economic, political, even spiritual — is felt in every city, every State house, every office of the Federal government. We recognize the imperative need for this development. Yet we must not fail to comprehend its grave implications. Our toil, resources and livelihood are all involved; so is the very structure of our society.

In the councils of government, we must guard against the acquisition of unwarranted influence, whether sought or unsought, by the military-industrial complex. The potential for the disastrous rise of misplaced power exists and will persist.

We must never let the weight of this combination endanger our liberties or democratic processes. We should take nothing for granted. Only an alert and knowledgeable citizenry can compel the proper meshing of the huge industrial and military machinery of defense with our peaceful methods and goals, so that security and liberty may prosper together.

Akin to, and largely responsible for the sweeping changes in our industrial-military posture, has been the technological revolution during recent decades.

In this revolution, research has become central; it also becomes more formalized, complex, and costly. A steadily increasing share is conducted for, by, or at the direction of, the Federal government.

Today, the solitary inventor, tinkering in his shop, has been overshadowed by task forces of scientists in laboratories and testing fields. In the same fashion, the free university, historically the fountainhead of free ideas and scientific discovery, has experienced a revolution in the conduct of research. Partly because of the huge costs involved, a government contract becomes virtually a substitute for intellectual curiosity. For every old blackboard there are now hundreds of new electronic computers.

The prospect of domination of the nation's scholars by Federal employment, project allocations, and the power of money is ever present — and is gravely to be regarded.

Yet, in holding scientific research and discovery in respect, as we should, we must also be alert to the equal and opposite danger that public policy could itself become the captive of a scientific-technological elite.

It is the task of statesmanship to mold, to balance, and to integrate these and other forces, new and old, within the principles of our democratic system — ever aiming toward the supreme goals of our free society.

Another factor in maintaining balance involves the element of time. As we peer into society's future, we — you and I, and our government — must avoid the impulse to live only for today, plundering, for our own ease and convenience, the precious resources of tomorrow. We cannot mortgage the material assets of our grandchildren without risking the loss also of their political and spiritual heritage. We want democracy to survive for all generations to come, not to become the insolvent phantom of tomorrow.

Down the long lane of the history yet to be written America knows that this world of ours, ever growing smaller, must avoid becoming a community of dreadful fear and hate, and be, instead, a proud confederation of mutual trust and respect.

Such a confederation must be one of equals. The weakest must come to the conference table with the same confidence as do we, protected as we are by our moral, economic, and military strength. That table, though scarred by many past frustrations, cannot be abandoned for the certain agony of the battlefield. Disarmament, with mutual honor and confidence, is a continuing imperative. Together we must learn how to compose differences, not with arms, but with intellect and decent purpose. Because this need is so sharp and apparent I confess that I lay down my official responsibilities in this field with a definite sense of disappointment. As one who has witnessed the horror and the lingering sadness of war — as one who knows that another war could utterly destroy this civilization which has been so slowly and painfully built over thousands of years — I wish I could say tonight that a lasting peace is in sight.

Happily, I can say that war has been avoided. Steady progress toward our ultimate goal has been made. But, so much remains to be done. As a private citizen, I shall never cease to do what little I can to help the world advance along that road. . . .

You and I — my fellow citizens — need to be strong in our faith that all nations, under God, will reach the goal of peace with justice. May we be ever unswerving in devotion to principle, confident but humble with power, diligent in pursuit of the Nation's great goals.

### QUESTIONS FOR READING AND DISCUSSION

1. What did Eisenhower identify as basic American goals and what was required to achieve them?
2. Why did he urge Americans to "guard against the acquisition of unwarranted influence . . . by the military-industrial complex"? What dangers did it pose?
3. To what extent did Eisenhower's address reflect the major historical legacies of the 1950s? Do you think his concerns are still relevant in the twenty-first century? Why or why not?

### COMPARATIVE QUESTIONS

1. How do Edith M. Stern's notions about women's enslavement compare with Rosa Parks's ideas and experiences? What might account for the differences?
2. In what ways do Dwight D. Eisenhower's views about the promise of America compare with the North Dakota civil defense plan and with the views of Stern, Parks, and Allen Ginsberg?
3. To what extent do the other documents in this chapter reflect Eisenhower's warnings about the dangers faced by America?
4. How did the era's relative economic abundance shape the ideas and experiences of the individuals described in these documents?

# CHAPTER 28

# REFORM, REBELLION, AND REACTION
## 1960–1974

During the 1960s, many Americans sought to make changes that many other Americans resisted. To those who wanted change, the times seemed right and the causes just. Presidents sympathetic to change occupied the Oval Office for most of the period, civil rights demonstrators confronted Jim Crow laws, black power advocates called for racial pride and revolution, and women's rights leaders outlined proposals for gender equality. The possibilities for change seemed extraordinary. The widespread sense that the American dream could be more fully realized is revealed in the following documents, as well as the lingering obstacles to achieving that goal.

## DOCUMENT 28-1

### President Lyndon B. Johnson Describes the Great Society

*During the 1960s, both Presidents John F. Kennedy and Lyndon B. Johnson tended to see government as an agent of change. Both presidents believed the government should take an active role in creating a better society. In 1964, President Johnson outlined his plans for the Great Society in a speech to students at the University of Michigan. Johnson's speech, excerpted here, illustrates the confidence many Americans had in the powers of government.*

### Address at the University of Michigan, May 22, 1964

I have come today from the turmoil of your Capital to the tranquility of your campus to speak about the future of your country.

---

*Public Papers of the President of the United States: Lyndon B. Johnson, 1963–65* (Washington, D.C.: U.S. Government Printing Office, 1965).

The purpose of protecting the life of our Nation and preserving the liberty of our citizens is to pursue the happiness of our people. Our success in that pursuit is the test of our success as a Nation.

For a century we labored to settle and to subdue a continent. For half a century we called upon unbounded invention and untiring industry to create an order of plenty for all of our people.

The challenge of the next half century is whether we have the wisdom to use that wealth to enrich and elevate our national life, and to advance the quality of our American civilization.

Your imagination, your initiative, and your indignation will determine whether we build a society where progress is the servant of our needs, or a society where old values and new visions are buried under unbridled growth. For in your time we have the opportunity to move not only toward the rich society and the powerful society, but upward to the Great Society.

The Great Society rests on abundance and liberty for all. It demands an end to poverty and racial injustice, to which we are totally committed in our time. But that is just the beginning.

The Great Society is a place where every child can find knowledge to enrich his mind and to enlarge his talents. It is a place where leisure is a welcome chance to build and reflect, not a feared cause of boredom and restlessness. It is a place where the city of man serves not only the needs of the body and the demands of commerce but the desire for beauty and the hunger for community.

It is a place where man can renew contact with nature. It is a place which honors creation for its own sake and for what it adds to the understanding of the race. It is a place where men are more concerned with the quality of their goals than the quantity of their goods.

But most of all, the Great Society is not a safe harbor, a resting place, a final objective, a finished work. It is a challenge constantly renewed, beckoning us toward a destiny where the meaning of our lives matches the marvelous products of our labor.

So I want to talk to you today about three places where we begin to build the Great Society — in our cities, in our countryside, and in our classrooms.

Many of you will live to see the day, perhaps 50 years from now, when there will be 400 million Americans — four-fifths of them in urban areas. In the remainder of this century urban population will double, city land will double, and we will have to build homes, highways, and facilities equal to all those built since this country was first settled. So in the next 40 years we must rebuild the entire urban United States.

Aristotle said: "Men come together in cities in order to live, but they remain together in order to live the good life." It is harder and harder to live the good life in American cities today.

The catalog of ills is long: there is the decay of the centers and the despoiling of the suburbs. There is not enough housing for our people or transportation for our traffic. Open land is vanishing and old landmarks are violated.

Worst of all expansion is eroding the precious and time honored values of community with neighbors and communion with nature. The loss of these values breeds loneliness and boredom and indifference.

Our society will never be great until our cities are great. Today the frontier of imagination and innovation is inside those cities and not beyond their borders.

New experiments are already going on. It will be the task of your generation to make the American city a place where future generations will come, not only to live but to live the good life. . . .

A second place where we begin to build the Great Society is in our countryside. We have always prided ourselves on being not only America the strong and America the free, but America the beautiful. Today that beauty is in danger. The water we drink, the food we eat, the very air that we breathe, are threatened with pollution. Our parks are overcrowded, our seashores overburdened. Green fields and dense forests are disappearing, . . .

A few years ago we were greatly concerned about the "Ugly American." Today we must act to prevent an ugly America.

For once the battle is lost, once our natural splendor is destroyed, it can never be recaptured. And once man can no longer walk with beauty or wonder at nature his spirit will wither and his sustenance be wasted.

A third place to build the Great Society is in the classrooms of America. There your children's lives will be shaped. Our society will not be great until every young mind is set free to scan the farthest reaches of thought and imagination. We are still far from that goal.

Today, 8 million adult Americans, more than the entire population of Michigan, have not finished 5 years of school. Nearly 20 million have not finished 8 years of school. Nearly 54 million — more than one-quarter of all America — have not even finished high school.

Each year more than 100,000 high school graduates, with proved ability, do not enter college because they cannot afford it. . . .

In many places, classrooms are overcrowded and curricula are outdated. Most of our qualified teachers are underpaid, and many of our paid teachers are unqualified. So we must give every child a place to sit and a teacher to learn from. Poverty must not be a bar to learning, and learning must offer an escape from poverty.

But more classrooms and more teachers are not enough. We must seek an educational system which grows in excellence as it grows in size. This means better training for our teachers. It means preparing youth to enjoy their hours of leisure as well as their hours of labor. It means exploring new techniques of teaching, to find new ways to stimulate the love of learning and the capacity for creation.

These are three of the central issues of the Great Society. While our Government has many programs directed at those issues, I do not pretend that we have the full answer to those problems.

But I do promise this: We are going to assemble the best thought and the broadest knowledge from all over the world to find those answers for America. I intend to establish working groups to prepare a series of White House conferences and meetings — on the cities, on natural beauty, on the quality of education, and on other emerging challenges. And from these meetings and from this inspiration and from these studies we will begin to set our course toward the Great Society.

The solution to these problems does not rest on a massive program in Washington, nor can it rely solely on the strained resources of local authority. They require us to create new concepts of cooperation, a creative federalism, between the National Capital and the leaders of local communities. . . .

For better or for worse, your generation has been appointed by history to deal with those problems and to lead America toward a new age. You have the chance never before afforded to any people in any age. You can help build a society where the demands of morality, and the needs of the spirit, can be realized in the life of the Nation.

So, will you join in the battle to give every citizen the full equality which God enjoins and the law requires, whatever his belief, or race, or the color of his skin?

Will you join in the battle to give every citizen an escape from the crushing weight of poverty?

Will you join in the battle to make it possible for all nations to have in enduring peace — as neighbors and not as mortal enemies?

Will you join in the battle to build the Great Society, to prove that our material progress is only the foundation on which we will build a richer life of mind and spirit?

There are those timid souls who say this battle cannot be won; that we are condemned to a soulless wealth. I do not agree. We have the power to shape the civilization that we want. But we need your will, your labor, your hearts, if we are to build that kind of society.

Those who came to this land sought to build more than just a new country. They sought a new world. So I have come here today to your campus to say that you can make their vision our reality. So let us from this moment begin our work so that in the future men will look back and say: It was then, after a long and weary way, that man turned the exploits of his genius to the full enrichment of his life.

QUESTIONS FOR READING AND DISCUSSION

1. What were the goals of Johnson's Great Society? Why would the Great Society be "a place where men are more concerned with the quality of the goals than the quantity of their goods"?

2. How could the Great Society be realized, according to Johnson? What did he mean by "new concepts of cooperation, a creative federalism between the National Capital and the leaders of local communities"?

3. What political groups did Johnson hope would respond to his message? Who were the "timid souls," and why were they important?

4. Johnson repeatedly referred to "the battle." To what extent did this military metaphor have significance for his Great Society plan and for his audience? Who were the enemies in the battle?

DOCUMENT 28-2

# Martin Luther King Jr. Explains Nonviolent Resistance

*Participants in the civil rights demonstrations that swept across the South during the 1960s used tactics of nonviolent resistance. Many white Americans, North and South, condemned the demonstrators as extremists and law-breakers whose ends may have been admirable but whose means were deplorable. Martin Luther King Jr. responded to those views in 1963 in a letter he wrote while in jail in Birmingham, Alabama, where he had been arrested for participating in demonstrations. King's letter, excerpted here, was directed to a group of white clergymen who had criticized the Birmingham demonstrations. King's letter set forth the ideals of nonviolence embraced by many civil rights activists.*

## *Letter from Birmingham City Jail,* 1963

My dear Fellow Clergymen,

While confined here in the Birmingham city jail, I came across your recent statement calling our present activities "unwise and untimely.". . . . [S]ince I feel that you are men of genuine good will and your criticisms are sincerely set forth, I would like to answer your statement in what I hope will be patient and reasonable terms.

I think I should give the reason for my being in Birmingham, since you have been influenced by the argument of "outsiders coming in." I have the honor of serving as president of the Southern Christian Leadership Conference, an organization operating in every southern state, with headquarters in Atlanta, Georgia. We have some eighty-five affiliate organizations all across the South. . . . Several months ago our local affiliate here in Birmingham invited us to be on call to engage in a nonviolent direct-action program if such were deemed necessary. . . .

Beyond this, I am in Birmingham because injustice is here. . . . I cannot sit idly by in Atlanta and not be concerned about what happens in Birmingham. Injustice anywhere is a threat to justice everywhere. . . .

You deplore the demonstrations that are presently taking place in Birmingham. But I am sorry that your statement did not express a similar concern for the conditions that brought the demonstrations into being. . . .

Birmingham is probably the most thoroughly segregated city in the United States. Its ugly record of police brutality is known in every section of this country. Its injust treatment of Negroes in the courts is a notorious reality. There have been more unsolved bombings of Negro homes and churches in Birmingham than any city in this nation. These are the hard, brutal and unbelievable facts. . . .

You may well ask, "Why direct action? Why sit-ins, marches, etc.? Isn't negotiation a better path?" You are exactly right in your call for negotiation. Indeed, this is the purpose of direct action. Nonviolent direct action seeks to create such a crisis and establish such creative tension that a community that has constantly refused to negotiate is forced to confront the issue. It seeks so to dramatize the issue that it can no longer be ignored. . . . So the purpose of the direct action is to create a situation so crisis-packed that it will inevitably open the door to negotiation. . . .

One of the basic points in your statement is that our acts are untimely. . . . My friends, I must say to you that we have not made a single gain in civil rights without determined legal and nonviolent pressure. History is the long and tragic story of the fact that privileged groups seldom give up their privileges voluntarily. . . .

We know through painful experience that freedom is never voluntarily given by the oppressor; it must be demanded by the oppressed. Frankly, I have never yet engaged in a direct action movement that was "well-timed," according to the timetable of those who have not suffered unduly from the disease of segregation. For years now I have heard the words "Wait!" It rings in the ear of every Negro with a piercing familiarity. This "Wait" has almost always meant "Never." . . . We have waited for more than 340 years for our constitutional and God-given rights. The nations of Asia and Africa are moving with jetlike speed toward the goal of political

Martin Luther King Jr., "Letter from Birmingham City Jail," in *Why We Can't Wait* (New York: Harper & Row, 1984).

independence, and we still creep at horse and buggy pace toward the gaining of a cup of coffee at a lunch counter. I guess it is easy for those who have never felt the stinging darts of segregation to say, "Wait." But when you have seen vicious mobs lynch your mothers and fathers at will and drown your sisters and brothers at whim; when you have seen hate-filled policemen curse, kick, brutalize and even kill your black brothers and sisters with impunity; when you see the vast majority of your twenty million Negro brothers smothering in an airtight cage of poverty in the midst of an affluent society; when you suddenly find your tongue twisted and your speech stammering as you seek to explain to your six-year-old daughter why she can't go to the public amusement park that has just been advertised on television, and see tears welling up in her little eyes when she is told that Funtown is closed to colored children, and see the depressing clouds of inferiority begin to form in her little mental sky, and see her begin to distort her little personality by unconsciously developing a bitterness toward white people; when you have to concoct an answer for a five-year-old son asking in agonizing pathos: "Daddy, why do white people treat colored people so mean?"; when you take a cross-country drive and find it necessary to sleep night after night in the uncomfortable corners of your automobile because no motel will accept you; when you are humiliated day in and day out by nagging signs reading "white" and "colored"; when your first name becomes "nigger" and your middle name becomes "boy" (however old you are) and your last name becomes "John," and when your wife and mother are never given the respected title "Mrs."; when you are harried by day and haunted by night by the fact that you are a Negro, living constantly at tiptoe stance never quite knowing what to expect next, and plagued with inner fears and outer resentments; when you are forever fighting a degenerating sense of "nobodiness"; then you will understand why we find it difficult to wait. There comes a time when the cup of endurance runs over, and men are no longer willing to be plunged into an abyss of injustice where they experience the blackness of corroding despair. I hope, sirs, you can understand our legitimate and unavoidable impatience.

You express a great deal of anxiety over our willingness to break laws. This is certainly a legitimate concern. Since we so diligently urge people to obey the Supreme Court's decision of 1954 outlawing segregation in the public schools, it is rather strange and paradoxical to find us consciously breaking laws. One may well ask, "How can you advocate breaking some laws and obeying others?" The answer is found in the fact that there are two types of laws: there are *just* and there are *unjust* laws. I would agree with Saint Augustine that "An unjust law is no law at all."

Now what is the difference between the two? How does one determine when a law is just or unjust? A just law is a man-made code that squares with the moral law or the law of God. An unjust law is a code that is out of harmony with the moral law. To put it in the terms of Saint Thomas Aquinas, an unjust law is a human law that is not rooted in eternal and natural law. Any law that uplifts human personality is just. Any law that degrades human personality is unjust. All segregation statutes are unjust because segregation distorts the soul and damages the personality. It gives the segregator a false sense of superiority, and the segregated a false sense of inferiority. . . . So segregation is not only politically, economically and sociologically unsound, but it is morally wrong and sinful. . . . So I can urge men to disobey segregation ordinances because they are morally wrong. . . .

I hope you can see the distinction I am trying to point out. In no sense do I advocate evading or defying the law as the rabid segregationist would do. This would lead to anarchy. One who breaks an unjust law must do it *openly, lovingly* . . . and with a willingness to accept the penalty. I submit that an individual who breaks a law that conscience tells him is unjust, and willingly accepts the penalty by staying in jail to arouse the conscience of the community over its injustice, is in reality expressing the very highest respect for law.

Of course, there is nothing new about this kind of civil disobedience. . . . It was practiced superbly by the early Christians who were willing to face hungry lions and the excruciating pain of chopping blocks, before submitting to certain unjust laws of the Roman Empire. . . .

I must make two honest confessions to you, my Christian and Jewish brothers. First, I must confess that over the last few years I have been gravely disappointed with the white moderate. I have almost reached the regrettable conclusion that the Negro's great stumbling block in the stride toward freedom is not the White Citizen's Counciler or the Ku Klux Klanner, but the white moderate who is more devoted to order than to justice; who prefers a negative peace which is the absence of tension to a positive peace which is the presence of justice; who constantly says, "I agree with you in the goal you seek, but I can't agree with your methods of direct action"; who paternalistically feels that he can set the timetable for another man's freedom; who lives by the myth of time and who constantly advised the Negro to wait until a "more convenient season." Shallow understanding from people of good will is more frustrating than absolute misunderstanding from people of ill will. Lukewarm acceptance is much more bewildering than outright rejection.

I had hoped that the white moderate would understand that law and order exist for the purpose of establishing justice, and that when they fail to do this they become dangerously structured dams that block the flow of social progress. I had hoped that the white moderate would understand that the present tension of the South is merely a necessary phase of the transition from an obnoxious negative peace, where the Negro passively accepted his unjust plight, to a substance-filled positive peace, where all men will respect the dignity and worth of human personality. Actually, we who engage in nonviolent direct action are not the creators of tension. We merely bring to the surface the hidden tension that is already alive. We bring it out in the open where it can be seen and dealt with. . . .

In your statement you asserted that our actions, even though peaceful, must be condemned because they precipitate violence. But can this assertion be logically made? Isn't this like condemning the robbed man because his possession of money precipitated the evil act of robbery? . . .

You spoke of our activity in Birmingham as extreme. At first I was rather disappointed that fellow clergymen would see my nonviolent efforts as those of the extremist. I started thinking about the fact that I stand in the middle of two opposing forces in the Negro community. One is a force of complacency made up of Negroes who, as a result of long years of oppression, have been so completely drained of self-respect and a sense of "somebodiness" that they have adjusted to segregation, and, of a few Negroes in the middle class who, because of a degree of academic and economic security, and because at points they profit by segregation, have unconsciously become insensitive to the problems of the masses. The other force is one of bitterness and hatred, and comes perilously close to advocating violence. It is expressed in the various black nationalist groups that are springing up over the nation, the largest and best known being Elijah Muhammad's Muslim movement. This movement is nourished by the contemporary frustration over the continued existence of racial discrimination. It is made up of people who have lost faith in America, who have absolutely repudiated Christianity, and who have concluded that the white man is an incurable "devil." I have tried to stand between these two forces, saying that we need not follow the "do-nothingism" of the complacent or the hatred and despair of the black nationalist. There is the more excellent way of love and nonviolent protest. I'm grateful to God that, through the Negro church, the dimension of nonviolence entered our struggle. If this philosophy had not emerged, I am convinced that by now many streets of the South would be flowing with floods of blood. And I am further convinced that if our white brothers dismiss us as "rabble-rousers" and "outside agitators" those of us who are working through the channels of nonviolent direct action and refuse to support our nonviolent efforts, millions of Negroes, out of frustration and despair, will seek solace and security in black nationalist ideologies, a development that will lead inevitably to a frightening racial nightmare.

Oppressed people cannot remain oppressed forever. The urge for freedom will eventually come. This is what happened to the American Negro. . . .

But as I continued to think about the matter I gradually gained a bit of satisfaction from being considered an extremist. Was not Jesus an extremist in love — "Love your enemies, bless them that curse you, pray for them that despitefully use you.". . . Was not Abraham Lincoln an extremist — "This nation cannot survive half slave and half free." Was not Thomas Jefferson an extremist — "We hold these truths to be self-evident, that all men are created equal." So the question is not whether we will be extremist but what kind of extremist will we be. Will we be extremists for hate or will we be extremists for love? Will we be extremists for the preservation of injustice — or will we be extremists for the cause of justice? . . .

But before closing I am impelled to mention one other point in your statement that troubled me profoundly. You warmly commended the Birmingham police force for keeping "order" and "preventing violence." I don't believe you would have so warmly commended the police force if you had seen its angry violent dogs literally biting six unarmed, nonviolent Negroes. I don't believe you would so quickly commend the policemen if you would observe their ugly and inhuman treatment of Negroes here in the city jail; if you would watch them push and curse old Negro women and young Negro girls; if you would see them slap and kick old Negro men and young boys; if you will observe them, as they did on two occasions, refuse to give us food because we wanted to sing our grace together. I'm sorry that I can't join you in your praise for the police department. . . .

I wish you had commended the Negro sit-inners and demonstrators of Birmingham for their sublime courage, their willingness to suffer and their amazing discipline in the midst of the most inhuman provocation. One day the South will recognize its real heroes. They will be the James Merediths,[1] courageously and with a majestic sense of purpose facing jeering and hostile mobs and the agonizing loneliness that characterizes the life of the pioneer. They will be old, oppressed, battered Negro women, symbolized in a seventy-two-year-old woman of Montgomery, Alabama, who rose up with a sense of dignity and with her people decided not to ride the segregated buses, and responded to one who inquired about her tiredness with ungrammatical profundity: "My feet is tired, but my soul is rested." They will be the young high school and college students, young ministers

---

[1]**James Meredith:** The first black student to attend the University of Mississippi, Meredith had to be escorted by U.S. marshalls to protect him from a rioting mob of segregationists in 1962.

of the gospel and a host of their elders courageously and nonviolently sitting-in at lunch counters and willingly going to jail for conscience's sake. One day the South will know that when these disinherited children of God sat down at lunch counters they were in reality standing up for the best in the American dream and the most sacred values in our Judeo-Christian heritage, and thusly, carrying our whole nation back to those great wells of democracy which were dug deep by the Founding Fathers in the formulation of the Constitution and the Declaration of Independence.

### QUESTIONS FOR READING AND DISCUSSION

1. In what ways did segregation generate a "sense of 'nobodiness'" and "a false sense of superiority"? Why?
2. King distinguished between just and unjust laws. How could one tell whether segregation was just or unjust? What was the difference between "civil disobedience" and criminal activity? Why did it express "the very highest respect for law"?
3. Why did white moderates disappoint King? What historical and religious examples did he invoke as admirable? Would white moderates have found King's arguments persuasive? Why or why not?
4. Where did King position himself and his followers along the spectrum of black society? What alternatives to nonviolence were advocated by others? Why did he gain "a bit of satisfaction from being considered an extremist"?
5. King intended to reach an audience far beyond Birmingham with his letter. What groups did he hope to appeal to with his arguments, and why were they important to the civil rights movement?

## DOCUMENT 28-3
# Black Power

*To some activists, the doctrines of nonviolence seemed self-defeating and dangerous. The violence that civil rights demonstrators repeatedly suffered convinced many younger activists that the strength of white racism made racial integration hopeless. In 1967, the Chicago office of the Student Non-Violent Coordinating Committee (SNCC) published a manifesto calling for black power. The SNCC leaflet, excerpted here, embodied ideas that appealed to many African Americans and other activists in the later 1960s.*

## Chicago Student Non-Violent Coordinating Committee Leaflet, 1967

### Black Men of America Are a Captive People

The black man in America is in a perpetual state of slavery no matter what the white man's propaganda tells us.

The black man in America is exploited and oppressed the same as his black brothers are all over the face of the earth by the same white man. . . .

---

Chicago Office of SNCC, *We Want Black Power* (1967); reprinted in *Black Protest Thought in the Twentieth Century,* 2d ed. eds., August Meier, Elliott Rudwick, and Frances L. Broderick (Indianapolis: Bobbs-Merrill, 1971), 484–90.

We are not alone in this fight, we are a part of the struggle for self-determination of all black men everywhere. We here in America must unite ourselves to be ready to help our brothers elsewhere.

We must first gain BLACK POWER here in America. Living inside the camp of the leaders of the enemy forces, it is our duty to our Brothers to revolt against the system and create our own system so that we can live as MEN.

We must take over the political and economic systems where we are in the majority in the heart of every major city in this country as well as in the rural areas. We must create our own black culture to erase the lies the white man has fed our minds from the day we were born.

## The Black Man in the Ghetto Will Lead the Black Power Movement

The black Brother in the ghetto will lead the Black Power Movement and make the changes that are necessary for its success.

The black man in the ghetto has one big advantage that the bourgeois Negro does not have despite his "superior" education. He is already living outside the value system white society imposes on all black Americans.

He has to look at things from another direction in order to survive. He is ready. He received his training in the streets, in the jails, from the ADC[1] check his mother did not receive in time and the head-beatings he got from the cop on the corner.

Once he makes that first important discovery about the great pride you feel inside as a BLACK MAN and the great heritage of the mother country, Africa, there is no stopping him from dedicating himself to fight the white man's system.

This is why the Black Power Movement is a true revolutionary movement with the power to change men's minds and unmask the tricks the white man has used to keep black men enslaved in modern society.

## The Bourgeois Negro Cannot be a Part of the Black Power Movement

The bourgeois Negro has been force-fed the white man's propaganda and has lived too long in the half-world between white and phony black bourgeois society. He cannot think for himself because be is a shell of a man full of contradictions he cannot resolve. He is not to be trusted under any circumstances until he has proved himself to be "cured." There are a minute handful of these "cured" bourgeois Negroes in the Black Power Movement and they are most valuable but they must not be allowed to take control. They are aware intellectually but under stress will react emotionally to the pressures of white society in the same way a white "liberal" will expose an unconscious prejudice that he did not even realize he possessed.

## What Brother Malcolm X Taught Us about Ourselves

Malcolm X was the first black man from the ghetto in America to make a real attempt to get the white man's fist off the black man. He recognized the true dignity of man — without the white society prejudices about status, education and background that we all must purge from our minds.

Even today, in the Black Power Movement itself we find Brothers who look

---

[1]**ADC:** Aid to Families with Dependent Children.

down on another Brother because of the conditions that life has imposed upon him. The most beautiful thing that Malcolm X taught us is that once a black man discovers for himself a pride of his blackness, he can throw off the shackles of mental slavery and become a MAN in the truest sense of the word. We must move on from the point our Great Black Prince had reached.

### We Must Become Leaders for Ourselves

We must not get hung-up in the bag of having one great leader who we depend upon to make decisions. This makes the Movement too vulnerable to those forces the white man uses to keep us enslaved, such as the draft, murder, prison or character assassination.

We have to all learn to become leaders for ourselves and remove all white values from our minds. When we see a Brother using a white value through error it is our duty to the Movement to point it out to him. We must thank our Brothers who show us our own errors. We must discipline ourselves so that if necessary we can leave family and friends at a moment's notice, maybe forever, and know our Brothers have pledged themselves to protect the family we have left behind.

As a part of our education, we must travel to other cities and make contracts with the Brothers in all the ghettos in America so that when the time is right we can unite as one under the banner of BLACK POWER.

### Learning to Think Black and Remove White Things from Our Minds

We have got to begin to say and understand with complete assuredness what black is. Black is an inner pride that the white man's language hampers us from expressing. Black is being a complete fanatic, who white society considers insane. We have to learn that black is so much better than belonging to the white race with the blood of millions dripping from their hands that it goes far beyond any prejudice or resentment. We must fill ourselves with hate for all white things. This is not vengeance or trying to take the white oppressors' place to become new black oppressors but is a oneness with a worldwide black brotherhood.

We must regain respect for the lost religion of our fathers, the spirits of the black earth of Africa. The white man has so poisoned our minds that if a Brother told you he practiced Voodoo you would roll around on the floor laughing at how stupid and superstitious be was.

We have to learn to roll around on the floor laughing at the black man who says he worships the white Jesus. He is truly sick.

We must create our own language for these things that the white man will not understand because a Black Culture exists and it is not the wood-carvings or native dancing it is the black strength inside of true men.

### Ideas on Planning for the Future of Black Power

We must infiltrate all government agencies. This will not be hard because black clerks work in all agencies in poor paying jobs and have a natural resentment of the white men who run these jobs.

People must be assigned to seek out these dissatisfied black men and women and put pressure on them to give us the information we need. Any man in overalls, carrying a tool box, can enter a building if he looks like he knows what he is doing.

Modern America depends on many complex systems such as electricity, water, gas, sewerage and transportation and all are vulnerable. Much of the government is run by computers that must operate in air conditioning. Cut off the air conditioning and they cannot function.

We must begin to investigate and learn all of these things so that we can use them if it becomes necessary. We cannot train an army in the local park but we can be ready for the final confrontation with the white man's system.

Remember your Brothers in South Africa and do not delude yourselves that it could not happen here. We must copy the white man's biggest trick, diversion, (Hitler taught them that) and infiltrate all civil rights groups, keep them in confusion so they will be neutralized and cannot be used as a tool of the white power structure.

The civil rights, integrationist movement says to the white man, "If you please, Sir, let us, the 10 percent minority of American have our rights. See how nice and nonviolent we are?"

This is why SNCC calls itself a Human Rights Organization. We believe that we belong to the 90 percent majority of the people on earth that the white man oppresses and that we should not beg the white man for anything. We want what belongs to us as human beings and we intend to get it through BLACK POWER.

## How to Deal with Black Traitors

Uncle Tom is too kind of a word. What we have are black traitors, quisslings, collaborators, sell-outs, white Negroes.

We have to expose these people for once and for all for what they are and place them on the side of the oppressor where they belong. Their black skin is a lie and their guilt the shame of all black men. We must ostracize them and if necessary exterminate them.

We must stop fighting a "fair game." We must do whatever is necessary to win BLACK POWER. We have to hate and disrupt and destroy and blackmail and lie and steal and become blood-brothers like the Mau-Mau.[2]

We must eliminate or render ineffective all traitors. We must make them fear to stand up like puppets for the white men, and we must make the world understand that these so-called men do not represent us or even belong to the same black race because they sold out their birthright for a mess of white society pottage. Let them choke on it.

## Pitfalls to Avoid on the Path to Black Power

We must learn how close America and Russia are politically. The biggest lie in the world is the cold-war. Money runs the world and it is controlled completely by the white man.

Russia and America run the two biggest money systems in the world and they intend to keep it under their control under any circumstances. Thus, we cannot except any help from Communism or any other "ism."

We must seek out poor peoples movements in South America, Africa and Asia and make our alliances with them. We must not be fooled into thinking that there is a ready-made doctrine that will solve all our problems.

There are only white man's doctrines and they will never work for us. We have to work out our own systems and doctrines and culture.

---

[2]**Mau-Mau:** A revolutionary tribal society in Kenya in the 1950s that engaged in terrorism in an effort to rid the country of Europeans.

### Why Propaganda is Our Most Important Tool

The one thing that the white man's system cannot stand is the TRUTH because his system is all based on lies.

There is no such thing as "justice" for a black man in America. The white man controls everything that is said in every book, newspaper, magazine, TV and radio broadcast.

Even the textbooks used in the schools and the bible that is read in the churches are designed to maintain the system for the white man. Each and every one of us is forced to listen to the white man's propaganda every day of our lives.

The political system, economic system, military system, educational system, religious system and anything else you name is used to preserve the status quo of white America getting fatter and fatter while the black man gets more and more hungry.

We must spend our time telling our Brothers the truth.

We must tell them that any black woman who wears a diamond on her finger is wearing the blood of her Brothers and Sisters in slavery in South Africa where one out of every three black babies die before the age of one, from starvation, to make the white man rich.

We must stop wearing the symbols of slavery on our fingers.

We must stop going to other countries to exterminate our Brothers and Sisters for the white man's greed.

We must ask our Brothers which side they are on.

Once you know the truth for yourself it is your duty to dedicate your life to recruiting your Brothers and to counteract the white man's propaganda.

We must disrupt the white man's system to create our own, We must publish newspapers and get radio stations. Black Unity is strength — let's use it now to get BLACK POWER.

#### QUESTIONS FOR READING AND DISCUSSION

1. According to this Chicago SNCC leaflet, why was "the Black Power Movement" a "true revolutionary movement"? What tactics would bring about the revolution?

2. Who was the Great Black Prince, and what did he teach? How did his teachings differ from nonviolence? Why? Who were black power's most important allies? Why?

3. What "white things" should be hated? Why was it necessary to be "a complete fanatic"? How did "white things" differ from "Black Culture"?

4. This SNCC document repeatedly declares the importance of black men. Where did women fit into the goals and tactics of the black power movement? Was the emphasis on men significant? If so, why?

## DOCUMENT 28-4

# Equal Rights for Women

*Justice and equality for women had far-reaching implications for social change. In 1966, the newly formed National Organization for Women adopted a statement of purpose — excerpted here — that identified the changes demanded by women's rights activists. The statement, drafted by feminist leader Betty Friedan, revealed the concerns of many American women in the 1960s.*

## National Organization for Women
## *Statement of Purpose,* October 29, 1966

We, men and women who hereby constitute ourselves as the National Organization for Women, believe that the time has come for a new movement toward true equality for all women in America, and toward a fully equal partnership of the sexes, as part of the world-wide revolution of human rights now taking place within and beyond our national borders.

The purpose of NOW is to take action to bring women into full participation in the mainstream of American society now, exercising all the privileges and responsibilities thereof in truly equal partnership with men.

We believe the time has come to move beyond the abstract argument, discussion and symposia over the status and special nature of women which has raged in America in recent years; the time has come to confront, with concrete action, the conditions that now prevent women from enjoying the equality of opportunity and freedom of choice which is their right as individual Americans, and as human beings.

NOW is dedicated to the proposition that women first and foremost are human beings, who, like all other people in our society, must have the chance to develop their fullest human potential. We believe that women can achieve such equality only by accepting to the full the challenges and responsibilities they share with all other people in our society, as part of the decision-making mainstream of American political, economic and social life.

We organize to initiate or support action, nationally or in any part of this nation, by individuals or organizations, to break through the silken curtain of prejudice and discrimination against women in government, industry, the professions, the churches, the political parties, the judiciary, the labor unions, in education, science, medicine, law, religion and every other field of importance in American society.

Enormous changes taking place in our society make it both possible and urgently necessary to advance the unfinished revolution of women toward true equality, now. With life span lengthened to nearly seventy-five years it is no longer either necessary or possible for women to devote the greater part of their lives to child-rearing; yet childbearing and rearing — which continues to be a most important part of most women's lives — still is used to justify barring women from equal professional and economic participation and advance.

Today's technology has reduced most of the productive chores which women once performed in the home and in mass-production industries based upon routine unskilled labor. This same technology has virtually eliminated the quality of muscular strength as a criterion for filling most jobs, while intensifying America's need for creative intelligence. In view of this new industrial revolution created by

*National Organization for Women Statement of Purpose;* reprinted in Betty Friedan, *It Changed My Life: Writings on the Women's Movement* (New York: Random House, 1976), 96–102.

automation in the mid-twentieth century, women can and must participate in old and new fields of society in full equality — or become permanent outsiders. . . .

There is no civil rights movement to speak for women, as there has been for Negroes and other victims of discrimination. The National Organization for Women must therefore begin to speak.

WE BELIEVE that the power of American law, and the protection guaranteed by the U.S. Constitution to the civil rights of all individuals, must be effectively applied and enforced to isolate and remove patterns of sex discrimination, to ensure equality of opportunity in employment and education, and equality of civil and political rights and responsibilities on behalf of women, as well as for Negroes and other deprived groups.

We realize that women's problems are linked to many broader questions of social justice; their solution will require concerted action by many groups. Therefore, convinced that human rights for all are indivisible, we expect to give active support to the common cause of equal rights for all those who suffer discrimination and deprivation, and we call upon other organizations committed to such goals to support our efforts toward equality for women.

WE DO NOT ACCEPT the token appointment of a few women to high-level positions in government and industry as a substitute for a serious continuing effort to recruit and advance women according to their individual abilities. To this end, we urge American government and industry to mobilize the same resources of ingenuity and command with which they have solved problems of far greater difficulty than those now impeding the progress of women.

WE BELIEVE that this nation has a capacity at least as great as other nations, to innovate new social institutions which will enable women to enjoy true equality of opportunity and responsibility in society, without conflict with their responsibilities as mothers and homemakers. In such innovations, America does not lead the Western world, but lags by decades behind many European countries. We do not accept the traditional assumption that a woman has to choose between marriage and motherhood, on the one hand, and serious participation in industry or the professions on the other. We question the present expectation that all normal women will retire from job or profession for ten or fifteen years, to devote their full time to raising children, only to reenter the job market at a relatively minor level. This in itself is a deterrent to the aspirations of women, to their acceptance into management or professional training courses, and to the very possibility of equality of opportunity or real choice, for all but a few women. Above all, we reject the assumption that these problems are the unique responsibility of each individual woman, rather than a basic social dilemma which society must solve. True equality of opportunity and freedom of choice for women requires such practical and possible innovations as a nationwide network of child-care centers, which will make it unnecessary for women to retire completely from society until their children are grown, and national programs to provide retraining for women who have chosen to care for their own children full time.

WE BELIEVE that it is as essential for every girl to be educated to her full potential of human ability as it is for every boy — with the knowledge that such education is the key to effective participation in today's economy and that, for a girl as for a boy, education can only be serious where there is expectation that it will be used in society. We believe that American educators are capable of devising means of imparting such expectations to girl students. Moreover, we consider the decline in the proportion of women receiving higher and professional education to be evidence of discrimination. This discrimination may take the form of quotas against the admission of women to colleges and professional schools; lack of encouragement by parents, counselors and educators; denial of loans or fellowships; or the traditional or arbitrary procedures in graduate and professional training geared in terms of men, which inadvertently discriminate against women. We believe that the same serious attention must be given to high school dropouts who are girls as to boys.

WE REJECT the current assumptions that a man must carry the sole burden of supporting himself, his wife, and family, and that a woman is automatically entitled to lifelong support by a man upon her marriage, or that marriage, home and family are primarily woman's world and responsibility — hers, to dominate, his to support. We believe that a true partnership between the sexes demands a different concept of marriage, an equitable sharing of the responsibilities of home and children and of the economic burdens of their support. We believe that proper recognition should be given to the economic and social value of homemaking and child care. To these ends, we will seek to open a reexamination of laws and mores governing marriage and divorce, for we believe that the current state of "half-equality" between the sexes discriminates against both men and women, and is the cause of much unnecessary hostility between the sexes.

WE BELIEVE that women must now exercise their political rights and responsibilities as American citizens. They must refuse to be segregated on the basis of sex into separate-and-not-equal ladies' auxiliaries in the political parties, and they must demand representation according to their numbers in the regularly constituted party committees — at local, state, and national levels — and in the informal power structure, participating fully in the selection of candidates and political decision-making, and running for office themselves.

IN THE INTERESTS OF THE HUMAN DIGNITY OF WOMEN, we will protest and endeavor to change the false image of women now prevalent in the mass media, and in the texts, ceremonies, laws, and practices of our major social institutions. Such images perpetuate contempt for women by society and by women for themselves. We are similarly opposed to all policies and practices — in church, state, college, factory, or office — which, in the guise of protectiveness, not only deny opportunities but also foster in women self-denigration, dependence, and evasion of responsibility, undermine their confidence in their own abilities and foster contempt for women.

NOW WILL HOLD ITSELF INDEPENDENT OF ANY POLITICAL PARTY in order to mobilize the political power of all women and men intent on our goals. We will strive to ensure that no party, candidate, President, senator, governor, congressman, or any public official who betrays or ignores the principle of full equality between the sexes is elected or appointed to office. If it is necessary to mobilize the votes of men and women who believe in our cause, in order to win for women the final right to be fully free and equal human beings, we so commit ourselves.

WE BELIEVE THAT women will do most to create a new image of women by acting now, and by speaking out in behalf of their own equality, freedom, and human dignity — not in pleas for special privilege, nor in enmity toward men, who are also victims of the current half-equality between the sexes — but in an active, self-respecting partnership with men. By so doing, women will develop confidence in their own ability to determine actively, in partnership with men, the conditions of their life, their choices, their future and their society.

QUESTIONS FOR READING AND DISCUSSION

1. Why did NOW reject the assumption that the solution to the inequality of women was "the unique responsibility of each individual woman, rather than a basic social dilemma"?

2. What social changes permitted advancing the "unfinished revolution"?

3. What goals did NOW seek, and what tactics did they intend to use? Who did they consider allies and enemies? What were the major barriers to achieving their goals?

4. How might men benefit if NOW's goals were realized?

## DOCUMENT 28-5

# Long Hot Summers of Urban Riots

*After Lyndon Johnson became president, riots repeatedly erupted in American cities creating numerous casualties, great property damage, and deep fears about civil disorder. Johnson appointed the Kerner Commission to study the causes of the urban riots. The commission's long report, excerpted below, reflected the thinking of many Americans that the "nation is moving toward two societies, one black, one white — separate and unequal." The assassination of Martin Luther King Jr. in Memphis in 1968, shortly after the release of the Kerner Commission report, caused riots in more than one hundred cities, including Washington, D.C. The commission report expressed the views of many people that the urban riots were caused by American society's deep-seated racial problems rather than, as critics argued, by dangerous criminals and soft-hearted, irresolute government officials.*

## The Kerner Commission Report on Civil Disorders, 1968

The summer of 1967 again brought racial disorders to American cities, and with them shock, fear and bewilderment to the nation.

The worst came during a two-week period in July, first in Newark and then in Detroit. Each set off a chain reaction in neighboring communities.

On July 28, 1967, the President of the United States established this Commission and directed us to answer three basic questions:

What happened? Why did it happen? What can be done to prevent it from happening again?

To respond to these questions, we have undertaken a broad range of studies and investigations. We have visited the riot cities; we have heard many witnesses; we have sought the counsel of experts across the country.

This is our basic conclusion: Our nation is moving toward two societies, one black, one white — separate and unequal.

Reaction to last summer's disorders has quickened the movement and deepened the division. Discrimination and segregation have long permeated much of American life; they now threaten the future of every American.

---

*Kerner Commission,* Report of the National Advisory Commission on Civil Disorders *(Washington, D.C.: U.S. Government Printing Office, 1968).*

This deepening racial division is not inevitable. The movement apart can be reversed. Choice is still possible. Our principal task is to define that choice and to press for a national resolution.

To pursue our present course will involve the continuing polarization of the American community and, ultimately, the destruction of basic democratic values.

The alternative is not blind repression or capitulation to lawlessness. It is the realization of common opportunities for all within a single society.

This alternative will require a commitment to national action — compassionate, massive and sustained, backed by the resources of the most powerful and the richest nation on this earth. From every American it will require new attitudes, new understanding, and, above all, new will.

The vital needs of the nation must be met; hard choices must be made, and, if necessary, new taxes enacted.

Violence cannot build a better society. Disruption and disorder nourish repression, not justice. They strike at the freedom of every citizen. The community cannot — it will not — tolerate coercion and mob rule.

Violence and destruction must be ended — in the streets of the ghetto and in the lives of people.

Segregation and poverty have created in the racial ghetto a destructive environment totally unknown to most white Americans.

What white Americans have never fully understood — but what the Negro can never forget — is that white society is deeply implicated in the ghetto. White institutions created it, white institutions maintain it, and white society condones it. . . .

It is time to make good the promises of American democracy to all citizens — urban and rural, white and black, Spanish-surname, American Indian, and every minority group. . . .

There can be no higher priority for national action and no higher claim on the nation's conscience. . . .

## Patterns of Disorder

The "typical" riot did not take place. The disorders of 1967 were unusual, irregular, complex and unpredictable social processes. Like most human events, they did not unfold in an orderly sequence. However, an analysis of our survey information leads to some conclusions about the riot process.
In general:

The civil disorders of 1967 involved Negroes acting against local symbols of white American society, authority and property in Negro neighborhoods — rather than against white persons.

Of 164 disorders reported during the first nine months of 1967, eight (5 percent) were major in terms of violence and damage; 33 (20 percent) were serious but not major; 123 (75 percent) were minor and undoubtedly would not have received national attention as "riots" had the nation not been sensitized by the more serious outbreaks.

In the 75 disorders studied by a Senate subcommittee, 83 deaths were reported. Eighty-two percent of the deaths and more than half the injuries occurred in Newark and Detroit. About 10 percent of the dead and 38 percent of the injured were public employees, primarily law officers and firemen. The overwhelming majority of the persons killed or injured in all the disorders were Negro civilians.

Initial damage estimates were greatly exaggerated. In Detroit, newspaper damage estimates at first ranged from $200 million to $500 million; the highest recent estimate is $45 million. In Newark, early estimates ranged from $15 to $25 million. A month later damage was estimated at $10.2 million, over 80 percent in inventory losses.

In the 24 disorders in 23 cities which we surveyed:

The final incident before the outbreak of disorder, and the initial violence itself, generally took place in the evening or at night at a place in which it was normal for many people to be on the streets.

Violence usually occurred almost immediately following the occurrence of the final precipitating incident, and then escalated rapidly. With but few exceptions, violence subsided during the day, and flared rapidly again at night. The night-day cycles continued through the early period of the major disorders.

Disorder generally began with rock and bottle throwing and window breaking. Once store windows were broken, looting usually followed.

Disorder did not erupt as a result of a single "triggering" or "precipitating" incident. Instead, it was generated out of an increasingly disturbed social atmosphere, in which typically a series of tension-heightening incidents over a period of weeks or months became linked in the minds of many in the Negro community with a reservoir of underlying grievances. At some point in the mounting tension, a further incident — in itself often routine or trivial — became the breaking point and the tension spilled over into violence. . . .

The typical rioter was a teenager or young adult, a lifelong resident of the city in which he rioted, a high school dropout; he was, nevertheless, somewhat better educated than his nonrioting Negro neighbor, and was usually underemployed or employed in a menial job. He was proud of his race, extremely hostile to both whites and middle-class Negroes and, although informed about politics, highly distrustful of the political system.

A Detroit survey revealed that approximately 11 percent of the total residents of two riot areas admitted participation in the rioting, 20 to 25 percent identified themselves as "bystanders," over 16 percent identified themselves as "counter-rioters" who urged rioters to "cool it," and the remaining 48 to 53 percent said they were at home or elsewhere and did not participate. In a survey of Negro males between the ages of 15 and 35 residing in the disturbance area in Newark, about 45 percent identified themselves as rioters, and about 55 percent as "noninvolved."

Most rioters were young Negro males. Nearly 53 percent of arrestees were between 15 and 24 years of age; nearly 81 percent between 15 and 35.

In Detroit and Newark about 74 percent of the rioters were brought up in the North. In contrast, of the noninvolved, 36 percent in Detroit and 52 percent in Newark were brought up in the North.

What the rioters appeared to be seeking was fuller participation in the social order and the material benefits enjoyed by the majority of American citizens. Rather than rejecting the American system, they were anxious to obtain a place for themselves in it.

Numerous Negro counter-rioters walked the streets urging rioters to "cool it." The typical counter-rioter was better educated and had higher income than either the rioter or the noninvolved.

The proportion of Negroes in local government was substantially smaller than the Negro proportion of population. Only three of the 20 cities studied had more than one Negro legislator; none had ever had a Negro mayor or city manager. In only four cities did Negroes hold other important policy-making positions or serve as heads of municipal departments.

Although almost all cities had some sort of formal grievance mechanism for handling citizen complaints, this typically was regarded by Negroes as ineffective and was generally ignored. . . .

The background of disorder is often as complex and difficult to analyze as the disorder itself. But we find that certain general conclusions can be drawn:

Social and economic conditions in the riot cities constituted a clear pattern of severe disadvantage for Negroes compared with whites, whether the Negroes lived in the area where the riot took place or outside it. Negroes had completed fewer years of education and fewer had attended high school. Negroes were twice as likely to be unemployed and three times as likely to be in unskilled and service jobs. Negroes averaged 70 percent of the income earned by whites and were more than twice as likely to be living in poverty. Although housing cost Negroes relatively more, they had worse housing — three times as likely to be overcrowded and substandard. When compared to white suburbs, the relative disadvantage is even more pronounced. . . .

## The Basic Causes

In addressing the question "Why did it happen?" we shift our focus from the local to the national scene, from the particular events of the summer of 1967 to the factors within the society at large that created a mood of violence among many urban Negroes.

These factors are complex and interacting; they vary significantly in their effect from city to city and from year to year; and the consequences of one disorder, generating new grievances and new demands, become the causes of the next. . . .

Despite these complexities, certain fundamental matters are clear. Of these, the most fundamental is the racial attitude and behavior of white Americans toward black Americans.

Race prejudice has shaped our history decisively; it now threatens to affect our future.

White racism is essentially responsible for the explosive mixture which has been accumulating in our cities since the end of World War II. Among the ingredients of this mixture are:

*Pervasive discrimination and segregation* in employment, education and housing, which have resulted in the continuing exclusion of great numbers of Negroes from the benefits of economic progress.

*Black in-migration and white exodus,* which have produced the massive and growing concentrations of impoverished Negroes in our major cities, creating a growing crisis of deteriorating facilities and services and unmet human needs.

*The black ghettos* where segregation and poverty converge on the young to destroy opportunity and enforce failure. Crime, drug addiction, dependency on welfare, and bitterness and resentment against society in general and white society in particular are the result.

At the same time, most whites and some Negroes outside the ghetto have prospered to a degree unparalleled in the history of civilization. Through television and other media, this affluence has been flaunted before the eyes of the Negro poor and the jobless ghetto youth.

Yet these facts alone cannot be said to have caused the disorders. Recently, other powerful ingredients have begun to catalyze the mixture:

*Frustrated hopes* are the residue of the unfulfilled expectations aroused by the great judicial and legislative victories of the Civil Rights Movement and the dramatic struggle for equal rights in the South.

*A climate that tends toward approval and encouragement of violence* as a form of protest has been created by white terrorism directed against nonviolent protest; by the open defiance of law and federal authority by state and local officials resisting desegregation; and by some protest groups engaging in civil disobedience who turn their backs on nonviolence, go beyond the constitutionally protected rights of petition and free assembly, and resort to violence to attempt to compel alteration of laws and policies with which they disagree.

*The frustrations of powerlessness* have led some Negroes to the conviction that there is no effective alternative to violence as a means of achieving redress of grievances, and of "moving the system." These frustrations are reflected in alienation and hostility toward the institutions of law and government and the white society which controls them, and in the reach toward racial consciousness and solidarity reflected in the slogan "Black Power."

*A new mood* has sprung up among Negroes, particularly among the young, in which self-esteem and enhanced racial pride are replacing apathy and submission to "the system."

*The police are not merely a "spark" factor.* To some Negroes police have come to symbolize white power, white racism and white repression. And the fact is that many police do reflect and express these white attitudes. The atmosphere of hostility and cynicism is reinforced by a widespread belief among Negroes in the existence of police brutality and in a "double standard" of justice and protection — one for Negroes and one for whites.

## QUESTIONS FOR READING AND DISCUSSION

1. According to the Kerner Commission, why did the urban riots occur? Why did the commission believe, "Our nation is moving toward two societies, one black, one white — separate and unequal." In what ways did they think that trend contributed to the riots? Did the commission's statement that "White racism is essentially responsible for the explosive mixture which has been accumulating in our cities since the end of World War II" mean that white people caused the riots?

2. According to the commission, were the riots criminal acts? If so, who were the criminals? If not, why not?

3. To what extent did the civil rights movement influence the riots? How did "self-esteem and enhanced racial pride" contribute to the riots, according to the commission?

4. How might police, judges, or rioters have responded to the commission's report? To what extent did the commission examine the responsibility of individuals for the riots?

5. What were the political consequences of the riots and the commission report? To what extent did the commission's analysis of the riots change government policies?

COMPARATIVE QUESTIONS

1. To what extent were Lyndon B. Johnson's aspirations for the Great Society compatible with the goals of Martin Luther King Jr., the Chicago SNCC, and NOW?

2. Judging from the documents in this chapter, how would King have responded to the arguments for black power and to the Kerner Commission report? How and why did the arguments of the advocates of black power differ from King's analysis and from the Kerner Commission report?

3. In what ways did NOW's call for the reeducation of women compare with the SNCC's advocacy of black culture or King's belief in nonviolence?

4. Each of the documents in this chapter makes assumptions about the state of American society and what it means to be an American. To what extent do the documents agree and disagree about these matters? Each document called for changes in the state of American society. Did the documents also advocate changes in what it meant to be an American? If so, what changes did they seek? Why?

# CHAPTER 29

# VIETNAM AND THE LIMITS OF POWER
## 1961–1975

T he war in Vietnam began almost unnoticed by most Americans, but by the mid-1960s it had become the dominating fact of American political life. American views of the war conflicted profoundly. Presidents justified American involvement in Vietnam in public speeches and private letters. Policymakers tried to devise a military strategy that would also win political support for the war effort. Generals grappled with the complexities of a guerrilla conflict. Officers struggled with maintaining military discipline in an unpopular war. Soldiers encountered the horrifying realities of combat. The following documents illustrate the vantage points of President John F. Kennedy, Secretary of Defense Robert McNamara, and the commanding general in Vietnam, William Westmoreland, as well as of officers and soldiers in the field and Americans at home.

### DOCUMENT 29-1
## *President Kennedy Explains Why We Are in Vietnam*

*Many Americans wondered why the United States had soldiers in Vietnam, and the question became more pointed as more and more soldiers were killed and wounded in the line of duty. The following correspondence between the sister of an American helicopter pilot killed in Vietnam and President John F. Kennedy illustrates the questions asked by many ordinary Americans and the responses of government officials. The correspondence highlights the very personal costs of the conflict in Vietnam that had to be weighed against the abstract and long-term rewards that officials claimed would result from American involvement.*

## Bobbie Lou Pendergrass
### *Letter to President John F. Kennedy,* **February 18, 1963**

Dear President Kennedy,

My brother, Specialist James Delmas McAndrew, was one of the seven crew members killed on January 11 in a Viet Nam helicopter crash.

The Army reports at first said that communist gunfire was suspected. Later, it said that the helicopter tragedy was due to malfunction of aircraft controls. I've wondered if the "malfunction of aircraft controls" wasn't due to "communist gunfire." However, that's neither important now, nor do I even care to know.

My two older brothers entered the Navy and the Marine Corps in 1941 immediately after the war started. They served all during the war and in some very important battles. Then Jim went into the Marines as soon as he was old enough and was overseas for a long time. During those war years and even all during the Korean conflict we worried about all of them — but that was all very different. They were wars that our <u>country</u> were fighting, and everyone here <u>knew</u> that our sons and brothers were giving their lives for their country.

I can't help but feel that giving one's life for one's country is one thing, but being sent to a country where half <u>our</u> country never even <u>heard</u> of and being shot at without even a chance to shoot back is another thing altogether!

Please, I'm only a housewife who doesn't even claim to know all about the international situation — but we have felt so bitter over this — can the small number of our boys over in Vietnam possibly be doing enough good to justify the <u>aw-ful</u> number of casualties? It seems to me that if we are going to have our boys over there, that we should send enough to have a <u>chance</u> — or else stay home. Those fellows are just sitting <u>ducks</u> in those darn helicopters. If a war is worth fighting — isn't it worth fighting to <u>win</u>?

Please answer this and help me and my family to reconcile ourselves to our loss and to feel that even though Jim died in Viet Nam — and it isn't our war — it wasn't in vain.

I am a good Democrat — and I'm not criticizing. I think you are doing a wonderful job — and God Bless You —

Very sincerely,
Bobbie Lou Pendergrass

## President John F. Kennedy
### *Letter to Bobbie Lou Pendergrass,* **March 6, 1963**

Dear Mrs. Pendergrass,

I would like to express to you my deep and sincere sympathy in the loss of your brother. I can, of course, well understand your bereavement and the feelings which prompted you to write.

The questions which you posed in your letter can, I believe, best be answered by realizing why your brother — and other American men — went to Viet Nam

Andrew Carroll, ed., *War Letters: Extraordinary Correspondence from American Wars* (New York: Washington Square Press, 2001), 391–93.

in the first place. When this is understood, I am sure that the other related questions will be answered.

Americans are in Viet Nam because we have determined that this country must not fall under Communist domination. Ever since Viet Nam was divided, the Viet Namese have fought valiantly to maintain their independence in the face of the continuing threat from the North. Shortly after the division eight years ago it became apparent that they could not be successful in their defense without extensive assistance from other nations of the Free World community.

In the late summer of 1955, with the approval of President Eisenhower, an Advisory group was established in Viet Nam to provide them with adequate weapons and equipment and training in basic military skills which are essential to survival in the battlefield. Even with this help, the situation grew steadily worse under the pressure of the Viet Cong. By 1961 it became apparent that the troubles in Laos and the troubles in Viet Nam could easily expand. It is also apparent that the Communist attempt to take over Viet Nam, is only part of a larger plan for bringing the entire area of Southeast Asia under their domination. Though it is only a small part of the area geographically, Viet Nam is the most crucial.

If Viet Nam should fall, it will indicate to the people of Southeast Asia that complete Communist domination of their part of the world is almost inevitable. Your brother was in Viet Nam because the threat to the Viet Namese people is, in the long run, a threat to the Free World community, and ultimately a threat to us also. For when freedom is destroyed in one country, it is threatened throughout the world.

I have written to you at length because I know that it is important to you to understand why we are in Viet Nam. James McAndrew must have foreseen that his service could take him into a war like this; a war in which he took part not as a combatant but as an advisor. I am sure that he understood the necessity of such a situation, and I know that as a soldier, he knew full scale war in Viet Nam is at the moment unthinkable.

I believe if you can see this as he must have seen it, you will believe as he must have believed, that he did not die in vain. Forty-five American soldiers, including your brother, have given their lives in Viet Nam. In their sacrifice, they have earned the eternal gratitude of this Nation and other free men throughout the world.

Again, I would like to express to you and the members of your family my deepest personal sympathy.

Sincerely,
John F. Kennedy

## QUESTIONS FOR READING AND DISCUSSION

1. Which of Bobbie Lou Pendergrass's questions did President Kennedy address and which ones did he ignore or avoid?

2. When Kennedy stated that, "Americans are in Viet Nam because we have determined that this country must not fall under Communist domination," what did he mean by "we have determined"? Who determined what and how? Did Pendergrass consider herself or her brother a participant in such a determination?

3. According to Kennedy, why were Pendergrass's brother and other U.S. "advisors" in Vietnam? How did Kennedy balance the ultimate "threat to us" in Vietnam against the personal loss of James McAndrew and his family?

4. Did Kennedy's statement that, "when freedom is destroyed in one country, it is threatened throughout the world" respond adequately to Pendergrass's comment that, "it isn't our war"?

## DOCUMENT 29-2

# A Secret Government Assessment of the Vietnam War

*Policymakers in Washington, D.C., directed the military operations of the Vietnam War more closely than any previous war in American history. Advanced technology made it possible for politicians and generals to communicate readily and to gather and analyze vast quantities of information. The political sensitivity of the war made that communication necessary. In October 1966, Secretary of Defense Robert S. McNamara drafted a secret memorandum for President Lyndon B. Johnson about the current status of the war in Vietnam. McNamara's memorandum, excerpted here, expressed the misgivings of one of the most influential political managers of the war — misgivings that remained confined to secret documents until the leaking of and subsequent publication of* The Pentagon Papers *in 1971.*

## Robert S. McNamara

### Actions Recommended for Vietnam, October 14, 1966

#### 1. Evaluation of the Situation.

In the report of my last trip to Vietnam almost a year ago, I stated that the odds were about even that, even with the then-recommended deployments, we would be faced in early 1967 with a military stand-off at a much higher level of conflict and with "pacification" still stalled. I am a little less pessimistic now in one respect. We have done somewhat better militarily than I anticipated. We have by and large blunted the communist military initiative — any military victory in South Vietnam the Viet Cong [VC] may have had in mind 18 months ago has been thwarted by our emergency deployments and actions. And our program of bombing the North has exacted a price.

My concern continues, however, in other respects. This is because I see no reasonable way to bring the war to an end soon. Enemy morale has not broken — he apparently has adjusted to our stopping his drive for military victory and has adopted a strategy of keeping us busy and waiting us out (a strategy of attriting our national will). He knows that we have not been, and he believes we probably will not be, able to translate our military successes into the "end products" — broken enemy morale and political achievements by the GVN [government of Vietnam].

The one thing demonstrably going for us in Vietnam over the past year has been the large number of enemy killed-in-action resulting from the big military operations. Allowing for possible exaggeration in reports, the enemy must be taking losses — deaths in and after battle — at the rate of more than 60,000 a year.

Robert S. McNamara, "Actions Recommended for Vietnam," October 14, 1966; reprinted in *The Pentagon Papers*, ed. George C. Herring (New York: McGraw Hill, 1971), 554–72.

The infiltration routes would seem to be one-way trails to death for the North Vietnamese. Yet there is no sign of an impending break in enemy morale and it appears that he can more than replace his losses by infiltration from North Vietnam and recruitment in South Vietnam.

Pacification is a bad disappointment. We have good grounds to be pleased by the recent elections, by Ky's[1] 16 months in power, and by the faint signs of development of national political institutions and of a legitimate civil government. But none of this has translated itself into political achievements at Province level or below. Pacification has if anything gone backward. As compared with two, or four, years ago, enemy full-time regional forces and part-time guerrilla forces are larger; attacks, terrorism and sabotage have increased in scope and intensity; more railroads are closed and highways cut; the rice crop expected to come to market is smaller; we control little, if any, more of the population; the VC political infrastructure thrives in most of the country, continuing to give the enemy his enormous intelligence advantage; full security exists nowhere (not even behind the U.S. Marines' lines and in Saigon); in the countryside, the enemy almost completely controls the night.

Nor has the ROLLING THUNDER program of bombing the North either significantly affected infiltration or cracked the morale of Hanoi. There is agreement in the intelligence community on these facts. . . .

In essence, we find ourselves . . . no better, and if anything worse off. This important war must be fought and won by the Vietnamese themselves. We have known this from the beginning. But the discouraging truth is that, as was the case in 1961 and 1963 and 1965, we have not found the formula, the catalyst, for training and inspiring them into effective action.

## 2. Recommended Actions.

In such an unpromising state of affairs, what should we do? We must continue to press the enemy militarily; we must make demonstrable progress in pacification; at the same time, we must add a new ingredient forced on us by the facts. Specifically, we must improve our position by getting ourselves into a military posture that we credibly would maintain indefinitely — a posture that makes trying to "wait us out" less attractive. I recommend a five-pronged course of action to achieve those ends.

### a. Stabilize U.S. Force-Levels in Vietnam.

It is my judgment that, barring a dramatic change in the war, we should limit the increase in U.S. forces . . . in 1967 to 70,000 men and we should level off at the total of 470,000. . . . It is my view that this is enough to punish the enemy at the large-unit operations level and to keep the enemy's main forces from interrupting pacification. I believe also that even many more than 470,000 would not kill the enemy off in such numbers as to break their morale so long as they think they can wait us out. It is possible that such a 40 percent increase over our present level of 325,000 will break the enemy's morale in the short term; but if it does not, we must, I believe, be prepared for and have underway a long-term program premised on more than breaking the morale of main force units. A stabilized U.S. force level

---

[1]**Ky:** Nguyen Cao Ky was premier of the Republic of South Vietnam from 1965 to 1967 [Ed.].

would be part of such a long-term program. It would put us in a position where negotiations would be more likely to be productive, but if they were not we could pursue the all-important pacification task with proper attention and resources and without the spectre of apparently endless escalation of U.S. deployments.

## b. Install a Barrier.

A portion of the 470,000 troops — perhaps 10,000 to 20,000 — should be devoted to the construction and maintenance of an infiltration barrier. Such a barrier would lie near the 17th parallel — would run from the sea, across the neck of South Vietnam (choking off the new infiltration routes through the DMZ [demilitarized zone]) and across the trails in Laos. . . .

## c. Stabilize the ROLLING THUNDER Program Against the North.

Attack sorties in North Vietnam have risen from about 4,000 per month at the end of last year to 6,000 per month in the first quarter of this year and 12,000 per month at present. Most of our 50 percent increase of deployed attack-capable aircraft has been absorbed in the attacks on North Vietnam. In North Vietnam, almost 84,000 attack sorties have been flown (about 25 percent against fixed targets), 45 percent during the past seven months.

Despite these efforts, it now appears that the North Vietnamese-Laotian road network will remain adequate to meet the requirements of the Communist forces in South Vietnam — this is so even if its capacity could be reduced by one-third and if combat activities were to be doubled. North Vietnam's serious need for trucks, spare parts and petroleum probably can, despite air attacks, be met by imports. The petroleum requirement for trucks involved in the infiltration movement, for example, has not been enough to present significant supply problems, and the effects of the attacks on the petroleum distribution system, while they have not yet been fully assessed, are not expected to cripple the flow of essential supplies. Furthermore, it is clear that, to bomb the North sufficiently to make a radical impact upon Hanoi's political, economic and social structure, would require an effort which we could make but which would not be stomached either by our own people or by world opinion; and it would involve a serious risk of drawing us into open war with China. . . .

At the proper time . . . I believe we should consider terminating bombing in all of North Vietnam, or at least in the Northeast zones, for an indefinite period in connection with covert moves toward peace.

## d. Pursue a Vigorous Pacification Program.

As mentioned above, the pacification (Revolutionary Development) program has been and is thoroughly stalled. The large-unit operations war, which we know best how to fight and where we have had our successes, is largely irrelevant to pacification as long as we do not lose it. By and large, the people in rural areas believe that the GVN when it comes will not stay but that the VC will; that cooperations with the GVN will be punished by the VC; that the GVN is really indifferent to the people's welfare; that the low-level GVN are tools of the local rich; and that the GVN is ridden with corruption.

Success in pacification depends on the interrelated functions of providing physical security, destroying the VC apparatus, motivating the people to cooperate and establishing responsive local government. An obviously necessary but not sufficient requirement for success of the Revolutionary Development cadre and police is vigorously conducted and adequately prolonged clearing operations by military troops, who will "stay" in the area, who behave themselves decently and who show some respect for the people.

This elemental requirement of pacification has been missing.

In almost no contested area designated for pacification in recent years have ARVN [Army of the Republic of Vietnam] forces actually "cleared and stayed" to a point where cadre teams, if available, could have stayed overnight in hamlets and survived, let alone accomplish their mission. VC units of company and even battalion size remain in operation, and they are more than large enough to over-run anything the local security forces can put up.

Now that the threat of a Communist main-force military victory has been thwarted by our emergency efforts, we must allocate far more attention and a por-tion of the regular military forces (at least half of the ARVN and perhaps a portion of the U.S. forces) to the task of providing an active and permanent security screen behind which the Revolutionary Development teams and police can operate and behind which the political struggle with the VC infrastructure can take place.

The U.S. cannot do this pacification security job for the Vietnamese. All we can do is "Massage the heart." For one reason, it is known that we do not intend to stay; if our efforts worked at all, it would merely postpone the eventual con-frontation of the VC and GVN infrastructures. The GVN must do the job; and I am convinced that drastic reform is needed if the GVN is going to be able to do it.

The first essential reform is in the attitude of GVN officials. They are gener-ally apathetic, and there is corruption high and low. Often appointments, promo-tions, and draft deferments must be bought; and kickbacks on salaries are common. Cadre at the bottom can be no better than the system above them.

The second needed reform is in the attitude and conduct of the ARVN. The image of the government cannot improve unless and until the ARVN improves markedly. They do not understand the importance (or respectability) of pacifica-tion nor the importance to pacification of proper, disciplined conduct. Promo-tions, assignments and awards are often not made on merit, but rather on the basis of having a diploma, friends or relatives, or because of bribery. The ARVN is weak in dedication, direction and discipline. . . .

## e. Press for Negotiations.

I am not optimistic that Hanoi or the VC will respond to peace overtures now. . . . The ends sought by the two sides appear to be irreconcilable and the relative power balance is not in their view unfavorable to them. But three things can be done, I believe, to increase the prospects:

(1) Take steps to increase the credibility of our peace gestures in the minds of the enemy. There is considerable evidence both in private statements by the Com-munists and in the reports of competent Western officials who have talked with them that charges of U.S. bad faith are not solely propagandistic, but reflect deeply held beliefs. Analyses of Communists' statements and actions indicate that they firmly believe that American leadership really does not want the fighting to stop, and, that we are intent on winning a military victory in Vietnam and on maintain-ing our presence there through a puppet regime supported by U.S. military bases.

As a way of projective U.S. bona fides, I believe that we should consider two possibilities with respect to our bombing program against the North, to be un-dertaken, if at all, at a time very carefully selected with a view to maximizing the chances of influencing the enemy and world opinion and to minimizing the chances that failure would strengthen the hand of the "hawks" at home: First, without fanfare, conditions, or avowal, whether the stand-down was permanent or temporary, stop bombing all of North Vietnam. It is generally thought that Hanoi will not agree to negotiations until they can claim that the bombing has stopped unconditionally. We should see what develops, retaining freedom to resume the bombing if nothing useful was forthcoming. . . . [A footnote:] Any limitation on the bombing of North Vietnam will cause serious psychological problems among the men who are risking their lives to help achieve our political objectives; among their commanders up to and including the JCS [Joint Chiefs of Staff]; and among those of our people who cannot understand why we should withhold punishment from the enemy. General Westmoreland, as do the JCS, strongly believes in the military value of the bombing program. Further, Westmoreland reports that the morale of his Air Force personnel may already be showing signs of erosion — an erosion resulting from current operational restrictions.

To the same end of improving our credibility, we should seek ways — through words and deeds — to make believable our intention to withdraw our forces once the North Vietnamese aggression against the South stops. In particular, we should avoid any implication that we will stay in South Vietnam with bases or to guarantee any particular outcome to a solely South Vietnamese struggle. . . .

### 3. The Prognosis.

The prognosis is bad that the war can be brought to a satisfactory conclusion within the next two years. The large-unit operations probably will not do it; negotiations probably will not do it. *While we should continue to pursue both of these routes in trying for a solution in the short run, we should recognize that success from them is a mere possibility, not a probability.*

The solution lies in girding, openly, for a longer war and in taking actions immediately which will in 12 to 18 months give clear evidence that the continuing costs and risks to the American people are acceptably limited, that the formula for success has been found, and that the end of the war is merely a matter of time.

QUESTIONS FOR READING AND DISCUSSION

1. Why did McNamara "see no reasonable way to bring the war to an end soon"? What was the difference, if any, between ending the war and winning the war?
2. To what extent could McNamara's assessment be said to reflect the success of the North Vietnamese "strategy of attriting our national will"?
3. What goals did McNamara hope to achieve? What actions did he recommend? To what extent were those actions within the capability of American military forces?
4. What assumptions did McNamara make about the support for the war among the South Vietnamese, American military personnel, and Americans at home?

## DOCUMENT 29-3

# *Military Commander Reassures Americans That the End Is in View*

*The Vietnam War generated dissent unprecedented in previous American wars. Antiwar activists burned draft cards and tried to impede military production. Hawks argued that nuclear weapons should be used to bomb the enemy back to the stone age.*

*Doves declared that the United States should immediately and unilaterally withdraw from the war. To bolster eroding political support for the war, General William C. West-moreland, commander of U.S. forces in Vietnam, gave a public address in November 1967. Westmoreland's optimistic assessment of the war, excerpted here, reflected the desire of policymakers to assure Americans that the war was being won and would soon be over.*

## General William C. Westmoreland
## *Public Address*, November 1967

With 1968, a new phase is now starting. We have reached an important point when the end begins to come into view. What is this third phase we are about to enter?

In Phase III, in 1968, we intend to do the following:

Help the Vietnamese Armed Forces to continue improving their effectiveness.

Decrease our advisers in training centers and other places where the professional competence of Vietnamese officers makes this possible.

Increase our advisory effort with the younger brothers of the Vietnamese Army: the Regional Forces and Popular Forces.

Use U.S. and free-world forces to destroy North Vietnamese forays while we assist the Vietnamese to reorganize for territorial security.

Provide the new military equipment to revitalize the Vietnamese Army and prepare it to take on an ever-increasing share of the war.

Continue pressure on [the] North to prevent rebuilding and to make infiltration more costly.

Turn a major share of frontline DMZ defense over to the Vietnamese Army.

Increase U.S. support in the rich and populated delta.

Help the Government of Viet-Nam single out and destroy the Communist shadow government.

Continue to isolate the guerrilla from the people.

Help the new Vietnamese government to respond to popular aspirations and to reduce and eliminate corruption.

Help the Vietnamese strengthen their policy forces to enhance law and order.

Open more roads and canals.

Continue to improve the Vietnamese economy and standard of living.

Now for phase IV — the final phase. That period will see the conclusion of our plan to weaken the enemy and strengthen our friends until we become progressively superfluous. The object will be to show the world that guerrilla warfare and invasion do not pay as a new means of Communist aggression.

I see phase IV happening as follows:

Infiltration will slow.

The Communist infrastructure will be cut up and near collapse.

The Vietnamese Government will prove its stability, and the Vietnamese Army will show that it can handle Viet Cong.

---

General William C. Westmoreland, "Address on Vietnam," *Department of State Bulletin*, December 11, 1967; reprinted in *Vietnam: A History in Documents*, ed. Gareth Porter (New York: New American Library, 1981), 352–54.

The Regional Forces and Popular Forces will reach a higher level of professional performance.

U.S. units can begin to phase down as the Vietnamese Army is modernized and develops its capacity to the fullest.

The military physical assets, bases and ports, will be progressively turned over to the Vietnamese.

The Vietnamese will take charge of the final mopping up of the Viet Cong (which will probably last several years). The U.S., at the same time, will continue the developmental help envisaged by the President for the community of Southeast Asia.

You may ask how long phase III will take, before we reach the final phase. We have already entered part of phase III. Looking back on phases I and II, we can conclude that we have come a long way.

I see progress as I travel all over Viet-Nam.

I see it in the attitudes of the Vietnamese.

I see it in the open roads and canals.

I see it in the new crops and the new purchasing power of the farmer.

I see it in the increasing willingness of the Vietnamese Army to fight North Vietnamese units and in the victories they are winning.

Parenthetically, I might say that the U.S. press tends to report U.S. actions; so you may not be as aware as I am of the victories won by South Vietnamese forces.

The enemy has many problems:

He is losing control of the scattered population under his influence.

He is losing credibility with the population he still controls.

He is alienating the people by his increased demands and taxes, where he can impose them.

He sees the strength of his forces steadily declining.

He can no longer recruit in the South to any meaningful extent; he must plug the gap with North Vietnamese.

His monsoon offensives have been failures.

He was dealt a mortal blow by the installation of a freely elected representative government.

And he failed in his desperate effort to take the world's headlines from the inauguration by a military victory.

Lastly, the Vietnamese Army is on the road to becoming a competent force. . . .

We are making progress. We know you want an honorable and early transition to the fourth and last phase. So do your sons and so do I.

It lies within our grasp — the enemy's hopes are bankrupt. With your support we will give you a success that will impact not only on South Viet-Nam but on every emerging nation in the world.

## QUESTIONS FOR READING AND DISCUSSION

1. Why did Westmoreland contend that "the end begins to come into view"? What were the features of the new phase of the war in 1968?

2. What evidence of progress did he see? Why did the progress indicate that phase IV was likely to begin soon? To what extent did phase IV represent victory?

3. Why did Westmoreland believe "the enemy's hopes are bankrupt"? To what extent were the enemy's "problems" attributable to U.S. policies, according to Westmoreland?

4. Although Westmoreland did not explicitly identify problems American military forces and policymakers confronted, to what extent might his list of the features of phases III and IV be considered an implicit recognition of problems that had yet to be solved? In what ways might Westmoreland's speech have inspired confidence among Americans about the war in Vietnam?

## DOCUMENT 29-4

# Military Discipline in an Unpopular War

*Soldiers in Vietnam knew that they were fighting in a controversial war — one that did not have overwhelming public support at home, that seemed confusing and deadly in the field, and that seemed to be poorly supported by the Vietnamese army, government, and general population. The perceptions and experiences of American soldiers had important consequences for military discipline. In 1971 Colonel Robert D. Heinl Jr., a twenty-seven-year veteran of the Marine Corps, cataloged in an army publication the state of military discipline among troops in Vietnam. Heinl's article, excerpted here, illustrates the demoralization within the armed forces while peace negotiators huddled with representatives of North Vietnam and the fighting continued.*

## Robert D. Heinl Jr.
### The Collapse of the Armed Forces, June 7, 1971

The morale, discipline and battleworthiness of the U.S. Armed Forces are, with a few salient exceptions, lower and worse than at any time in this century and possibly in the history of the United States.

By every conceivable indicator, our army that now remains in Vietnam is in a state approaching collapse, with individual units avoiding or having refused combat, murdering their officers and noncommissioned officers, drug-ridden, and dispirited where not near-mutinous. . . .

Intolerably clobbered and buffeted from without and within by social turbulence, pandemic drug addiction, race war, sedition, civilian scapegoatise, draftee recalcitrance and malevolence, barracks theft and common crime, unsupported in their travail by the general government, in Congress as well as the executive branch, distrusted, disliked, and often reviled by the public, the uniformed services today are places of agony for the loyal, silent professionals who doggedly hang on and try to keep the ship afloat. . . .

While no senior officer (especially one on active duty) can openly voice any such assessment, the foregoing conclusions find virtually unanimous support in numerous non-attributable interviews with responsible senior and midlevel officers, as well as career noncommissioned officers and petty officers in all services.

Historical precedents do exist for some of the services' problems, such as desertion, mutiny, unpopularity, seditious attacks, and racial troubles. Others, such as drugs, pose difficulties that are wholly new. Nowhere, however, in the

Colonel Robert D. Heinl Jr., "The Collapse of the Armed Forces," *Armed Forces Journal,* June 7, 1971; reprinted in *Vietnam and America: A Documentary History,* ed. Marvin E. Gettleman (New York: Grove Atlantic, 1995), 323–31.

history of the Armed Forces have comparable past troubles presented themselves in such general magnitude, acuteness, or concentrated focus as today. . . .

To understand the military consequences of what is happening to the U.S. Armed Forces, Vietnam is a good place to start. It is in Vietnam that the rear-guard of a 500,000-man army, in its day (and in the observation of the writer) the best army the United States ever put into the field, is numbly extricating itself from a nightmare war the Armed Forces feel they had foisted on them by bright civilians who are now back on campus writing books about the folly of it all.

"They have set up separate companies," writes an American soldier from Cu Chi, . . . "for men who refuse to go out into the field. It is no big thing to refuse to go. If a man is ordered to go to such and such a place he no longer goes through the hassle of refusing; he just packs his shirt and goes to visit some buddies at another base camp. Operations have become incredibly ragtag. Many guys don't even put on their uniforms any more. . . . The American garrisons on the larger bases are virtually disarmed. The lifers have taken our weapons from us and put them under lock and key. . . . There have also been quite a few frag incidents in the battalion."

Can all this really be typical or even truthful? Unfortunately the answer is yes.

"Frag incidents" or just "fragging" is current soldier slang in Vietnam for the murder or attempted murder of strict, unpopular, or just aggressive officers and NCOs. With extreme reluctance (after a young West Pointer from Senator Mike Mansfield's Montana was fragged in his sleep) the Pentagon has now disclosed that fraggings in 1970 (209) have more than doubled those of the previous year (96).

Word of the deaths of officers will bring cheers at troop movies or in bivouacs of certain units. In one such division . . . fraggings during 1971 have been authoritatively estimated to be running about one a week. . . .

Bounties, raised by common subscription in amounts running anywhere from $50 to $1,000, have been widely reported put on the heads of leaders whom the privates . . . want to rub out.

Shortly after the costly assault on Hamburger Hill in mid-1969, the GI underground newspaper in Vietnam, GI Says, publicly offered a $10,000 bounty on LCol Weldon Honeycutt, the officer who ordered (and led) the attack. Despite several attempts, however, Honeycutt managed to live out his tour and return Stateside.

"Another Hamburger Hill" (i.e., toughly contested assault), conceded a veteran major, "is definitely out."

The issue of "combat refusal" an official euphemism for disobedience of orders to fight — the soldier's gravest crime — has only recently been again precipitated on the frontier of Laos. . . .

"Search and evade" (meaning tacit avoidance of combat by units in the field) is now virtually a principle of war, vividly expressed by the GI phrase, "CYA (cover your ass) and get home!"

That "search-and-evade" has not gone unnoticed by the enemy is underscored by the Viet Cong delegation's recent statement at the Paris Peace Talks that communist units in Indochina have been ordered not to engage American units which do not molest them. The same statement boasted — not without foundation in fact — that American defectors are in the VC ranks.

Symbolic anti-war fasts (such as the one at Pleiku where an entire medical unit, led by its officers, refused Thanksgiving turkey), peace symbols, "V"-signs not for victory but for peace, booing and cursing of officers and even of hapless entertainers such as Bob Hope, are unhappily commonplace.

As for drugs and race, Vietnam's problems today not only reflect but reinforce those of the Armed Forces as a whole. In April, for example, members of a Congressional investigating subcommittee reported that 10 to 15% of our troops in Vietnam are now using high-grade heroin, and that drug addiction there is "of epidemic proportions."

Only last year an Air Force major and command pilot for Ambassador Bunker was apprehended at Tan Son Nhut air base outside Saigon with $8-million worth of heroin in his aircraft. This major is now in Leavenworth. . . .

It is a truism that national armies closely reflect societies from which they have been raised. It would be strange indeed if the Armed Forces did not today mirror the agonizing divisions and social traumas of American society, and of course they do.

For this very reason, our Armed Forces outside Vietnam not only reflect these conditions but disclose the depths of their troubles in an awful litany of sedition, disaffection, desertion, race, drugs, breakdowns of authority, abandonment of discipline, and, as a cumulative result, the lowest state of military morale in the history of the country.

Sedition — coupled with disaffection within the ranks, and externally fomented with an audacity and intensity previously inconceivable — infests the Armed Services:

At best count, there appear to be some 144 underground newspapers published on or aimed at U.S. military bases in this country and overseas. Since 1970 the number of such sheets has increased 40% (up from 103 last fall). These journals are not mere gripe-sheets that poke soldier fun . . . at the brass and the sergeants. "In Vietnam," writes the Ft Lewis-McChord Free Press, "the Lifers, the Brass, are the true Enemy, not the enemy." Another West Coast sheet advises readers: "Don't desert. Go to Vietnam and kill your commanding officer."

At least 14 GI dissent organizations (including two made up exclusively of officers) now operate more or less openly. Ancillary to these are at least six antiwar veterans' groups which strive to influence GIs. . . .

By present count at least 11 (some go as high as 26) off-base antiwar "coffee houses" ply GIs with rock music, lukewarm coffee, antiwar literature, how-to-do-it tips on desertion, and similar disruptive counsels. . . .

Internally speaking, racial conflicts and drugs — also previously insignificant — are tearing the services apart today. . . .

Racial conflicts (most but not all sparked by young black enlisted men) are erupting murderously in all services.

At a recent high commanders' conference, General Westmoreland and other senior generals heard the report from Germany that in many units white soldiers are now afraid to enter barracks alone at night for fear of "head-hunting" ambushes by blacks. . . . All services are today striving energetically to cool and control this ugly violence which in the words of one noncommissioned officer, has made his once taut unit divide up "like two street gangs.". . .

The drug problem — like the civilian situation from which it directly derives — is running away with the services. In March, Navy Secretary John H. Chafee, speaking for the two sea services, said bluntly that drug abuse in both the Navy and Marines is out of control.

In 1966, the Navy discharged 170 drug offenders. Three years later (1969), 3,800 were discharged. Last year in 1970, the total jumped to over 5,000.

Drug abuse in the Pacific Fleet — with Asia on one side, and kinky California on the other — gives the Navy its worst headaches. To cite one example, a destroyer due to sail from the West Coast last year for the Far East nearly had to postpone deployment when, five days before departure, a ring of some 30 drug users (over 10 percent of the crew) was uncovered. . . .

What those statistics say is that the Armed Forces (like their parent society) are in the grip of a drug pandemic — a conclusion underscored by the one fact that, just since 1968, the total number of verified drug addiction cases throughout the Armed Forces has nearly doubled. One other yardstick: according to military medical sources, needle hepatitis now poses as great a problem among young soldiers as VD. . . .

With conditions what they are in the Armed Forces, and with intense efforts on the part of elements in our society to disrupt discipline and destroy morale the consequences can be clearly measured in two ultimate indicators: manpower retention (reenlistments and their antithesis, desertions); and the state of discipline.

In both respects the picture is anything but encouraging. . . . Desertion rates are going straight up. . . .

In 1970, the Army had 65,643 deserters, or roughly the equivalent of four infantry divisions. This desertion rate (52.3 soldiers per thousand) is well over twice the peak rate for Korea (22.5 per thousand). It is more than quadruple the 1966 desertion-rate (14.7 per thousand) of the then well-trained, high-spirited professional Army. . . .

Admiral Elmo R. Zumwalt, Jr., Chief of Naval Operations, minces no words. "We have a personnel crisis," he recently said, "that borders on disaster.". . .

The trouble of the services — produced by and also in turn producing the dismaying conditions described in this article — is above all a crisis of soul and backbone. It entails — the word is not too strong — something very near a collapse of the command authority and leadership George Washington saw as the soul of military forces. This collapse results, at least in part, from a concurrent collapse of public confidence in the military establishment.

### Questions for Reading and Discussion

1. According to Heinl, why was the army in Vietnam "in a state approaching collapse"? What caused fragging, bounties, combat refusal, and search and evade?

2. What did Heinl believe were the sources of sedition, racial strife, and drug abuse? How did such problems influence the military effort in Vietnam?

3. What did Heinl mean by saying, "The trouble of the services . . . is above all a crisis of soul and backbone"?

## Document 29-5

# *An American Soldier in Vietnam*

*Hundreds of thousands of Americans served in uniform in Vietnam. Their experiences varied enormously, depending on when and where they served and what they were assigned to do. Arthur E. Woodley Jr., who served as a special forces ranger in Vietnam in 1968 and 1969, recalled in an interview more than a decade later how the war changed him. Woodley's interview, excerpted here, reveals experiences confronted by many young Americans in combat in Vietnam.*

## Arthur E. Woodley Jr.
### *Oral History of a Special Forces Ranger*

I went to Vietnam as a basic naïve young man of eighteen. Before I reached my nineteenth birthday, I was a animal. . . .

It began on my fourteenth day in country. The first time I was ever in a combat situation at all. . . .

I was a cherry boy. Most cherry boys went on point. . . . I adapted so well to bein' a point man that that became my permanent position after this first mission.

We was in very thick elephant grass. We had sat down for a ten-minute break. And we heard the Vietn'ese talking, coming through the elephant grass. So we all sat ready for bein' attacked.

I heard this individual walking. He came through the elephant grass, and I let loose on my M-16 and hit him directly in his face. Sixteen rounds. The whole clip. And his face disappeared. From the chin up. Nothing left. And his body stood there for 'proximately somewhere around ten, fifteen seconds. And it shivers. And it scared me beyond anyone's imagination.

Then it was chaos from then on. Shooting all over. We had a approximate body count of five VC. Then we broke camp and head for safer ground.

After thinkin' about that guy with no face, I broke into a cold sweat. I knew it could've been me that was in his place instead of me in my place. But it changed me. Back home I had to defend myself in the streets, with my fist, with bottles, or whatever. But you don't go around shooting people. As physical as I had been as a teenager, there were never life-threatening situations. I had never experienced anything quite as horrible as seeing a human being with his face blown apart. I cried. I cried because I killed somebody.

You had to fight to survive where I grew up. Lower east Baltimore. . . . It was very difficult for us to go from one neighborhood to another without trying to prove your manhood.

It was a mixed-up neighborhood of Puerto Ricans, Indians, Italians, and blacks. Being that I'm light-skinned, curly hair, I wasn't readily accepted in the black community. I was more accepted by Puerto Ricans and some rednecks. They didn't ask what my race classification was. I went with them to white movies, white restaurants, and so forth. But after I got older, I came to the realization that I was what I am and came to deal with my black peers. . . .

Being from a hard-core neighborhood, I decided I was gonna volunteer for the toughest combat training they had. I went to jump school, Ranger school, and Special Forces training. I figured I was just what my country needed. A black patriot who could do any physical job they could come up with. Six feet, one hundred and ninety pounds, and healthy. . . .

We got to Cam Ranh in November 1968. And I got the biggest surprise of my life. There was water surfing. There was big cars being driven. There was women with fashionable clothes and men with suits on. It was not like being in a war zone. I said, Hey, what's this? Better than being home.

When I got there, my basic job was combat infantryman, paratrooper, 5th Special Forces Group. . . . We were like a unit of misfits who were sort of throwed

Arthur E. Woodley, Jr., interview, in Wallace Terry, *Bloods: An Oral History of the Vietnam War by Black Veterans* (New York: Ballantine, 1984), 243–63.

together and made into a strike combat unit. We would go out and capture prisoners, destroy a certain village, or kill a certain party because it was necessary for the war effort.

I didn't ask no questions about the war. I thought communism was spreading, and as an American citizen, it was my part to do as much as I could to defeat the Communist from coming here. Whatever America states is correct was the tradition that I was brought up in. And I, through the only way I could possibly make it out of the ghetto, was to be the best soldier I possibly could. . . .

Then came the second week of February of '69.

This was like three days after we had a helicopter go down in some very heavy foliage where they couldn't find no survivors from the air. . . . We were directed to find the wreckage, report back. They see if we can find any enemy movement and find any prisoners. . . .

The helicopter, it was stripped. All the weaponry was gone. There was no bodies. It looked like the helicopter had been shot out of the air. It had numerous bullet holes in it. . . .

We recon this area, and we came across this fella, a white guy, who was staked to the ground. His arms and legs tied down to stakes. And he had a leather band around his neck that's staked in the ground so he couldn't move his head to the left or right.

He had numerous scars on his face where he might have been beaten and mutilated. And he had been peeled from his upper part of chest to down to his waist. Skinned. Like they slit your skin with a knife. And they take a pair of pliers or a instrument similar, and they just peel the skin off your body and expose it to the elements. . . .

The man was within a couple of hours of dying on his own.

And we didn't know what to do, because we couldn't move him. There was no means. We had no stretcher. There was only six of us. And we went out with the basic idea that it was no survivors. We was even afraid to unstake him from the stakes, because the maggots and flies were eating at the exposed flesh so much. . . .

It was a heavy shock on all of us to find that guy staked out still alive. . . .

And he start to cryin', beggin' to die.

He said, "I can't go back like this. I can't live like this. I'm dying. You can't leave me here like this dying."

It was a situation where it had to be remove him from his bondage or remove him from his suffering. Movin' him from this bondage was unfeasible. It would have put him in more pain than he had ever endured. There wasn't even no use talkin' 'bout tryin' and takin' him back, because there was nothing left of him. It was that or kill the brother, and I use the term "brother" because in a war circumstance, we all brothers.

The man pleaded not only to myself but to other members of my team to end his suffering. He made the plea for about half an hour, because we couldn't decide what to do. . . .

It took me somewhere close to 20 minutes to get my mind together. Not because I was squeamish about killing someone, because I had at that time numerous body counts. Killing someone wasn't the issue. It was killing another American citizen, another GI.

I tried my best not to.

I tried to find a thousand and one reasons why I shouldn't do this. . . .

I put myself in his situation. In his place. I had to be as strong as he was, because he was askin' me to kill him, to wipe out his life. He had to be a hell of a man to do that. I don't think I would be a hell of a man enough to be able to do that. I said to myself, I couldn't show him my weakness, because he was showin' me his strength.

The only thing that I could see that had to be done is that the man's sufferin' had to be ended.

I put my M-16 next to his head. Next to his temple.

I said, "You sure you want me to do this?"

He said, "Man, kill me. Thank you."

I stopped thinking. I just pulled the trigger. I cancelled his suffering.

When the team came back, we talked nothing about it.

We buried him. We buried him. Very deep.

Then I cried. . . .

Now it begins to seem like on every mission we come across dead American bodies, black and white. I'm seeing atrocities that's been done on them. Markings have been cut on them. Some has been castrated, with their penises sewed up in their mouth with bamboo.

I couldn't isolate myself from all this. I had gotten to the conclusion today or tomorrow I'll be dead. So it wasn't anything I couldn't do or wouldn't do. . . .

. . . [T]he Vietn'ese, they called me Montagnard,[1] because I would dress like a Montagnard. I wouldn't wear conventional camouflage fatigues in the field. I wore a dark-green loincloth, a dark-green bandana to blend in with the foliage, and a little camouflage paint on my face. And Ho Chi Minh sandals. And my grenades and ammunition. That's the way I went to the field.

I dressed like that specifically as the point man, because if the enemy saw anyone first, they saw myself. They would just figure I was just another jungle guy that was walking around in the woods. And I would catch 'em off guard.

When we first started going into the fields, I would not wear a finger, ear, or mutilate another person's body. Until I had the misfortune to come upon those American soldiers who were castrated. Then it got to be a game between the Communists and ourselves to see how many fingers and ears that we could capture from each other. After a kill we would cut his finger or ear off as a trophy, stuff our unit patch in his mouth, and let him die.

I collected about 14 ears and fingers. With them strung on a piece of leather around my neck, I would go downtown, and you would get free drugs, free booze, free pussy because they wouldn't wanna bother with you 'cause this man's a killer. It symbolized that I'm a killer. And it was, so to speak, a symbol of combat-type manhood. . . .

Some days when we came back on a POW snatch we played this game called Vietn'ese Roulette on the helicopter. We wouldn't be told how many to capture. Maybe they only wanted one. But we would get two or three to find out which one is gonna talk. You would pull the trigger on one. Throw the body out. Or you throw one without shooting 'im. You place fear into the other Vietn'ese mind. This is you. This is next if you don't talk. . . .

---

[1]**Montagnard:** A French term used to describe a member of a dark-skinned people living in the highland regions of North and South Vietnam.

I guess my team got rid of about eight guys out of the chopper one way or another, but I only remember pushing two out myself. . . .

With 89 days left in country, I came out of the field.

At the time you are in the field you don't feel anything about what you are doin'. It's the time that you have to yourself that you sit back and you sort and ponder.

What I now felt was emptiness.

Here I am. I'm still eighteen years old, a young man with basically everything in his life to look forward to over here in a foreign country with people who have everything that I think I should have. They have the right to fight. I've learned in this country that you don't have the right to gather forces and fight back the so-called oppressor. You have the right to complain. They had the right. They fought for what they thought was right.

I started to recapture some of my old values. I was a passionate young man before I came into the Army. I believed that you respect other people's lives just as much as I respect my own. I got to thinkin' that I done killed around 40 people personally and maybe some others I haven't seen in the fire fights. I was really thinkin' that there are people who won't ever see their children, their grandchildren.

I started seeing the atrocities that we caused each other as human beings. I came to the realization that I was committing crimes against humanity and myself. That I really didn't believe in these things I was doin'. I changed.

I stopped wearing the ears and fingers. . . .

I left Vietnam the end of '69. . . .

The same day I left Vietnam, I was standin' back on the corner in Baltimore. Back in the States. A animal. And nobody could deal with me.

I got out January '71. Honorable discharge. Five Bronze Stars for valor. . . .

I couldn't deal with goin' to school, because I wasn't motivated. The only friends I made were militant types, because they were the only ones could relate to what I was tryin' to say. I took all the money I saved up and bought weapons. Fifteen hundred dollars' worth. Rifles, guns. I joined the Black Panthers group basically because it was a warlike group. With the Panthers we started givin' out free milk and other community help things. But I was thinkin' we needed a revolution. A physical revolution. And I was thinkin' about Vietnam. All the time. . . .

I don't have a job now. But I would take any human service job, especially where I could show the black kids and the black people that we ought to stop looking toward the stars and start looking toward each other. That our greatest horizons is in our children. And if we don't bring our children up to believe in themselves, then we'll never have anything to believe in.

But they turn their backs on a lot of us Vietnam vet'rans. They say the only way to success is through education. I wanna go back in school and get my B.A., but I can't afford to. I gotta get out there and get a job. Ain't no jobs out there. So what I'm gon' do now? Only thing else I know how to do is pick up a gun. Then I'm stupid. I'm being stupid again. I'm not going forward. I'm going backwards. And can't go any further backwards. I done been so damn far back, I'm listenin' to the echoes in the tunnel.

One day I'm down on Oliver and Milton Avenue. Go in this grocery store. In my neighborhood.

This Vietn'ese owns the store.

He say, "I know you?"

I say, "You know me from where?"

"You Vietnam?"

"Yeah, I was in Vietnam."

"When you Vietnam."

"'68, '69."

"Yeah, me know you An Khe. You be An Khe?"

"Yeah, I was in An Khe."

"Yeah, me know you. You Montagnard Man."

Ain't that some shit?

I'm buyin' groceries from him.

I ain't been in the store since. I'm still pissed off.

He's got a business, good home, drivin' cars. And I'm still strugglin'.

## QUESTIONS FOR READING AND DISCUSSION

1. According to Woodley, how did he become "a animal" in Vietnam? To what extent did he consider himself a "black patriot" while he was in Vietnam?

2. Why did Woodley come to "the realization that I was committing crimes against humanity and myself"?

3. In what ways did Woodley relate his service in Vietnam to his belief back in Baltimore that "we needed a revolution"?

4. To what extent did Woodley's experiences in Vietnam change his ideas about America?

## COMPARATIVE QUESTIONS

1. How did General William Westmoreland's public assessment of the war differ from Robert S. McNamara's private evaluation? How did McNamara's assessment compare to President Kennedy's? What accounts for the differences? Did such differences influence American policy in Vietnam?

2. Robert Heinl, Westmoreland, and McNamara all stressed the importance of morale, but they differed sharply on the morale problems that existed and why. What accounts for these differences? Was morale an issue in Bobbie Pendergrass's correspondence with President Kennedy?

3. To what extent were Arthur Woodley's experiences in Vietnam consistent with the goals of American policy described by Kennedy, McNamara, and Westmoreland? Would Kennedy, McNamara, and Westmoreland have seen Woodley as a model soldier? What did Woodley think of the policies designed and implemented by Kennedy, Westmoreland, and McNamara?

4. To what extent did Woodley's experiences conform to Heinl's observations? What accounts for the differences, if any?

5. Judging from the documents in this chapter, to what extent do you think the Vietnam War called into question or reaffirmed fundamental American values?

# CHAPTER 30

# AMERICA MOVES TO THE RIGHT
## 1969–1989

The powerful currents of change that swept the nation during the 1960s created even stronger countercurrents that dominated the politics of subsequent decades. Most of the activist groups that had worked for social change succumbed to bitter in-fighting, fracturing their unity and sapping their political vitality. Their opponents mobilized effectively to redirect power, so they claimed, from the government to the people and to stymie what they regarded as further decay in American values. The Watergate affair, however, revealed that quite un-American values were used routinely at the highest levels of the Nixon administration. The following documents illustrate that the crosscurrents of the time raised questions about the nation's basic values and institutions: Should the Supreme Court decide whether abortions were legal? Could government provide solutions to national problems? What did America mean to the rest of the world and the millions of new immigrants from all parts of the globe?

## DOCUMENT 30-1

## *The Watergate Tapes: Nixon, Dean, and Haldeman Discuss the Cancer within the Presidency*

*President Richard M. Nixon used the powers of the presidency to violate the law and spy on political opponents. When the burglars who broke into the office of the Democratic National Committee in the Watergate building on June 17, 1972, were caught and arrested, they quickly began to demand financial help from their employers in the Republican party. They also threatened to tell what they knew about other dirty tricks they had perpetrated. On March 21, 1973, John Dean, the president's counsel, met with Nixon in the Oval Office to inform him of the demands of the Watergate burglars and the dangers they posed to his presidency. Secret tape-recordings of that meeting and others were made public in April 1974 by President Nixon. He announced in an address to the nation that "I know in my own heart that, through the long painful and difficult process revealed in these transcripts, I was trying in that period to discover what was right and to do what was right." The transcript of the March 21 meeting, excerpted here, demonstrates instead deep involvement in criminal activities by Nixon and leading members of his administration. The transcripts of the Watergate tapes provided all Americans with a detailed, word-by-word portrait of the inner workings of the Nixon White House.*

## Transcript from Tape-recorded Meeting, March 21, 1973

D[ean]: The reason that I thought we ought to talk this morning is because in our conversations, I have the impression that you don't know everything I know and it makes it very difficult for you to make judgments that only you can make on some of these things and I thought that —

P[resident]: In other words, I have to know why you feel that we shouldn't unravel something?

D: Let me give you my overall first.

P: In other words, your judgment as to where it stands, and where we will go,

D: I think that there is no doubt about the seriousness of the problem we've got. We have a cancer within, close to the Presidency, that is growing. It is growing daily. It's compounded, growing geometrically now, because it compounds itself. That will be clear if I, you know, explain some of the details of why it is. Basically, it is because (1) we are being blackmailed; (2) people are going to start perjuring themselves very quickly that have not had to perjure themselves to protect other people in the line. And there is no assurance —

P: That that won't bust?

D: That that won't bust. So let me give you the sort of basic facts, talking first about the Watergate; and then about Segretti; and then about some of the peripheral items that have come up. First of all on the Watergate: how did it all start, where did it start? OK! It started with an instruction to me from Bob Haldeman[1] to see if we couldn't set up a perfectly legitimate campaign intelligence operation over at the Re-Election Committee. . . . That is when I came up with Gordon Liddy.[2] They needed a lawyer. Gordon had an intelligence background from his FBI service. I was aware of the fact that he had done some extremely sensitive things for the White House while he had been at the White House and he had apparently done them well. Going out into Ellsberg's[3] doctor's office —

P: Oh, yeah.

D: And things like this. He worked with leaks. He tracked these things down. So the report that I got . . . was that he was a hell of a good man and not only that

---

*Submission of Recorded Presidential Conversations to the Committee on the Judiciary of the House of Representatives by President Richard M. Nixon,* April 1974.

[1]**Bob Haldeman:** H. Robert Haldeman, one of Nixon's top aides.

[2]**Gordon Liddy:** A former FBI agent who led a secret unit set up by the Nixon administration and nicknamed the "plumbers" because their mission was to stop the kind of "leaks" that had led to the publication of the *Pentagon Papers.*

[3]**Ellsberg:** Daniel Ellsberg, a former aide who had leaked the *Pentagon Papers* to the *New York Times* in 1971. In an attempt to discredit Ellsberg, the Nixon administration hired men to break into Ellsberg's psychiatrist's office, steal confidential records, and leak them to the press.

a good lawyer and could set up a proper operation. . . . Magruder[4] called me in January and said I would like to have you come over and see Liddy's plan.

P: January of '72?

D: January of '72.

D: . . . So I came over and Liddy laid out a million dollar plan that was the most incredible thing I have ever laid my eyes on: all in codes, and involved black bag operations, kidnapping, providing prostitutes to weaken the opposition, bugging, mugging teams. It was just an incredible thing. . . .

So there was a second meeting. . . . I came into the tail end of the meeting. . . . [T]hey were discussing again bugging, kidnapping and the like. At this point I said right in front of everybody, very clearly, I said, "These are not the sort of things (1) that are ever to be discussed in the office of the Attorney General of the United States — that was where he still was — and I am personally incensed. " And I am trying to get Mitchell[5] off the hook. . . . So I let it be known. I said "You all pack that stuff up and get it the hell out of here. You just can't talk this way in this office and you should re-examine your whole thinking."

P: Who all was present?

D: It was Magruder, Mitchell, Liddy and myself. I came back right after the meeting and told Bob, "Bob, we have a growing disaster on our hands if they are thinking this way," and I said, "The White House has got to stay out of this and I, frankly, am not going to be involved in it." He said, "I agree, John." I thought at that point that the thing was turned off. That is the last I heard of it and I thought it was turned off because it was an absurd proposal. . . . I think Bob was assuming that they had something that was proper over there, some intelligence gathering operation that Liddy was operating. . . . They were going to infiltrate, and bug, and do this sort of thing to a lot of these targets. This is knowledge I have after the fact. Apparently after they had initially broken in and bugged the DNC they were getting information. . . .

P: They had never bugged Muskie,[6] though, did they?

D: No, they hadn't, but they had infiltrated it by a secretary.

P: By a secretary?

D: By a secretary and a chauffeur. There is nothing illegal about that. So the information was coming over here. . . . The next point in time that I became aware of anything was on June 17th when I got the word that there had been this break in at the DNC and somebody from our Committee had been caught in the DNC. And I said, "Oh, (expletive deleted)." You know, eventually putting the pieces together —

P: You knew what it was.

D: I knew who it was. . . .

P: Why at that point in time I wonder? I am just trying to think. We had just finished the Moscow trip.

---

[4]**Magruder:** Jeb Magruder worked for the Committee to Re-elect the President.

[5]**Mitchell:** John Mitchell, Nixon's former attorney general, who ran the Committee to Re-elect the President, the organization that authorized the Watergate break-in.

[6]**Muskie:** Edmund Muskie, a Democratic senator from Maine who had hoped to run against Nixon in the 1972 election. Watergate hearings in 1973 revealed that his bid for the Democratic nomination had been sabotaged by the Committee to Re-elect the President.

The Democrats had just nominated [Geroge] McGovern — I mean, (expletive deleted), what in the hell were these people doing? I can see their doing it earlier. I can see the pressures, but I don't see why all the pressure was on then.

D: I don't know, other than the fact that they might have been looking for information about the conventions.

P: That's right. . . .

P: What did they say in the Grand Jury?

D: They said, as they said before the trial in the Grand Jury, that . . . we knew [Liddy] had these capacities to do legitimate intelligence. We had no idea what he was doing. . . . We had no knowledge that he was going to bug the DNC.

P: The point is, that is not true?

D: That's right.

P: Magruder did know it was going to take place?

D: Magruder gave the instructions to be back in the DNC.

P: He did?

D: Yes.

P: You know that?

D: Yes.

P: I see. OK.

D: I honestly believe that no one over here knew that. I know that as God is my maker, I had no knowledge that they were going to do this.

P: Bob didn't either, or wouldn't have known that either. You are not the issue involved. Had Bob known, he would be.

D: Bob — I don't believe specifically knew that they were going in there.

P: I don't think so.

D: I don't think he did. I think he knew that there was a capacity to do this but he was not given the specific direction. . . .

D: So, those people are in trouble as a result of the Grand Jury and the trial. . . . Now what has happened post June 17? I was under pretty clear instructions not to investigate this, but this could have been disastrous on the electorate if all hell had broken loose. I worked on a theory of containment —

P: Sure.

D: To try to hold it right where it was.

P: Right.

D: There is no doubt that I was totally aware of what the Bureau was doing at all times. I was totally aware of what the Grand Jury was doing. I knew what witnesses were going to be called. I knew what they were asked, and I had to. . . . Now post June 17th: These guys . . . started making demands. "We have to have attorneys fees. We don't have any money ourselves, and you are asking us to take this through the election." Alright, so arrangements were made through Mitchell, initiating it. And I was present in discussions where these guys had to be taken care of. Their attorneys fees had to be done. Kalmbach was brought in. Kalmbach raised some cash.

P: They put that under the cover of a Cuban Committee, I suppose?

D: Well, they had a Cuban Committee and . . . some of it was given to Hunt's[7] lawyer, who in turn passed it out. . . .

---

[7]**Hunt:** E. Howard Hunt, a former CIA agent who, along with Liddy, led the "plumbers."

P: (unintelligible) — but I would certainly keep that cover for whatever it is worth. . . .

D: . . . Here is what is happening right now. . . . One, this is going to be a continual blackmail operation by Hunt and Liddy and the Cubans. No doubt about it. And McCord,[8] . . . Hunt has now made a direct threat against Ehrlichman,[9] . . . He says, "I will bring John Ehrlichman down to his knees and put him in jail. I have done enough seamy things for he and [Egil] Krogh, they'll never survive it."

P: Was he talking about Ellsberg?

D: Ellsberg, and apparently some other things. I don't know the full extent of it.

P: I don't know about anything else.

D: I don't know either, and I hate to learn some of these things. So that is that situation. Now, where are we at the soft points? How many people know about this? Well, let me go one step further in this whole thing. The Cubans that were used in the Watergate were also the same Cubans that Hunt and Liddy used for this California Ellsberg thing, for the break in out there. So they are aware of that. How high their knowledge is, is something else. Hunt and Liddy, of course, are totally aware of it, of the fact that it is right out of the White House.

P: I don't know what the hell we did that for!

D: I don't know either. . . . So that is it. That is the extent of the knowledge. So where are the soft spots on this? Well, first of all, there is the problem of the continued blackmail which will not only go on now, but it will go on while these people are in prison, and it will compound the obstruction of justice situation. It will cost money. It is dangerous. People around here are not pros at this sort of thing. This is the sort of thing Mafia people can do: washing money, getting clean money, and things like that. We just don't know about those things, because we are not criminals and not used to dealing in that business.

P: That's right.

D: It is a tough thing to know how to do.

P: Maybe it takes a gang to do that.

D: That's right. There is a real problem as to whether we could even do it. Plus there is a real problem in raising money. Mitchell has been working on raising some money. He is one of the ones with the most to lose. But there is no denying the fact that the White House, in Ehrlichman, Haldeman and Dean are involved in some of the early money decisions.

P: How much money do you need?

D: I would say these people are going to cost a million dollars over the next two years.

P: We could get that. On the money, if you need the money you could get that. You could get a million dollars. You could get it in cash. I know where it could be gotten. It is not easy, but it could be done. But the question is who the hell would handle it? Any ideas on that? . . .

D: Now we've got [Herbert] Kalmbach. Kalmbach received, at the close of the '68 campaign in January of 1969, he got a million $700,000 to be custodian for. That came down from New York, and was placed in safe deposit boxes here. Some other people were on the boxes. And ultimately, the money was taken out

---

[8]**"Cubans . . . McCord"**: Refers to the four Cuban Americans who, together with former CIA agent James McCord, were arrested in the Watergate break-in.

[9]**John Ehrlichman:** John Ehrlichman, a top Nixon aide.

to California. Alright, there is knowledge of the fact that he did start with a million seven. Several people know this. Now since 1969, he has spent a good deal of this money and accounting for it is going to be very difficult for Herb [Kalmbach]. For example, he has spent close to $500,000 on private polling. That opens up a whole new thing. It is not illegal, but more of the same thing.

P: Everybody does polling.

D: That's right. There is nothing criminal about it. It's private polling. . . . I don't know of anything that Herb has done that is illegal. . . .What really bothers me is this growing situation. As I say, it is growing because of the continued need to provide support for the Watergate people who are going to hold us up for everything we've got, and the need for some people to perjure themselves as they go down the road here. If this thing ever blows, then we are in a cover up situation. I think it would be extremely damaging to you and the —

P: Sure. The whole concept of Administration justice. Which we cannot have! . . .

D: That's right. I am coming down to what I really think, is that Bob and John and John Mitchell and I can sit down and spend a day, or however long, to figure out one, how this can be carved away from you, so that it does not damage you or the Presidency. It just can't! You are not involved in it and it is something you shouldn't —

P: That is true! . . .

D: What really troubles me is one, will this thing not break some day and the whole thing — domino situation — everything starts crumbling, fingers will be pointing. Bob will be accused of things he has never heard of and deny and try to disprove it. It will get real nasty and just be a real bad situation. And the person who will be hurt by it most will be you and the Presidency, and I just don't think —

P: First, because I am an executive I am supposed to check these things.

D: That's right.

P: Let's come back to this problem. What are your feelings yourself, John? You know what they are all saying. What are your feelings about the chances?

D: I am not confident that we can ride through this. I think there are soft spots. . . .

P: . . . But just looking at it from a cold legal standpoint: you are a lawyer, you were a counsel — doing what you did as counsel. You were not — What would you go to jail for?

D: The obstruction of justice.

P: The obstruction of justice?

D: That is the only one that bothers me.

P: Well, I don't know. I think that one. I feel it could be cut off at the pass, maybe, the obstruction of justice. . . .Talking about your obstruction of justice, though, I don't see it.

D: Well, I have been a conduit for information on taking care of people out there who are guilty of crimes.

P: Oh, you mean like the blackmailers?

D: The blackmailers. Right.

P: Well, I wonder if that part of it can't be — I wonder if that doesn't — let me put it frankly: I wonder if that doesn't have to be continued? Let me put it this way: let us suppose that you get the million bucks, and you get the proper way to handle it. You could hold that side?

D: Uh, huh.

P: It would seem to me that would be worthwhile. . . .

D: There are two routes. One is to figure out how to cut the losses and minimize the human impact and get you up and out and away from it in any way. In a way it would never come back to haunt you. That is one general alternative. The other is to go down the road, just hunker down, fight it at every corner, every turn, don't let people testify — cover it up is what we really are talking about. Just keep it buried, and just hope that we can do it, hope that we make good decisions at the right time, keep our heads cool, we make the right moves.

P: And just take the heat?

D: And just take the heat. . . .

[H. R. Haldeman joins the meeting.]

P: . . . You see, John is concerned, as you know, about the Ehrlichman situation. It worries him a great deal because, and this is why the Hunt problem is so serious, because it had nothing to do with the campaign. It has to do with the Ellsberg case. I don't know what the hell the — (unintelligible)

H[aldeman]: But what I was going to say —

P: What is the answer on this? How you keep it out, I don't know. You can't keep it out if Hunt talks. You see the point is irrelevant. It has gotten to this point —

D: You might put it on a national security basis.

H: It absolutely was.

D: And say that this was —

H: (unintelligible) — CIA —

D: Ah —

H: Seriously.

P: National Security. We had to get information [from Ellsberg's psychiatrist's office] for national security grounds.

D: Then the question is, why didn't the CIA do it or why didn't the FBI do it?

P: Because we had to do it on a confidential basis.

H: Because we were checking them.

P: Neither could be trusted.

H: It has basically never been proven. There was reason to question their position.

P: With the bombing thing coming out and everything coming out, the whole thing was national security.

D: I think we could get by on that.

P: On that one I think we should simply say this was a national security investigation that was conducted. And on that basis, I think . . . Krogh could say he feels he did not perjure himself. He could say it was a national security matter. That is why — . . . You really only have two ways to go. You either decide that the whole (expletive deleted) thing is so full of problems with potential criminal liabilities, which most concern me. I don't give a damn about the publicity. We could rock that through that if we had to let the whole damn thing hang out, and it would be a lousy story for a month. But I can take it. The point is, that I don't want any criminal liabilities. That is the thing that I am concerned about for members of the White House staff, and I would trust for members of the Committee. . . .

H: Well, the thing we talked about yesterday. You have a question where you cut off on this. There is a possibility of cutting it at Liddy, where you are now.

P: Yeah.

D: But to accomplish that requires a continued perjury by Magruder and requires —

P: And requires total commitment and control over all of the defendants which — in other words when they are let down — . . . Another way to do it then Bob, and John realizes this, is to continue to try to cut our losses. Now we have to take a look at that course of action. First it is going to require approximately a million dollars to take care of the jackasses who are in jail. That can be arranged. That could be arranged. But you realize that after we are gone, and assuming we can expend this money, then they are going to crack and it would be an unseemly story. Frankly, all the people aren't going to care that much.

D: That's right.

P: People won't care, but people are going to be talking about it, there is no question. . . . And my point is that I think it is good, frankly, to consider these various options. And then, once you decide on the right plan, you say, "John," you say, "No doubts about the right plan before the election. You handled it just right. You contained it. And now after the election we have to have another plan. Because we can't for four years have this thing eating away." We can't do it.

H: We should change that a little bit. John's point is exactly right. The erosion here now is going to you, and that is the thing that we have to turn off at whatever cost. We have to turn it off at the lowest cost we can, but at whatever cost it takes.

D: That's what we have to do.

P: Well, the erosion is inevitably going to come here, apart from anything and all the people saying well the Watergate isn't a major issue. It isn't. But it will be. It's bound to. (Unintelligible) has to go out. Delaying is the great danger to the White House area. We don't, I say that the White House can't do it. Right?

D: Yes, Sir.

## QUESTIONS FOR READING AND DISCUSSION

1. What "cancer within" did Dean worry about? Why did Nixon and Dean believe they were being blackmailed, and how did they plan to respond? What were the "soft spots" that worried Dean?

2. Did Dean and Attorney General Mitchell entertain plans to break the law? Did Nixon?

3. How did President Nixon obtain information about political opponents? How did Nixon hope to use arguments about "national security"?

4. Did Nixon declare his opposition to a "cover-up"? Did he demand that all members of his administration strictly adhere to the law? Why or why not?

5. Nixon knew the conversations in his office were being taped, but none of the other officials were aware that their remarks were being recorded. To what extent might this knowledge have influenced what Nixon said?

## DOCUMENT 30-2

# Roe v. Wade and Abortion Rights

*One of the important activities of the women's rights movement was setting up clinics to advise women about birth control, pregnancy, and abortion. In many states, abortions were illegal. In 1970, Sarah Weddington, a lawyer from the Women's Liberation Birth Control Information Center in Austin, Texas, filed suit in federal court to overturn the*

*Texas antiabortion law. Weddington's client took the name Jane Roe in the legal documents to preserve her privacy. Jane Roe was actually Norma McCorvey, a pregnant young high school dropout who sought an abortion, an action opposed by Henry Wade, the district attorney of Dallas County. In 1973, a 7 to 2 majority of the U.S. Supreme Court decided the case of Roe v. Wade. Justice Harry A. Blackmun wrote the majority opinion, the source of the following selection.*

## Supreme Court Decision, 1973

We forthwith acknowledge our awareness of the sensitive and emotional nature of the abortion controversy, of the vigorous opposing views, even among physicians, and of the deep and seemingly absolute convictions that the subject inspires. One's philosophy, one's experiences, one's exposure to the raw edges of human existence, one's religious training, one's attitudes toward life and family and their values, and the moral standards one establishes and seeks to observe, are all likely to influence and to color one's thinking and conclusions about abortion.

In addition, population growth, pollution, poverty, and racial overtones tend to complicate and not to simplify the problem.

Our task, of course, is to resolve the issue by constitutional measurement free of emotion and of predilection. We seek earnestly to do this, and, because we do, we have inquired into, and in this opinion place some emphasis upon, medical and medical-legal history and what that history reveals about man's attitudes toward the abortive procedure over the centuries. . . .

Jane Roe, a single woman who was residing in Dallas County, Texas, instituted this federal action in March 1970 against the District Attorney of the county. She sought a declaratory judgment that the Texas criminal abortion statutes were unconstitutional on their face, and an injunction restraining the defendant from enforcing the statutes.

Roe alleged that she was unmarried and pregnant; that she wished to terminate her pregnancy by an abortion "performed by a competent, licensed physician, under safe, clinical conditions"; that she was unable to get a "legal" abortion in Texas because her life did not appear to be threatened by the continuation of her pregnancy; and that she could not afford to travel to another jurisdiction in order to secure a legal abortion under safe conditions. She claimed that the Texas statutes were unconstitutionally vague and that they abridged her right of personal privacy, protected by the First, Fourth, Fifth, Ninth, and Fourteenth Amendments. By an amendment to her complaint Roe purported to sue "on behalf of herself and all other women" similarly situated. . . .

On the merits, the District Court held that the "fundamental right of single women and married persons to choose whether to have children is protected by the Ninth Amendment, through the Fourteenth Amendment," and that the Texas criminal abortion statutes were void on their face because they were both unconstitutionally vague and constituted an overbroad infringement of the plaintiffs' Ninth Amendment rights. . . .

---

*Roe v. Wade,* 410 U.S. 113 (1973).

It perhaps is not generally appreciated that the restrictive criminal abortion laws in effect in a majority of States today are of relatively recent vintage. Those laws, generally proscribing abortion or its attempt at any time during pregnancy except when necessary to preserve the pregnant woman's life, are not of ancient or even of common law origin. Instead, they derive from statutory changes effected, for the most part, in the latter half of the 19th century. . . .

Three reasons have been advanced to explain historically the enactment of criminal abortion laws in the 19th century and to justify their continued existence. . . .

It has been argued occasionally that these laws were the product of a Victorian social concern to discourage illicit sexual conduct. Texas, however, does not advance this justification in the present case, and it appears that no court or commentator has taken the argument seriously. . . .

A second reason is concerned with abortion as a medical procedure. When most criminal abortion laws were first enacted, the procedure was a hazardous one for the woman. This was particularly true prior to the development of antisepsis. . . . Abortion mortality was high. . . . Thus it has been argued that a State's real concern in enacting a criminal abortion law was to protect the pregnant woman, that is, to restrain her from submitting to a procedure that placed her life in serious jeopardy. . . .

The third reason is the State's interest — some phrase it in terms of duty — in protecting prenatal life. . . .

. . . [A]s long as at least *potential* life is involved, the State may assert interests beyond the protection of the pregnant woman alone. . . .

It is with these interests, and the weight to be attached to them, that this case is concerned.

The Constitution does not explicitly mention any right of privacy. In a line of decisions, however, going back perhaps as far as . . . [1891], the Court has recognized that a right of personal privacy, or a guarantee of certain areas or zones of privacy, does exist under the Constitution. . . .

This right of privacy, whether it be founded in the Fourteenth Amendment's concept of personal liberty and restrictions upon state action, as we feel it is, or, as the District Court determined, in the Ninth Amendment's reservation of rights to the people, is broad enough to encompass a woman's decision whether or not to terminate her pregnancy. The detriment that the State would impose upon the pregnant woman by denying this choice altogether is apparent. Specific and direct harm medically diagnosable even in early pregnancy may be involved. Maternity, or additional offspring, may force upon the woman a distressful life and future. Psychological harm may be imminent. Mental and physical health may be taxed by child care. There is also the distress, for all concerned, associated with the unwanted child, and there is the problem of bringing a child into a family already unable, psychologically and otherwise, to care for it. In other cases, as in this one, the additional difficulties and continuing stigma of unwed motherhood may be involved. . . .

On the basis of elements such as these, appellants and some *amici*[1] argue that the woman's right is absolute and that she is entitled to terminate her

---

[1]**Amici:** A legal term for "friends of the court," people who are not party to the litigation but offer advice to the court on the litigation.

pregnancy at whatever time, in whatever way, and for whatever reason she alone chooses. With this we do not agree. . . . [A] state may properly assert important interests in safeguarding health, in maintaining medical standards, and in protecting potential life. At some point in pregnancy, these respective interests become sufficiently compelling to sustain regulation of the factors that govern the abortion decision. The privacy right involved, therefore, cannot be said to be absolute. . . .

We therefore conclude that the right of personal privacy includes the abortion decision, but that this right is not unqualified and must be considered against important state interests in regulation. . . .

Where certain "fundamental rights" are involved, the Court has held that regulation limiting these rights may be justified only by a "compelling state interest,". . . and that legislative enactments must be narrowly drawn to express only the legitimate state interests at stake. . . .

. . . The appellee and certain *amici* argue that the fetus is a "person" within the language and meaning of the Fourteenth Amendment. . . .

The Constitution does not define "person" in so many words. . . . All this, together with our observation . . . that throughout the major portion of the 19th century prevailing legal abortion practices were far freer than they are today, persuades us that the word "person," as used in the Fourteenth Amendment, does not include the unborn. . . .

Texas urges that, apart from the Fourteenth Amendment, life begins at conception and is present throughout pregnancy, and that, therefore, the State has a compelling interest in protecting that life from and after conception. We need not resolve the difficult question of when life begins. When those trained in the respective disciplines of medicine, philosophy, and theology are unable to arrive at any consensus, the judiciary, at this point in the development of man's knowledge, is not in a position to speculate as to the answer.

It should be sufficient to note briefly the wide divergence of thinking on this most sensitive and difficult question. . . .

In areas other than criminal abortion the law has been reluctant to endorse any theory that life, as we recognize it, begins before live birth or to accord legal rights to the unborn except in narrowly defined situations and except when the rights are contingent upon live birth. . . . [T]he unborn have never been recognized in the law as persons in the whole sense.

. . . [T]he State does have an important and legitimate interest in preserving and protecting the health of the pregnant woman, whether she be a resident of the State or a nonresident who seeks medical consultation and treatment there, and that it has still another important and legitimate interest in protecting the potentiality of human life. These interests are separate and distinct. Each grows in substantiality as the woman approaches term and, at a point during pregnancy, each becomes "compelling."

With respect to the State's important and legitimate interest in the health of the mother, the "compelling" point, in the light of present medical knowledge, is at approximately the end of the first trimester. This is so because of the now established medical fact, referred to above, that until the end of the first trimester mortality in abortion is less than mortality in normal childbirth. It follows that, from and after this point, a State may regulate the abortion procedure to the extent that the regulation reasonably relates to the preservation and protection of maternal health. . . .

With respect to the State's important and legitimate interest in potential life, the "compelling" point is at viability. This is so because the fetus then presumably has the capability of meaningful life outside the mother's womb. State regulation protective of fetal life after viability thus has both logical and biological justifications. If the State is interested in protecting fetal life after viability, it may go so far as to proscribe abortion during that period except when it is necessary to preserve the life or health of the mother. . . .

To summarize and to repeat:

1. A state criminal abortion statute of the current Texas type, that excepts from criminality only a *life saving* procedure on behalf of the mother, without regard to pregnancy stage and without recognition of the other interests involved, is violative of the Due Process Clause of the Fourteenth Amendment.

(a) For the stage prior to approximately the end of the first trimester, the abortion decision and its effectuation must be left to the medical judgment of the pregnant woman's attending physician.

(b) For the stage subsequent to approximately the end of the first trimester, the State, in promoting its interest in the health of the mother, may, if it chooses, regulate the abortion procedure in ways that are reasonably related to maternal health.

(c) For the stage subsequent to viability the State, in promoting its interest in the potentiality of human life, may, if it chooses, regulate, and even proscribe, abortion except where it is necessary, in appropriate medical judgment, for the preservation of the life or health of the mother. . . .

The decision leaves the State free to place increasing restrictions on abortion as the period of pregnancy lengthens, so long as those restrictions are tailored to the recognized state interests. The decision vindicates the right of the physician to administer medical treatment according to his professional judgment up to the points where important state interests provide compelling justifications for intervention. Up to those points the abortion decision in all its aspects is inherently, and primarily, a medical decision, and basic responsibility for it must rest with the physician. If an individual practitioner abuses the privilege of exercising proper medical judgment, the usual remedies, judicial and intraprofessional, are available.

It is so ordered.

## QUESTIONS FOR READING AND DISCUSSION

1. Why did Jane Roe seek a decision from the Supreme Court? Why did the state of Texas oppose Roe's lawsuit?

2. According to the court, why were criminal abortion laws enacted?

3. What was the basis of the court's declaration that "a right of personal privacy, or a guarantee of certain areas or zones of privacy . . . exist under the Constitution"? Was that right absolute, according to the court?

4. To what extent did the state have "important and legitimate" interests in regulating abortions, according to the court? How should the boundary between a woman's right to privacy and a state's interests be defined?

5. What is the significance of the court's statement that "the word 'person,' as used in the Fourteenth Amendment, does not include the unborn"?

DOCUMENT 30-3

# President Ronald Reagan Declares Government the Problem

*Many Americans shared the conviction that government caused problems for the nation, rather than solving them, a conviction President Ronald Reagan made the centerpiece of his first inaugural address and acted upon throughout his two terms in office. Reagan's theme of individual rather than government solutions to major national problems appealed to voters in both Republican and Democratic parties. Reagan linked small-government ideas to optimistic patriotism, suggesting that proponents of government programs were pessimists of dubious American loyalty.*

## Inaugural Address, January 20, 1981

. . . [M]y fellow citizens: To a few of us here today, this is a solemn and most momentous occasion; and yet, in the history of our Nation, it is a commonplace occurrence. The orderly transfer of authority as called for in the Constitution routinely takes place as it has for almost two centuries and few of us stop to think how unique we really are. In the eyes of many in the world, this every-4-year ceremony we accept as normal is nothing less than a miracle. . . .

The business of our nation goes forward. These United States are confronted with an economic affliction of great proportions. We suffer from the longest and one of the worst sustained inflations in our national history. It distorts our economic decisions, penalizes thrift, and crushes the struggling young and the fixed-income elderly alike. It threatens to shatter the lives of millions of our people.

Idle industries have cast workers into unemployment, causing human misery and personal indignity. Those who do work are denied a fair return for their labor by a tax system which penalizes successful achievement and keeps us from maintaining full productivity.

But great as our tax burden is, it has not kept pace with public spending. For decades, we have piled deficit upon deficit, mortgaging our future and our children's future for the temporary convenience of the present. To continue this long trend is to guarantee tremendous social, cultural, political, and economic upheavals.

You and I, as individuals, can, by borrowing, live beyond our means, but for only a limited period of time. Why, then, should we think that collectively, as a nation, we are not bound by that same limitation?

We must act today in order to preserve tomorrow. And let there be no misunderstanding — we are going to begin to act, beginning today.

The economic ills we suffer have come upon us over several decades. They will not go away in days, weeks, or months, but they will go away. They will go away because we, as Americans, have the capacity now, as we have had in the past, to do whatever needs to be done to preserve this last and greatest bastion of freedom.

In this present crisis, government is not the solution to our problem.

Ronald Reagan, First Inaugural Address, January 20, 1981.

From time to time, we have been tempted to believe that society has become too complex to be managed by self-rule, that government by an elite group is superior to government for, by, and of the people. But if no one among us is capable of governing himself, then who among us has the capacity to govern someone else? All of us together, in and out of government, must bear the burden. The solutions we seek must be equitable, with no one group singled out to pay a higher price.

We hear much of special interest groups. Our concern must be for a special interest group that has been too long neglected. It knows no sectional boundaries or ethnic and racial divisions, and it crosses political party lines. It is made up of men and women who raise our food, patrol our streets, man our mines and our factories, teach our children, keep our homes, and heal us when we are sick — professionals, industrialists, shopkeepers, clerks, cabbies, and truckdrivers. They are, in short, "We the people," this breed called Americans.

Well, this administration's objective will be a healthy, vigorous, growing economy that provides equal opportunity for all Americans, with no barriers born of bigotry or discrimination. Putting America back to work means putting all Americans back to work. Ending inflation means freeing all Americans from the terror of runaway living costs. All must share in the productive work of this "new beginning" and all must share in the bounty of a revived economy. With the idealism and fair play which are the core of our system and our strength, we can have a strong and prosperous America at peace with itself and the world.

So, as we begin, let us take inventory. We are a nation that has a government — not the other way around. And this makes us special among the nations of the Earth. Our Government has no power except that granted it by the people. It is time to check and reverse the growth of government which shows signs of having grown beyond the consent of the governed.

It is my intention to curb the size and influence of the Federal establishment and to demand recognition of the distinction between the powers granted to the Federal Government and those reserved to the States or to the people. All of us need to be reminded that the Federal Government did not create the States; the States created the Federal Government.

Now, so there will be no misunderstanding, it is not my intention to do away with government. It is, rather, to make it work — work with us, not over us; to stand by our side, not ride on our back. Government can and must provide opportunity, not smother it; foster productivity, not stifle it.

If we look to the answer as to why, for so many years, we achieved so much, prospered as no other people on Earth, it was because here, in this land, we unleashed the energy and individual genius of man to a greater extent than has ever been done before. Freedom and the dignity of the individual have been more available and assured here than in any other place on Earth. The price for this freedom at times has been high, but we have never been unwilling to pay that price.

It is no coincidence that our present troubles parallel and are proportionate to the intervention and intrusion in our lives that result from unnecessary and excessive growth of government. It is time for us to realize that we are too great a nation to limit ourselves to small dreams. We are not, as some would have us believe, doomed to an inevitable decline. I do not believe in a fate that will fall on us no matter what we do. I do believe in a fate that will fall on us if we do nothing. So, with all the creative energy at our command, let us begin an era of national renewal. Let us renew our determination, our courage, and our strength. And let us renew our faith and our hope.

We have every right to dream heroic dreams. Those who say that we are in a time when there are no heroes just don't know where to look. You can see heroes every day going in and out of factory gates. Others, a handful in number, produce enough food to feed all of us and then the world beyond. You meet heroes across a counter — and they are on both sides of that counter. There are entrepreneurs with faith in themselves and faith in an idea who create new jobs, new wealth and opportunity. They are individuals and families whose taxes support the Government and whose voluntary gifts support church, charity, culture, art, and education. Their patriotism is quiet but deep. Their values sustain our national life.

I have used the words "they" and "their" in speaking of these heroes. I could say "you" and "your" because I am addressing the heroes of whom I speak — you, the citizens of this blessed land. Your dreams, your hopes, your goals are going to be the dreams, the hopes, and the goals of this administration, so help me God. . . .

Can we solve the problems confronting us? Well, the answer is an unequivocal and emphatic "yes." . . .

In the days ahead I will propose removing the roadblocks that have slowed our economy and reduced productivity. Steps will be taken aimed at restoring the balance between the various levels of government. Progress may be slow — measured in inches and feet, not miles — but we will progress. It is time to reawaken this industrial giant, to get government back within its means, and to lighten our punitive tax burden. And these will be our first priorities, and on these principles, there will be no compromise. . . .

And as we renew ourselves here in our own land, we will be seen as having greater strength throughout the world. We will again be the exemplar of freedom and a beacon of hope for those who do not now have freedom. . . .

As for the enemies of freedom, those who are potential adversaries, they will be reminded that peace is the highest aspiration of the American people. We will negotiate for it, sacrifice for it; we will not surrender for it — now or ever.

Our forbearance should never be misunderstood. Our reluctance for conflict should not be misjudged as a failure of will. When action is required to preserve our national security, we will act. We will maintain sufficient strength to prevail if need be, knowing that if we do so we have the best chance of never having to use that strength.

Above all, we must realize that no arsenal, or no weapon in the arsenals of the world, is so formidable as the will and moral courage of free men and women. It is a weapon our adversaries in today's world do not have. It is a weapon that we as Americans do have. Let that be understood by those who practice terrorism and prey upon their neighbors.

I am told that tens of thousands of prayer meetings are being held on this day, and for that I am deeply grateful. We are a nation under God, and I believe God intended for us to be free. It would be fitting and good, I think, if on each Inauguration Day in future years it should be declared a day of prayer. . . .

Standing here, one faces a magnificent vista, opening up on this city's special beauty and history. At the end of this open mall are those shrines to the giants on whose shoulders we stand. . . .

Beyond those monuments to heroism is the Potomac River, and on the far shore the sloping hills of Arlington National Cemetery with its row on row of simple white markers bearing crosses or Stars of David. They add up to only a tiny fraction of the price that has been paid for our freedom.

Each one of those markers is a monument to the kinds of hero I spoke of earlier. Their lives ended in places called Belleau Wood, The Argonne, Omaha Beach, Salerno and halfway around the world on Guadalcanal, Tarawa, Pork Chop Hill, the Chosin Reservoir, and in a hundred rice paddies and jungles of a place called Vietnam.

Under one such marker lies a young man — Martin Treptow — who left his job in a small town barber shop in 1917 to go to France with the famed Rainbow Division. There, on the western front, he was killed trying to carry a message between battalions under heavy artillery fire.

We are told that on his body was found a diary. On the flyleaf under the heading, "My Pledge," he had written these words: "America must win this war. Therefore, I will work, I will save, I will sacrifice, I will endure, I will fight cheerfully and do my utmost, as if the issue of the whole struggle depended on me alone."

The crisis we are facing today does not require of us the kind of sacrifice that Martin Treptow and so many thousands of others were called upon to make. It does require, however, our best effort, and our willingness to believe in ourselves and to believe in our capacity to perform great deeds; to believe that together, with God's help, we can and will resolve the problems which now confront us.

And, after all, why shouldn't we believe that? We are Americans. God bless you, and thank you.

#### QUESTIONS FOR READING AND DISCUSSION

1. Why did President Reagan believe that, "In this present crisis, government is not the solution to our problem"? What, for example, would improve the economy?
2. What "special interest groups" did Reagan oppose and what did he favor? Why?
3. What was the significance of Reagan's statement that, "the States created the Federal Government"? Did state governments offer solutions to national problems, while the federal government did not? Why or why not?
4. Reagan declared, "We are a nation under God, and I believe God intended for us to be free." What significance did such views have for Reagan's views about government and individuals?

## DOCUMENT 30-4

## *President Ronald Reagan Defends American Morality*

*President Ronald Reagan portrayed America as the embodiment of morality. He attributed American morality to traditional values he associated with Christianity. Reagan believed his views represented 100 percent Americanism and that those who differed were either deluded or suspect. Millions of Americans agreed with him and voted for him. Reagan drew upon his ideas of American morality in his speech — excerpted here — to the annual convention of the National Association of American Evangelicals in Orlando, Florida, in 1983. The speech illustrates Reagan's concept of history as a struggle between good and evil and his certainty that America was on the side of good.*

# Address to the National Association of American Evangelicals, 1983

Those of you in the National Association of Evangelicals are known for your spiritual and humanitarian work. And I would be especially remiss if I didn't discharge right now one personal debt of gratitude. Thank you for your prayers. . . .

So I tell you there are a great many God-fearing, dedicated, noble men and women in public life, present company included. And yes, we need your help to keep us ever mindful of the ideas and the principles that brought us into the public arena in the first place. The basis of those ideals and principles is a commitment to freedom and personal liberty that, itself, is grounded in the much deeper realization that freedom prospers only where the blessings of God are avidly sought and humbly accepted.

The American experiment in democracy rests on this insight. . . .

Well, I'm pleased to be here today with you who are keeping America great by keeping her good. Only through your work and prayers and those of millions of others can we hope to survive this perilous century and keep alive this experiment in liberty, this last, best hope of man.

I want you to know that this administration is motivated by a political philosophy that sees the greatness of America in you, her people, and in your families, churches, neighborhoods, communities — the institutions that foster and nourish values like concern for others and respect for the rule of law under God.

Now, I don't have to tell you that this puts us in opposition to, or at least out of step with, a prevailing attitude of many who have turned to a modern-day secularism, discarding the tried and time-tested values upon which our very civilization is based. No matter how well intentioned, their value system is radically different from that of most Americans. And while they proclaim that they're freeing us from superstitions of the past, they've taken upon themselves the job of superintending us by government rule and regulation. Sometimes their voices are louder than ours, but they are not yet a majority.

An example of that vocal superiority is evident in a controversy now going on in Washington. And since I'm involved, I've been waiting to hear from the parents of young America. How far are they willing to go in giving to government their prerogatives as parents?

Let me state the case as briefly and simply as I can. An organization of citizens, sincerely motivated and deeply concerned about the increase in illegitimate births and abortions involving girls well below the age of consent, some time ago established a nationwide network of clinics to offer help to these girls and, hopefully, alleviate this situation. Now, again, let me say, I do not fault their intent. However, in their well-intentioned effort, these clinics have decided to provide advice and birth control drugs and devices to underage girls without the knowledge of their parents. . . .

Well, we have ordered clinics receiving federal funds to notify the parents such help has been given. . . . I've watched TV panel shows discuss this issue, seen columnists pontificating on our error, but no one seems to mention morality as playing a part in the subject of sex.

---

Ronald Reagan, "Remarks at the Annual Convention of the National Association of Evangelicals." The Public Papers of President Ronald Reagan, The Reagan Library. Http://www.reagan.utexas.edu/resource/_vti_script/speeches_rrpubpap.asp0.idq

Is all of Judeo-Christian tradition wrong? Are we to believe that something so sacred can be looked upon as a purely physical thing with no potential for emotional and psychological harm? . . .

Many of us in government would like to know what parents think about this intrusion in their family by government. We're going to fight in the courts. The right of parents and the rights of family take precedence over those of Washington-based bureaucrats and social engineers.

But the fight against parental notification is really only one example of many attempts to water down traditional values and even abrogate the original terms of American democracy. Freedom prospers when religion is vibrant and the rule of law under God is acknowledged. When our Founding Fathers passed the First Amendment, they sought to protect churches from government interference. They never intended to construct a wall of hostility between government and the concept of religious belief itself.

The evidence of this permeates our history and our government. The Declaration of Independence mentions the Supreme Being no less than four times. "In God We Trust" is engraved on our coinage. The Supreme Court opens its proceedings with a religious invocation. And the members of Congress open their sessions with a prayer. I just happen to believe the schoolchildren of the United States are entitled to the same privileges as Supreme Court justices and congressmen.

Last year, I sent the Congress a constitutional amendment to restore prayer to public schools. Already this session, there's growing bipartisan support for the amendment, and I am calling on the Congress to act speedily to pass it and to let our children pray. . . .

More than a decade ago, a Supreme Court decision literally wiped off the books of fifty states statutes protecting the rights of unborn children. Abortion on demand now takes the lives of up to one and a half million unborn children a year. Human life legislation ending this tragedy will someday pass the Congress, and you and I must never rest until it does. Unless and until it can be proven that the unborn child is not a living entity, then its right to life, liberty, and the pursuit of happiness must be protected. . . .

Now, I'm sure that you must get discouraged at times, but you've done better than you know, perhaps. There's a great spiritual awakening in America, a renewal of the traditional values that have been the bedrock of America's goodness and greatness.

One recent survey by a Washington-based research council concluded that Americans were far more religious than the people of other nations; 95 percent of those surveyed expressed a belief in God and a huge majority believed the Ten Commandments had real meaning in their lives. And another study has found that an overwhelming majority of Americans disapprove of adultery, teenage sex, pornography, abortion, and hard drugs. And this same study showed a deep reverence for the importance of family ties and religious belief.

I think the items that we've discussed here today must be a key part of the nation's political agenda. For the first time the Congress is openly and seriously debating and dealing with the prayer and abortion issues — and that's enormous progress right there. I repeat: America is in the midst of a spiritual awakening and a moral renewal. . . .

Now, obviously, much of this new political and social consensus I've talked about is based on a positive view of American history, one that takes pride in our country's accomplishments and record. But we must never forget that no government schemes are going to perfect man. We know that living in this world means dealing with what philosophers would call the phenomenology of evil or, as theologians would put it, the doctrine of sin.

There is sin and evil in the world, and we're enjoined by Scripture and the Lord Jesus to oppose it with all our might. Our nation, too, has a legacy of evil with which it must deal. The glory of this land has been its capacity for transcending the moral evils of our past. For example, the long struggle of minority citizens for equal rights, once a source of disunity and civil war, is now a point of pride for all Americans. We must never go back. There is no room for racism, anti-Semitism, or other forms of ethnic and racial hatred in this country.

I know that you've been horrified, as have I, by the resurgence of some hate groups preaching bigotry and prejudice. Use the mighty voice of your pulpits and the powerful standing of your churches to denounce and isolate these hate groups in our midst. The commandment given us is clear and simple: "Thou shalt love thy neighbor as thyself."

But whatever sad episodes exist in our past, any objective observer must hold a positive view of American history, a history that has been the story of hopes fulfilled and dreams made into reality. Especially in this century, America has kept alight the torch of freedom, but not just for ourselves but for millions of others around the world.

And this brings me to my final point today. During my first press conference as president, in answer to a direct question, I pointed out that, as good Marxist-Leninists, the Soviet leaders have openly and publicly declared that the only morality they recognize is that which will further their cause, which is world revolution. . . .

Well, I think the refusal of many influential people to accept this elementary fact of Soviet doctrine illustrates a historical reluctance to see totalitarian powers for what they are. We saw this phenomenon in the 1930s. We see it too often today.

This doesn't mean we should isolate ourselves and refuse to seek an understanding with them. I intend to do everything I can to persuade them of our peaceful intent, to remind them that it was the West that refused to use its nuclear monopoly in the forties and fifties for territorial gain and which now proposes a 50-percent cut in strategic ballistic missiles and the elimination of an entire class of land-based, intermediate-range nuclear missiles.

At the same time, however, they must be made to understand we will never compromise our principles and standards. We will never give away our freedom. We will never abandon our belief in God. And we will never stop searching for a genuine peace. But we can assure none of these things America stands for through the so-called nuclear freeze solutions proposed by some.

The truth is that a freeze now would be a very dangerous fraud, for that is merely the illusion of peace. The reality is that we must find peace through strength. . . .

A number of years ago, I heard a young father, a very prominent young man in the entertainment world, addressing a tremendous gathering in California. It was during the time of the cold war, and communism and our own way of life were very much on people's minds. And he was speaking to that subject. And suddenly . . . I heard him saying, "I love my little girls more than anything.". . . . He went on: "I would rather see my little girls die now, still believing in God, than have them grow up under communism and one day die no longer believing in God."

There were thousands of young people in that audience. They came to their feet with shouts of joy. They had instantly recognized the profound truth in what he had said, with regard to the physical and the soul and what was truly important.

Yes, let us pray for the salvation of all of those who live in that totalitarian darkness — pray they will discover the joy of knowing God. But until they do, let us be aware that while they preach the supremacy of the state, declare its omnipotence over individual man, and predict its eventual domination of all peoples on the earth, they are the focus of evil in the modern world. . . .

But if history teaches anything, it teaches that simpleminded appeasement or wishful thinking about our adversaries is folly. It means the betrayal of our past, the squandering of our freedom.

So, I urge you to speak out against those who would place the United States in a position of military and moral inferiority. . . . I urge you to beware the temptation of pride — the temptation of blithely declaring yourselves above it all and label both sides equally at fault, to ignore the facts of history and the aggressive impulses of an evil empire, to simply call the arms race a giant misunderstanding and thereby remove yourself from the struggle between right and wrong and good and evil.

I ask you to resist the attempts of those who would have you withhold your support for our efforts, this administration's efforts, to keep America strong and free, while we negotiate real and verifiable reductions in the world's nuclear arsenals and one day, with God's help, their total elimination.

While America's military strength is important, let me add here that I've always maintained that the struggle now going on for the world will never be decided by bombs or rockets, by armies or military might. The real crisis we face today is a spiritual one; at root, it is a test of moral will and faith. . . .

I believe we shall rise to the challenge. I believe that communism is another sad, bizarre chapter in human history whose last pages even now are being written. I believe this because the source of our strength in the quest for human freedom is not material, but spiritual. And because it knows no limitation, it must terrify and ultimately triumph over those who would enslave their fellow man.

## Questions for Reading and Discussion

1. According to Reagan, why did freedom prosper "only where the blessings of God are avidly sought and humbly accepted"? What evidence did he cite that the founders "never intended to construct a wall of hostility between government and the concept of religious belief"?

2. Reagan identified his opponents as advocates of "modern-day secularism." What did they believe, and why did their views threaten the "Judeo-Christian tradition"?

3. Why did Reagan call the Soviet Union "the focus of evil in the modern world"? What did he think the United States should do to oppose the evil Soviets?

4. Reagan advocated "a positive view of American history." What view was Reagan arguing against? What did he believe made the United States different from other nations?

# A Vietnamese Immigrant on the West Coast

*Following the Vietnam War, hundreds of thousands of immigrants came to the United States from Vietnam and elsewhere in Southeast Asia. The following interview, conducted in 1983, describes the experiences of one immigrant, a man from central Vietnam who preferred to remain anonymous. His statements reflect the experiences of millions of new immigrants who came to America seeking political asylum, reunion with family members, and, above all, a better life.*

## Anonymous Man
### Oral History

On our third attempt, my wife, children, and I escaped by boat from Vietnam and arrived in Hong Kong, where we remained for three months. Then my brother, who came to America in 1975, sponsored us, and we arrived in America in 1978.

We stayed with my brother and his family for five months. Neither I nor anyone in our family spoke any English before our arrival in America. I realized that I must study to communicate. Even though my brother was in one place, I decided to move to the West Coast. For nine months we lived in one town, where my children went to school. My wife and I also attended school to learn English. Although we received public assistance, we were always short each month by $20, $30, or even $40. If the situation continued like this, we'd have no money for clothes for the family. Even then, what we bought were old clothes that cost 20 or 25 cents apiece.

We made a visit to one of my sisters who lived in a small city that was surrounded by a lot of farmland. I saw that many of the people worked as farmers. I thought, "Maybe it's better for us to move here because I am used to working hard. God made me a hard-working man."

In 1980 we moved to that farming town. As soon as we arrived, I started to grow vegetables in the small backyard of the house we rented. In the meantime, I also worked as a farm laborer. We earned $35 to $45 a day, and that made me feel at ease. During the day I worked outside; in the evening I worked in my backyard. We began to sell what we grew, and from this we earned $200 a month. We liked to have our portion of land to do something, but we did not have enough money to buy.

We received help from the Public Housing Authority. The new house we moved into has four bedrooms. Each month we pay $50. The rest . . . is paid for by the government. The owner who rents us the house likes me very much because we keep the house very clean. . . . I moved all of the fruit trees from the old to the new house, and also planted a larger garden of vegetables and herbs. We have very good relations with our neighbors. They like us very much. They hire us to work on their backyards. That's the reason our income has increased. I grew too much to sell only to our neighbors. I needed to find a market.

James M. Freeman, *Hearts of Sorrow: Vietnamese-American Lives* (Stanford, CA: Stanford University Press, 1989), 382–90.

One day I went to the farmer's market. I didn't know how to do it. I brought my vegetables there but they chased me away. . . . The second time I went back, they chased me away again. But that time I asked, "Can you help me so I can sell vegetables like other people?"

That man told me, "Okay, you come with me; I'll show you how."

He gave me an application form, his business card, and an appointment. He explained to me during the appointment how I should do it and what kind of product I should have. He told me, "I want to come and see your garden, if it fulfills the requirements."

I agreed. He came down to inspect everything and wrote down on a piece of paper all the vegetables I grew. Then he gave me a permit. I brought my vegetables to the market, and nobody chased me any more. We earned some more money. . . .

After two years of this, we can save some [a lot]. Then we decided to have a fish truck. I borrowed some from my brother because it costs $4,000 to $5,000 to have a fish truck. During my work as a fish merchant our income was better. . . .

I am very happy in America for three reasons. First, I am very proud that I can do many things that other people could not do. Even though I do not know English very well, I did not bother anyone in dealing with paperwork or with translations. I myself did everything. I am very pleased by that. My English is not fluent, but when I speak with American people, they understand me, even though my grammar is not very good.

Second, I am at ease about living in America. Americans treat Vietnamese very well. I suppose if Americans had to live in Vietnam as refugees, the Vietnamese would not help them as much as the Americans helped me. We are very happy to live in America. I have received letters from Vietnamese refugees living in other countries. I am able to compare my life with theirs. Life in the United States is much better than in other countries of the Free World.

Third, what I like most is freedom, to move, to do business, and the freedom to work. I have freedom for myself, to work, to live, freedom to do everything you want. You can apply for a job or you can do a small business. You can apply for a license for a small business with no difficulties, no obstacles.

Although in America we live with everything free, to move, to do business, we still have the need to return to Vietnam one day. This is our dream. In Vietnam, before the Communists came, we had a sentimental life, more . . . comfortable and cozy, more joyful. To go out on the street, in the market in Vietnam, makes us more comfortable in our minds, spiritually.

Here in America, we have all the material comforts, very good. But the joy and sentiment are not like we had in Vietnam. There, when we went out from the home, we laughed, we jumped. And we had many relatives and friends to come to see us at home. Here in America, I only know what goes on in my home; my neighbor knows only what goes on in his home. We have a saying, "One knows only one's home." In America, when we go to work, we go in our cars. When we return, we leave our cars and enter our homes. . . . We do not need to know what goes on in the houses of our neighbors. That's why we do not have the kind of being at ease that we knew in Vietnam. . . .

When my sister came to America, she did as I am doing now. She and her family grew vegetables. Now they have two Vietnamese grocery stores and are the most successful Vietnamese refugees in their area. . . .

Another sister lives in the same town as I do. She and her husband are old, but their children are doing very well too. So four of my mother's children are now in America; four remain in Vietnam.

To live in America means that our life has changed. In Vietnam my family was very poor. We had to work very hard. We didn't have enough food or clothes. Under the Communist regime we were not free to do anything. If we made more than we needed, then the rest belonged to the revolutionary government. They did not want us to become rich. We needed to use old clothes. If we had new clothes, that's not good under the new regime because it showed that we had the capitalistic spirit.

My family living in America has everything complete and happy, and a new chance. I hope that my children become new people. My daughter in the eighth grade is the smartest of my children; she always gets A's. My youngest boy, who is eight years old, always is first in math in his class. My two oldest sons are not so good, but are above average and are preparing for electronics careers.

But the children are different here in America when compared with Vietnam. There is this big difference. Children growing up in Vietnam are afraid of their parents. Even when they marry, they still have respect and fear of their parents. In America, when they become 18, they lose their fear. They depend on the law of the land and go out of the house.

The one most difficult problem is the American law, and the American way to educate children. This is a big obstacle for the Vietnamese family. In Vietnam, in educating our children, if we cannot get success telling them what to do, we would punish them with a beating. By doing so, they would become good people. Here we cannot beat the children. That's the reason there's a big obstacle for us. When a child doesn't want to study, but likes to play with friends, if they want to smoke marijuana, when they do such bad things and parents tell them not to do so, the first, second, and third time, if they still don't listen, then parents *put them on the floor and beat them*. By doing so, this is the best way to prevent them from doing bad things, to get them to become good people. But here we cannot do that.

In my opinion, the Vietnamese have a lot of bad children because of American law, which is not like Vietnamese law. There are so many Vietnamese teenagers who came to America and who became not good people because of American law. When parents beat the child, the police come and arrest the parent. In the Vietnamese view, this is *the most dangerous and difficult obstacle*.

This is the *one most important thing* I want Americans to realize about the Vietnamese. The problem with educating and rearing the children is difficult because of American law. There's a second important point. Vietnamese life is not like American life. The Vietnamese have *villages, neighbors, and sentiment*. The father-child and mother-child relationship lasts forever, until the parents are very old. Children have the duty to take care of their parents. When the children were young, parents had the duty to raise and educate them. When the parents are old, duty is reversed: children take care of the parents. This is not like in America, where adult children leave the home, and old parents go to the nursing home. I'd like Americans to know that. I have met and talked with a lot of old American people. They have said to me, "When we become old, we . . . live together. When we become sick, nobody knows. When the postman comes, makes a surprise visit, only then does someone know we are sick. Sometimes our children aren't close by, or they live in a different state."

I ask the old people, "Do your children give you money?"

They reply, "No." These children do not think very much about their parents. This is very different from Vietnam; when children are married, they stay at home. When the parents become old, the children are together and take care of them.

But there are good lessons to be learned in America, such as *public sanitation.* That is what I have learned from America. At home, everything is arranged orderly and clean. Also, my American friends say what they think. This is different from what a Vietnamese would do. The American way, that's what I want my children to do. When we have one, we say "one." When we have two, we say "two." If that is a cow, we say it is a cow; if it's a goat, we say it's a goat. Vietnamese can learn this from Americans. I don't want to say what Americans can learn from the Vietnamese.

## QUESTIONS FOR READING AND DISCUSSION

1. How did this Vietnamese immigrant come to the United States? What kind of work did he do after arriving?

2. Why was he "very happy in America"? How did his life in America differ from that in Vietnam and the experiences of other Vietnamese immigrants "in other countries of the Free World"?

3. Why did he believe the "most difficult" problems were "the American law, and the American way to educate children"?

4. This man hinted that "Americans can learn from the Vietnamese." What lessons do you think he might urge Americans to learn?

## COMPARATIVE QUESTIONS

1. How did the concept of national security discussed by Richard Nixon and the optimistic complacency of Ronald Reagan compare with the experiences of the Vietnamese immigrant? What did each identify as the source of security? Why?

2. To what extent did the Watergate tapes reflect changes in, or deviations from, American ideas about democracy expressed in Reagan's speeches? What special interests are revealed in each? What views of government?

3. How did the constitutional protection of privacy in *Roe v. Wade* extend to the lives of working people such as the Vietnamese immigrant and to politicians and the government, as documented in the Watergate tapes?

4. To what extent do the documents in this chapter provide evidence of a retreat from liberalism?

# CHAPTER 31

# THE END OF THE COLD WAR AND THE CHALLENGES OF GLOBALIZATION AND TERRORISM

## 1989–2003

After World War II, the cold war set the basic parameters of American foreign policy. When the United States withdrew from Vietnam and Communist forces swept across much of Southeast Asia, many Americans called for greater military spending and a renewed commitment to turn back communism elsewhere in the world. When the Soviet Union collapsed, the appeal of communism in most of the world collapsed with it. The dominance of the United States in what President George H. W. Bush called the "new world order" was undisputed, but the foreign policy implications of American supremacy remained unclear. The election of 2000 elevated George W. Bush to the White House, after the Supreme Court intervened, and on September 11, 2001, Bush confronted the terrible realities of terrorism. The religious and political impulses motivating Islamic terrorists became the focus of worldwide attention and led the United States to announce a new national security strategy.

## DOCUMENT 31-1

## *President George Bush Declares a New World Order*

*By 1989, the disintegration of the Soviet Union and the collapse of Communist govern-
ments throughout Eastern Europe ended the cold war that had dominated American
foreign policy since World War II. The United States now stood alone as the world's only
superpower. In his 1991 State of the Union Address, President George Bush proclaimed a
new world order structured by American ideals of freedom and democracy. Delivered only
a few days after U.S. armed forces and a broad coalition of allies attacked Iraq in the Gulf
War, Bush's speech offered a sweeping vision of the United States as the model for the rest
of the world and the ultimate defender of order and harmony. The speech reflected a
renewed sense of optimism and confidence among many Americans that victory in the
cold war was the prelude to a triumphal future for the nation and the world.*

## *State of the Union Address,* January 29, 1991

Mr. President, Mr. Speaker, members of the United States Congress. I come to this House of the people, to speak to you and all Americans, certain that we stand at a defining hour. Halfway around the world, we are engaged in a great struggle in the skies and on the seas and sands. We know why we're there. We are Americans: part of something larger than ourselves.

For two centuries, we've done the hard work of freedom. And tonight we lead the world in facing down a threat to decency and humanity. What is at stake is more than one small country, it is a big idea: a new world order, where diverse nations are drawn together in common cause to achieve the universal aspirations of mankind: peace and security, freedom and the rule of law. Such is a world worthy of our struggle and worthy of our children's future.

The community of nations has resolutely gathered to condemn and repel lawless aggression. [Iraqi President] Saddam Hussein's unprovoked invasion, his ruthless, systematic rape of a peaceful neighbor, violated everything the community of nations holds dear. The world has said this aggression would not stand — and it will not stand.

Together, we have resisted the trap of appeasement, cynicism and isolation that gives temptation to tyrants. The world has answered Saddam's invasion with 12 United Nations resolutions, starting with a demand for Iraq's immediate and unconditional withdrawal — and backed up by forces from 28 countries of six continents. With few exceptions, the world now stands as one.

The end of the Cold War has been a victory for all humanity. A year and a half ago, in Germany, I said that our goal was a Europe whole and free. Tonight, Germany is united. Europe has become whole and free — and America's leadership was instrumental in making it possible.

Our relationship with the Soviet Union is important, not only to us but to the world. That relationship has helped to shape these and other historic changes. But like many other nations, we have been deeply concerned by the violence in the Baltics, and we have communicated that concern to the Soviet leadership.

The principle that has guided us is simple: Our objective is to help the Baltic peoples achieve their aspirations, not to punish the Soviet Union.

In our recent discussions with the Soviet leadership, we have been given representations, which, if fulfilled, would result in the withdrawal of some Soviet forces, a reopening of dialogue with the republics and a move away from violence. We will watch carefully as the situation develops. And we will maintain our contact with the Soviet leadership to encourage continued commitment to democratization and reform.

If it is possible, I want to continue to build a lasting basis for U.S.-Soviet cooperation, for a more peaceful future for all mankind. The triumph of democratic ideas in Eastern Europe and Latin America — and the continuing struggle for freedom elsewhere all around the world — all confirm the wisdom of our nation's founders. Tonight, we work to achieve another victory, a victory over tyranny and savage aggression.

---

George Bush, "State of the Union Address," January 29, 1991, *Historic Documents of 1991* (Washington, D.C.: Congressional Quarterly, 1992), 37–45.

We in this union enter the last decade of the 20th century thankful for our blessings, steadfast in our purpose, aware of our difficulties and responsive to our duties at home and around the world.

For two centuries, America has served the world as an inspiring example of freedom and democracy. For generations, America has led the struggle to preserve and extend the blessings of liberty. And today, in a rapidly changing world, American leadership is indispensable. Americans know that leadership brings burdens and sacrifices.

But we also [know] why the hopes of humanity turn to us.

We are Americans: We have a unique responsibility to do the hard work of freedom. And when we do — freedom works.

The conviction and courage we see in the Persian Gulf today is simply the American character in action. The indomitable spirit that is contributing to this victory for world peace and justice is the same spirit that gives us the power and the potential to meet our toughest challenges at home.

We are resolute and resourceful. If we can selflessly confront the evil for the sake of good in a land so far away, then surely we can make this land all that it should be.

If anyone tells you that America's best days are behind her, they're looking the wrong way.

Tonight, I come before this House and the American people with an appeal for renewal. This is not merely a call for new government initiatives, it is a call for new initiative in government, in our communities and from every American to prepare for the next American century.

America has always led by example. So who among us will set the example? Which of our citizens will lead us in this American century? Everyone who steps forward today to get one addict off drugs, to convince one troubled teenager not to give up on life, to comfort one AIDS patient, to help one hungry child.

We have within our reach the promise of a renewed America. We can find meaning and reward by serving some higher purpose than ourselves — a shining purpose, the illumination of a thousand points of light. And it is expressed by all who know the irresistible force of a child's hand, of a friend who stands by you and stays there, a volunteer's generous gesture, an idea that is simply right.

The problems before us may be different, but the key to solving them remains the same: It is the individual — the individual — who steps forward. And the state of our union is the union of each of us, one to the other; the sum of our friendships, marriages, families and communities.

We all have something to give. So if you know how to read, find someone who can't. If you've got a hammer, find a nail. If you're not hungry, not lonely, not in trouble — seek out someone who is.

Join the community of conscience. Do the hard work of freedom. And that will define the state of our union.

Since the birth of our nation, "We, the people" has been the source of our strength. What government can do alone is limited, but the potential of the American people knows no limits.

We are a nation of rock-solid realism and clear-eyed idealism. We are Americans: We are the nation that believes in the future; we are the nation that can shape the future.

And we've begun to do just that — by strengthening the power and choice of individuals and families.

Together, these last two years, we've put dollars for child care directly in the hands of parents, instead of bureaucracies. Unshackled the potential of Americans with disabilities. Applied the creativity of the marketplace in the service of the environment, for clean air. And made home ownership possible for more Americans.

The strength of a democracy is not in bureaucracy, it is in the people and their communities. In everything we do, let us unleash the potential of our most precious resource — our citizens, our citizens themselves. We must return to families, communities, counties, cities, states and institutions of every kind the power to chart their own destiny, and the freedom and opportunity provided by strong economic growth. And that's what America is all about. . . .

This nation was founded by leaders who understood that power belongs in the hands of people. And they planned for the future. And so must we, here and all around the world. As Americans, we know there are times when we must step forward and accept our responsibility to lead the world away from the dark chaos of dictators toward the brighter promise of a better day. Almost 50 years ago we began a long struggle against aggressive totalitarianism. Now we face another defining hour for America and the world.

There is no one more devoted, more committed to the hard work of freedom, than every soldier and sailor, every Marine, airman, and Coast Guardsman, every man and woman now serving in the Persian Gulf.

[Bush interrupted by extended applause.]

What a wonderful fitting tribute to them. Each of them has volunteered, volunteered to provide for this nation's defense — and now they bravely struggle, to earn for America, for the world, and for future generations a just and lasting peace.

Our commitment to them must be the equal of their commitment to their country. They are truly America's finest.

The war in the gulf is not a war we wanted. We worked hard to avoid war. . . . But time and again, Saddam Hussein flatly rejected the path of diplomacy and peace. The world well knows how this conflict began and when: It began on Aug. 2nd, when Saddam invaded and sacked a small, defenseless neighbor. And I am certain of how it will end. So that peace can prevail, we will prevail.

Tonight, I am pleased to report that we are on course. Iraq's capacity to sustain war is being destroyed. . . . Our purpose in the Persian Gulf remains constant: to drive Iraq out of Kuwait, to restore Kuwait's legitimate government and to ensure the stability and security of this critical region. Let me make clear what I mean by the region's stability and security. We do not seek the destruction of Iraq, its culture or its people. Rather, we seek an Iraq that uses its great resources not to destroy, not to serve the ambitions of a tyrant, but to build a better life for itself and its neighbors. We seek a Persian Gulf where conflict is no longer the rule, where the strong are neither tempted nor able to intimidate the weak.

Most Americans know instinctively why we are in the gulf. They know we had to stop Saddam now, not later. They know that this brutal dictator will do anything, will use any weapon, will commit any outrage, no matter how many innocents must suffer. They know we must make sure that control of the world's oil resources does not fall into his hands, only to finance further aggression. They know that we need to build a new, enduring peace — based not on arms races and confrontation, but on shared principles and the rule of law. And we all realize that our responsibility to be the catalyst for peace in the region does not end with the successful conclusion of this war.

Democracy brings the undeniable value of thoughtful dissent — and we have heard some dissenting voices here at home — some, a handful, reckless; most responsible. But the fact that all voices have the right to speak out is one of the reasons we've been united in purpose and principle for 200 years. . . .

But the world has to wonder what the dictator of Iraq is thinking. If he thinks that by targeting innocent civilians in Israel and Saudi Arabia, that he will gain advantage, he is dead wrong.

And if he thinks that he will advance his cause through tragic and despicable environmental terrorism — he is dead wrong.

And if he thinks that by abusing the coalition prisoners of war, he will benefit — he is dead wrong.

We will succeed in the gulf. And when we do, the world community will have sent an enduring warning to any dictator or despot, present or future, who contemplates outlaw aggression. The world can therefore seize this opportunity to fulfill the long-held promise of a new world order — where brutality will go unrewarded and aggression will meet collective resistance.

Yes, the United States bears a major share of leadership in this effort. Among the nations of the world, only the United States of America has had both the moral standing and the means to back it up. We are the only nation on this Earth that could assemble the forces of peace. This is the burden of leadership — and the strength that has made America the beacon of freedom in a searching world. This nation has never found glory in war. Our people have never wanted to abandon the blessings of home and work for distant lands and deadly conflict. If we fight in anger, it is only because we have to fight at all. And all of us yearn for a world where we will never have to fight again.

Each of us will measure, within ourselves, the value of this great struggle. Any cost in lives, any cost, is beyond our power to measure. But the cost of closing our eyes to aggression is beyond mankind's power to imagine. This we do know: Our cause is just, our cause is moral, our cause is right.

Let future generations understand the burden and the blessings of freedom. Let them say, we stood where duty required us to stand. Let them know that together, we affirmed America and the world as a community of conscience.

The winds of change are with us now. The forces of freedom are together and united. And we move toward the next century more confident than ever that we have the will at home and abroad to do what must be done — the hard work of freedom. . . .

## QUESTIONS FOR READING AND DISCUSSION

1. How did the "new world order" represent "the hard work of freedom"? What did Bush mean by saying that "freedom works"?

2. In what ways did the attack on Iraq exemplify the new world order? What were the "burdens and sacrifices" of American leadership?

3. What sort of "renewal" did Bush advocate? What was the proper relationship between individuals and government, according to Bush? What significance did "a thousand points of light" have for the new world order? Who belonged to "the community of conscience" and who did not?

4. To what extent was the new world order a defense of the political status quo rather than a vision for a more just and humane world? How might a "responsible" rather than a "reckless" critic disagree with Bush's new world order?

## DOCUMENT 31-2

# Supreme Court Dissents from Deciding 2000 Presidential Election

*In the 2000 presidential election, the Democrats' Albert Gore Jr. received a half million more popular votes than the Republicans' George W. Bush, but the disputed electoral votes of Florida were awarded to Bush by a 5 to 4 decision of the U.S. Supreme Court, the first time in American history the Supreme Court has decided a presidential election. The majority of the Court retreated from its rhetoric of judicial restraint and the constitutional limits of federal power to decide the outcome of Florida's balloting. Dissents from Supreme Court justices in the minority, excerpted below, criticized the reasoning and the consequences of the majority's partisan activism.*

## Supreme Court Dissents in George W. Bush v. Albert Gore Jr., December 12, 2000

JUSTICE STEVENS, with whom JUSTICE GINSBURG AND JUSTICE BREYER join, dissenting.

The Constitution assigns to the States the primary responsibility for determining the manner of selecting the Presidential electors. . . . When questions arise about the meaning of state laws, including election laws, it is our settled practice to accept the opinions of the highest courts of the States as providing the final answers. On rare occasions, however, either federal statutes or the Federal Constitution may require federal judicial intervention in state elections. This is not such an occasion.

The federal questions that ultimately emerged in this case are not substantial. Article II provides that "each State shall appoint, in such Manner as the Legislature thereof may direct, a Number of Electors." . . . It does not create state legislatures out of whole cloth, but rather takes them as they come — as creatures born of, and constrained by, their state constitutions. . . .

In the same vein, we also observed that "the States' legislative power is the supreme authority except as limited by the constitution of the State." . . . Moreover, the Florida Legislature's own decision to employ a unitary code for all elections indicates that it intended the Florida Supreme Court to play the same role in Presidential elections that it has historically played in resolving electoral disputes. . . .

Neither [federal law] . . . nor Article II [of the U.S. Constitution] grants federal judges any special authority to substitute their views for those of the state judiciary on matters of state law.

Nor are petitioners correct in asserting that the failure of the Florida Supreme Court to specify in detail the precise manner in which the "intent of the voter" . . . is to be determined rises to the level of a constitutional violation. We found such a violation when individual votes within the same State were weighted unequally, . . . but we have never before called into question the substantive standard by which a State determines that a vote has been legally cast.

---

Supreme Court of the United States, no. 00-949, *George W. Bush et al., Petitioners v. Albert Gore Jr. et al, on writ of certiorari to the Florida Supreme Court,* December 12, 2000.

And there is no reason to think that the guidance provided to the fact-finders, specifically the various canvassing boards, by the "intent of the voter" standard is any less sufficient — or will lead to results any less uniform — than, for example, the "beyond a reasonable doubt" standard employed every day by ordinary citizens in courtrooms across this country. . . .

Of course, as a general matter, "the interpretation of constitutional principles must not be too literal. We must remember that the machinery of government would not work if it were not allowed a little play in its joints." . . .

As the majority [of the Court] explicitly holds, once a state legislature determines to select electors through a popular vote, the right to have one's vote counted is of constitutional stature. As the majority further acknowledges, Florida law holds that all ballots that reveal the intent of the voter constitute valid votes. Recognizing these principles, the majority nonetheless orders the termination of the contest proceeding before all such votes have been tabulated. Under their own reasoning, the appropriate course of action would be to remand [to the Florida Supreme Court] to allow more specific procedures for implementing the legislature's uniform general standard to be established.

In the interest of finality, however, the majority effectively orders the disenfranchisement of an unknown number of voters whose ballots reveal their intent — and are therefore legal votes under state law but were for some reason rejected by ballot-counting machines. It does so on the basis of the deadlines. . . .

Thus, nothing prevents the majority, even if it properly found an equal protection violation, from ordering relief appropriate to remedy that violation without depriving Florida voters of their right to have their votes counted.

As the majority notes, "a desire for speed is not a general excuse for ignoring equal protection guarantees." . . . [T]he Florida Supreme Court [did not] make any substantive change in Florida electoral law.

Its decisions were rooted in long-established precedent and were consistent with the relevant statutory provisions, taken as a whole. It did what courts do — it decided the case before it in light of the legislature's intent to leave no legally cast vote uncounted.

In so doing, it relied on the sufficiency of the general "intent of the voter" standard articulated by the state legislature, coupled with a procedure for ultimate review by an impartial judge, to resolve the concern about disparate evaluations of contested ballots. If we assume — as I do — that the members of that court and the judges who would have carried out its mandate are impartial, its decision does not even raise a colorable[1] federal question.

What must underlie [the Bush] petitioners' entire federal assault on the Florida election procedures is an unstated lack of confidence in the impartiality and capacity of the state judges who would make the critical decisions if the vote count were to proceed. Otherwise, their position is wholly without merit. The endorsement of that position by the majority of this Court can only lend credence to the most cynical appraisal of the work of judges throughout the land.

It is confidence in the men and women who administer the judicial system that is the true backbone of the rule of law. Time will one day heal the wound to that confidence that will be inflicted by today's decision. One thing, however, is certain. Although we may never know with complete certainty the identity of the

---

[1]**Colorable:** Plausible.

winner of this year's Presidential election, the identity of the loser is perfectly clear. It is the Nation's confidence in the judge as an impartial guardian of the rule of law. I respectfully dissent.

JUSTICE BREYER, with JUSTICE STEVENS and JUSTICE GINSBURG and JUSTICE SOUTER

The Court was wrong to take this case. It was wrong to grant a stay[2]. It should now vacate that stay and permit the Florida Supreme Court to decide whether the recount should resume.

The political implications of this case for the country are momentous. But the federal legal questions presented, with one exception, are insubstantial. . . .

The majority justifies stopping the recount entirely on the ground that there is no more time. In particular, the majority relies on the lack of time for the [Florida] Secretary [of State] to review and approve equipment needed to separate under-votes. But the majority reaches this conclusion in the absence of any record evidence that the recount could not have been completed in the time allowed by the Florida Supreme Court. . . .

Given this detailed, comprehensive scheme for counting electoral votes, there is no reason to believe that federal law either foresees or requires resolution of such a political issue by this Court. Nor, for that matter, is there any reason to think that the Constitution's Framers would have reached a different conclusion. Madison, at least, believed that allowing the judiciary to choose the presidential electors "was out of the question.". . .

The decision by both the Constitution's Framers and the 1886 Congress to minimize this Court's role in resolving close federal presidential elections is as wise as it is clear. However awkward or difficult it may be for Congress to resolve difficult electoral disputes, Congress, being a political body, expresses the people's will far more accurately than does an unelected Court. And the people's will is what elections are about.

Moreover, Congress was fully aware of the danger that would arise should it ask judges, unarmed with appropriate legal standards, to resolve a hotly contested Presidential election contest. Just after the 1876 Presidential election, Florida, South Carolina, and Louisiana each sent two slates of electors to Washington.

Without these States, Tilden, the Democrat, had 184 electoral votes, one short of the number required to win the Presidency. With those States, Hayes, his Republican opponent, would have had 185. In order to choose between the two slates of electors, Congress decided to appoint an electoral commission composed of five Senators, five Representatives, and five Supreme Court Justices. Initially the Commission was to be evenly divided between Republicans and Democrats, with Justice David Davis, an Independent, to possess the decisive vote.

However, when at the last minute the Illinois Legislature elected Justice Davis to the United States Senate, the final position on the Commission was filled by Supreme Court Justice Joseph P. Bradley. The Commission divided along partisan lines, and the responsibility to cast the deciding vote fell to Justice Bradley. He decided to accept the votes by the Republican electors, and thereby awarded the Presidency to Hayes. Justice Bradley immediately became the subject of vociferous attacks.

---

[2]**Stay:** Suspension of judicial proceedings, in this case the proceedings of the Florida Supreme Court.

Bradley was accused of accepting bribes, of being captured by railroad interests, and of an eleventh-hour change in position after a night in which his house "was surrounded by the carriages" of Republican partisans and railroad officials. . . .

[T]he legal question upon which Justice Bradley's decision turned was not very important in the contemporaneous political context. . . . For present purposes, the relevance of this history lies in the fact that the participation in the work of the electoral commission by five Justices, including Justice Bradley, did not lend that process legitimacy.

Nor did it assure the public that the process had worked fairly, guided by the law. Rather, it simply embroiled Members of the Court in partisan conflict, thereby undermining respect for the judicial process. And the Congress that later enacted the Electoral Count Act knew it. This history may help to explain why I think it not only legally wrong, but also most unfortunate, for the Court simply to have terminated the Florida recount.

Those who caution judicial restraint in resolving political disputes have described the quintessential case for that restraint as a case marked, among other things, by the "strangeness of the issue," its "intractability to principled resolution," its "sheer momentousness, . . . which tends to unbalance judicial judgment," and "the inner vulnerability, the self-doubt of an institution which is electorally irresponsible and has no earth to draw strength from." . . .

Those characteristics mark this case. At the same time, as I have said, the Court is not acting to vindicate a fundamental constitutional principle, such as the need to protect a basic human liberty. No other strong reason to act is present. Congressional statutes tend to obviate the need.

And, above all, in this highly politicized matter, the appearance of a split decision runs the risk of undermining the public's confidence in the Court itself. That confidence is a public treasure. It has been built slowly over many years, some of which were marked by a Civil War and the tragedy of segregation. It is a vitally necessary ingredient of any successful effort to protect basic liberty and, indeed, the rule of law itself.

We run no risk of returning to the days when a President (responding to this Court's efforts to protect the Cherokee Indians) might have said, "John Marshall has made his decision; now let him enforce it!" . . . But we do risk a self-inflicted wound — a wound that may harm not just the Court, but the Nation.

I fear that in order to bring this agonizingly long election process to a definitive conclusion, we have not adequately attended to that necessary "check upon our own exercise of power," "our own sense of self-restraint." . . . Justice Brandeis once said of the Court, "The most important thing we do is not doing." . . .

What it does today, the Court should have left undone. I would repair the damage done as best we now can, by permitting the Florida recount to continue under uniform standards. I respectfully dissent.

## QUESTIONS FOR READING AND DISCUSSION

1. According to Justice Stevens, who was the "loser" in the presidential election of 2000 and why?
2. According to Justice Breyer, what should the Court have done in "this highly politicized matter"? Why did he believe the majority acted otherwise?

3. To what extent did the justices use historical judgments and interpretations in writing these dissents?

4. Do you think the concerns of Stevens, Breyer, and the other dissenting justices about the "Nation's confidence in the judge as an impartial guardian of the rule of law" were justified? Why or why not?

## DOCUMENT 31-3

# *President George W. Bush Receives CIA Warning about al Qaeda and Addresses Congress after 9/11 Terrorist Attacks*

*On August 6, 2001, President George W. Bush received a document from the Central Intelligence Agency (CIA), termed a President's Daily Brief (PDB), that was titled "Bin Laden Determined to Strike in the U.S." Reprinted below, this PDB was one of more than forty PDBs from the CIA that President Bush received before September 11, 2001 that mentioned the possibility of terrorist attacks by al Qaeda. After the terrorist attacks on September 11, President Bush addressed Congress and the American people and outlined his plan to protect the nation's security. His address targeted the Taliban government in Afghanistan and warned terrorists throughout the world that the United States would track them down. Bush's speech, excerpted below, expressed the nation's outrage and resolution, defining the contrast between freedom and evil that shaped Bush's subsequent policies.*

## President's Daily Brief

## *Bin Laden Determined to Strike in the U.S.*, August 6, 2001

Clandestine, foreign government, and media reports indicate bin Laden since 1997 has wanted to conduct terrorist attacks in the U.S. Bin Laden implied in U.S. television interviews in 1997 and 1998 that his followers would follow the example of World Trade Center bomber Ramzi Yousef and "bring the fighting to America."

After U.S. missile strikes on his base in Afghanistan in 1998, bin Laden told followers he wanted to retaliate in Washington, according to a . . . [this and subsequent deletions were made by the government for reasons of national security] service.

An Egyptian Islamic Jihad (E.I.J.) operative told an . . . . service at the same time that bin Laden was planning to exploit the operative's access to the U.S. to mount a terrorist strike.

The millennium plotting in Canada in 1999 may have been part of bin Laden's first serious attempt to implement a terrorist strike in the U.S. Convicted plotter Ahmed Ressam has told the F.B.I. that he conceived the idea to attack Los Angeles International Airport himself, but that bin Laden lieutenant Abu Zubaydah encouraged him and helped facilitate the operation. Ressam also said that in 1998 Abu Zubaydah was planning his own U.S. attack.

---

The White House, *New York Times*, April 11, 2004; U.S. Government Web site, George W. Bush, "Address to a Joint Session of Congress and the American People," September 20, 2001.

Ressam says bin Laden was aware of the Los Angeles operation.

Although bin Laden has not succeeded, his attacks against the U.S. embassies in Kenya and Tanzania in 1998 demonstrate that he prepares operations years in advance and is not deterred by setbacks. Bin Laden associates surveilled our embassies in Nairobi and Dar es Salaam as early as 1993, and some members of the Nairobi cell planning the bombings were arrested and deported in 1997.

Al Qaeda members — including some who are U.S. citizens — have resided in or traveled to the U.S. for years, and the group apparently maintains a support structure that could aid attacks. Two Al Qaeda members found guilty in the conspiracy to bomb our embassies in East Africa were U.S. citizens, and a senior E.I.J. member lived in California in the mid-1990's.

A clandestine source said in 1998 that a bin Laden cell in New York was recruiting Muslim-American youth for attacks.

We have not been able to corroborate some of the more sensational threat reporting, such as that from a . . . service in 1998 saying that bin Laden wanted to hijack a U.S. aircraft to gain the release of "Blind Sheik" Omar Abdel Rahman and other U.S.-held extremists.

Nevertheless, F.B.I. information since that time indicates patterns of suspicious activity in this country consistent with preparations for hijackings or other types of attacks, including recent surveillance of federal buildings in New York.

The F.B.I. is conducting approximately 70 full field investigations throughout the U.S. that it considers bin Laden-related. C.I.A. and the F.B.I. are investigating a call to our embassy in the U.A.E. in May saying that a group of bin Laden supporters was in the U.S. planning attacks with explosives.

# President George W. Bush

## *Address to a Joint Session of Congress and the American People, September 20, 2001*

In the normal course of events, Presidents come to this chamber to report on the state of the Union. Tonight, no such report is needed. It has already been delivered by the American people.

We have seen it in the courage of passengers, who rushed terrorists to save others on the ground — passengers like an exceptional man named Todd Beamer. . . .

We have seen the state of our Union in the endurance of rescuers, working past exhaustion. We have seen the unfurling of flags, the lighting of candles, the giving of blood, the saying of prayers — in English, Hebrew, and Arabic. We have seen the decency of a loving and giving people who have made the grief of strangers their own.

My fellow citizens, for the last nine days, the entire world has seen for itself the state of our Union —and it is strong.

Tonight we are a country awakened to danger and called to defend freedom. Our grief has turned to anger, and anger to resolution. Whether we bring our enemies to justice, or bring justice to our enemies, justice will be done.

I thank the Congress for its leadership at such an important time. . . . And you . . . acted, by delivering $40 billion to rebuild our communities and meet the needs of our military. . . .

And on behalf of the American people, I thank the world for its outpouring of support. America will never forget the sounds of our National Anthem

playing at Buckingham Palace, on the streets of Paris, and at Berlin's Branden-
burg Gate. . . .

Nor will we forget the citizens of 80 other nations who died with our own:
dozens of Pakistanis; more than 130 Israelis; more than 250 citizens of India; men
and women from El Salvador, Iran, Mexico and Japan; and hundreds of British
citizens. America has no truer friend than Great Britain. Once again, we are joined
together in a great cause — [I am] so honored the British Prime Minister has crossed
an ocean to show his unity of purpose with America. Thank you for coming, friend.

On September the 11th, enemies of freedom committed an act of war against
our country. Americans have known wars — but for the past 136 years, they have
been wars on foreign soil, except for one Sunday in 1941. Americans have known
the casualties of war — but not at the center of a great city on a peaceful morning. Americans have known surprise attacks — but never before on thousands of
civilians. All of this was brought upon us in a single day — and night fell on a
different world, a world where freedom itself is under attack.

Americans have many questions tonight. Americans are asking: Who attacked our country? The evidence we have gathered all points to a collection of
loosely affiliated terrorist organizations known as al Qaeda. They are the same
murderers indicted for bombing American embassies in Tanzania and Kenya, and
responsible for bombing the U.S.S. *Cole.*

Al Qaeda is to terror what the mafia is to crime. But its goal is not making
money; its goal is remaking the world — and imposing its radical beliefs on people everywhere.

The terrorists practice a fringe form of Islamic extremism that has been rejected by Muslim scholars and the vast majority of Muslim clerics — a fringe
movement that perverts the peaceful teachings of Islam. The terrorists' directive
commands them to kill Christians and Jews, to kill all Americans, and make no
distinction among military and civilians, including women and children.

This group and its leader — a person named Osama bin Laden — are linked
to many other organizations in different countries, including the Egyptian Islamic
Jihad and the Islamic Movement of Uzbekistan. There are thousands of these terrorists in more than 60 countries. They are recruited from their own nations and
neighborhoods and brought to camps in places like Afghanistan, where they are
trained in the tactics of terror. They are sent back to their homes or sent to hide in
countries around the world to plot evil and destruction.

The leadership of al Qaeda has great influence in Afghanistan and supports
the Taliban regime in controlling most of that country. In Afghanistan, we see al
Qaeda's vision for the world.

Afghanistan's people have been brutalized — many are starving and many
have fled. Women are not allowed to attend school. You can be jailed for owning
a television. Religion can be practiced only as their leaders dictate. A man can be
jailed in Afghanistan if his beard is not long enough.

The United States respects the people of Afghanistan — after all, we are currently its largest source of humanitarian aid — but we condemn the Taliban
regime. It is not only repressing its own people, it is threatening people everywhere by sponsoring and sheltering and supplying terrorists. By aiding and abet-
ting murder, the Taliban regime is committing murder.

And tonight, the United States of America makes the following demands on
the Taliban: Deliver to United States authorities all the leaders of al Qaeda who
hide in your land. Release all foreign nationals, including American citizens, you

have unjustly imprisoned. Protect foreign journalists, diplomats and aid workers in your country. Close immediately and permanently every terrorist training camp in Afghanistan, and hand over every terrorist, and every person in their support structure, to appropriate authorities. Give the United States full access to terrorist training camps, so we can make sure they are no longer operating.

These demands are not open to negotiation or discussion. The Taliban must act, and act immediately. They will hand over the terrorists, or they will share in their fate.

I also want to speak tonight directly to Muslims throughout the world. We respect your faith. It's practiced freely by many millions of Americans, and by millions more in countries that America counts as friends. Its teachings are good and peaceful, and those who commit evil in the name of Allah blaspheme the name of Allah. The terrorists are traitors to their own faith, trying, in effect, to hijack Islam itself. The enemy of America is not our many Muslim friends; it is not our many Arab friends. Our enemy is a radical network of terrorists, and every government that supports them.

Our war on terror begins with al Qaeda, but it does not end there. It will not end until every terrorist group of global reach has been found, stopped and defeated.

Americans are asking, why do they hate us? They hate what we see right here in this chamber — democratically elected government. Their leaders are self-appointed. They hate our freedoms — our freedom of religion, our freedom of speech, our freedom to vote and assemble and disagree with each other.

They want to overthrow existing governments in many Muslim countries, such as Egypt, Saudi Arabia, and Jordan. They want to drive Israel out of the Middle East. They want to drive Christians and Jews out of vast regions of Asia and Africa.

These terrorists kill not merely to end lives, but to disrupt and end a way of life. With every atrocity, they hope that America grows fearful, retreating from the world and forsaking our friends. They stand against us, because we stand in their way.

We are not deceived by their pretenses to piety. We have seen their kind before. They are the heirs of all the murderous ideologies of the 20th century. By sacrificing human life to serve their radical visions — by abandoning every value except the will to power — they follow in the path of fascism, and Nazism, and totalitarianism. And they will follow that path all the way, to where it ends: in history's unmarked grave of discarded lies.

Americans are asking: How will we fight and win this war? We will direct every resource at our command — every means of diplomacy, every tool of intelligence, every instrument of law enforcement, every financial influence, and every necessary weapon of war — to the disruption and to the defeat of the global terror network.

This war will not be like the war against Iraq a decade ago, with a decisive liberation of territory and a swift conclusion. It will not look like the air war above Kosovo two years ago, where no ground troops were used and not a single American was lost in combat.

Our response involves far more than instant retaliation and isolated strikes . . . We will starve terrorists of funding, turn them one against another, drive them from place to place, until there is no refuge or no rest. And we will pursue nations that provide aid or safe haven to terrorism. Every nation, in every region, now has a decision to make. Either you are with us, or you are with the terrorists. From this day forward, any nation that continues to harbor or support terrorism will be regarded by the United States as a hostile regime.

Our nation has been put on notice: We are not immune from attack. We will take defensive measures against terrorism to protect Americans. . . .

These measures are essential. But the only way to defeat terrorism as a threat to our way of life is to stop it, eliminate it, and destroy it where it grows.

Many will be involved in this effort, from FBI agents to intelligence operatives to the reservists we have called to active duty. All deserve our thanks, and all have our prayers. And tonight, a few miles from the damaged Pentagon, I have a message for our military: Be ready. I've called the Armed Forces to alert, and there is a reason. The hour is coming when America will act, and you will make us proud.

This is not, however, just America's fight. And what is at stake is not just America's freedom. This is the world's fight. This is civilization's fight. This is the fight of all who believe in progress and pluralism, tolerance and freedom.

We ask every nation to join us. We will ask, and we will need, the help of police forces, intelligence services, and banking systems around the world. . . . An attack on one is an attack on all.

The civilized world is rallying to America's side. They understand that if this terror goes unpunished, their own cities, their own citizens may be next. Terror, unanswered, can not only bring down buildings, it can threaten the stability of legitimate governments. And you know what — we're not going to allow it.

Americans are asking: What is expected of us? I ask you to live your lives, and hug your children. I know many citizens have fears tonight, and I ask you to be calm and resolute, even in the face of a continuing threat.

I ask you to uphold the values of America, and remember why so many have come here. We are in a fight for our principles, and our first responsibility is to live by them. No one should be singled out for unfair treatment or unkind words because of their ethnic background or religious faith. . . .

After all that has just passed — all the lives taken, and all the possibilities and hopes that died with them — it is natural to wonder if America's future is one of fear. Some speak of an age of terror. I know there are struggles ahead, and dangers to face. But this country will define our times, not be defined by them. As long as the United States of America is determined and strong, this will not be an age of terror; this will be an age of liberty, here and across the world.

Great harm has been done to us. We have suffered great loss. And in our grief and anger we have found our mission and our moment. Freedom and fear are at war. The advance of human freedom — the great achievement of our time, and the great hope of every time — now depends on us. Our nation — this generation — will lift a dark threat of violence from our people and our future. We will rally the world to this cause by our efforts, by our courage. We will not tire, we will not falter, and we will not fail. . . .

## QUESTIONS FOR READING AND DISCUSSION

1. What action do you think it was appropriate for President Bush to take after receiving the August 6, 2001, PDB from the CIA? Obviously, neither President Bush nor any other U.S. government official knew in advance that the September 11 attacks would occur. But, given the warning in the PDB and other intelligence reports, why did American authorities fail to prevent the attacks?

2. According to President Bush, who was responsible for the terrorist attacks of September 11 and why?

3. Why did many other nations express sympathy and support for the United States? What did Bush mean by, "Either you are with us, or you are with the terrorists"? Did that mean critics of American policy or the Bush administration were "with the terrorists"? Why or why not?

4. What sacrifices did Bush call for from Americans? Why? To what extent did American values conflict with terrorists' aims?

5. To what extent was Bush correct that, "The enemy of America is not our many Muslim friends; it is not our many Arab friends"?

## DOCUMENT 31-4

# Al Qaeda Training Manual Declares Jihad

*A police raid on an al Qaeda member's home in Manchester, England, located an al Qaeda training manual in a computer file titled "Declaration of Jihad." To Muslims, jihad has several meanings, including "spiritual struggle." In the al Qaeda training manual, however, jihad refers to holy war against non-Muslims sanctioned by Allah, Muslims' God. The al Qaeda manual was translated from Arabic into English by government officials and used as evidence in legal proceedings in New York. The manual outlines the religious authority claimed by al Qaeda as well as the targets of the organization's terrorism. The manual raises important questions about the motivation for the September 11 attacks in the United States.*

## Al Qaeda Training Manual, Declaration of Jihad against the Country's Tyrants

In the name of Allah, the merciful and compassionate. . . .

### Presentation

To those champions who avowed the truth day and night. . . . And wrote with their blood and sufferings these phrases. . . .

The confrontation that we are calling for with the apostate regimes does not know Socratic debate . . . , Platonic ideals . . . , nor Aristotelian diplomacy. But it knows the dialogue of bullets, the ideals of assassination, bombing, and destruction, and the diplomacy of the cannon and machine-gun. . . .

Islamic governments have never and will never be established through peaceful solutions and cooperative councils. They are established as they [always] have been by pen and gun, by word and bullet, by tongue and teeth. . . .

### Pledge, O Sister

To the sister believer whose clothes the criminals have stripped off.
To the sister believer whose hair the oppressors have shaved.
To the sister believer who's body has been abused by the human dogs. . . .

---

United States Department of Justice, Al Qaeda Training Manual, http://www.usdoj.gov/ag/trainingmanual.htm.

### Pledge, O Sister

Covenant, O Sister . . . to make their women widows and their children orphans.

Covenant, O Sister . . . to make them desire death and hate appointments and prestige. Covenant, O Sister . . . to slaughter them like lambs and let the Nile, al-Asi, and Euphrates rivers flow with their blood.

Covenant, O Sister . . . to be a pick of destruction for every godless and apostate regime.

Covenant, O Sister . . . to retaliate for you against every dog who touches you even with a bad word.

### In the name of Allah, the merciful and compassionate

Thanks be to Allah. We thank him, turn to him, ask his forgiveness, and seek refuge in him from our wicked souls and bad deeds. Whomever Allah enlightens will not be misguided, and the deceiver will never be guided. I declare that there is no god but Allah alone; he has no partners. I also declare that Mohammed is his servant and prophet. . . .

The most truthful saying is the book of Allah and the best guidance is that of Mohammed, God bless and keep him. The worst thing is to introduce something new, for every novelty is an act of heresy and each heresy is a deception.

### Introduction

Martyrs were killed, women were widowed, children were orphaned, men were handcuffed, chaste women's heads were shaved, harlots' heads were crowned, atrocities were inflicted on the innocent, gifts were given to the wicked, virgins were raped on the prostitution altar. . . .

After the fall of our orthodox caliphate on March 3, 1924[1] and after expelling the colonialists, our Islamic nation was afflicted with apostate rulers who took over in the Moslem nation. These rulers turned out to be more infidel and criminal than the colonialists themselves. Moslems have endured all kinds of harm, oppression, and torture at their hands.

These apostate rulers threw thousands of the Haraka Al-Islamyia [Islamic Movement] youth in gloomy jails and detention centers that were equipped with the most modern torture device and [manned with] experts in oppression and torture. Those youth had refused to move in the rulers' orbit, obscure matters to the youth, and oppose the idea of rebelling against the rulers. But they [the rulers] did not stop there; they started to fragment the essence of the Islamic nation by trying to eradicate its Moslem identity. Thus, they started spreading godless and atheistic views among the youth. We found some that claimed that socialism was from Islam, democracy was the [religious] council, and the prophet — God bless and keep him — propagandized communism.

Colonialism and its followers, the apostate rulers, then started to openly erect crusader centers, societies, and organizations like Masonic Lodges, Lions and Rotary clubs, and foreign schools. They aimed at producing a wasted generation that pursued everything that is western and produced rulers, ministers, leaders,

---

[1]**March 3, 1924:** The Turkish parliament, led by Mustafa Ataturk, abolished the Ottoman caliphate, separating Islam from the government, and Turkey became a secular republic four years later.

physicians, engineers, businessmen, politicians, journalists, and information specialists. [Koranic verse:] "And Allah's enemies plotted and planned, and Allah too planned, and the best of planners is Allah."

They [the rulers] tried, using every means and [kind of] seduction, to produce a generation of young men that did not know [anything] except what they [the rulers] want, did not say [anything] except what they [the rulers] think about, did not live except according to their [the rulers'] way, and did not dress except in their [the rulers'] clothes. However, majestic Allah turned their deception back on them, as a large group of those young men who were raised by them [the rulers] woke up from their sleep and returned to Allah, regretting and repenting.

The young men returning to Allah realized that Islam is not just performing rituals but a complete system: Religion and government, worship and Jihad [holy war], ethics and dealing with people, and the Koran and the sword. The bitter situation that the nation has reached is a result of its divergence from Allah's course and his righteous law for all places and times. That [bitter situation] came about as a result of its children's love for the world, their loathing of death, and their abandonment of Jihad.

Unbelief is still the same. . . . It is the same unbelief that drove Sadat, Hosni Mubarak, Gadhafi, Hafez Assad, Saleh, Fahed — Allah's curse be upon the non-believing leaders — and all the apostate Arab rulers to torture, kill, imprison, and torment Moslems.

These young men realized that an Islamic government would never be established except by the bomb and rifle. Islam does not coincide or make a truce with unbelief, but rather confronts it.

The confrontation that Islam calls for with these godless and apostate regimes, does not know Socratic debates, Platonic ideals, nor Aristotelian diplomacy. But it knows the dialogue of bullets, the ideals of assassination, bombing, and destruction, and the diplomacy of the cannon and machine-gun.

The young came to prepare themselves for Jihad, commanded by the majestic Allah's order in the holy Koran. [Koranic verse:] "Against them make ready your strength to the utmost of your power, including steeds of war, to strike terror into [the hearts of] the enemies of Allah and your enemies and others besides whom ye may not know, but whom Allah doth know."

I present this humble effort [the training manual] to these young Moslem men who are pure, believing, and fighting for the cause of Allah. It is my contribution toward paving the road that leads to majestic Allah and establishes a caliphate according to the prophecy. . . .

### First Lesson

We cannot resist this state of ignorance unless we unite our ranks, and adhere to our religion. Without that, the establishment of religion would be a dream or illusion that is impossible to achieve or even imagine. . . . Sheik Ibn Taimia —may Allah have mercy on him — said. . . ." It should be understood that governing the people's affairs is one of the greatest religious obligations. In fact, without it, religion and world [affairs] could not be established. The interests of Adam's children would not be achieved except in assembly, because of their mutual need. When they assemble, it is necessary to [have] a leader. Allah's prophet — God bless and keep him — even said, 'If three [people] come together let them pick a leader.' . . . Since Allah has obligated us to do good and avoid the unlawful, that would not be done except through force and lording. Likewise, the rest of what he [God] obligated [us with] would not be accomplished except by force and lordship, be it Jihad, justice, pilgrimage, assembly, holidays, support of the oppressed, or the establishment of boundaries. That is why it has been said, "the sultan is Allah's shadow on earth." . . .

## Necessary Qualifications and Characteristics for the Organization's Member

1. Islam:
   The member of the Organization must be Moslem. How can an unbeliever, someone from a revealed religion [e.g., Christian or Jew] a secular person, a communist, etc. protect Islam and Moslems and defend their goals and secrets when he does not believe in that religion [Islam]? . . .
2. Commitment to the Organization's Ideology:
   This commitment frees the Organization's member from conceptional problems.
3. Maturity:
   The requirements of military work are numerous, and a minor cannot perform them. The nature of hard and continuous work in dangerous conditions requires a great deal of psychological, mental, and intellectual fitness, which are not usually found in a minor. . . .
4. Sacrifice:
   He [the member] has to be willing to do the work and undergo martyrdom for the purpose of achieving the goal and establishing the religion of majestic Allah on earth.
5. Listening and Obedience:
   In the military, this is known today as discipline. It is expressed by how the member obeys the orders given to him. This is what our religion urges. The Glorious [Koran] says, "O, ye who believe! Obey Allah and obey the messenger and those charged with authority among you." . . .
6. Keeping Secrets and Concealing Information
   [This secrecy should be used] even with the closest people for deceiving the enemies is not easy. . . . Allah's messenger — God bless and keep him — says, "Seek Allah's help in doing your affairs in secrecy." . . .
7. Free of Illness . . .
8. Patience
   [The member] should have plenty of patience for [enduring] afflictions if he is overcome by the enemies. He should not abandon this great path and sell him self and his religion to the enemies for his freedom. He should be patient in performing the work, even if it lasts a long time.
9. Tranquility and "Unflappability"
   [The member] should have a calm personality that allows him to endure psychological traumas such as those involving bloodshed, murder, arrest, imprisonment, and reverse psychological traumas such as killing one or all of his Organization's comrades. [He should be able] to carry out the work.
10. Intelligence and Insight. . . .
11. Caution and Prudence. . . .

12. Truthfulness and Counsel

The Commander of the faithful, Omar Ibn Al-Khattab — may Allah be pleased with him — asserted that this characteristic was vital in those who gather information and work as spies against the Moslems' enemies . . . saying, "If you step foot on your enemies' land, get spies on them. Choose those whom you count on for their truthfulness and advice, whether Arabs or inhabitants of that land. Liars' accounts would not benefit you, even if some of them were true; the deceiver is a spy against you and not for you."

13. Ability to Observe and Analyze. . . .

14. Ability to Act, Change Positions, and Conceal Oneself. . . .

## Third Lesson

How can a Muslim spy live among enemies if he maintains his Islamic characteristics? How can he perform his duties to Allah and not want to appear Muslim?

Concerning the issue of clothing and appearance, Ibn Taima — may Allah have mercy on him — said, "If a Muslim is in a combat or godless areas, he is not obligated to have a different appearance from [those around him]". . . .

Resembling the polytheist in religious appearance is a kind of "necessity permits the forbidden" even though they [forbidden acts] are basically prohibited. As for the visible duties, like fasting and praying, he can fast by using any justification not to eat with them [polytheists]. As for prayer . . . Al-Bakhari [says], . . . the prophet — Allah bless and keep him — combined [noon, afternoon, sunset, and evening prayers] in Medina without fear or hesitation. . . .

It is noted, however, that it is forbidden to do the unlawful, such as drinking wine or fornicating. There is nothing that permits those.

Guidelines for Beating and Killing Hostages: Religious scholars have permitted beating. . . .

In this tradition, we find permission to interrogate the hostage for the purpose of obtaining information.

It is permitted to strike the nonbeliever who has no covenant until he reveals the news, information, and secrets of his people. . . .

The religious scholars have also permitted the killing of a hostage if he insists on withholding information from Moslems. They permitted his killing so that he would not inform his people of what he learned about the Muslim condition, number, and secrets. . . .

### QUESTIONS FOR READING AND DISCUSSION

1. Who are considered "apostate rulers"? Was the United States singled out as an "apostate" government? Why or why not?

2. Why did such things as "Lions and Rotary clubs" pose a threat to Islam? Who were the "wasted generation" and how did "majestic Allah" turn "their deception back on them"?

3. What intellectual traits are demanded by "the Organization," namely al Qaeda? How, for example, is a member freed from "conceptional problems"?

4. Does the al Qaeda training manual encourage dissent and democratic decision making? Why or why not?

5. What kinds of killing does the al Qaeda training manual expect its members to do? Why?

## DOCUMENT 31-5

# National Security of the United States Requires Preemptive War

*A year after the terrorist attacks of September 11, 2001, the Bush administration announced a national security strategy that asserted the doctrine of preemptive war against possible threats to the United States and declared the goal of making the nation the world's greatest military power for the indefinite future. The excerpts below document the explanations for such policies.*

## The National Security Strategy of the United States, September 2002

The United States of America is fighting a war against terrorists of global reach. The enemy is not a single political regime or person or religion or ideology. The enemy is terrorism — premeditated, politically motivated violence perpetrated against innocents.

In many regions, legitimate grievances prevent the emergence of a lasting peace. Such grievances deserve to be, and must be, addressed within a political process. But no cause justifies terror. The United States will make no concessions to terrorist demands and strike no deals with them. We make no distinction between terrorists and those who knowingly harbor or provide aid to them.

The struggle against global terrorism is different from any other war in our history. It will be fought on many fronts against a particularly elusive enemy over an extended period of time. Progress will come through the persistent accumulation of successes — some seen, some unseen.

Today our enemies have seen the results of what civilized nations can, and will, do against regimes that harbor, support, and use terrorism to achieve their political goals. Afghanistan has been liberated; coalition forces continue to hunt down the Taliban and al-Qaida. But it is not only this battlefield on which we will engage terrorists. Thousands of trained terrorists remain at large with cells in North America, South America, Europe, Africa, the Middle East, and across Asia.

Our priority will be first to disrupt and destroy terrorist organizations of global reach and attack their leadership; command, control, and communications; material support; and finances. This will have a disabling effect upon the terrorists' ability to plan and operate. . . .

We will disrupt and destroy terrorist organizations by:

- direct and continuous action using all the elements of national and international power. Our immediate focus will be those terrorist organizations of global reach and any terrorist or state sponsor of terrorism which attempts to gain or use weapons of mass destruction (WMD) or their precursors;

---

The National Security Strategy of the United States of America, September 2002, http://www.whitehouse.gov/nsc/nssall.html.

- defending the United States, the American people, and our interests at home and abroad by identifying and destroying the threat before it reaches our borders. While the United States will constantly strive to enlist the support of the international community, we will not hesitate to act alone, if necessary, to exercise our right of self defense by acting preemptively against such terrorists, to prevent them from doing harm against our people and our country; and
- denying further sponsorship, support, and sanctuary to terrorists by convincing or compelling states to accept their sovereign responsibilities.

We will also wage a war of ideas to win the battle against international terrorism. This includes:

- using the full influence of the United States, and working closely with allies and friends, to make clear that all acts of terrorism are illegitimate so that terrorism will be viewed in the same light as slavery, piracy, or genocide: behavior that no respectable government can condone or support and all must oppose;
- supporting moderate and modern government, especially in the Muslim world, to ensure that the conditions and ideologies that promote terrorism do not find fertile ground in any nation;
- diminishing the underlying conditions that spawn terrorism by enlisting the international community to focus its efforts and resources on areas most at risk; and
- using effective public diplomacy to promote the free flow of information and ideas to kindle the hopes and aspirations of freedom of those in societies ruled by the sponsors of global terrorism. . . .

The nature of the Cold War threat required the United States — with our allies and friends — to emphasize deterrence of the enemy's use of force, producing a grim strategy of mutual assured destruction. With the collapse of the Soviet Union and the end of the Cold War, our security environment has undergone profound transformation.

Having moved from confrontation to cooperation as the hallmark of our relationship with Russia, the dividends are evident: an end to the balance of terror that divided us; an historic reduction in the nuclear arsenals on both sides; and cooperation in areas such as counterterrorism and missile defense that until recently were inconceivable.

But new deadly challenges have emerged from rogue states and terrorists. None of these contemporary threats rival the sheer destructive power that was arrayed against us by the Soviet Union. However, the nature and motivations of these new adversaries, their determination to obtain destructive powers hitherto available only to the world's strongest states, and the greater likelihood that they will use weapons of mass destruction against us, make today's security environment more complex and dangerous.

In the 1990s we witnessed the emergence of a small number of rogue states that, while different in important ways, share a number of attributes. These states:

- brutalize their own people and squander their national resources for the personal gain of the rulers;
- display no regard for international law, threaten their neighbors, and callously violate international treaties to which they are party;

- are determined to acquire weapons of mass destruction, along with other advanced military technology, to be used as threats or offensively to achieve the aggressive designs of these regimes;
- sponsor terrorism around the globe; and
- reject basic human values and hate the United States and everything for which it stands.

At the time of the Gulf War, we acquired irrefutable proof that Iraq's designs were not limited to the chemical weapons it had used against Iran and its own people, but also extended to the acquisition of nuclear weapons and biological agents. In the past decade North Korea has become the world's principal purveyor of ballistic missiles, and has tested increasingly capable missiles while developing its own WMD arsenal. Other rogue regimes seek nuclear, biological, and chemical weapons as well. These states' pursuit of, and global trade in, such weapons has become a looming threat to all nations.

We must be prepared to stop rogue states and their terrorist clients before they are able to threaten or use weapons of mass destruction against the United States and our allies and friends. Our response must take full advantage of strengthened alliances, the establishment of new partnerships with former adversaries, innovation in the use of military forces, modern technologies, including the development of an effective missile defense system, and increased emphasis on intelligence collection and analysis.

Our comprehensive strategy to combat WMD includes:

- *Proactive counterproliferation efforts.* We must deter and defend against the threat before it is unleashed. We must ensure that key capabilities — detection, active and passive defenses, and counterforce capabilities — are integrated into our defense transformation and our homeland security systems. . . .
  It has taken almost a decade for us to comprehend the true nature of this new threat. Given the goals of rogue states and terrorists, the United States can no longer solely rely on a reactive posture as we have in the past. The inability to deter a potential attacker, the immediacy of today's threats, and the magnitude of potential harm that could be caused by our adversaries' choice of weapons, do not permit that option. We cannot let our enemies strike first.
- In the Cold War, especially following the Cuban missile crisis, we faced a generally status quo, risk-averse adversary. Deterrence was an effective defense. But deterrence based only upon the threat of retaliation is less likely to work against leaders of rogue states more willing to take risks, gambling with the lives of their people, and the wealth of their nations.
- In the Cold War, weapons of mass destruction were considered weapons of last resort whose use risked the destruction of those who used them. Today, our enemies see weapons of mass destruction as weapons of choice. For rogue states these weapons are tools of intimidation and military aggression against their neighbors. These weapons may also allow these states to attempt to blackmail the United States and our allies to prevent us from deterring or repelling the aggressive behavior of rogue states. Such states also see these weapons as their best means of overcoming the conventional superiority of the United States.

- Traditional concepts of deterrence will not work against a terrorist enemy whose avowed tactics are wanton destruction and the targeting of innocents; whose so-called soldiers seek martyrdom in death and whose most potent protection is statelessness. The overlap between states that sponsor terror and those that pursue WMD compels us to action.

For centuries, international law recognized that nations need not suffer an attack before they can lawfully take action to defend themselves against forces that present an imminent danger of attack. Legal scholars and international jurists often conditioned the legitimacy of preemption on the existence of an imminent threat — most often a visible mobilization of armies, navies, and air forces preparing to attack.

We must adapt the concept of imminent threat to the capabilities and objectives of today's adversaries. Rogue states and terrorists do not seek to attack us using conventional means. They know such attacks would fail. Instead, they rely on acts of terror and, potentially, the use of weapons of mass destruction — weapons that can be easily concealed, delivered covertly, and used without warning.

The targets of these attacks are our military forces and our civilian population, in direct violation of one of the principal norms of the law of warfare. As was demonstrated by the losses on September 11, 2001, mass civilian casualties is the specific objective of terrorists and these losses would be exponentially more severe if terrorists acquired and used weapons of mass destruction.

The United States has long maintained the option of preemptive actions to counter a sufficient threat to our national security. The greater the threat, the greater is the risk of inaction — and the more compelling the case for taking anticipatory action to defend ourselves, even if uncertainty remains as to the time and place of the enemy's attack. To forestall or prevent such hostile acts by our adversaries, the United States will, if necessary, act preemptively.

The United States will not use force in all cases to preempt emerging threats, nor should nations use preemption as a pretext for aggression. Yet in an age where the enemies of civilization openly and actively seek the world's most destructive technologies, the United States cannot remain idle while dangers gather.

We will always proceed deliberately, weighing the consequences of our actions. . . .

The purpose of our actions will always be to eliminate a specific threat to the United States or our allies and friends. The reasons for our actions will be clear, the force measured, and the cause just. . . .

It is time to reaffirm the essential role of American military strength. We must build and maintain our defenses beyond challenge. Our military's highest priority is to defend the United States. . . .

The unparalleled strength of the United States armed forces, and their forward presence, have maintained the peace in some of the world's most strategically vital regions. However, the threats and enemies we must confront have changed, and so must our forces. A military structured to deter massive Cold War-era armies must be transformed to focus more on how an adversary might fight rather than where and when a war might occur. . . .

The presence of American forces overseas is one of the most profound symbols of the U.S. commitments to allies and friends. Through our willingness to use force in our own defense and in defense of others, the United States demonstrates its resolve to maintain a balance of power that favors freedom. . . .

The United States must and will maintain the capability to defeat any attempt by an enemy — whether a state or non-state actor — to impose its will on the United States, our allies, or our friends. We will maintain the forces sufficient to support our obligations, and to defend freedom. Our forces will be strong enough to dissuade potential adversaries from pursuing a military build-up in hopes of surpassing, or equaling, the power of the United States. . . .

In exercising our leadership, we will respect the values, judgment, and interests of our friends and partners. Still, we will be prepared to act apart when our interests and unique responsibilities require. . . .

## QUESTIONS FOR READING AND DISCUSSION

1. To what extent are the doctrines of preemptive war and military supremacy new in American foreign policy, according to the national security strategy? How has the United States previously dealt with the "imminent danger of attack"?

2. To what extent is the national security strategy described in the excerpt above a response to the September 11, 2001, terrorist attacks in the United States? To what extent is it a response to the end of the cold war?

3. Do you think this policy influenced the Bush administration's war on Iraq? Why or why not? To what extent does the plan depend on weapons of mass destruction in the hands of terrorists? What weapons of mass destruction did the 9/11 terrorists employ?

4. Do you believe this national security strategy protects the "interests and unique responsibilities" of the American people? Why or why not?

5. What are the limits to the strategy of preemptive war? Should America be the world's police force, according to the strategy? Do you agree? Why or why not?

## COMPARATIVE QUESTIONS

1. In what ways did the new world order envisioned by George H. W. Bush compare with the views of his son, George W. Bush, and the national security strategy of his administration?

2. How do the dissents in *Bush v. Gore* compare to the defense of American values in George W. Bush's speech following 9/11?

3. Were the Muslim and Arab friends of the United States referred to by George W. Bush the "apostate rulers" targeted by al Qaeda? If so, to what extent were U.S. friends responsible for terrorists such as al Qaeda? What, according to the documents here, motivated the terrorist attacks on the United States?

4. How does the world order envisioned by the al Qaeda training manual compare to that envisioned by both presidents Bush?

5. Do you think that the September 11, 2001, terrorist attacks changed the world and American thinking about the world as much as the end of the cold war did? Why or why not?

## ACKNOWLEDGMENTS

*Chapter 18*   18–2. "Ida Lindgren, Letters 1870–1824." Excerpts from *Letters from the Promised Land: Swedes in America, 1840–1914* by H. Arnold Barton, editor. copyright © 1975 by the University of Minnesota Press. Reprinted by permission of the publisher.

18–5. "Richard Pratt, 'Kill the Indian . . . and save the man . . .'" edited excerpt from "The Advantage of Mingling Indians with Whites" in *Americanizing the American Indians: Writings by the "Friends of the Indian 1880–1900"* by Francis Paul Prucha. Copyright © 1973 by Harvard University Press. Reprinted with permission of the publisher.

*Chapter 19*   19–2. "Interviews with Journalist Helen Campbell, 1880s." Originally from *Prisoners of Poverty* (1900). Reprinted in *Root of Bitterness: Documents in the Social History of American Women*, edited by Nancy F. Cott. Copyright © 1996 by Northeastern University Press. Reprinted by permission of Northwestern University Press.

19–3. "Michael Gold , Jews Without Money, 1890s." Excerpt from *Jews Without Money* by Michael Gold. Copyright © 1984, 1930 by Michael Gold. Reprinted by permission of Carroll & Graf Publishers Inc.

*Chapter 21*   21–4. "Why I Am a Member of the I.W.W." From *Four L Bulletin* (1992). Reprinted in *Rebel Voices: An I.W.W. Anthology*, edited by Joyce L. Kornbluh. Copyright © 1964 by Joyce L. Kornbluh. Reprinted by permission of the author.

*Chapter 22*   22–3. "Anonymous Soldier's Letter to Elmer J. Sutters," (1918). Edited text from *War Letters: Extraordinary Correspondence from American Wars* edited by Andrew Carroll. Copyright © 2001 by Washington Square Press. Reprinted by permission of the author.

22–5. "Stanley B. Norvell, Letter to Victor F. Lawson, 1919." Excerpted from "Views of a Negro During the Red Summer of 1919" from *Journal of Negro History* 51 (July 1966), edited by William Tuttle. Copyright © 1966 by the Association for the Study of African American Life and History. Reprinted by permission.

*Chapter 23*   23–1. "Address before the New York Chamber of Commerce, November 19, 1925." From *Foundations of the Republic: Speeches and Addresses*. Copyright © 1926. Reprinted by permission of Simon & Schuster, Inc.

23–2. "Diary Entries, 1925–1928" Excerpt from *Leaves from a Notebook of a Tamed Cynic* by Reinhold Niebuhr. Copyrignt © 1929 by Reinhold Niebuhr. Reprinted by permission of Presbyterian Publishing Corporation.

*Chapter 24*   24–4. "Let the Mexicans Organize" From *The Nation*, December 19, 1936. Copyright © 1936 by The Nation Magazine. Reprinted by permission of the publisher.

24–5. "Herbert Hoover, Anti-New Deal Campaign Speech, 1936." From *The New York Times*, October 31, 1936. "Minnie Hardin, Letter to Eleanor Roosevelt, December 14, 1937." From *The New York Times*, December 14, 1937. Copyright © 1936, 1937 by The New York Times Company, Inc. Reprinted by permission.

*Chapter 25*   25–2. "Monica Sone, Nisei Daughter." Excerpt from *Nisei Daughter* by Monica Sone. Copyright © 1953 by Monica Sone. Copyright © renewed 1981 by Monica Sone. Reprinted by permission of Little , Brown & Company, Inc.

25–3. Varian, Fry, " The massacre of the Jews." From *New Republic*, December 21, 1942. Copyright © 1942. Reprinted by permission of The New Republic, Inc.